W9-AUT-593

THE CRITICS RAVE ABOUT
THE STRAIGHT DOPE

THE STRAIGHT DOPE

A Compendium of Human Knowledge
by Cecil Adams

Edited and with
an introduction by
Ed Zotti
Illustrated by
Slug Signorino

BALLANTINE BOOKS • NEW YORK

My thanks to Mike, Dave, and Ed, who slaved over my copy as if it were their own; to Pat, a font of knowledge and good counsel; to Slug, Michigan City's answer to Hieronymus Bosch; to Bobo, for finally saying yes; to Mary, for moral and immoral support; and to Mark, my agent, to McC, ace designer and computer king, and to Frank, Renaldo, Susan, Jim, the Mikes, A.J., Ric, Gregg, Joel, Bert, and the rest of the painstaking *Reader* minions, for their patience during this, the Stalingrad of American literature. And finally, to America's finest book reviewer. You know who you are.

Table of Contents

Introduction

I first became acquainted with Cecil Adams, self-proclaimed omniscient, in the fall of 1978, when I was asked to become his editor. The previous occupant of that post, the noted film critic Dave Kehr, had been driven to the brink of madness by Cecil's obnoxious personality, and desperately wanted out. Being young and foolish, I accepted the job without hesitation. It was a decision that changed my life. I was innocent then; now I am hardened and brutal. Dealing with Cecil on a regular basis will do that to you.

Cecil first surfaced in February, 1973, in the pages of the Chicago *Reader*, a weekly alternative newspaper. The format of the Straight Dope, as Cecil's column was called, was (and remains) straightforward: readers submitted questions on whatever oddball topics struck their fancy, and Cecil answered them, inevitably managing to work in numerous wisecracks, insults, and rambling digressions in the process. At first *Reader* management (and no doubt the reading public) was skeptical that the column would be anything more than a trendy Action Line. But it soon became clear that Cecil possessed two remarkable qualifications: he was never wrong, and he knew *everything*. Moreover, he had a prose style that was strangely addictive, in an irritating sort of way. The first clear demonstration of these qualities came only a few months after the column started running, when someone inquired about the calorie content of the average male ejaculation. Cecil's reply drew a vitriolic response accusing him of cheap sensationalism and inaccuracy. It was a challenge that Cecil could not afford to ignore, and he rose to the occasion majestically. (The exchange is reproduced on pages 54 and 55 of this volume.) His reputation thereafter was assured.

Cecil's editor in the early years was Mike Lenehan, who has

since gone on to glory as a contributor to the *Atlantic* magazine. Lenehan found working with Cecil a bizarre experience. It was a full year before the two ever met face to face, Cecil preferring to conduct his business via phone and anonymous mail drops. As often as not, the columnist wrote his weekly opuses in crabbed longhand on the backs of old envelopes, sandwich wrappers, or bus transfers, which Lenehan had to decipher as best he could. As a result, errors occasionally found their way into print. Cecil was livid on these occasions, but the unflappable Lenehan pointed out that if Cecil would simply behave like an ordinary human being instead of a two-bit combination of Horace Greeley and James Bond, such problems could be readily avoided.

Cecil eventually saw the wisdom of this, and consented to show up from time to time in the paper's editorial offices—usually about three minutes before deadline, and invariably with copy that looked like it had been sitting underneath the canary all night. He would stroll around in Bermuda shorts, sandals, and shirts with the sleeves torn out, muttering incongruous non sequiturs to himself. No one ever actually saw him at work, but Lenehan reported after a visit to Cecil's house that tottering mounds of mildewed newsprint were piled everywhere, the rugs were worn through as though from incessant nervous pacing, and dirty coffee cups and fast-food containers were scattered all over the place. Cecil himself sat at his battered desk in the middle of the room rummaging through heaps of papers, mumbling, "Wait a second, I know I've got it here somewhere."

At an early stage of the game the *Reader* was fortunate enough to obtain the services of Slug Signorino to illustrate the Straight Dope. This was a shrewd move in two respects. Not only was Slug an artist of authority and vision, as a glance through these pages will confirm, but he also possessed a personality nearly as poisonous as Cecil's own. The two took to one another with the enthusiasm of the Apaches for the First Cavalry, thus deflecting much misery and aggravation from the rest of us. Cecil over the years has been particularly peeved at Slug's habit of depicting him as a turkey with a mortarboard, which he does not feel adequately conveys his stature in contemporary American culture. "It's a good thing the guy's a genius," Cecil has been heard to say, "or I would have murdered him in his sleep long ago." Slug, for his part, merely grins evilly.

Their personal feuds notwithstanding, the Cecil-Slug combination has proven to be enduringly popular. The column presently appears in the Baltimore *City Paper*, the Dallas *Observer*, the Los Angeles *Reader*, the Phoenix *New Times*, and the Washington,

D.C., *City Paper*, as well as the Chicago *Reader*. Cecil now spends the bulk of his time shuttling between the cities, while Slug stays home in Michigan City, Indiana, where, he says, "the humidity is good for the Rapidographs."

Of his life and methods, Cecil will say little, preferring to let his work speak for itself. "Before my arrival, people would go to their graves without ever knowing why wintergreen Life Savers make clouds of sparks when you chew them in the dark," he says. "Now they know—or they will once they read this book—and their lives are the richer for it. Ditto for the many other vital questions on politics, culture, and reproductive physiology that I have dealt with over the years. In fact, I think it is safe to say that no one today can hope to achieve a fully satisfactory and meaningful life without reading the Straight Dope regularly."

That may be putting it a bit strongly, but we're sure you'll find the present volume, a collection of the best columns from the last eleven years, a useful addition to your library, coffee table, or bathroom. Oh, and if you like the book, be sure to tell your friends. This has been a labor of love, but if we make a few bucks off the deal, it sure wouldn't hurt.

—Ed Zotti

Chapter 1

≈≈≈≈≈≈≈≈≈≈≈≈≈≈≈≈≈≈≈≈≈≈≈≈

All God's Creatures

While gazing recently at my Hubert the Harris (stuffed) Lion, I noticed it comes complete with a belly button and glasses. The glasses are obviously to provide a dignified effect, but is it anatomically correct to put a belly button on a lion? How about cats in general? Dogs? Primates other than man, such as apes? Some of my friends say all mammals have umbilical cords and therefore must have belly buttons. Others say dogs and cats are born in a sac and therefore have no belly button. Please shed some light on this issue for us urbanites.—T.J., Chicago

I'm not trying to discourage people from writing their Uncle Cecil, T., but it seems to me the easiest way to find out whether cats have belly buttons would have been to inspect a cat. If you had, you would have found that cats are indeed equipped with navels, notwithstanding the fact that they (along with dogs) are born in amnionic sacs. Admittedly, cat belly buttons don't look quite like the human version, being basically an elongated scar, often hidden by hair, located just astern of the rib cage. Virtually all mammals, including apes and lions, have umbilical cords and hence navels, the principal exceptions reportedly being our distinguished forebears Adam and Eve, for reasons that a moment's thought will make obvious.

The other day I told some friends a story about how when I was 14 and living near Washington, D.C., I saw this 90-pound monkey at a carnival who could literally pick a grown man up and toss him out of a boxing ring. A crowd of people listened to a man (probably the trainer) dare anyone to stay three minutes in the ring with what appeared to be a large chimp. There was a fee to try your luck and a $100 reward if you stayed in the three minutes.

1

Well, I'll tell you, I saw these guys get in there with this monkey and get tossed right out. It seems the trainer had this whistle and whenever he felt inclined he would blow it, which was the signal for the chimp to do his thing. It was a delightful experience (to watch, at least). Anyway, I don't think my friends believed me. So you have to back me up, Cece: isn't it true that a 90-pound chimpanzee can throw a full-grown man through the air?—Tom M., Chicago

P.S.: Their great strength notwithstanding, is it possible to keep chimps as pets?

Chimpanzees look mighty cute trucking around on their roller skates, wearing funny hats, and going "ook, ook," but when roused they are vicious little bastards and not to be trifled with. Blessed with a muscle structure considerably superior to *homo sapiens* (if not nearly as fetching in a bathing suit), chimpanzees can handle almost anything that comes along. Three drunks at a carnival would be no sweat.

It's a lot easier to get a chimp in roller skates than it is to get him to pump iron—hence, most of the data on chimp strength is anecdotal and decidedly unscientific. In tests at the Bronx Zoo in 1924, a dynamometer—a scale that measures the mechanical force of a pull on a spring—was erected in the monkey house. A 165-pound male chimpanzee named "Boma" registered a pull of 847 pounds, using only his right hand (although he did have his feet braced against the wall, being somewhat hip, in his simian way, to the principles of leverage). A 165-pound man, by comparison, could manage a one-handed pull of about 210 pounds. Even more frightening, a female chimp, weighing a mere 135 pounds and going by the name of Suzette, checked in with a one-handed pull of 1,260 pounds. (She was in a fit of passion at the

2

time; one shudders to think what her boyfriend must have looked like next morning.) In dead lifts, chimps have been known to manage weights of 600 pounds without even breaking into a sweat. A male gorilla could probably heft an 1,800-pound weight and not think twice about it.

As you might deduce, therefore, the word on keeping chimps as pets is a big negatory. Chimpanzees can never be fully domesticated; they're aggressive by nature and sooner or later they'll start to threaten their keepers in subtle ape ways that the untrained eye won't recognize, until one day—blammo.

But maybe you're thinking, I'll just keep the little beast until it starts to act tough, and then toss it back into the jungle. Wrong. A chimpanzee brought up in captivity won't be accepted by its brothers in the wild. Shunned, the citified chimp will either starve to death or be set upon by a simian hit squad. No matter how you look at it, keeping a chimp as a pet is dangerous and inhumane.

My question is simple: how can a mother hen, which must weigh around five pounds or more, sit on a fragile item like an egg without crushing it to pieces?—Rick G., Zirndorf, West Germany

Mama hens do not crush their chilluns mainly because they are not exactly sitting on them, at least not in the sense that humans sit. They are more or less squatting on them; their feet continue to bear most of the weight. Nesting material also supplies a certain amount of support.

We are used to thinking of chickens as rather blimplike creatures from seeing the bloated carcasses on sale in the supermarket, but in reality a nesting hen is not quite so corpulent. Its underside is not rounded so much as V-shaped, the point of the V being the chicken's breastbone. In addition, the area around the breastbone is devoid of feathers. Together these two features give you a couple off shallow troughlike areas that permit the hen to apply maximum warmth to the eggs without making an omelet out of them. Not that the average hen in a commercial chicken farm has to worry about such things—her eggs are whisked away immediately for processing and packaging.

Do all mammals have tongues?—Cathy B., Baltimore
    Yes.

Regarding the expression "deeper than whale shit," just how deep is whale shit? What would be the weight of the average bowel movement of the world's largest whale?—Larry Lujack, Superjock, Chicago

3

Whale excrement is largely liquid in consistency and thus, like Top 40 radio and other effluvia, has little substance and no depth. The world's largest whales are blue whales, and these excrete a minimum of 2 percent of their body weight—about 3 tons—each day.

I've been looking at bulldogs for longer than I care to remember, but damn if I can see how they're supposed to look like bulls. To me, they've always resembled decaying watermelons. What's the connection? And speaking of animals (deft segue, huh?), whence comes the expression "crocodile tears"? From crocodiles, no doubt, but a little elaboration would be appreciated.—Mike K., Los Angeles

Bulldogs, the world's ugliest canines, are the products of centuries of selective breeding. The name doesn't come from any actual resemblance to a bull, but refers instead to the bulldogs' mission in life—they were bred specifically to attack and maim bulls, of all things, and were used in a popular spectator sport of the Middle Ages, known as "bull-baiting." The dog's assignment was to sink his teeth as far into the bull's nose as he could and hold on. The bull would counter by attempting to disembowel the dog. All of this was considered a real hoot at the time. The fourteenth century, we should remember, did not have the benefit of *Charley's Angels* or *Masterpiece Theater*. The winning dog was the one who managed to hold on the longest. The owners of the dogs, naturally, would pay a service charge to the bull's manager to cover wear and tear.

Just as we now scientifically breed basketball players, the sportsmen of the Middle Ages bred their dogs to conform to the requirements of the game. Short, squat dogs were favored because they were harder to tackle than the more willowy breeds. The bull owners, for their part, preferred dogs with short teeth, so the bull's snout wouldn't suffer excessive damage. But the real triumph of the bulldog lay in the design of the head. Ordinary dogs had a problem: the bull's nose would swell when bitten, often to the point where the ballooning flesh would block the dog's nostrils—and when you're choking, it's hard to maintain a grip on an irritated bull. The bulldog's nose, though, is turned up and set back a bit from the teeth, affording plenty of breathing space between the jaws and the expanding bull snout.

As for "crocodile tears," crocodiles, it seems, actually do cry, not because of their sensitive natures but in order to lubricate their food. The tears run from the eyes down into the mouth and throat, softening the fragments of Great White Hunter or whatever and helping them down the chute. The tears, naturally enough, were often confused with shows of emotion in the first accounts of the animals to reach England. Sir John Mandeville writes, "In many places of Inde are many crocodiles—that is, a manner of long serpent. These serpents slay men and eat them weeping." Another writer, Edward Topsell, passes along a more cynical interpretation: "There are not many brute beasts that can weep, but such is the nature of the crocodile that, to get a man within his danger, he will sob, sigh, and weep as though he were in extremity, but suddenly he destroyeth him." It was Topsell's version that was adapted by Shakespeare, Spenser, and other poets as a metaphor for an insincere show of feeling, and through that route the expression entered common currency.

Topsell, we note parenthetically, continues with some helpful advice on how to avoid unwanted crocodile confrontations: "Some have written that the crocodile runneth away from a man if he wink with his left eye and look steadfastly upon him with his right eye; but if this be true, it is not attributed to the virtue of the right eye, but only to the rareness of sight which is conspicuous to the serpent from one." Got that?

There are some (my girlfriend for one) who say cats are smarter than dogs, and others (I think most) who say that dogs are definitely more intelligent. Which is, and why?—Bruce T., Chicago

Judging the relative intelligence of cats and dogs is like deciding which is better looking—there's just not much basis for comparison. Psychologists have a tough enough time coming up with a culture-blind IQ test for humans, who all belong to the same species; designing a *species*-blind test for dogs and cats is just about impossible. What people take to be signs of intelligence in their pets usually are just specialized survival skills that say nothing about innate brainpower. A cat, for instance, is much more dexterous with its paw than a dog. This dexterity fascinates cat lovers, who also cite the cat's legendary standoffishness as proof of its mental superiority. The dog, on the other hand, is much more of a social animal; dog advocates claim this proves the dog is more civilized, ergo, more intelligent.

Animal ethologists (they're the professionals in this line of work) regard such arguments as rubbish. Cats are loners because they have always hunted alone—one mouse won't feed more than one cat. Without his nimble paws, a cat couldn't corner, catch, and eat his prey. Dogs, though, hunted in packs because they picked on game bigger than they were. They used their teeth to kill their prey and dismember the carcass. (Admittedly, not all cats hunt alone—lions don't, for instance—but let's not make this discussion any more confusing than it already is.) Ethologists don't even like to weigh one *breed* against another, within the same species. If a bloodhound smells better, or a greyhound sees better—well, that's what they were bred for.

But surely, you querulously cry, there must be *some* way to compare cats and dogs. Maybe, but it hasn't turned up yet. Obedience and trainability, I should note, aren't considered reliable measures of intelligence. Newborn cats open their eyes a little sooner than dogs do, but the dog gets into solid foods sooner than the cat. Overall, puppies and kittens grow into adulthood at virtually identical rates. Mama cats toilet train their young, and mama dogs don't, but that doesn't prove anything. In sum, to hell with it.

Is there really such a thing as a flea circus? What do circus fleas do? And how does one train a flea? Surely not with a rolled-up newspaper and a choke chain?—Joyce K., Seattle

There is most certainly such a thing as a flea circus, Joyce. However (joke coming), there ain't no such thing as a (joke imminent) *flea lunch!* (Pause for big laffs.) Now then. The intimate association of fleas and humankind down through the ages has given rise to many strange and wonderful things, of which the flea circus is by no means the most bizarre. Ask me about erotic flea art sometime. No kidding. Anyway, flea circuses appear to have originated in England in the 16th century, but they entered their golden age in the 1830s through the efforts of an entrepreneur named L. Bertolotto who ran flea exhibitions in London. The P.T. Barnum of his day, Bertolotto had flea orchestras playing audible flea music, flea foursomes in games of flea whist, and flea dancing

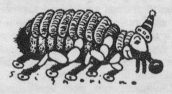

companies complete with dresses and frock coats for a flea ball. Other fleas drew miniature coaches or warships, and still others portrayed Napoleon and the Duke of Wellington. By way of finale, the fleas were often allowed to sup upon the arm of their manager, a man whose dedication to his art can only be described as awesome.

Flea circuses were a fixture of carnivals and circus sideshows in the U.S. for decades; as late as the mid-1950s there was a flea circus near Times Square in New York. As one might suppose, given the scale of the performers, the size of the potential audience at a given showing was necessarily limited. The typical flea coliseum consisted of a small table surrounded by a few chairs. Supposedly, though, a determined promoter could squeeze in as many as 50 ten-minute shows a day. Training the fleas consisted in the main of rigging them up with wire harnesses so that they could only move in a particular way. If necessary—say, in a flea orchestra—the fleas might also be glued to their seats. And what did the anticruelty people have to say about these unseemly practices? Not a thing. We are surrounded by hypocrisy. Changing tastes and a scarcity of human-fed fleas (the only kind with enough stamina for the job) eventually doomed the flea circus. American theater has been but a pale shadow ever since.

Why do cats purr? And while we're on the subject, what is the pedigree of the Cheshire cat?—T.S., Dallas

Cats don't purr just when they're feeling chipper—they also purr when they're frightened or badly hurt. Purring doesn't have any specific emotional connotation; rather it seems to be a kind of homing device. Cats learn the signal in the first few days of kittenhood, when they can't see, hear, or smell very well. The mother cat purrs to call the kittens to nurse—unable to hear the sound, the kitten can feel the vibrations.

There are two schools of thought on exactly *how* a cat purrs. One theory traces the vibrations to a set of "false vocal cords," a bundle of membranes that lies above the genuine vocal cords and seems to have no other clear function. The other opinion locates the purr in the vibrations of the hyoid apparatus, a series of small bones connecting the skull and the larynx that nominally serves to support the tongue. Since it's very difficult to induce a cat to purr while you are examining his hyoid apparatus, the truth may never be known.

As for the Cheshire cat—well, keeds, there ain't no such thing. The Cheshire cat in *Alice in Wonderland* is Lewis Carroll's play on a popular expression—"to grin like a Cheshire cat"—of obscure origin. Cheshire is a dairy county in western England famous for its cheese—cheese that once, according to legend, came molded in the shape of a grinning cat. A rival theory finds

the Cheshire cat in the coat of arms of the area's Grosvenor family. What started out as a lion on the crest came to resemble, in the bumbling hands of the Cheshire sign painters, an inebriated alley cat. The phrase first appears in print in Peter Pindar's "Pair of Lyric Epistles" in 1795: "Lo, like a Cheshire cat our court will grin."

A two-part question: we all know cats freak out over catnip—but why? What is it about catnip that gives our feline friends such pleasure? One of my cats, a neutered male named Ivan, also gets off on the scent of imported Spanish olives—once to the point of incontinence. What gives? Is there some chemical similarity between catnip and olive juice?—Bob J., Chicago

Catnip research, not too surprisingly, has not kept pace with the other branches of biology, and consequently very little is known about the workings of this exotic drug, if drug it be. The odor released from the crushed leaves of *Nepeta cataria*, as this small mint plant is known, seems to affect only members of the cat family, lions and tigers not excepted. Even cats from parts of the world where catnip is unknown immediately succumb to the aroma.

Catnip seems to have the effect of a stimulant, accelerating the victim's heartbeat and inducing an uncontrollable urge to "frisk" and/or "scamper," to put it in technical terms. Root of valerian (which, interestingly enough, was once used as a sedative for humans) has a similar effect on cats, but the scent of Spanish olives seems to be a weakness exclusive to Ivan. It seems less likely that Ivan is in the grip of a catnip-like euphoria than that he's possessed by another emotion not entirely foreign to house-cats, namely "hunger."

When I pet my girlfriend's cat I'm left with a layer of cat hairs on my hand. She (the cat) always seems to be shedding. How can the thing stand to have all those hairs in its mouth when it grooms itself with its tongue? The thought of it makes me gag; why doesn't the cat? Is this some kind of special adaptive behavior? Should I learn a Heimlich maneuver for cats just in case?—John J., Baltimore

House cats *are* always shedding, they *do* gag (after a fashion) on all the hair they insist on swallowing, and if it weren't for the legions of humans willing to bail them out of the jams they repeatedly get themselves into, the whole feline race would surely have perished long ago, and good riddance. As your girlfriend can doubtless tell you, cats periodically regurgitate things called hair balls, which look like tiny hot dogs made of damp felt. These are made of hair the cat has accumulated in its stomach. Cat apologists claim hair balls are indeed an adaptive mechanism, the theory being that cats in the wild protect their stomachs by wrapping hair around bones, claws, and other indigestible components of their lunches, which they subsequently expectorate. Personally I regard this as a flimsy rationalization for a peculiarly repulsive habit, but never mind. Sometimes the hair balls work their way from the stomach into the intestine, where they get stuck, causing the cat untold gastric distress. The only cure is for the cat's owner to administer one of several intestinal lubricants. Cats thus have the singular distinction of being the only animal species ecologically dependent on an allegedly superior race (e.g., us) to save it from itself. And humans think it's the *cats* that are the domesticated animal.

Watching people feeding squirrels in the park, it occurs to me that, since squirrels are unlikely to find many peanuts in their natural woodland habitat, peanuts may not be the best food in the world for them—not to mention the candy, crackers, and Fritos that some people indiscriminately toss to them. Are we really doing the squirrels a favor by feeding them this junk? Or have they managed to adapt to us?—Morris S., Baltimore

After decades of city dwelling, the urban squirrel has become quite a different creature from his woodland brother—he'll eat anything, and like it. A researcher at the American Museum of Natural History, an institution that conveniently borders on New

York's Central Park, conducted an informal survey in 1957, placing the two nuts that squirrels seem to prefer in the wild—hazelnuts and acorns—among a row of more citified fare: peanuts, popcorn, and Cracker Jacks. Without fail, the subject squirrels would select whichever tidbit happened to be closest to them, a sign that they have not only lost their natural taste but become fairly indolent as well.

Several naturalists have postulated that a peanut diet is genuinely harmful to the squirrels: it seems to result in a weakening of eyesight and a definite thinning of the pelt. Luckily, the parks continue to offer a passable selection of organic delights for more health-minded squirrels: the tender staminate flowers of oak and pine trees, the buds of young plants, and even, now and again, a touch of maple sap.

While passing an Arco station the other day, I thought of the old Sinclair sign with the dinosaur on it—Dino the Big Green Brontosaurus. What I want to know is, how do they know that dinosaurs were green? Are they just guessing or does someone actually have a piece of dinosaur skin? Also, it's common to see dinosaur bones at a museum, but has anyone ever found a frozen piece of hide or meat in a glacier somewhere? If so, would it be possible to take this 100,000,000-year-old tissue and clone a living dinosaur from its cells?—Michael J., Chicago

Mike, do you honestly think the Sinclair people made their company symbol green because they had some serious scientific notion that *real dinosaurs* were green—and kelly green at that? They just thought it was an appealing color, and not as implausible as, say, lavender. Apart from their association with fossil fuels, dinosaurs are widely thought (by children at least) to be cuddly. You may recall that Sinclair at one time distributed inflatable plastic replicas of Dino. I had one, and found it inexplicably charming. It is not known with any certainty what color brontosauruses were. No pieces of dinosaur skin have ever been found; like other soft tissue, it decays rapidly. The vertebrate fossil record is almost entirely in the form of bones and other durable items, and even then the original material has frequently been salted out and replaced by various minerals. There have been a couple of skin *impressions* found, where a dinosaur sat down, one supposes, but these give no clue as to color.

As for preservation in ice, dinosaurs resided on this planet from 225,000,000 to 65,000,000 years ago. It is generally thought that the oldest ice formations on earth are those of Antarctica, which are perhaps 50,000,000 years old. From this we deduce that no brontosaurus-bearing ice has survived to the present day. Mammoths, bison, and other critters found in polar ice are relics from the most recent interglacial period, and are between 10,000 and 70,000 years old, which is quite youthful, relatively speaking. You may recall reading some time ago that Russian scientists were attempting to clone a mammoth from some preserved cells. Don't hold your breath.

When we came home this evening we found that a foul odor thoroughly pervaded our large apartment. We have reason to suspect that this odor (it's still here) is none other than that of the "spray" commonly attributed to male cats—in this case, our three-years-neutered male cat Mudhead. What exactly is cat "spray"? Is it different from cat urine? Is it possible that our neutered Mudhead was capable of such a feat after three years?— World Gato Headquarters, Chicago

Spray is but one of several odious secretions associated with cats, whose reputation for cleanliness is greatly exaggerated. Spray consists of urine mixed with a viscous, fatty material whose extraordinary pungency has been most charitably characterized as "musky," although more colorful terms have also been used. The accepted method of application is for the cat to back up to some prominent domestic landmark, such as a door frame, sofa, or curtain, raise its tail, and let squirt. This is unquestionably a bit on the disgusting side, but things could be worse. The hippopotamus, for instance, is said to mark jungle trails by excreting a lethal mixture of urine and feces while twirling its tail like a propeller. This may explain the historically sluggish market for pet hippopotamuses. Cats are motivated to spray principally by a desire to: (1) denote their turf, (2) exhibit their studliness (if the cat is a male), and (3) be a pain in the nuts. Motive number 3 comes into play whenever the cat feels its precious self is being neglected, such as when its owner(s) changes jobs, has a baby, or what have you. In the case of a new baby, incidentially, one of my cat manuals here urges that "guests who come to visit the infant should be encouraged to make a fuss over the cat first[!]" Personally I would be inclined to threaten the cat with lingering death rather than resort to this kind of appeasement, but I admit to having some prejudice in the matter. Neutering supposedly reduces the incidence of spraying, particularly if undertaken before the cat reaches puberty, but as you can see it does not always work. In any event it's claimed that vinegar will neutralize the smell.

It should be noted that another source of kitty odor could be an infection of the anal sacs, yet another dubious feature of the cat physiology. If Mudhead has been skidding his little bottom over the carpet lately, you might be well advised to hie yourself (and him) over to the vet. Otherwise just pound on him for a while with the newspaper. It may not cure him, but it has a wonderfully tranquilizing effect on the owner, I find.

During a recent movie at a local theater, there was a short feature in which this guy laid a chicken on its stomach, moved his finger in a straight line away from the chicken's beak, and thereby hypnotized the poor critter. Can this really be done? How does it work? Have you ever hypnotized a chicken?—Randy K., Lisle, Illinois

Up until now I have pretty much had my hands full contending with turkeys, Randy my son, but should chickens become equally worrisome you may be sure I will give hypnosis a shot. Remarkably enough, the technique described does work. In the old days it was thought you had to draw a line in front of the chicken with chalk, but modern masters of the art have learned you can dispense with the props. The trick seems to require physically restraining the chicken and administering some strong stimulus, e.g., drawing lines. This induces total sensory overload in the chicken's two-volt brain, putting him/her/it under for anywhere from 15 seconds to 30 minutes. Alternatively, I understand, you can pop the chicken's cork with a beady-eyed stare. If it's pigeons you're after, a small piece of white putty on the end of the beak is recommended. Allegedly it is also possible to put the nod on a vicious horse by grabbing its nose, pulling its head down, and blowing "strongly and steadily into its ear for about five minutes," it says here. You first, buddy.

It is doubtful whether putting an animal into an apparent trance state can legitimately be regarded as hypnosis, in the sense that humans are hypnotized. Some regard it simply as a sort of freeze reaction, while others claim it's an attempt to feign death in hopes that the hypnotizer will lose interest and scoot.

Chapter 2

~~~~~~

Urban Studies

With the price of meat as high as it is these days, I wondered how I, as a city dweller, might hunt and eat my own game. I'm thinking of squirrels. There seem to be enough to go around. Assuming I could catch one, how should I clean and cook it?—E. Hemingway, Los Angeles

This isn't such a hot idea, E. City squirrels are inordinately fond of rabies and other diseases, some of which can be transmitted through mere skin contact. If your diet lacks meat protein but you lack cash, I suggest you develop a taste for a meat substitute, such as soybeans or Jack-in-the-Box hamburgers.

Country-bred squirrels are another matter, however, and if you ever have the chance to try one you might wish to employ the following foolproof preparation method (note to weak-stomached readers—skip to the next question pronto): Wearing gloves at all times (to protect against other, less insidious, infections), take a sharp knife and cut lengthwise through the squirrel's tailbone from the underside, stopping before you reach the skin of the back. Next, hold the tail away from the body (the squirrel's) and make slices across the lower back to widen the strip of skin that connects the tail to the body. You can now peel your squirrel like a banana—grasp the hind legs, step on the tail, and pull slowly, peeling the skin off the head and front legs. After cutting the remaining skin from the hind legs, remove the head and feet, then slit the body down the front and remove the internal organs. The squirrel has small, elusive glands in the small of his back and in the pits of his forelegs—these too must be removed. Wash the body thoroughly with a mixture of water and vinegar.

So, your mouth is watering, right? OK, now you can cook the squirrel meat just as you would cook chicken, using whatever your favorite recipe may be. (Shake 'N' Bake, however, is not in keeping with the true spirit of the endeavor.) The tastiest squirrels are the grey ones, red squirrels being both too skinny and too gamey. For a more tender squirrel, hang the cleaned body up by what's left of the legs for two or three days.

Bon appetit.

We are sitting around talking about pigeon excrement and Cecil Adams and now we are wondering: (1) what is unique about the pigeon that can allow it to survive in or select for the urban environment? And please don't give us bullshit about how pigeons can survive in rubbish or excrement, or enjoy crowds and noises. We are interested in physiological and ecological answers, not conclusions based on observational behavior. (2) What are the mechanics of The Straight Dope? Do you have a staff? Where do you find out all this stuff? What percentage of questions can you, can't you, and do you answer?—Gary S., Baltimore

(1) Your attempt at writing prose that appears to be scientific intimidates me no end—I guess I'm pretty lucky that there are, indeed, a couple of "ecological" factors involved in the pigeon question and not just "conclusions based on observational behavior" (by which I presume you mean "observed behavior," unless you're referring to documented cases of peeping Tom-ism by pigeons or the observance of pigeon religious holidays, in which case I'm afraid you've really got me stumped). Common urban pigeons, *Columba livia*, appear to be native to North Africa, where they usually dwell on narrow cliff ledges that might be compared to the urban roosts they take up in the nooks and crannies of large stone buildings. Pigeons are also among the first birds to have been domesticated, and a large proportion of any urban pigeon population is assumed to be "feral," or once domestic and now—by virtue of escape—wild. Instead of being afraid of humans, these pigeons are used to being fed by them; they know how to take advantage of food sources that other species of birds do not—specifically, little old ladies in tennis shoes.

(2) *Fat chance!*

Where are all the baby pigeons? All the ones you ever see are growed up and flapping. Don't they ever have a childhood or a nest? Are they all imported full-grown from New Jersey?—T.B., Washington, D.C.

Sorry to disappoint you, T.B., but there's not much of a mystery—the common street pigeon builds a nest like your normal bird. But pigeons, living up to the urbanologists' nickname "flying rats," are both a little sloppier and a little more devious than the average avian; they construct small, flimsy nests, barely large enough to hold Mother Pigeon's usual two eggs, in cornices and other out-of-the-way places. While the eggs incubate (for about two weeks) the nest is kept constantly covered—by the male during the day, and by the female on the night shift. Once the little suckers hatch, they spend another two weeks in the nest feeding off a protein substance called "pigeon's milk" secreted from the crop of the adult (both sexes, interestingly). When they're all growed up and flapping, they hit the road. Well, what did you expect—test tubes?

Can you in your infinite yet magnanimous wisdom explain something that's been troubling me for years? When pigeons bob their heads as they walk is it because their legs are connected to their necks or what?—Dennis A., Highland Park, Illinois

Of course not. As any fool can see, a pigeon's legs are connected to its body—and it's a good thing, too, because the pigeon would look mighty funny if it were assembled according to the offhand anatomy you described. Basically the pigeon's back-and-forth head motion—not exactly a bob—helps it keep its balance when walking. The pigeon's legs are located pretty far astern, and if it kept its head forward all the time it would probably tip over. This would expose the pigeon to the ridicule of the community. Instead, what it does is move its chest forward in time with one leg, and its head forward in time with the other leg. Thus some weight is always trailing a little abaft the port beam, as we say. Many fowl have similarly peculiar gaits, because they cannot afford orthopedic shoes.

GRATUITOUS INSULTS FROM THE STEAMING MILLIONS

Cecil, you dunderhead, where'd you dig up that story about pigeons bobbing their heads to maintain balance? Any text of ornithology (Pettingill's, for example) will tell you pigeons, like most birds, have eyes on the sides of their heads, their vision's basically monocular, and they bob their heads for depth perception. Birds with front-faced eyes, like owls, have binocular vision, and, like people, don't have to bob their heads. Straight dope, indeed!—Paul G., Chicago

Listen, you chump, it happens that I have had an intimate association with pigeons since my earliest days and I know everything there is to know about them, or pretty nearly, anyway. My father used to send me out to feed the damn pigeons in his damn pigeon loft all the time, and I want to know who you are going to believe, some stupid internationally famous ornithologist or me, veteran pigeon feeder. I will admit this Pettingill fellow may have something with this depth perception business, but it is my undying conviction that balance has as much to do with it. It is well known that pigeons, along with most other birds, have enormous fields of vision—they can see 340 degrees around without moving, owing to the peculiar construction of the eyeball and the way the eyes are placed in the head. The peripheral vision of each eye is so great that the two visual fields overlap, giving the pigeon a binocular field of 24 degrees when it looks straight ahead. So if the pigeon is walking straight toward say, a tasty piece of corn, it does not need to bob its head to maintain depth perception. On the other hand, like all bipedal creatures, its ability to maintain balance is a delicate thing, and since its "arms" are occupied being wings, it is not unreasonable to suppose that the back-and-forth motion of the head helps maintain balance. So there. See if I ever answer any of your questions again, fella.

FURTHER ENLIGHTENMENT ON THE GREAT PIGEON HEAD-BOBBING CONTROVERSY

The diffuse speculation on the function of pigeon head movements recently aired in your column demands comment. Unfortunately, both you and your steaming ornithological detractor err grievously. The bobbing actually takes place to preserve monocular acuity. Here's how it works, swine. For an animal with side-mounted eyes, forward movements result in parallax shifts (apparent motion of near objects relative to distant objects). Now, vertebrate eyes—and retinas—work much better with completely stationary images. So what happens is that the bird's body walks on while the head is temporarily left behind to stabilize the image. The head is then jerked forward at the start of the next step. Owls and humans, by contrast, have front-facing eyes, and thus, no parallax problem while walking. Heavy-headed creatures with side-mounted eyes (pigs, cows), for which the avian solution is impractical, apparently were dumb to start with and have grown to enjoy parallax shifts. If the aforementioned blather continues, maybe you and your critic along with Pettingrill should consider having your eyes remounted to match your wits.—Martin S., Chicago

It's Pettingill, not Pettingrill, my son. Try not to get so excited about these things. In light of the fact that we now have three separate theories on why pigeons bob their heads, it is apparent that the definitive answer to this question continues to elude the great minds of this century. Unless there are any pigeons out there who wish to contribute to the discussion, we will leave this issue to future generations to decide.

ABSOLUTELY THE LAST THING YOU WILL EVER HAVE TO READ ON THIS RIDICULOUS SUBJECT

I read your column in the discarded alternative newspapers—of which, I might add, there is no small supply—that blow my way across the pavement. About the pigeon controversy—i.e., why pigeons jerk their heads when they walk—the answer is really quite simple. We do it because it feels good.

Walter Pigeon
Equitable Plaza, Chicago

For me, spring brings robins—and silverfish. What do these little buggers want with me? Do they really "eat books?"—Bob, Chicago

The silverfish, known to insect fans as *Lepisma saccharina,* enjoys starch as the main staple of its diet. Starch is most readily available to household bugs in paste, particularly the kind used to hang wallpaper and bind books. Hence, the silverfish's reputation as a litterateur.

Like undergraduates at the University of Chicago, the silverfish may come by his intellectual predilections as the consequence of an unhappy sex life. The poor things don't copulate—the male, as the grand finale to a series of wriggling "courtship movements," merely drops a "sperm packet," which the female then tucks away in her vagina. Not much fun, which could explain why singles bars for silverfish do such lousy business.

The other day some friends and I were discussing cockroaches and we discovered all three of our apartments had been infested with the vermin at approximately the same time—i.e., September-October. Do you have any explanation for this remarkable coincidence? Don't say they were coming in for the winter; we all lived in the same apartments last winter and had nary a roach.—Curious Citizen, Baltimore

Before we continue with this discussion of "vermin," I feel obliged to remind you, in fairness to the little buggers, that cock-

roaches are among the most primitive insects known to science—
they beat you to the planet a good 300,000,000 years ago—and
thus we might reasonably inquire who is infesting whom. In addition, various peoples of the world have found the cockroach to
be quite useful—a mash of dead cockroach and sugar has been
used to cure ulcers of the skin; a tonic containing cockroach ashes
has been drunk to eliminate worms; cockroaches fried in oil and
garlic have been eaten to aid digestion. Today, many cockroaches
grow up to become public relations executives.

Cockroaches don't normally enter a building of their own
volition; they have to be brought in. The best explanation for your
problem is that one of you carried a mama roach—or possibly
just some eggs (the eggs aren't susceptible to pesticides)—into
your building with the groceries or something. Judging from the
autumnal appearance of the hordes, I'd mark the arrival of the
contraband roach around early summer (the eggs take 30-60 days
to hatch). Although roaches have no real "season" all their own,
summer is their most active time.

*I'm tired of Roach Motels, Baygon, boric acid and other pansy-
ass roach killers. I want a recipe for some stuff they will eat gladly
and die of quickly. I have no kids or pets to worry about. I don't
care if the active ingredient is a little dangerous to handle, or
hard (even illegal) to get. I want the little suckers dead. What
will do it?—Hayden J., Chicago*

Calm yourself, Hayden, and pay attention to your Uncle
Cecil. There are two proven approaches to dealing with *la cucar-
acha:* (1) borax, and (2) arson. Assuming your landlord objects
to the latter line of attack, hie yourself down to the basement and
mix up the following recipe: 4 parts borax, 2 parts flour, and 1
part cocoa powder. Now, you may regard borax as "pansy-ass,"
my boy, but that is because you are young and ignorant and have
not yet grasped the subtleties of Total Insect Warfare, which requires
fanatical dedication. You must mix up oodles of this stuff and
apply it with the enthusiasm of Robert S. McNamara dumping
Agent Orange on the Mekong Delta. Pour it in a continuous line
along the walls. Put an extra dose under sinks and around kitchen
cabinets. Hell, fill your damned house to a depth of one foot with
the stuff. The little bastards will die piteously, I promise.

Incidentally, should you also happen to be troubled by rats,
I have here an ingenious formula for inducing rat death: Mix equal
parts cement and flour. Place a pan of this powder out next to a
pan of water. The rats eat the cement, then they drink the water,

and by the next morning their bowels have turned to concrete. Sadistic, eh? I knew you'd love it.

FIELD REPORTS FROM THE TEEMING MILLIONS, PART ONE

With regard to your answer to the cockroach problem, there is an easier way. The cocoa powder mixture is rather messy and probably sticky with excessive moisture. What you should do instead is get DAP putty and some steel wool. Put the steel wool in every (and I mean every) hole you find in your apartment. Seal well with the putty or even cement. After all, if the roaches can't get in, you don't have to worry about killing them. The roaches eat the steel wool to get to you and die of a very bad case of indigestion.

If that isn't enough, apply Roach Prufe powder (about $8 a can). This miracle powder works like a charm because it sticks to the little varmints and they take it back to their homes and kids, where they lick the stuff and die. What's best is that the roaches don't recognize this light blue odorless powder as poison.

Death to roaches.—R.S., Baltimore

Listen, doofus, what do you suppose is the active ingredient in Roach Prufe? Boric acid, that's what. What did I tell you to dump all over your house to kill roaches with? A mixture containing borax, which for our purposes is equivalent to boric acid. Now, if you use Roach Prufe, it'll cost you a jillion dollars to get enough to do the job right. If you use my method, and mix up some *generic* Roach Prufe, so to speak, you'll save beaucoups bucks. It's people like you that make me despair of ever rescuing this country from the clutches of ignorance.

FIELD REPORTS FROM THE TEEMING MILLIONS, PART TWO

This young and ignorant 39-year-old, who has tried (among other things) the three poisons most used by professionals against roaches, has tried your borax stuff for two weeks. The problems are (1) the gritty junk gets tracked all over the house, (2) if it gets wet it forms a dark crusty mess (not easy to avoid around sinks and tubs), (3) there have been no dead bodies, and (4) there have been more live *bodies. I wrote you for the Straight Dope—not more pansy-ass folklore. Please try again.—Hayden J., Chicago*

Two weeks? *Two lousy weeks?* Hayden, for Jah's sake, we're talking about eradicating a bug that has lived on this planet for *three hundred million years,* give or take a couple million. Have a little patience. In the meantime, caulk those cracks with steel wool, per recommendation of R.S. (see above).

FIELD REPORTS FROM THE TEEMING MILLIONS, PART THREE

In view of the constant criticism you have been receiving concerning your surefire roach-killing concoction, I felt that I should write. We tried it, and at first the results were discouraging. But gradually we noticed an improvement in the situation. I don't know if the little buggers died or not, but they've stopped frolicking in and around my living quarters. The mixture does *work, but, like all boric-acid-based mixtures, including Roach Prufe, it needs time to take effect. However, as Hayden J. points out, it does make a helluva mess when it gets wet.—Patricia L., Chicago*

Thanks, Mom.

FIELD REPORTS FROM THE TEEMING MILLIONS, PART FOUR

I imagine you're probably getting a little tired of this topic, but I thought I would write in with one more comment about cockroach extermination. The only way to succeed is to be persistent and use all *the methods. First, find all the holes in the apartment (especially the bathroom and kitchen) that lead to another apartment. Caulk them up tightly. Cockroaches need water, so never leave water in the sink or dirty dishes anywhere. Put boric acid around the baseboards and especially around the sink. Put Roach Motels (they* do *work) under the sink and/or on the counter near the sink. There are also small black strips that can be put in places that cockroaches walk, which will poison them when they cross.*

21

And don't give up looking for entrances from other apartments, because roaches can leave a trail for others to follow. One last point about boric acid. I heard it gives the roaches indigestion, they can't fart, and so they explode!—Rufus B., Baltimore

They *explode*? Where do you guys come up with this stuff, anyway? I have two possible explanations for what borax does, both given to me by supposedly reputable scientists. Take your pick: (1) The stuff gets on the waxy coating on the critter's hide (or "exoskeleton") and partially dissolves it. Whereupon the cockroach dehydrates and croaks. (2) The borax acts as an abrasive, causing microscratches in said coating. Cockroach dehydrates, etc. Inasmuch as the Teeming Millions seem to have some doubts as to the efficacy of borax, I might mention that there *is* a more drastic method, for those who are into the take-no-prisoners approach. Unfortunately, it also renders your house uninhabitable (temporarily, anyway), so I have some qualms about recommending it. It's called a "carbamate bomb," carbamates being a class of particularly deadly bug poisons. You seal up your house, light the "bomb" (it looks and works something like a roadside flare), and scoot yourself out the door. The fumes from the bomb kill every living thing, and 48 hours later, if you're lucky, you can move back in. The drawbacks are that the bombs are expensive, you have to stay with friends for a couple days, and after you move back in you have to swab poison off every exposed surface. In addition, if your slobbola next-door neighbor doesn't improve his housekeeping practices, his cockroaches will just migrate over to your place and two months later you'll be back where you started. Personally, I think you'd be better off sticking with borax.

As an only child, I was forced to be ingenious about inventing solitary diversions. While reading an old diary recently, I found that on July 1, 1969, I went on a murderous binge which resulted in the untimely death of 52 houseflies. Knowing how degenerate their reproductive habits are, I got to wondering how many of their descendants would be around to plague us today had it not been for this prodigious feat of dipterocide. Can you enlighten me? For obvious reasons, I prefer to remain . . .—Anonymous, Chicago

If it's awesome statistical fireworks you're looking for, buddy, come to the right place. The female *Musca domestica*, or common housefly, typically lays 600-1,000 eggs in the course of her roughly two-month lifetime, most of which grow to maturity in 10-12 days, upon which they can set about raising little maggots of their own. Under ideal conditions (which invariably prevail in this column), you may get as many as 12 generations a year. Let us suppose that 132 generations would have been born, or laid, or whatever the appropriate term might be, had you not committed the aforementioned massacre 11 years ago. Let us further suppose that half of the 52 flies were female, that half of all subsequent generations were female, and finally that each female deposited 1,000 eggs, a nice round number. The total number of female descendants is 26×500^{132}, and the total fly population, of course, is twice that many. Having performed various subtle mathematical manipulations on my handy calculator, I may categorically state that your house would presently be infested by roughtly 9.550892×10^{357} flies. At 128 flies to the cubic inch, we get 3.25×10^{16} per cubic mile, or 2.292×10^{56} per cubic parsec, which means that all the flies would fit into a cube a little more than 3.45×10^{100} parsecs on a side. The galaxy in which we presently reside, by way of comparison, is 25-30 parsecs across. It is easy to scramble up your decimal points in calculations of this type and I may have lost a few billion parsecs here and there, but the implication in general is clear: with that selfless act long ago, you singlehandedly saved the cosmos.

The lesson in all this, of course, is the futility of trying to predict the future by projecting a single factor. Most fly eggs, fortunately, do not survive to achieve senior citizenhood, succumbing at some point to parasites, disease, predators, starvation, unhappily situated roller-skates, and so on. Northern winters kill most adult flies, leaving only those in the larval and pupal stages to maintain the Muscidate race. The humbling truth is that, regardless of your efforts in the way of wholesale slaughter, at any given time there are about as many flies as the planet has room for, ecologically speaking. It is enough to drive you to racquetball.

I am sure that many of your readers would appreciate an answer to this most perplexing problem. All my marijuana plants are infested with tiny black bugs that suck out the juices, leaving them at first a speckled white, then yellow and worthless. Do you know of any non-toxic (to humans) spray or insecticide, preferably concocted from natural ingredients, that would get rid of them? Hurry, these mites are spreading to my other plants.—A Reader, Dallas

You don't describe the little buggers very completely, but my guess is that you've got aphids—some species of aphids are dark green or black, and sucking is their forte. Just like this job,

23

sometimes. The best "natural" deterrent to aphids is the ladybug. You'll find several suppliers listed in almost any issue of *Organic Gardening*. If this idea doesn't appeal to you, try cigarette butts. No kidding. Drop two or three cigarette butts in a quart of warm water, let sit overnight, strain, and spray the plants completely. Repeat after six days. Supposedly the butts contain nicotine sulfate, which kills any bug—mite, aphid, you name it. Several of Cecil's devoted readers swear by this method. Alternatively, you can try 'most any house and garden spray containing pyrethrum (made 'from chrysanthemums) as the main active ingredient. It's safe as long as you use it according to directions. Make sure you spray several times to make sure you nail each generation as it hatches. If *that* doesn't work—Cecil is a great believer in contingency plans—you'll have to escalate to Diazinon, which breaks down (and is thus safe for eating and smoking, if you catch my drift) in three to four days. Malathion, the strontium–90 of aphid control, takes a week or more to break down and should be used only as a last resort.

While working part-time in the food service at USC, I had the opportunity to see thousands of dead cockroaches. One thing about these roaches intrigues me: why did they all die on their backs? Is it programmed into their tiny little genes, or do they do it just to bug us?—Leslie, University of Southern California, Los Angeles

Frankly, Leslie, if I saw thousands of dead cockroaches at the food service where I went to school, I would have other things on my mind than why they all died on their backs. In any case, they don't always die that way—basically it depends on how the little scumbags happen to meet their Maker. I have been studying up on this subject with the crack bug scientists at some of the nation's leading institutions of higher learning, and we have formulated the following Roach Mortality Scenarios, which represent a major step forward in our understanding of roach postmortem postioning: (1) *Roach has heart attack while crawling on the wall.* OK, so maybe roaches don't have heart attacks. Just suppose the roach expires somehow and tumbles earthward. The aerodynamics of the roach corpse (smooth on the back, or wing side; irregular on the front, or leg side) are such that the critter will tend to land on its back. Or so goes the theory. Admittedly the study of bug airfoil characteristics is not as advanced as it might be. (2) *Roach dessicates*, i.e., dries out, after the manner of Lucille Ball. This is what happens when you use Cecil's Guaranteed Roach Assassination Technique, described elsewhere in this volume. The roach saunters carelessly through the lethal borax crystals, causing him to lose precious bodily fluids and eventually die. Since this process is gradual, it may happen that the roach simply conks out and dies on its belly. (3) *Roach dies after ingesting potent neurotoxins,* e.g., Diet Coke, some traditional bug poison like pyrethrum, or the food served at USC cafeterias. Neurotoxins basically cause the roach to twitch itself to death, in the course of which it will frequently kick over on its back, there to flail helplessly until the end comes. No doubt this accounts for the supine position of the deceased cockroaches at USC, although what they are doing there in the first place is another question.

Once again I feel compelled to solicit your enlightenment. Your answer to my inquiry regarding my childhood slaughter of house-flies was most impressive. While it did not drive me to racquetball, neither did it repress what appears to be a deeply rooted psychotic desire to decimate the insect population. I have killed again. Last week I visited my cousin, who is at least as deviate as myself, and whose domicile is infested with cockroaches. We conceived the notion of putting one of the verminous creatures into the micro-wave oven. When one strolled conspicuously onto the counter top, we seized it, imprisoned it in a bottle, and inserted it into the death chamber. Two minutes passed without result. Four minutes. Five. Disgruntled, we persevered for ten more minutes before it became apparent that we had a corpse on our hands. Our question is this: if water boils in three minutes, what took so long for our odious deed to be accomplished?—Two Malefactors in Suspense, Chicago

The study of the effects of microwave ovenry on bugs is still in its infancy, unfortunately, so we cannot provide a definitive answer to this inquiry. However, several possible explanations come to mind. (1) You did not have the microwave plugged in. In the end the cockroach may simply have died of boredom. Many worthwhile experiments have come to grief because of carelessness with the scientific apparatus. (2) The insect you were attempting to incinerate was not really a cockroach. Your basic member of the Blattidae (or cockroach) family goes into a heat stupor at about 105 degrees Fahrenheit and expires a couple degrees above that. The larvae of certain West African midges, though, will recover at least briefly from five-minute exposures to 392 degrees Fahrenheit. Possibly, therefore, what you thought was a cockroach was really a West African midge traveling incognito. (3) Your cousin has a Popeil pocket microwave or some similar el cheapo brand that heats unevenly. Uneven heating to some extent is inherent in microwave cookery, but most manufacturers provide various methods to eliminate the problem. Even so, some ovens have cold spots. Your intended victim may have been the beneficiary of one. Alternatively, if there was a metal cap on the bottle you trapped the cockroach in—metal in microwaves, incidentally, is definitely contraindicated—the metal may have deflected the lethal radiation, delaying the onset of death. (4) What you took to be evidence that the cockroach was still alive was really its death throes. Permanent nerve damage generally results early on in tests of this nature. If you administered an IQ test to the cockroach at the three-minute mark you would quite possibly have discovered that it had been reduced to imbecility. But who knows. Finally, lads, while one appreciates your efforts, I feel compelled to point out that using a 1,000-watt microwave to snuff bugs is a bit . . . Vietnamesque, if you take my meaning. I prefer a good swift shot to the exoskeleton myself. Does wonders for that ancient bloodlust.

Recently a condominium in my neighborhood put signs on their front lawn reading, "This Lawn Is Chemically Treated—Keep Pets Off." I'd like to know, chemically treated with what? That is, if it's chemically treated at all. I have a hunch that there is nothing on the lawn at all and the signs are there to scare away people walking their dogs. If the lawn is treated with something, what most likely is it, and what does it do to the animals? Also, if an animal or child is poisoned or harmed by the chemicals, aren't they responsible? Is there a company or something that goes around treating lawns and sticking up ominous signs to keep dogs off?— J.K., Washington, D.C.

The chemical used may be, as you suspect, no chemical at all, or it may be any of a myriad of herbicides and pesticides. Assuming, for the sake of argument, that there is a real chemical there, and assuming it is not prohibited for use near residences by the federal government, and assuming that the landscaper who put it there has followed the directions for dilution, application, etc., specified for the product's use, and assuming that the treatment is not being repeated every two days or so . . . assuming all these things, none of which is a very risky assumption, there's a very good chance that the sign is pure hokum. Some commonly used lawn-treatment chemicals are toxic—2,4-Dichlorophenoxyacetic acid, a broadleaf weed killer, is a good example—but when they're used properly their danger passes within 24 hours or so as they are washed or absorbed into the soil.

Even in the small number of cases in which signs like this warn of real danger, the chemicals referred to are put there to treat the lawn rather than to chase or harm animals. Anti-animal preparations do exist, but their purpose is to chase only, and they are harmless. One particularly charming concoction I've heard tell of consists of napthalene (in harmless amounts), tobacco dust, and dried animal blood. The blood attracts the offending varmint to the site so it can be scared away forever by the tobacco dust (which causes sneezing) and the napthalene (which causes an unpleasant tingly sensation in the genital area—I told you this stuff was charming). As devious as all this may seem, the product—like others that work on the odor or taste principle—cannot harm any person or thing that eats less that 70 or 80 pounds of it. In sum, this "chemically treated lawn" business is just a cheap psychological ploy calculated to make you keep your goddamn dog off the lawn. Having scooped a fair amount of puppy poop in my day, I think it's a wonderful idea.

While maintaining a tenuous foothold on a space in the vestibule of a commuter train during yesterday's afternoon rush hour stampede, I struggled to recollect what I had once read or heard about the Japanese solution to commuter congestion. Cecil, can you give me the straight dope on (forgive me) "pushers" on the Tokyo subway platforms? Also, what is the meaning of life?—Les E., Chicago

No need to apologize for "pushers"—that's the literal translation of "oshiya," the Japanese term for the guys who make their living cramming commuters into Tokyo's overcrowded subways and trains. As a rule, two oshiya are assigned to every downtown station, each man covering half of each two-car subway train. Since there are two doors per car, the oshiya have to be fast on their feet to stuff as many bodies as possible. They also have to be, shall we say, fairly intimidating fellows: it's said that many oshiya are recruited from the ranks of unemployed sumo wrestlers. But they're nice guys, too—during slack hours, they remain on duty to help little old ladies and other frail types on and off the trains. The Japanese have been putting up with pushers since the early 30s and seem perfectly content to go on doing so.

As for the meaning of life, Luigi Pirandello once wrote: 'Life is little more than a loan shark: it exacts a very high rate of interest for the few pleasures it concedes." But he was probably drunk at the time.

Are the yellow lights on the traffic intersections getting briefer, or am I just getting slower as I inch toward 30? Several times lately I've been nearly run over while crossing the street. I tried watching carefully and found that if the light turned yellow when I was exactly in the middle of the street I could just barely get to the other side. Presumably, then, if it turns yellow just after you've stepped off the curb, you could get yourself killed. Was there a change?—C.M., Baltimore

Light sequencing is carefully calculated according to a formula found in the *Traffic Engineer's Handbook,* which is accepted as a national standard. The formula takes into account the width of the intersection and the speed of traffic, but not the speed of pedestrians—the yellow light, you see, is for cars, not people. If you're on foot you're supposed to be watching the "Walk-Don't Walk" signals, which do take pedestrians into account: about six feet per second in most neighborhoods, four feet per second in neighborhoods that have predominantly elderly residents.

My friends and I were trapped in the middle of the Santa Monica freeway, unable to move in any direction, when the conversation turned to the cause of our condition. "Why," one friend asked, "does traffic come to a stop on a highway that presumably offers nothing to stop it? We should be able to drive across the country without stopping, except for gas." It sounds like a silly question, but what stops the first car in the daily freeway tie-up?—D.S., nearing the Vermont off-ramp, Los Angeles

Actually, D., engineers have devoted considerable study to

expressway traffic, and they have concluded that there is a compelling psychological principle that causes the cars to stop, namely the fear of flaming death. Here's what happens. In theory, given the old rule about maintaining one car length ahead of you for each ten miles per hour of driving speed, the capacity of a single lane of expressway is 40 cars per minute (2,400 per hour) at 60 MPH. In practice, however, drivers instinctively begin to slow down at loads higher than 25 cars per minute (1,500 per hour). At 33 cars per minute (2,000 per hour), average speed drops to 35 MPH. At this critical juncture, drivers are extremely jumpy, and they will slam on the brakes at the slightest provocation—anything from an accident or a stall to a couple extra cars trying to merge into traffic at an on-ramp. The first guy slows down a little, the second guy slows down a lot, and the third, fourth, or fifth guy may stop altogether, bringing traffic to a halt. That's why you almost never find smoothly flowing expressway traffic at speeds below 35 MPH—it's usually stop-and-go, or, at best, speed-up-and-then-slow-down-real-quick. It also explains why relatively minor increases in the traffic volume, such as those caused by mass transit fare increases, frequently result in chaos on the highways. Keep this in mind next time you are tempted to bitch about transit subsidies.

At 4:30 this morning I awoke to an unusual sloshing sound coming from the bathroom. Being the 'fraidy cat that I am, I forced my husband to investigate. Sure enough, we had a large (approximately 12 inches) rat practicing for the Summer Olympics in our toilet! Yucko! After dealing with the immediate situation (I will spare you the details), we started wondering: how did the rat get into the toilet in the first place? Did he climb up the pipe from the sewer? (Bear in mind that we live in a third-floor apartment.) As it turns out, we discovered that he had gotten in through a hole underneath our bathroom sink, which has a cupboard under it. Which raised another question: just how did he manage to scrabble into a porcelain toilet bowl? How clever are these little monsters, anyway? Can they in fact climb through pipes? The thought of having one swim up from below while you're sitting there reading Cosmopolitan *is too horrible to contemplate.—K.B., Chicago*

This is going to gross you out of existence, K.B., but duty demands that the facts be revealed, come what may. First the good news: although some people claim otherwise, Cecil's buddies in the rat annihilation biz say rats probably can't crawl up through toilet soil pipes, because the inside of the pipe is ordinarily wet and slick and because the diameter of said pipe—usually six inches—is too great to permit the rat to chimney its way up, if you follow me. On the other hand, rats are very agile critters and it's quite possible for one to crawl up inside a three- or-four-inch rainspout on a dry day. And rats can certainly crawl up the *outside* of a one-or-two-inch pipe, or, for that matter, up a brick wall using the seams of mortar as pawholds. Rats can also do a tightrope number into your house via the telephone wire. Getting back to toilets, you *do* have a problem if your john is at ground level or in the basement—that is, where the soil pipe runs horizontally or at a very shallow angle to the sewer. Rats are good underwater swimmers, and it's no problem—believe it or not, they actually have movies of this—for rats to stroll along a horizontal soil pipe from the sewer, swim through the water-filled piping inside the toilet, and emerge in the toilet bowl. If the soil pipe runs vertically for five or six feet or more, though, you're probably safe. I underline the word "probably." I have a note here from a Teeming Millionth employed as a janitor who claims that every rat he has ever found in a toilet during his professional career was in a top-floor apartment. From this he deduces that the rats get up on the roof, enter the soil pipe through the roof vent, and *lower themselves down the pipe* and into the john. Screening off the roof vent supposedly cures the problem. Just thought I'd mention it.

Supposing your rat got into the house via more conventional means, such as a hole in the wall, getting into the toilet bowl is no problem; rats are great jumpers. Some can bound as high as three feet or so, which is why people are told to keep lids on their garbage cans. What probably happened in your case was that the rat was looking for a drink of water, fell into the toilet bowl, and couldn't get out.

Now for the remedial measures. Having determined that rats are in the building, we first caulk up the rat holes leading in from outdoors, using steel wool (a temporary measure), cement (where appropriate), tin, or a meshlike material called hardware cloth. This traps all the rats inside the house with you. At this point you have two options: (1) *Learn to live with them.* Rats make wonderfully cuddly pets, so long as you do not mind the threat of rabies, typhus, or bubonic plague. I recall reading a story a while back of two women who kept hundreds of rats as pets in their home, feeding them 10 to 12 loaves of bread per day. The city was finally notified after the telephone company got tired of replacing wires that the rats had chewed through. (2) *Massacre the bastards.* First, starve 'em. Rats basically eat what people eat (they don't like insects and such), so store all food in metal or glass containers or else in the refrigerator. This includes things like flour, sugar, spaghetti, and cereal. Next, wash all dishes and empty all garbage immediately after each meal. Finally, get a snap trap or a glue board (works like flypaper), and bait it with peanut butter, preferably Skippy crunch style. Light a couple candles and put on some Mantovani (rats are suckers for cheap romance). Put the traps near any likely rat habitat, meaning any cool, dark, moist, concealed place, such as under a cupboard or in the wall (rat droppings are a giveaway). Then await the pitter-patter of little feet.

POISON PEN LETTERS FROM THE TEEMING MILLIONS
Pleeeease—rodents are not, I repeat not a source of rabies transmission. Check with the Centers for Disease Control in Atlanta. Perhaps you were thinking of those other warm furry critters, my friends the bats, which are the largest reservoir of rabies in the good old U.S. of A.—George K., M.D., Arkansas

Christ, leave it to the Teeming Millions to speak up for the rats. Listen, George, according to my trusty *Encyclopedia Americana,* rats can carry or transmit typhus, spirochetal jaundice, tularemia, trichinosis, leishmaniasis, leptospirosis, bubonic plague—and rabies. The CDC confirm this. As for bats—well, let me tell you, buddy, they don't take kindly to being libeled by disreputable rat lovers such as yourself. Bat biologist Edward Stashko of Oakton College, Des Plaines, Illinois, estimates that less than one-half of 1 percent of bats are rabid. He says many common misconceptions about bats, such as that they can carry rabies and infect humans without themselves being affected by the disease, grew out of faulty scientific research from the 30s, no doubt conducted at the behest of the rat lobby. According to a 1982 report in *National Wildlife,* only ten people in the U.S. and Canada have contracted rabies from bats in more than 30 years. Exclaims Dr. Stashko: "More people have died from lawn mowers than bats. Statistically you have a better chance of being hit by lightning than being bitten by a rabid bat." Dr. Merlin D. Tuttle, curator of mammals at the Milwaukee Public Museum and founder of the noted philanthropic group, Bat Conservation International (I am not making this up), further elaborates: "You have a greater chance of dying from poisoning at a church picnic than from a bat. Are we going to outlaw those? Thousands of people die at the hands of their spouses every year, yet we're not about to wipe marriage out. Cats and dogs in the neighborhood are more likely to give you rabies. You have to put these dangers in perspective. Statistically, you have a better chance *in this country* of dying from being hit on the head with a coconut than from a bat biting you." According to the CDC, by far the highest incidence of rabies among animals tested occurs not in bats but in skunks. So let's watch it with the smart remarks, eh, punk?

THE TEEMING MILLIONS REPLY IN A RESPECTFUL AND CIVILIZED MANNER. TOMORROW: SUN RISES IN WEST, POPE DISCOVERED TO BE JEWISH
I was flattered to rank no worse than "punk" in your pantheon of ne'er-do-wells, but I have always been one to do my homework on matters such as bats, and I would not want people to get the impression from your answer that they have nothing to fear from bats.

To clarify a few matters (I would not be so presumptuous as to attempt to correct you again), I am no rat lover. Indeed, I am a card-carrying caver, and have a special fondness for all forms of cave life, particularly bats. However, I have also received pre-exposure rabies prophylaxis, and doctors Stashko and Tuttle no doubt have also—they would be fools not to. Any bat bite is presumed to be rabid, for good reason. Have you ever tried to catch a bat after it bites you? What about recognizing him in a lineup of several hundred thousand bats—not uncommon numbers in Texas and New Mexico caves? Skunks are slow-witted surface dwellers and much easier to catch. Besides, they're not on the endangered species list yet and several American bats are. With only 1-5 cases of rabies per year since 1960 in the U.S., 10 cases of bat-transmitted rabies is a pretty significant number, particularly since cavers are about the only people that regularly come up against the critters (not so with skunks!). Even if only one half of one percent of bats are rabid, it's been estimated that the Mexican free-tailed bat population of Texas alone was over 100 million in 1957. One half of one percent is still a lot of bats. You should also know that no rodent rabies transmission has ever been reported in the U.S.—George K., Imboden, Arkansas

No need to be so reasonable about it.

Chapter 3

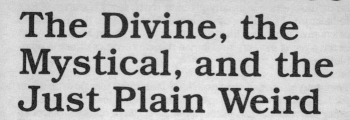

The Divine, the Mystical, and the Just Plain Weird

How come people always say "Jesus H. Christ"? Why not Jesus Q. Christ or Jesus R. Christ or something else? Does the H really stand for something? My future peace of mind depends on your answer.—W.B.T., Chicago

The *H* stands for Harold, as in, "Our Father, Harold be they name" (snort).

Actually, I've heard numerous explanations for the *H* over the years. The first is that it stands for "Holy," as in Jesus Holy Christ, a common enough blasphemy in the South, abridged to *H* by fast-talking Northerners. Other colorful southern epithets include Jesus Hebe Christ and Jesus Hebrew Christ, which abbreviate similarly. The drawback of this account is that it is so hopelessly unimaginative that I can barely type it without falling asleep. Luckily, the other theories are more entertaining: (1) It stands for "Haploid." This is an old bio major joke, referring to the unique (not to say immaculate) circumstances of Christ's conception. Having no biological father, J.C. was shortchanged in the chromosome department to the tune of one half. Ingenious, I'll admit, but whimsy has no place in a serious investigation such as this. (2) It recalls the *H* in the IHS logo emblazoned on much Christian paraphernalia. IHS dates from the earliest years of Christianity, being an abbreviation of "Jesus" in classical Greek characters. The Greek pronunciation is "Iesous," with the *E* sound being represented by the character eta, which looks like an *H*. When the symbol passed to Christian Romans, for whom an *H* was an *H*, the unaccountable character eventually became accepted as Jesus's middle initial. (3) Finally, a reader makes the claim that the *H*

33

derives from the taunting Latin inscription INRH that was supposedly tacked on the cross by Roman soldiers: Iesus Nazarenus, Rex Hebrei (Jesus the Nazarene, King of the Hebrews). Trouble is, the inscription is usually given as INRI: Iesus Nazarenus, Rex Iudaeorum (J.C., King of the Jews). Nonetheless, this is the kind of creative thinking I like to see from my Teeming Millions. With every passing day, my mission on this earth comes closer to completion.

They taught us in grammar school that sightseers have to stoop for fear of braining themselves while exploring the Mayflower *and other historical ships, because our forefathers apparently tended to be a lot shorter than we are today. A while back, I was glancing at Anthony Burgess's book* Jesus of Nazareth; *in it Christ is portrayed as a physically tall and powerful man. A special on the Shroud of Turin the other night described the spooky image as five feet, ten inches tall. If Jesus Christ were this height, would he have been literally a big man in his time?—Blair G., Phoenix*

He'd have been somewhat bigger than the average, but not exceptionally so. Based on the somewhat limited fossil evidence we have from the Middle East—mainly Egyptian mummies and the like—average height in Christ's time was probably around five feet six. There were people who were quite a bit taller, though; Ramses III, pharaoh of Egypt from 1198 to 1166 BC, is said to have been around six feet even.

So far as can be determined, height didn't start to increase significantly until well into the Industrial Revolution. The most dramatic increase has occurred within the last 50 years or so due to advances in nutrition, notably the invention of Wheaties, the breakfast of champions.

I hear Jesus wasn't really a Capricorn, but that he was either a Pisces or a Leo instead—that his birthday is observed in December because the Catholic Church took over the ancient Saturnalia debauch. What's the lowdown?—Jerry M., Los Angeles

History records no observation of Christmas before 354, and by that time there was no one around who remembered exactly when Jesus was born. Today, historians have all but given up trying to figure it out. They give his birth date as 6-8 BC (good trick, but this was no ordinary dude) and leave it at that.

Nobody knows exactly why Christ's birthday is celebrated on December 25. One theory holds that this is the *right* date, postulating that Zachary was high priest and that the Day of Atonement fell on September 24, ergo, John the Baptist was born on June 24 and Christ dropped in exactly six months later on December 25. Modern scholars use this theory to get laughs at cocktail parties. Another guess works backward from the supposed date of crucifixion (March 25), figuring that Christ was conceived exactly 33 years before he died, True Believers having no use for fractional numbers. According to the most tenable hypothesis, Christ's birthday was assigned to the winter solstice (December 25 in the Julian calendar, January 6 in the Egyptian) because the date had a ready-made pagan holiday, the "Birthday of the Invincible Sun" (or "ancient Saturnalia debauch," as you put it).

The idea that Jesus was a Pisces probably comes from the characterization of that sign as one of spiritualism, humility, compassion, sacrifice, etc. Students of astrology will tell you it's not kosher to work the formula backwards that way.

During the TV series I, Claudius, *mentions of Jesus Christ were mostly couched in allusions to "the Nazarene." In one of the later episodes, however, he was referred to as "Joshua bar-Joseph." Was this his true natal name, and if so, how did it get transformed into Jesus?—John S., Chicago*

"Jesus" is the Greek form of the Hebrew "Joshua" (meaning "Jehovah saves"), which is the name (roughly) The Boss went by in his heyday. Galileans during the time of Christ spoke Aramaic, but apparently they used Hebrew names for their kids the way Italian-Americans, say, might use an Italian name today. By the time the Gospels were written in 60 AD or so, Greek had come into general use for literary purposes, and "Joshua" became "Jesus." The prefix *bar*-means "son of" in Aramaic, and "bar-Joseph" is thus roughly comparable to "O'Shaughnessy," to put it in terms that the average citizen can relate to.

I don't want to get your column embroiled in biblical debates, but I must know the answer to a question that has been bothering me for some time. I need to know if the Egyptians record the Jewish Exodus in their ancient historical documents. If so, does it differ from the historical accounts? Do they record a "Moses" raised as a pharoah's son? Did they notice that they were hit with ten plagues? Finally, do they record the destruction of the Egyptian army in the Red Sea?—Rufino O., Chicago

If you're hoping for a clipping from the Egyptian *News-Gazette* reporting a spate of singular weather—e.g., partly sunny with occasional torrents of fire (giggle)—I'm afraid I'll have to disappoint you. Apart from the Old Testament and related sources, there are only a few surviving records of any sort from the Mosaic era, mostly in the form of inscribed stone slabs called stelae. There is a large body of Hellenic literature dealing with Moses, but all of it was written long after the fact and was considerably embroidered in the process. One stela from the reign of Merneptah (1235-1227 BC, thought to be roughly the time of the Exodus) does refer to the nomad tribe of Israel, but claims to have destroyed it. Plainly the war correspondence of the time was no more reliable than that of the present era.

Depsite the lack of primary source material, there have been innumerable efforts over the years to relate biblical places and events to their historical counterparts, with mixed success. To this day there remains wide disagreement as to the precise identity of such basic landmarks as the Sea of Reeds (it certainly wasn't the Red Sea) and Mount Sinai. One school of thought holds that Moses cunningly led his people across the Gulf of Suez at ebb tide, then watched as the water rose to its customary six and a half feet and drowned the pursuing Egyptians. This hypothesis fails to account for the mighty wind that supposedly parted the waters to begin with. Another theory has it that the Israelites crossed Lake Subonis, which is (or was) separated from the Mediterranean by a narrow isthmus. The surrounding land is swampy and treacherous and the isthmus itself is frequently submerged during storms; no doubt the reader can imagine an appropriate scenario.

Of course, the fact that there is no historical evidence for the existence of Moses or the ten plagues does not necessarily mean that they were purely mythical; there is precious little historical evidence to establish the existence of anybody from the period, except for those who happened to be head honcho at one time or another. On the other hand, it seems likely that much of the detail of the biblical account was drawn from Egyptian sources. The name "Moses" apparently derives from the common Egyptian suffix –mose, "born of," as in Thut–mose, "born of the god Thut." The Old Testament claim that the name comes from the Hebrew mashah is thought to be an example of Judaic wishful thinking. The story of the infant Moses's rescue from the canebrake, interestingly, parallels the Egyptian legend of the goddess Isis, who hid her son Horus in a delta papyrus thicket to protect him from some nasty fate.

The various plagues described in the Old Testament, such as lice, pestilence, locusts, boils, and whatnot, are all commonplace features of Egyptian life, which may account for the eagerness of the Israelites to leave in the first place. The first plague, for instance, when Moses turns the waters of the Nile to blood, most likely recalls the fact that the Nile turns red during the spring floods because of the various microorganisms floating around in it. How Moses arranged to have this phenomenon operate on command is beyond me. Maybe he knew Mayor Daley.

While it hadn't occured to me that you might be the font of knowledge from which this information might flow, it did occur to my best friend. The mystery surrounds the message the Blessed Virgin left to the children when she miraculously appeared to them in Fatima, Portugal. It was to be opened some 50 years later, but curiosity got the better of the pope and it was opened before the time elapsed. The message was never revealed. What's the secret? Was it that horrible? Do you think the National Enquirer *might know?—M.R., Washington, D.C.*

Before loosing my mighty torrent of knowledge, M., I'll have to provide a little background for those Teeming Millions who never learned the charming story of Fatima because they were wasting their formative years having impure thoughts and eating hamburger on Fridays. You might do well to pay attention yourself, because your letter contains a couple of regrettable misconceptions.

Though the Catholic Church is naturally reluctant to recognize tales of miracles, cures, apparitions, and the like, it has deemed credible the story of the Blessed Virgin's appearances at Fatima to three Portuguese children: Lucia dos Santos, aged ten, and her cousins Francisco and Jacinta Marto, nine and seven. After the first of these appearances—they occurred monthly from May through October 1917—word got around that something neat was going on, and with each subsequent visit increasing numbers of people came to Fatima to have a look. Only the children could see and hear the Lady, however; the rest had to be content with a moving cloud, a rustling tree, and—on the final visit—a grand miracle, witnessed by up to 100,000 people, in which the sun danced around the sky for ten minutes.

Among other things, the Lady allegedly told the children that World War I would end soon, that another great war was coming, and that two of the children, Francisco and Jacinta, would be taken into heaven shortly. They died of influenza within three years. The third child, Lucia, entered the convent in 1925. Though the Lady of Fatima had told the children to keep certain of their conversations secret, Lucia eventually succumbed to pressure from her religious superiors and set down the three-part "Secret of Fatima" in various written memoranda beginning in 1941. The first two parts, which Lucia revealed relatively freely, were quickly made public: (1) The Lady of Fatima showed the children a vision of hell, including demons that "could be distinguished by their terrifying and repellent likeness to frightful and unknown animals." (2) In order to prevent "war, famine and persecutions of the church and of the Holy Father," the Lady said she would return to ask for the "Consecration of Russia to my Immaculate Heart."

Lucia wrote down the third part of the secret, much more reluctantly, after Christmas of 1943, and it is this part that remains a mystery. Her memoir was sealed in an envelope and given to the bishop of Leiria, Portugal, to whom Lucia expressed her wish— not, as far as anyone has been able to determine, the Lady of Fatima's wish—that it remain sealed at least until 1960, when it would "seem clearer." Later, Lucia apparently extracted a promise that it would definitely be opened and made public in 1960. Before the year of truth arrived, however, the document was passed to Rome, under circumstances that do not shine very clearly through the mist of history. Pope Pius XII, who died in 1958, may have read it, and Pope John XXIII and a few cronies certainly did, probably in 1959. John said, "This makes no reference to my time"; though Lucia was still alive, he dispatched the document to the archives and left the matter to his successors, none of whom has yet seen fit to come clean.

The papal cover-up, combined with the red-baiting, fire-and-brimstone nature of the revealed parts of the secret, has led many observers to speculate that the message is one of nuclear apocalypse. I, however, have it on good authority that it was a personal missive to Pope John. To wit:

Dear Jack—What's all this nonsense about birth control? We never said anything about birth control. Please check your files and advise ASAP.—Regards, G. P.S.: Kennedy for President!

I got a certain morbid thrill from watching the Spanish nuns who were briefly released from their vows of silence to act as cheerleaders for the pope during one of his visits. This led to curiosity about vows of silence, and I asked my parochial-schooled husband about the matter, but he claimed to have no knowledge of the subject. So it's up to you: why do some monks and nuns have vows of silence? Do the vocal cords atrophy after, say, 50 years of this? Do you get expelled if you talk in your sleep? And how about everyday, mundane activities and communications? How do

38

*you get someone to pass the sugar (or hair shirt)? Sign language?
Scribbled messages?—Joyce K., Seattle*

Let us eschew snottiness here, Joyce; there are many among us who would profit from a little enforced quietude. Jesse Jackson, for instance. Silence teaches self-discipline, and has been a prominent feature of many religious and monastic regimens down through the ages, in both Eastern and Western cultures. Although there are Indian ascetics who claim (via notes, I presume) not to have spoke a word in years, usually silence of this kind is not total. Trappist monks, for instance, sing hymns and recite prayers on a daily basis, and are permitted to talk when addressed by superiors, when a work assignment demands it, or when escorting guests. Casual conversation is forbidden, but brief dispensations are granted on special occasions. A rudimentary sign language is used when necessary. Talking in your sleep, needless to say, is not punished, and most minor infractions will earn you nothing more serious than some extra penance, although occasionally more elaborate punishments are prescribed. In one monastery, for instance, talkative monks are assigned lower-status jobs in the monastery shop, where the community earns extra income anodizing such things as animal figurines. Obedient monks are permitted to apply zinc to lions, eagles, and other imposing creatures. "Loose lips," however, zinc sheeps. Sorry, couldn't help myself.

*I have a question to which I need an immediate reply, which I
hope you publish, as others in the community may feel the need
to know this information. Please list in order the most preferred
ways to kill a vampire.—J. Pasquale, Baltimore*

I'll admit I've heard some horror stories about the crime rate in Baltimore, J., but *vampires*—land o'Goshen, honey, things are really getting out of hand. Grab your pencil. To kill a vampire it is first necessary to determine its ethnic origin. I regret that I cannot offer much useful information on how this might be accomplished, but I am sure you will think of something. Next, locate the vampire's daytime whereabouts, i.e., its grave. My vampire manual recommends placing "a young lad who is innocent of girls," such as Richard Simmons, atop a black virgin stallion, and leading the two through a likely graveyard. If the horse refuses to pass a certain grave, you've hit paydirt, so to speak. The telltale signs of a vampirous corpse are fluidity of the blood, lack of putrefaction, and flexibility of the limbs (we're talking about *corpses* now, mind you). Finally, administer treatment as prescribed below:

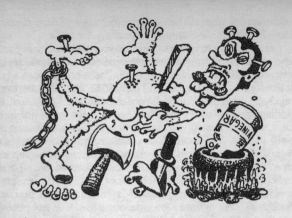

Species	Country	Approved Method of Disposal
Sampiro	Albania	Stake through heart
Nachtzehrer	Bavaria	Place coin in mouth, decapitate with ax
Ogoljen	Bohemia	Bury at crossroads
Krvoijac	Bulgaria	Chain to grave with wild roses
Kathakano	Crete	Boil head in vinegar
Brukulaco	Greece	Cut off and burn head
Vampir	Hungary	Stake through heart, nail through temples
Dearg-dul	Ireland	Pile stones on grave
Vryolakas	Macedonia	Pour boiling oil on, drive nail through navel
Upier	Poland	Bury face downwards
Gierach	Prussia	Put poppy seeds in grave
Strigoiul	Rumania	Remove heart, cut in two; garlic in mouth, nail in head
Vlkoslak	Serbia	Cut off toes, drive nail through neck
Neuntoter	Saxony	Lemon in mouth
Vampiro	Spain	No known remedy

I realize the above will not be much use in the case of a Third World vampire, but you cannot have everything. Incidentally, we will have none of this "preferred ways" business. There is a right way and a wrong way to do everything. Take some pride in your work.

Tell me about halo. How and where and when did this come about? Who decided? Why do Buddhist artifacts have halo? Who else used it?—S.C., Chicago

Your wish is my command, my little swamp turnip, but you might try to be a little less peremptory next time you write your

Unca Cecil, who after all has been certified by God as Font of Universal Wisdom. The halo (also called a *nimbus*) has been around since the time of the Greeks and Romans, and was incorporated into Christian art sometime in the fourth century AD. Actually, this halo business is pretty intricate. There are not only plain round halos, used to signify saints, there's also the cross within a halo, used for Christ; the triangular halo, used for representations of the Trinity; and the square halo, used to depict unusually saintly living personages, such as certain scandalously underpaid journalists I could name. (Square halos, I am obliged to report, look totally Polish. No offense.) Occasionally you also see things like the hexagonal halo, about which the less said the better.

Related to the halo is the aureole, a lemon-drop-shaped item that appears to radiate from the entire body of the holy being. There's also "glory," which is sort of a generalized effusion of blessedness used to cover up troublesome details in the vicinity of the saintly centerpiece that the artist does not feel like drawing. Similar ingenuity has been shown in the depiction of halos. In relatively crude medieval art, it was sufficient simply to sketch in a circle, but in naturalistic Renaissance art, it was deemed necessary to depict the halo in perspective, which resulted in a solid-looking object looking suspiciously like a coffee saucer suspended over the noggin of the elect. This ridiculous notion was soon abandoned in favor of rays of light and similarly mystical representation. I note, incidentally, that in the *Encyclopedia Britannica* there is a picture of an angel flipping a combination halo and Frisbee, clearly an attempt at a little ecclesiastical humor. (The title sez "Angel with a Millstone," but I wasn't born yesterday.) The Buddhists of India, finally, picked up the halo from Greek invaders in the third century AD.

As a child, my parents supplied me with books in order to keep me out of mischief. One of my earliest heroes was Harry Houdini, the colorful escape artist. Countless summer days were spent daydreaming and conjecturing on the secrets behind Harry's slipperiness. But regardless of my conclusions, I felt secure in the belief that Harry's special knowledge would one day become public, due (I had heard) to a provision in his will that his secrets be revealed after the passage of a certain number of years. Has that date come and gone? If so, where can I get my hands on this info? I need it in case my brother's parole falls through.—D.T.D., Chicago

Houdini's will must be second only to Jerry Mather's Vietnam demise as the all-time great Rumor That Would Not Die. For years I've heard stories about manuscripts withering away in bank vaults, waiting for the fiftieth anniversary of Houdini's death (which, by the way, was 1976) to be given to the world. But stories, alas, are all they are. Houdini left most of his apparatus to his brother, who toured for a few years after Houdini's death under the name "Hardeen." Houdini's will stipulated that all the tricks and manuscripts be burned after Hardeen's death, but some of the material has survived in private collections. Even so, none of Houdini's plans for his more spectacular effects has ever come to light— apparently the sonofabitch took them with him. So we may never know—for sure—how Houdini escaped after being lashed to the arm of a windmill in Holland, or stuffed down the gut of a dead "sea monster" in Boston, or sealed in a giant envelope in Chicago (he got out without making a tear), or, my personal favorite, sewn up inside a giant football by the University of Pennsylvania varsity squad.

Houdini published several books and pamphlets on magic during his lifetime. I particularly recommend *Miracle Mongers and Their Methods* (1920), a genuinely bizarre volume that gives the Straight Dope on such dubious entertainments as driving a steel spike through your cheek and setting your arm on fire. You'll be the life of the party. Some of Houdini's shorter articles were collected in a Dover paperback, *Houdini on Magic*, edited by Walter B. Gibson. A few books purporting to "expose" Houdini have also been published, such as J.D. Cannell's 1932 *Secrets of Houdini*, but these now seem to be wholly fraudulent.

There were two main schools of thought on Houdini's escapes. One, pushed by Cannell and others, held that Houdini was a mere contortionist, who could expand his muscles while restraints were being placed on him, then later relax and slip out of his bonds. The other explanation, which I mention here entirely for its entertainment value, was offered by Sir Arthur Conan Doyle, the creator of Sherlock Holmes, who claimed that Houdini was a full-fledged medium, performing his escapes with the help of the spirit world. How the spirit world felt about doing three-a-day vaudeville has not been recorded.

The plain truth, not surprisingly, seems to be that Houdini was merely an extraordinarily accomplished showman, who knew how to milk a few basic techniques of stage magic for all they were worth. Today, professional magicians say that most of Houdini's tricks could be reproduced, but his performances could never be.

Just exactly what event are the Russians and Red Chinese commemorating on May 1 each year? I have yet to find any birthday or important event relating to communism/socialism that occurred on May 1. Someone once told me, though, that May 1, 1776, was the birth date of a group called the Illuminati, which was alleged to be a clandestine group devoted to one-world government. Is it so? Please enlighten.—Bob B., Dallas

Better grab yourself a sandwich and a beer, Bobberino; this is going to take a while. The Illuminati play a leading role in what is without doubt the muthah conspiracy theory of all time, stretching back at least two centuries and probably as far as the Pleistocene Era, to hear some tell it. Adherents of the theory, who for the most part are right-wing fruitcakes, claim it explains every social upheaval from the French Revolution of 1789 through the Russian Revolution of 1917. The Illuminati are said to be the guiding force behind a vast international cabal involving the Masons, German and/or Jewish socialists, the Bolsheviks, and revolutionaries of every stripe, whose principal aim is either the establishment of a totalitarian one-world government, the destruction of Western civilization, or both. This ain't no foolin' around, apocalypse fans.

But let's start with the easy part first. May Day, an international celebration of worker solidarity observed principally in socialist countries, traces its origins back to the eight-hour-day movement in the U.S., and specifically commemorates the 1886 Haymarket Riot in Chicago, of all places (we learn this, incidentally, from the *Great Soviet Encyclopedia*). At an October 1884 convention in Chicago, the Federation of Organized Trades and Labor Unions, later to be reorganized as the American Federation of Labor, declared May 1, 1886, to be the date from which "eight hours shall constitute a legal day's work," as opposed to the nine- or ten-hour days then prevalent.

Why May 1 is chosen is not clear. Among other things, it happened to be the date of the traditional May Day spring festival, celebrated in Europe (and parts of the U.S.) since medieval times. But other American labor groups had earlier suggested other days, such as the Fourth of July.

In any event, the federation, which at the time was neither very powerful nor very radical, had no particular plans for May 1, 1886. As the day drew nearer, though, radical labor organizations began to agitate for a general strike. Sentiment for the strike was especially pronounced in Chicago, home of many leftist German immigrants and the leading center of the radical labor movement in the U.S. The strike and accompanying demonstrations in Chicago went off peacefully enough on May 1, but on May 4, at a workers' demonstration in Haymarket Square, someone threw a bomb into a crowd of policemen, killing seven. In the ensuing melee the cops killed two workers, and four radicals were later hanged for their roles on the basis of flimsy evidence. The Haymarket affair cemented the importance of May Day in the radical calendar. In Paris in 1889 the Second International, a federation of socialist organizations, called for demonstrations of labor solidarity on May 1, 1890, and May Day has been observed one way or another ever since—although not, ironically, in the U.S.

Coincidentally—although some would say it's no coincidence—May 1 is also the date that a secret society called the Illuminati was founded in 1776 by a Bavarian university professor named Adam Weishaupt. Although the group's precise aims are a little murky, the Illuminati were apparently dedicated to the abolition of organized religion and the nation-state—in short, they were anarchists. Such ideas were not uncommon at the time; Enlightenment thinkers like Rousseau had vaguely similar notions.

By and by it occurred to Weishaupt that he could multiply his influence by infiltrating existing lodges of Masons. The Masons, themselves a secret society, seem to have originated in England, and by Weishaupt's time were well established throughout Europe. Although they were decentralized and had no overriding political program, the Masons had attracted a fair number of freethinkers, who to some extent took advantage of the group's clandestine character to discuss Enlightenment ideas. Masons were suspected of being anticlerical, and had been condemned on several occasions by the Catholic Church

Weishaupt's minions succeeded in gaining influential positions in many Masonic lodges in Germany, Austria, and elsewhere. Characteristically, though, only the top leaders of the Illuminati knew the full extent of the group's radical plans. Weishaupt, who claimed to have been inspired partly by the Jesuits, set up an elaborate hierarchy complete with secret signs, ceremonies, and codes in which members were gradually given additional knowledge as they rose in rank. Eventually, though, some of the Illuminati quarreled, and disgruntled ex-members went to the authorities with lurid stories. In 1785, the alarmed Elector of Bavaria ordered both the Illuminati and the Masons suppressed. Numerous incriminating papers were confiscated and later published throughout Europe, creating a widespread panic that secret societies were plotting the violent overthrow of all civilization. This probably would have died down eventually, except for one thing: on July

14, 1789, the Bastille fell to a Paris mob, and the French Revolution began.

We now take leave of Reality, and enter the twilight world of Total Paranoia. Not much is known about what happened to the Illuminati after 1785. Some of them went underground, and several may have been involved in various plots over the following few years. Whatever the truth of the matter, rightists began churning out an immense volume of books and pamphlets blaming the Illuminati for . . . well, just about everything. The most famous of these was a five-volume work published in 1797-99 by Augustin de Barruel, a French cleric. A synthesis of nearly every plot theory that had appeared up to that time, Barruel's book traced the alleged conspiracy from the Manichean heresy of the third century AD down through the Knights Templars in the Middle Ages and finally to the Masons and the Illuminati, who (he said) were ultimately successful in fomenting the French Revolution.

Barruel's book was the foundation of a vast legend about the Illuminati and their allies, lackeys, and dupes that has continued, with considerable elaboration, down to the present day. Well into the 20th century, Barruel was still being quoted by other conspiracy writers. What is striking, though, is not just the longevity of the theory, but the extent to which it was wholeheartedly believed. Even so prominent a figure as the English statesman Disraeli accepted unquestioningly the notion that secret societies were behind everything.

Perhaps the most prominent of the conspiracy theorists writing in English was Nesta Webster. Her books, such as *World Revolution: The Plot Against Civilization* and *Secret Societies and Subversive Movements*, were immensely popular—the latter, first published in 1924, went into an eighth edition in 1964. It is difficult in a short space to do justice to the all-encompassing grandeur of Ms. Webster's version of the Theory, but basically she felt that all the revolutionary events of 1789 through 1917 were the work of "illuminized freemasons," many of them German, who were allied with a group of apostate Jews who, among other things, controlled international finance. Lenin, she wrote, was "the agent of the great German-Jewish company that hopes to rule the world." Zionism and the efforts to liberate Ireland were also part of the plot. Finally, she noted in *World Revolution*, "Was it again a mere coincidence that in July 1889 an International Socialist Congress in Paris decided that May 1, which was *the day on which Weishaupt founded the Illuminati* [her italics], should be chosen for an annual International Labour demonstration . . .?"

And so it goes. You hear less about the Illuminati today,

probably because the whole thing is so cornball, and let's face it, after 200 years even the best conspiracy theory starts to get a little old. I note here in my copy of *None Dare Call it Conspiracy* (1972), a crackpot classic that pins the one-world plot on the Council on Foreign Relations, that the Illuminati rate only a couple paragraphs. The tendency of late seems to be to play the whole Illuminati business for laughs. Several years ago a couple wise guys named Robert Shea (a onetime *Playboy* editor) and Robert Anton Wilson wrote an off-the-wall conspiracy satire called *Illuminatus!*, which among other things disclosed that the Illuminati had reached the *New York Times*. Now and then, Shea claimed, the word "fnord" will pop up in a news story. You can't consciously see it, he says, "but it's placed throughout the paper, and you notice it only subconsciously. Every time you see a 'fnord' you feel fear, so that by the time you have finished reading the paper you're in a state of chronic, low-grade emergency paranoia. Keeping people in that state is one of the main things the Illuminati do."

So much for the comic relief. What influence, if any, the Illuminati *really* had on the French Revolution or anything else is impossible to say, naturally, but you could make the case that some features of Illuminati organization, notably the use of front groups and the concept of a revolutionary elite, were an inspiration to later radicals. Undoubtedly their chief impact, however, was the climate of paranoia they engendered. For a fuller discussion of the whole business, see *The Mythology of the Secret Societies*, by J.M. Roberts (1972).

In high expectation of Valentine's Day, I'd like to get a guaranteed high potency love potion recipe and corresponding love spell. How about it, Cece?—Barb T., Chicago

Strictly no sweatski, Barbikins. I provide below a handy recipe for an herbal love charm, devised by one Miriam "Starhawk" Simos of San Francisco. I should point out that this is a sort of all-purpose cluster-bomb-type love charm, to be used only if you are not real fussy about who your prospective manchild turns out to be. If you already have some particular target in mind, there is probably some more salubrious method, but I do not know what it is, not having gotten that far in my witchcraft book yet. For the nonce, fake it.

LOVE CHARM RECIPE

Ingredients: A circle of rose-colored or (for more sexually passionate love) red cloth; acacia flowers, myrtle, rose petals or buds, jasmine flowers, and lavender; a red felt heart, and a copper coin

or ring. To tie them all up (in seven knots), use a blue thread or ribbon.

Directions: (1) Assemble all materials on your altar (you *do* have an altar, I assume). (2) Cast a circle. Easier said than done, judging from the instructions here. You have to recite this incantation about the Red Lion of the noon heat and all this other stuff, plus you have to make mystical gesticulations with your sacred witch's knife. Sounds pretty cornball to me. Personally I'd go with, "I hereby declare this circle cast. Amen and hallelujah." No muss, no fuss. (3) Light candle (incense optional). (4) Raise energy, it says here. In other words, get psyched. (5) With mortar and pestle, grind together herbs. (6) Gather herbs and other objects into cloth. Twist top and tie together with thread. (7) Breathe on charm, charge with air. Charge basically means recite more incantations. If I were you, I'd trash the incantation jive, but for those who insist on it, here is a representative sestet:

> HAR HAR HOU HOU
> DANCE Ici DANCE La!
> JOUE Ici JOUE La!
> HAR HAR HOU HOU!
> DANCE Here DANCE There!
> PLAY Here PLAY There!

El retardo supremo, if you want my opinion. Anyway: (8) Pass charm through candle flame, charge with fire. (9) Sprinkle a few drops of water on charm, charge with water. (10) Dip into salt, or touch to pentacle, if you happen to have one on you, and charge with earth. (11) Hold charm in hands, breathe on it, and charge fully with whatever energy is left over from 7, 8,

47

9, and 10, concentrating on your visualization. (12) Drop to the ground, relax, and earth the power. (I know this is cryptic. It is in the nature of witchcraft to be cryptic. If you want easy-to-follow directions, go buy a box of cake mix.) (13) Visualize tying knot. Actually tie knot (total of seven, remember). Recite as follows: "By all the power/Of three times three/This spell bound around/Shall be./To cause no harm/Nor return on me/As I do will/So mote it be!" Hip hip hooray, etc. (14) Open circle and await arrival of love. For further details, see *The Spiral Dance: A Rebirth of the Ancient Religion of the Great Goddess* by Starhawk, available at fine occult bookstores everywhere.

Didn't Jimmy Carter once claim he had seen a UFO? Was he all by himself, or did other people see it too? Has there been any subsequent investigation? Was it a "real" UFO, or did Jimmy get snookered by swamp gas?—Rhoda A., Baltimore

Two guesses, kiddo. In a report filed with the Center for UFO Studies in Evanston, Illinois, Carter claimed to have seen his UFO in October, 1969, when he was running (unsuccessfully, at that point) for governor of Georgia. Being a shrewd politician even then, he didn't file his report until September, 1973 (hell, look what happened to Eagleton). It was around 7:15, shortly after dark, when Carter and a group of about 10 or 12 people spotted the alleged UFO over the countryside near Leary, Georgia. The object stood still in the sky for a period of 10 or 12 minutes, slowly changing its color, size, and brightness, and then gradually retreated into the distance, disappearing from view. Carter estimated that the object, at its closest, was some 300 to 1,000 yards away.

Later research, however, has cast grave doubts on the Big Peanut's credibility. Robert Sheaffer, a volunteer researcher for the Committee for the Scientific Investigation of Claims of the Paranormal, reported in an issue of *Zetetic* magazine that what Carter actually saw on that fateful October eve was not a flying saucer, but the planet Venus, a notorious trickster in these matters. Nor was the fateful eve in October—apparently, during the four-year gap between the incident and Carter's report, the President confused his dates. By checking the files of the Lions Club chapter that Carter was scheduled to address that evening, Sheaffer discovered that the actual date was January 6, 1969—a night on which the planet would be sitting in precisely the spot where Carter saw his spaceship. "Either an extraterrestrial space vehicle was covering up Venus," Sheaffer concludes drily, "or Mr. Carter was looking at the planet."

We were having a heated argument the other day that it's impossible to clap without using both hands. But then someone piped up that the Chinese have found a way of clapping using one hand only. Can they do it? Can anyone?—Frank N., Baltimore

I notice, Frank, that you hail from Baltimore, a city whose residents fall into one of two categories, in my observation: (1) persons of exceeding wit and ingenuity, and (2) complete idiots. Your letter, quite honestly, lends itself equally well to either proposition. Let us start with the latter.

(1) *You are an idiot.* There is this thing called a "joke," Frank, that you may want to look into sometime. A joke is a display of cleverness intended to engender yux. There are, however, certain rather thick personages who require advance notice if they are to recognize a joke when they see one. In polite society it is customary when in the presence of these people to signal the onset of a joke by means of some subtle stratagem, such as a gong, large firecracker, or air-raid siren. Clearly your so-called friends could stand a lesson in thoughtfulness. For further insight, see (2) below.

(2) *You are a person of exceeding wit and ingenuity*, and your letter is actually a coy recasting of a famous Zen Buddhist koan, or riddle, such as Zen masters use to instruct their pupils. The koan in question, devised by the Japanese Zen master Hakuin (1686-1769), is as follows: *In clapping both hands, a sound is heard. What is the sound of one hand?* (In casual discussion this is usually corrupted to: *What is the sound of one hand clapping?*) Unsophisticated persons are generally inclined to answer with something like "half a clap," which signifies that they have not yet achieved Buddha nature. After several years of dedicated meditating, however, they learn the correct response, which is to face the questioner, assume an appropriate Buddhist posture, and without a word thrust one hand forward. I learn this from *The Sound of One Hand Clapping: 281 Zen Koans With Answers* (Yoel Hoffmann, translator), which is my idea of an admirably no-bullshit approach to cosmic enlightenment. I realize that the allegedly correct response in this case is a little on the enigmatic side, but that is Zen Buddhism for you. It is by ruminating assiduously on such mysteries that we learn to free our minds from the strictures of linear thinking and grasp the essence of the void. Other effective methods of combating linear thinking are Quaaludes and old *Magnum P.I.* reruns, two excellent examples of the way modern technology enriches ancient religious practice.

The other Zen koan you may want to take note of is said to have been composed by the Japanese Zen master Joshu (778-897), and goes as follows: *Does a dog have Buddha nature?* The correct answer is *Mooooo*, uttered in a sort of plaintive bellow. In the interest of perfect technical accuracy I suppose I should mention that the conventional spelling here is usually *Mu*, which is Zen Buddhist for "a question that is so dumb as not to be worth answering." However, *Mooooo* seems to me to be infinitely more expressive and meaningful to noble children of the sod such as ourselves, particularly those who live in Iowa. Anyway, Frank, I am glad you brought up the subject. We cannot learn about foreign cultures unless we ask.

FURTHER INSIGHT FROM THE TEEMING MILLIONS

Re your recent discussion, the sound of one hand clapping is, as any true friend of Jimmy Rockford can tell you, the sound of a slap in the face.—Evelyn M., San Quentin, California

Once again I marvel at the subtle ways in which Westerners assimilate the wisdom of the Orient.

Whilst reading of the yoga practice of swallowing a long strip of cloth and pulling it back up again in order to clean the stomach passage, I was struck with a most intriguing idea. What if one were to feed in enough string to extend from one's mouth to one's posterior, cheek to cheek as it were? Could this be done? What type of string would be best and how long would it have to be? If I attached Dixie cups to each end would I be able to talk to a friend? How much time would it take for it to run its course and could I pull it out of the orifice of my choice? Don't string me along on this one, Cecil, because I'm ...—Hanging by a Thread in Dallas

Dixie cups, eh? The disinterested scientific observer does not have time for Dixie cups. Dixie cups are for meatballs. We will forget you said it.

The yogic practice you refer to is called *dhauti*, the washing out of the stomach, and is one of the six purificatory acts prescribed for adherents of hatha yoga. In *dhauti* you swallow a damp cloth about four inches wide and 15 cubits (25 feet) long, ream out your plumbing with it, and pull it back out. Supposedly this will rid you of unhealthy impurities and cure you of various debilities, including coughs, an enlarged spleen, lymphatic afflictions, and even leprosy. There is another exercise called *vasti* in which you flush the equipment from the opposite end, by drawing water into the anus through a bamboo tube. This is guaranteed to make you a big hit at the frat house.

The project you describe is rather more elaborate than either of the preceding. The alimentary canal stretches some 30 feet from cheek to cheek, as you descriptively put it; most of this is intestine, coiled intricately in the abdomen. The general view of the Straight Dope Biomedical Research Team is that while you might be able to coax a string through your stomach and maybe a short distance into the small intestine, you wouldn't get much further than that. Peristalsis, the wavelike series of muscular contractions that normally propels material through the digestive tract, would be ineffective in overcoming all the friction that hauling a string would entail. It would probably just bunch up in your stomach.

If you are genuinely desirous of probing your innards with twine, however, I can suggest an alternative yogic exercise called *sutra neti*, which involves a dampened, waxed string that you snort through one nostril. After a few days practice, it is claimed, you should be able to inhale the string with such velocity that you can fish the far end out of your mouth. With both ends in hand, you can then engage in the practice of *gharshana-neti*, or string rubbing, which apparently is something like playing the Jew's harp. I presume this sates your curiosity on the subject.

Recently I saw a movie on cable TV called The Man Who Saw Tomorrow, *about Michael Nostradamus the prognosticator. That film scared the shit out of me. Nostradamus claims that first Halley's comet will screw up the entire world and then in the 1990s a Middle East/Russian collaboration will wage nuclear war on the West for 27 years, after which the U.S. and Russia will join together again to defeat the Islamic horde. Halley's comet is supposedly due in 1986—should I begin to say my prayers? How good was Nostradamus at predicting the future? Did Orson Welles (the film's narrator) con me again?—Lisa L., River Forest, Illinois*

There are two schools of thought on Nostradamus: either (1) he had supernatural powers which enabled him to prophesy the future with uncanny accuracy, or (2) he did for bullshit what Stonehenge did for rocks. I am inclined to the latter view, for reasons which will become clear presently.

Michel de Nostredame (Nostradamus in Latin) was born in southern France in 1503. Intelligent and well-educated, he worked as a traveling physician for many years, but late in life his reason failed him and he decided to become a free-lance writer. Among his works (which included a collection of jelly recipes, charmingly enough) were several books of prophecy, organized into sets of 100 quatrains, or "centuries." There were so many of these proph-

51

ecies and they were so vaguely written that they could be made to apply to nearly anything. For example, one quatrain predicted prosperity for Henry II, the king of France. Unfortunately, Henry was killed in a jousting accident a couple years later. No problem—someone discovered the following gem among the 940 or so other quatrains: "The young lion shall overcome the old/On the field of battle in single combat;/In a cage of gold he shall pierce his eyes:/Two knells one, then to die, a cruel death" (sic). It was pointed out that a sliver from the lance of Henry's opponent had penetrated the king's golden helmet and pierced his eye and brain. Furthermore, the king was seven years older than his opponent. Ergo, Nostradamus had really been on target after all. (After Nostradamus's death, some editors amended the enigmatic last line to read, "two *wounds* [from] one," which fits the circumstances even better.) Fast shuffles like this do wonders for a guy's reputation.

True believers have since applied Mike's predictions to nearly every significant event in the 400 years since his death in 1566. This effort has been aided, for those not fluent in French, by convenient mistranslations. For example, the well-known *People's Almanac* gives one verse as follows: "The captive prince, conquered, to Elba,/He will pass the Gulf of Genoa by sea to Marseilles,/He is completely conquered by a great effort of foreign forces,/Though he escapes the fire, the bees yield liquor by the barrel." The mention of Elba makes this otherwise ambiguous quatrain appear to apply to Napoleon. In fact, however, the original has "aux Itales," which is generally translated as "to Italy," not "to Elba." (The more imaginative, it must be conceded, claim "Itales" derives from "Aethalia," the classical name for Elba.) Similarly, some say the following verse predicts the Great Fire of London in 1666: "The blood of the just shall be dry in London./Burnt by fire of 3 times 20 and 6./The ancient dame shall fall from her high place,/Of the same sect many shall be killed." The ancient dame supposedly was the statue of the Virgin on St. Paul's cathedral. Sounds convincing, but a literal translation of the first two lines is far more cryptic: "The blood of the just will commit a fault at London,/Burnt through lightning of twenty three the sixes." Yet another verse mentions a certain "Hister," which some claim refers to Adolf Hitler. In fact, though, Hister is simply the classical name for the Lower Danube, and Nostradamus uses it as such in several instances.

Supposed predictions by Nostradamus of future wars and disasters are equally implausible. I didn't see the movie you allude to, but other scenarios I've come across talk about an alliance between the U.S. and the U.S.S.R. followed by a joint Arab-Chinese invasion of Europe. There's also something about a giant meteor falling in the Indian Ocean (maybe this is the reference to Halley's comet you mention). This last is based on a quatrain supposedly beginning, "A great spherical mountain [i.e., a meteor] about one mile in diameter/ . . . Will roll end over end, then sink great nations," etc. Once again an overenthusiastic translator has been at work—the first line is more plausibly rendered as "a great mountain seven stadia around," and many Nostradamus buffs say it refers to Vesuvius. In any case, it's not worth worrying about.

Chapter 4

S-E-X

This question is really going to blow your mind . . . but I'm on a diet and I have to know the answer: are there any calories in the average male ejaculation?—Name withheld and question reworded because I lost the letter. C.

Ah, the thirst for knowledge—it knows no bounds. Start by assuming that male ejaculate is roughly equivalent in nutritional composition to raw egg white (a safe assumption). The normal size egg is about 35 cubic centimeters in volume and contains about 14 calories and 3 grams of protein. The normal size ejaculation is about 5 cubic centimeters, or one-seventh the volume of an egg white; figure it, therefore, to contain about one-seventh the nutrients—approximately 2 calories and .1 gram of protein. Of course, you'll have to adjust those figures if you're talking about Jumbo Size (eggs, that is). Happy dieting.

THE TEEMING MILLIONS BITE BACK!
Dear Mr. Know-It-All:

First of all, let me comment upon the total contrivance of the question in order to be, shall we say, sensationalist—"name withheld," indeed. I can just see somebody's mother exclaiming, "My God, this person wants to know how many calories there are in semen, and that means—drum roll—ORAL SEX!" Anyway, I distinctly remember seeing this same question answered in the Playboy Advisor, although quite a bit less pretentiously, with the P.A. saying that semen was loaded with calories. However, even if by some chance I remember wrong, and you are correct, what right do you have to assume that semen is nutritionally equivalent to egg white and derive your answer from that? Is it because semen looks like egg white (after all, we know it certainly doesn't taste *like egg white)? Or is it because the real function of an egg is reproductive, and since semen has the same function it follows that they must have the same nutritional composition?*

Please, if you feel you have to deal with this kind of thing, go about it in a more competent manner.—Lynne W., Chicago

"Mr. Know-It-All"—I rather like the appellation. Did you make it up yourself?

I won't attempt to rebut your allegations in the order in which you present them. Rather, if you don't mind, I'll take them in descending order, starting with the most irrational. You accuse me, it seems, of (1) making up the question in order to be, shall we say, sensationalist, and (2) failing to answer the question correctly. In other words, I made up a question I could not answer—how foolish of me! And then, having contrived the question, I compounded my error by tipping off eagle-eyed observers such as yourself to the fact by including the "name withheld" business. How easy it would have been for me to invent a pair of initials and an address to go along with my invented question. I don't know what could have come over me.

The fact is that the question was not written by me or anybody I know. It came in the mail. Unfortunately, since I *did* lose the letter, I can prove this only by appealing to your sense of logic (unless, of course, said reader should come to my rescue at some time in the future).

As to what right I have to assume that semen and egg white are nutritionally equivalent, the answer, my dear, is every right in the world, since I know for a fact that semen and egg white *are* nutritionally equivalent, at least within the demands of precision imposed by the nature of the question (and I did say *roughly* equivalent). Although it is true that the nutritional elements in semen and egg white (protein, carbohydrates, lipids, etc.) do not correspond down the line, both substances are about 90 percent water, and in both the remaining 10 percent is composed of relatively high energy (calorie) yielding nutrients. Calculation will show that the substances are about equal in caloric content. (Actually, egg white is a little higher.)

Granted, my answer was less than rigorous. However, the problem defies rigor. The amount of nutritive substance in semen varies as much as 100 percent from sample to sample; the amount of fructose (one of the main sugars found in honey) in semen varies over a range of 400 percent. Finally, the volume of ejaculate itself varies from 3 to 5 cubic centimeters—not exactly a precise measurement. It is, however, a very small amount of stuff. It is true that semen is "loaded with calories," as you claim the Playboy Advisor reported. The point is that 5 cubic centimeters of *anything* is not going to make anybody fat, especially when 90 percent of the stuff is water. Five cubic centimeters of *pure sugar* has only 18 calories, for God's sake.

In the end, it seems that you are the one guilty of making unwarranted assumptions. You assumed I played a made-up question for kicks and that I didn't know what I was talking about. Neither of these, I can assure you, is what anyone would call a "safe assumption."

Several magazines advertise various devices and methods for penis enlargement. Are these a rip-off? Or is there actually a way to make it bigger and thicker, short of surgery?—John G., Baltimore

I have checked into the situation thoroughly, John, and the sad fact is that if nature has equipped us with a ding instead of a dong, well, we must just learn to live with it, and that is all there is to it. A consulting urologist at the sexual behavior consultation unit at Johns Hopkins Hospital in Baltimore tells me that there are no known methods, surgical or otherwise, of permanently increasing penis size for what we might call "cosmetic purposes." There is such a thing as *reconstructive* surgery, for men who have suffered some sort of injury to their privy members, but that is another matter. For instance, a recent article in the medical literature described the unfortunate case of a Saudi Arabian lad who at age two was the unfortunate victim of an inept practitioner of a ghastly home medical technique known as "guillotine-type circumcision," the details of which I leave to the imagination. Having been left with a three-quarter-inch "micropenis," as one doctor rather tactlessly put it, the poor fellow underwent reconstructive surgery in his 20s using skin grafts from his thigh. This gave him a penis that was about three inches long when fully erect, which I guess must be considered an improvement. However, the results, judging from the photos supplied with the article, leave something to be desired from an aesthetic standpoint.

There is also something called "implant" surgery, which is widely used to help impotent males achieve an erection. There are two basic techniques: semirigid rods and inflatable implants (we will have no snickering about this, if you don't mind). The simplest and consequently most widely used technique consists of a pair of silicone rods that are inserted into the penis via a surgical incision. The chief drawback of this method is that you are left with a permanent erection, which can be something of an embarrassment in public restrooms and whatnot. To get around this problem, an improved type of rod, which I regard as a splendid example of Yankee ingenuity, comes with a hinge in the middle. Yet another type consists of a silicone shell with a flexible silver braid inside, giving us what is basically a giant pipe cleaner, which can be bent to suit the occasion. Many interesting and artistic effects can be achieved with this device. Finally, there is the inflatable implant, whose advantage, according to its fans, is "a natural-appearing erection with increased penile girth," not to mention the fact that you only get an erection when you want one. What happens is that a pair of inflatable cylinders are installed in the penis, connected by tubing to a squeeze pump in the scrotum and a reservoir near the bladder filled with the penile equivalent of brake fluid. When you feel the situation demands an erection, you give the old scrotum a squeeze or two, and there you go, just like magic. Later you can use a release valve to get things back to normal. The disadvantage here is that the cylinders sometimes leak, resulting in a mortifying loss of pressure that all of us menfolk can readily identify with. Fortunately, the medical wizards at Johns Hopkins and elsewhere are experimenting with a new, improved implant which it is hoped will reduce this problem.

I should point out that none of these techniques is meant to increase the size of the penis beyond its natural length. In fact, oftentimes finding the right size implant is the touchiest part of the surgery (one manufacturer offers rods in something like eight sizes, ranging up to an awesome nine inches). So don't get your hopes up.

Finally, I ought to mention the fascinating art of *phalloplasty*, which is medicine's polite term for the procedure by which a woman undergoing a sex-change operation is outfitted with a surgically-constructed crank. The "neophallus"—medical terminology is such a stitch sometimes—is usually fashioned out of abdominal fat; the scrotum, complete with plastic testes, is made from the patient's labia. In bygone days, a piece of rib was used to make the appendage sexually serviceable, but now the job is usually done with a synthetic prosthesis along the lines described above. The artifical erection is usually imbedded permanently in the penis, but I understand in current practice it's more often fitted into a handy slip-in pouch that is cut into the underside of the organ. Now, you may think to yourself, hey, this wazoo I've got now is such an embarrassment, I might as well just bag it and have somebody phalloplast me a new one. OK, but I should warn you that phalloplasty is a particularly vexing surgical undertaking, primarily because of the penis's duality of function. Many sex-change counselors try to discourage it, and in fact most female-to-male transsexuals content themselves with less drastic measures (typically mastectomy, hysterectomy, and hormone treatments, in case you're interested). According to at least one educated guess, only about ten phalloplasties are performed yearly in this country. In short, your best bet is to reconcile yourself to your present equipment. Remember, it ain't the meat, it's the motion.

I'm 30, and so far my life has wasted away. So, I've decided to become a eunuch. Imagine, me a eunuch! Don't you just love it? Can I find a good-paying job, or will I end up a house pet? And, would it be advisable to keep my "private parts" in a little jar?—Larry W., Chicago

Frankly, Larry, I'm having quite a bit of trouble imagining you at all, much less as a eunuch. However, if I were you (and luckily, I'm not) I'd think this over carefully. Employment opportunities for eunuchs seem to be severely limited these days, and you could be left holding the bag (snicker).

The origin of the word "eunuch" (a combination of two Greek words: *enue* "bed," and *echein*, "to have charge of") refers to the eunuch's traditional role as a harem keeper; but the harem, the official sort at least, has gone by the wayside, cutting eunuchs off from the mass of the gainfully employable. For quite a while eunuchs found work as singers—a good amount of music was written expressly for the lilting voice of the castrato—but, unfortunately, show business has changed, and the only castrato who's found steady work since the turn of the century has been Frankie Valli.

Becoming a eunuch, for that matter, is no easy thing in itself. You can't just walk into your neighborhood GP's office, casually mention that you were thinking of making a change, and have it taken care of then and there. Reputable hospitals will only perform castrations in connection with complete sex-change operations, and then only after intensive psychiatric screening. Johns Hopkins, the hospital that for years handled most of the sex changes in the U.S. (they've since gotten out of the business), required a minimum of two years of psychological testing. But if you're impatient, you could travel to Casablanca, where at least up until a few years ago you could find a certain Dr. Georges Borou, the man who, by dint of extensive experience, is reputed to be the world's leading transsexual surgeon. Dr. Borou acquired all that experience by working strictly on a cash-and-carry basis (it's amazing how all these dumb puns just sort of pop up in a story like this), no questions asked. I don't have his number, but I assume he's listed in the Casablanca directory. Look under "Surgeons—Retail."

Finally, Larry, I don't care what you keep in your "little jar," as long as you keep it to yourself.

Two women friends of mine in Italy are intent on having a baby together. They insist that research has been done in the U.S. and that it is possible (even if the method can "only" produce girls). What can I tell them? Where could they go? What should they do?—Karin H., Los Angeles

They should quit reading those damned little squibs in the popular science magazines, for starters—I get enough screwball mail as it is. Your friends probably saw something about the work of Pierre Soupart, a reproductive physiologist at Vanderbilt University in Nashville. Soupart used a special process involving a virus to fuse two unfertilized mouse eggs, resulting in a single cell that subsequently began dividing as if it were an ordinary fertilized egg. Soupart stopped his experiment once the embryo (if that's what it was) got to the 64-cell stage, but it's possible the thing could have been implanted in a mommy mouse's womb, so that today we'd have some little rodent waltzing around with two mothers and no father. The mind reels.

Needless to say, Soupart's procedure is nowhere near the stage where it would be practical for humans—in fact, his real intention apparently was to come up with a way to guarantee a supply of cows, as opposed to bulls. (Your friends, incidentally, are correct in supposing that the product of a female/female union would necessarily also be female. Only sperm possess the Y chromosome necessary to produce males.) The last time Soupart published anything on the subject was in 1980, and I presume he hasn't made much progress since. If your friends want something small and cuddly around the house, tell them to go out and buy a cat.

This question came up recently in a conversation and was hotly discussed: does a pig have a corkscrew-shaped penis?—Joe C., Los Angeles

Only worthless California degenerates such as yourself are interested in things like this, Joe, but what the heck, I haven't gotten any threatening letters from the postal inspectors in weeks, and it's time to shake those suckers up. The answer to your question, incredibly enough, is yes—pigs *do* have corkscrew-shaped penises. You may think I am making this up, but Uncle Cecil is here to tell you he *never* makes things up. Permit me to quote from *Reproductive Behavior in Ungulates*, by A.F. Fraser: "The manner of intromission [i.e., hosing] in the pig is unique. In this species, the male, when mounted, makes thrusting actions with the penis, which repeatedly makes semi-rotary actions. Only when the *spiral glans penis* [my emphasis] of the boar becomes lodged tightly in the firm folds of the cervix does the action stop and ejaculation commence. It is clear, in fact, that the locking of the penis in the cervix acts as the essential stimulus to ejaculation in the boar."

Accompanying this passage is a helpful drawing revealing that not only does the male pig have a corkscrew-shaped wanker, the female pig has a corkscrew-shaped receptacle, as it were—actually, a corkscrew-shaped cervix. Cecil is aware that in humans the penis does not penetrate the cervix, but as should be obvious by now, there are many differences between human and porcine sexual practices, the principal exception being a girl I met in St. Louis in 1974. But I digress.

I regret to report that hours of diligent research have failed to turn up an actual photograph of the pig's amazing Roto-Rooter. For some reason, publishers of livestock breeding manuals prefer to publish lavish photo spreads of pigs' anuses, for which I cannot confess to having any particular fascination. Fortunately, cartoonist Slug Signorino, being the sensitive artistic genius that he is, has managed to come up with the lifelike representation shown here, which gives you the basic idea.

Much remains to be learned about pig reproductive physiology. For instance, it's unclear whether the male pig, in the midst of his amatory labors, employs a clockwise or a counterclockwise rotation. It may be that pigs come in both versions, as with right- and left-handed humans. We can only guess at the life of heartache and misery that must await the little Porky equipped with a left-handed tool in a world of right-handed Petunias. Furthermore, in view of the locking action of the male member in the cervix, we can imagine the danger of the male and female reproductive organs becoming cross-threaded during the heat of romance, resulting in the lovers being unable to separate themselves after completing the act. For this reason we should advise farmers to equip themselves with crowbars, graphite, and 3-in-1 oil, so that unintended tragedy may be prevented. Here at the Straight Dope, public service is our only goal.

What is the female equivalent of a wet dream called? Why do women have them? Are they very common? What I really want to know is: is sex mental or physical? Thanks very much for your kind response. I prefer to remain . . . —Anonymous, Chicago

I respectfully decline to get involved in a metaphysical debate on the nature of sex, Annie. Personally, I prefer mine warm, sticky, and covered with chocolate. However, to each his own.

If by "wet dream" you mean a nocturnal emission, there is no precise female equivalent, because women rarely ejaculate fluid at the point of orgasm (there allegedly are some exceptions to this, but we won't get into that right now). On the other hand, women do have nocturnal orgasms, though not so frequently as men. It's estimated that by age 45, 40 percent of all women have had a nocturnal orgasm at least once, compared to 80 percent of males. Fewer than 10 percent of women, compared to 50 percent of males, report having nocturnal orgasms more than five times a year. Men often experience their first orgasms during a wet dream, but women rarely have nocturnal orgasms until they have had orgasm by some other means first.

In both sexes, nocturnal orgasms are often accompanied by erotic dreams, but this is not invariably the case. Wet dreams usually make little impression on men, but women sometimes have quite vivid sexual dreams in connection with nocturnal orgasms, so much so that on occasion the dreamer may believe she has actually had sexual congress, as we may euphemistically put it. Medieval theologians posited the existence of "incubi," demons who had intercourse with women while they slept (the "succubus" is the equivalent for males). Witches claimed to have had intercourse with the devil in this way, and were frequently put to death on account of it. One might well launch into a feminist diatribe here on the extent to which witch trials and the like were a paranoid male response to the threat of female sexuality, as evidenced by the nocturnal orgasm. However, we scientists don't like to sermonize.

I remember reading, some years ago, a newspaper account of a woman who took her pedigreed bitch in for stud service, and was horrified to find a litter of mongrels nine weeks later. She sued the owner of the stud service, saying that the pedigree was irretrievable, and that therefore the bitch was no good as a source of purebred dogs. If this is true, does this mean that if a human female has ever been pregnant, she carries the father's genetic information in future pregnancies, even if a subsequent pregnancy is by a different man?—John S., Dallas

If ignorance were cornflakes, John, you'd be General Mills. As you'd know if you'd been paying attention in high school biology, pregnant females—whether human, canine, or wombat—retain no male residue once they expel the placenta after giving birth. The woman who filed the lawsuit obviously had a couple kinks in her cable, and it sounds like you could stand a little rest yourself.

What is it with those ads you see occasionally for "ear sex"? What is ear sex? Does the phone company complain? The FCC? Do the patrons of this service really get a MasterCard bill at the end of the month that says "$50 for ear sex"? What if it's their *wives who pay the bills? The whole thing sounds pretty bizarre to me.—Anonymous, Chicago*

There is only one way to deal with a question like this, A., and that is to ask someone who knows. Accordingly, I have recently concluded an interesting telephonic interlude with one Christa, known to some as Madame Christa, the proprietress of one of the leading ear sex services in the great city of Chicago. While our discussion was strictly of a nonrecreational nature, I would venture to say that this is a woman who is good at what she does. Christa initially worked for several ear sex services on the West Coast, but eventually decided to go into business on her own, ear sex being a very low-overhead type of operation. Presently Christa boasts a clientele that spans the continent.

The idea in ear sex, not to be overly bashful about it, is that you call up and have a woman talk dirty to you while you masturbate. When it seem advisable Christa will also mail you some of her unlaundered underwear. This is all a perfectly legal procedure, assuming that the relationship remains long-distance, as it were, which Christa assures me it does. While the phone company is not exactly an enthusiastic supporter of enterprises of this kind, to date is has not made any serious attempt to put a stop to it. What happens is you call up and give your credit card number plus your name, address, and phone number. If the credit card number checks out, Christa calls you back and you get down to serious business. The charge is $30 for up to 30 minutes. Christa says her firm, (she employs three other women part-time) averages about 80 calls a week, so you can see we are talking about a line of endeavor that is very nearly as lucrative (and honorable) as writing newspaper columns. One of the peak periods is 9 to 12 in the morning, when many customers call from the office. A fair number of them, Christa says, are lawyers, thus confirming the ancient dictum, "lawyers do it in their briefs." There is evidently a considerable degree of customer satisfaction; Christa estimates that 85 percent of the callers are repeaters. The charge is listed under an innocuous heading on the credit card bill, so as to avoid unnecessary friction on the home front.

Christa has various theories on why men choose to avail themselves of her services, which have to do with feminism, the lack of, shall we say, suitable outlets for certain kinds of expression, and so on. Apart from that, I must say that Christa appears to have an acute grasp of male psychology, which no doubt has contributed to her success. Many of her callers describe their fantasies in truly appalling detail, such as is best left to the imagination of the reader. Christa feels, not unreasonably, that this has a therapeutic effect on the men. If so, the women of this country, not to mention the mothers, 13-year-olds, young boys, dogs, and goats, should be everlastingly grateful. There is much weirdness amongst us, kids.

What is the function of pubic hair? This is something everyone seems to have, and just takes for granted. There are bodies that are virtually hairless, except for the pubic area, where suddenly there is a thick and luxurious patch. One explanation for pubic hair is that it acts as a cushion to prevent chafing during intercourse. But this seems unlikely to be true. If it were, we should have a lot of hair on the bottoms of our feet, for certainly we engage more in walking than in intercourse (most of us, anyway). So what is the real answer?—R.R., Baltimore

I wish to state, by way of preface, that I am not making any of these questions up. You ought to see the ones I *don't* answer. Various theories have been advanced regarding the purpose of pubic hair. For example, I have a Smithsonian monograph here— nothing like a little light reading in the john, you know—that presents the novel thesis that pubic and axillary (armpit) hair gives babies something to grab onto. *My* baby does this, it is true, but then she is 29 years old. More plausibly it has been suggested that pubic hair helps to retain certain glandular secretions that are supposed to be a powerful aphrodisiac. The nation's indefatigable corps of monkey testers has determined that armpit perfume has a direct stimulatory effect on the primate libido. The alluring fragrance of moldy T-shirts is thus accounted for, I guess. Clearly more scientific research is called for.

There is a rumor going around our office that female pigs have six minute orgasms. We're hoping to nip such distortions of truth in the bud and also keep the female workers here from feeling anxious with undue expectations of themselves. Also, do animals ever do it for fun?—Concerned reader, Los Angeles

Generally speaking, your nonhumanoid beasties, such as pigs, do not experience the Big O. We are talking about the female of the species here, of course. The males generally manage to get off, which to my mind confirms the fundamental sexism of the animal world. However, this is not to say that the lower orders necessarily are physiologically incapable of orgasm. A couple years ago some Dutch researchers noticed that female stump-tail macaques (macaques are a type of monkey) displayed what we must frankly describe as shit-eating grins while engaging in, ahh, lesbian episodes. The female on top, if you follow me, concluded the sessions with "ejaculation face," an expression of abandoned bliss that male macaques customarily assume when they climax. The researchers subsequently wired up the female macaques to test instruments and confirmed that what looked like an orgasm probably really was an orgasm, since the dominant female experienced uterine contractions and abruptly accelerated heartbeat, not to mention an intense craving for a cigarette immediately afterward. In later tests, the researchers also noticed that female macaques appeared to climax about 20 percent of the time during heterosexual encounters, a rather dismal percentage that we can no doubt chalk up to chronic sexual ineptitude on the part of the males.

As for your second question, we must point out that, scientifically speaking, animals *always* do it for fun. This is because they are not Catholics. Take it from your Unca Cecil.

Since you get into answering kinky questions, I think you'll have lots of fun with this one. I was watching the Tomorrow *show when they were doing a report on S&M and the following questions occurred to me: (1) Are S&M and bondage the same thing? Can the two expressions be used interchangeably? (2) Where did S&M in its present structured and rather ritualistic form evolve from? (3) What is the origin of bondage gear? (4) Is there any significance behind the black and silver color of bondage and S&M apparel? (5) Are there certain basic pieces of gear (a starter set, so to speak) that practitioners are expected to own? (6) What is this I hear about wearing certain objects or articles of clothing in a certain way that is supposed to indicate being into S&M? If you answer fully, I'll whip you in gratitude.—Aileen C., Baltimore*

I swear, half the people in Baltimore must be bent. I have notes here from residents of that city who want to know (among other things) how to get a job as a gigolo, the world's record for ejaculation volume, and who invented fellatio. Journalism school does not adequately prepare you for this. However, I persevere.

Let's start by defining our terms. *Sadomasochism* (S&M) in general means any sexual encounter in which someone inflicts pain and/or humiliation on a (usually willing) partner. Often these episodes are quite ritualized, involving a "master" punishing a disobedient "slave." The ritual aspect is sometimes referred to as *discipline*. *Bondage* simply means the use of restraining devices (handcuffs, ropes, shackles, harnesses) during sex. It has S&M

65

overtones but need not involve pain. S&M and bondage, therefore, are not interchangeable terms, although the two do tend to go hand in hand. *Fetishism* is a dependence on a substance (leather, rubber), object (lingerie, dirty socks,) or nonsexual body part (commonly the feet) to trigger sexual arousal. A male bondage enthusiast who has made a genuine fetish out of his sex toys will not be able to get an erection without them. *Flagellism* is dependence on whipping or caning to achieve sexual release. A *dominatrix* is a woman, often a prostitute, who specializes in disciplining men.

Deciding what is and isn't S&M can be a pretty arbitrary business at times. A certain amount of pain is common in many sexual relationships, but the distinction usually drawn is that "ordinary" pain is mild and mutual (each partner gives as good as he/she gets) whereas S&M pain is all one way (although it should be noted that switching roles between one encounter and the next is commonplace). But even this distinction doesn't always hold up. For instance, the delicate art of fist-fucking (forcing the fist into the anus) has become so widespread among gays in the last ten years or so that many no longer consider it S&M, although many straights would no doubt think otherwise. Then we have "water sports," involving urine, and "scat," involving feces. Neither is particularly painful, although they can involve a fair amount of humiliation.

Designation of equipment can be similarly arbitrary. Most traditional S&M and bondage gear is made of black leather and chrome steel, whose color and feel denote menace and brute force—the sensual juxtaposed with the mechanical, if you want to get literary about it. On the other hand, there's a whole other category of haberdashery made out of black latex (bras, corsets, briefs, etc.) that is not normally associated with S&M or bondage but some of which clearly has applications in that line—hoods and gags, for instance. (I'm told, in case you're wondering, that the kick in latex is that you *sweat* into it. Different strokes for different folks, right?)

S&M has been around for thousands of years; the Roman historian Tacitus is said to have made reference to it, and I suppose most of the basic gear involved traces back about as far. But many props are of fairly recent origin, notably motorcycle paraphernalia. You can also get something called a "Vietnamese basket" to hang your partner from the ceiling with—one of the many splendid legacies of the late war. In addition, many of the rituals, particularly the fantasies indulged in by heterosexuals, are inspired by relatively recent events. "Prisoner and concentration camp guard" is unfailingly popular. In Victorian England there grew up an elaborate ritual involving "governesses" who disciplined erring "students" with the birch rods then in general use in the public schools.

There's no such thing as an S&M or bondage "starter set," as you put it, but you can probably get going with a leather belt and some elementary restraining device, such as a rope. Gays tend to go in for fairly utilitarian items like cock rings, penis leashes, dildos, flails, and whatnot. Heterosexual couples are often wont to add elaborate costumery—for instance, the well-known kitten-with-a-whip number, complete with stiletto heels. You can get various gimmicks to attach to or pierce the nipples, labia, penis, or scrotum, from which you can then hang weights. There's also a speculum-like device for manipulating the anus. Some people invest in full-scale—how shall I say—"arenas," complete with stocks, rack, whipping post, and pulleys in the ceiling.

There are certain items you can wear to tip people off to your sexual preference, but for the most part they're only useful if you're gay. For instance there is (or there was at one time) an almost comically elaborate handkerchief code, which you used to find printed up and posted in gay hangouts and sex shops. Hanky in the left back pocket signified a dominant, the right pocket a submissive. Yellow means you're into water sports (get it?), red means fist-fucking, green means you expect payment, and so on. Keys and at one time earrings serve(d) a similar purpose. I'm told that in L.A. if you show up with a teddy bear it means you want to be cuddled. To each his own.

Heterosexuals have no such codes, and finding partners can be a real chore, with ads in swingers' publications and notices on sex shop bulletin boards perhaps the commonest methods. In some cities—the big three for this kind of thing are New York, San Francisco and Los Angeles—there are clubs that cater to various specialties, but in most towns you're on your own. Dominant women in particular are difficult to find and a submissive male whose wife or girlfriend won't cooperate usually has to avail himself of the services of a prostitute.

Up to a point I suppose we can regard certain aspects of this as good clean fun; simple bondage, for the most part, is harmless, and many whips create more noise than pain. But there are some obvious dangers. Piercing of the skin carries a substantial risk of hepatitis or AIDS, particularly for gays with multiple partners, and during anal manipulation you can rupture the intestine, tear the sphincter muscle, or, if nothing else, lose something inside, which means an embarrassing trip to the emergency room. And let's face it, children, when we get into knives, lighted cigarettes, and permanent mutilation we're getting positively pathological. A fair number of people get killed every year because they pick up some random hustler or because they try some strangulation stunt with a rope. The trick is finding a partner who knows when to quit. Personally, Aileen, I'm into whipped cream and wrestling, but if it's leather that does it for you, I'm certainly willing to be accommodating.

This question might seen like it's more up Ann Landers's alley than yours, but I have faith in you, Cece. What can I do with my roommate, who is so helplessly in love (with what I consider to be a perfectly useless girl, to boot) that he's in a continual daze? The dishes never get washed, the bathroom is a mess, his clothes are piling up in the kitchen, and all he can do is hold long, heavy phone conversations at weird hours of the night. Help!—T.C., Dallas

A touchy problem, to be sure. I recommend a remedy prescribed by the 14th-century physician Bernard of Gordon in his *Lilium medicinae*: "Finally . . . when we have no other counsel, let us employ the counsel of old women, who may slander and defame the girl as much as they can, for they are more sagacious in this than men. . . . Let there be sought a most horrible-looking old woman with great teeth, a beard, and evil and vile clothing who carries a menstrous napkin in her lap. And, approaching the lover, let her begin to pull up her dress, explaining that she is bony and drunken, that she urinates in bed, that she is epileptic and shameless, that there are great stinking excrescences on her body, and other enormities concerning which old women are well instructed. If the lover will not relent on account of this persuasion, let her suddenly take out the menstrous rag before his face and bear it aloft saying with a loud cry, 'Such is your love, such!' If he doesn't relent on account of these things, he is a devil incarnate. His fatuousness will be with him finally in perdition."

Let me know how it works.

Can you get cancer of the penis and clitoris?—Maggie B., Chicago

Not at the same time.

There is such a thing as cancer of the penis, but it is relatively rare—it accounts for only 1 or 2 percent of all male cancer cases, and it is much less likely to occur in males who are circumcised than in those who aren't. As for cancer of the clitoris, it's theoretically possible, but it virtually never happens that a tumor appears there and nowhere else. Generally when the clitoris is affected by cancer is is an advanced cancer of the vulva.

You-didn't-ask-me-but-I'm-telling-you-for-your-own-good department: Medical science chronicles cases of *cancer a deux*, which is the contraction of cancer simultaneously or consequently by two persons who live together. Statistical evidence suggests that the sexual partners of uncircumcised males are more likely to contract cancer of the cervix than those whose partners have been circumcised. Researchers believe than the problem isn't so much the lack of circumcision per se, but rather what we might tactfully describe as inadequate personal hygiene on the part of the male. A condom or simple soap and water regularly applied will minimize the risk.

When I first saw it in print it was being hailed as "an important new discovery." In practice it seems like the same old feature of earlier, less enlightened days. I definitely have the need to get it straight, Cecil: what is a Grafenberg spot and what's in it for me?—A.C., Washington, D.C.

Lotsa fun is in it for you, A.—maybe. Boosters say the G-spot is the key to the ultimate orgasm, but skeptics say it doesn't exist. Cecil, being the dispassionate scientific observer that he is, will merely present the claims of both sides, after which you can decide for yourself.

According to supporters, the Grafenberg spot is a long-neglected, recently rediscovered piece of feminine sexual equipment located in the upper front vaginal wall, near where the urethra meets the bladder. Stimulation of the spot has been shown to cause orgasm in many women, and these orgasms are often described as "deeper" or "more intense" than the old run-of-the-mill variety. In a small percentage of the women tested—about a tenth, according to one estimate—orgasm is accompanied by ejaculation through the urethra. For years this ejaculation has been interpreted by women, and their mostly male doctors, as urination, but in fact, G-spot buffs claim, the fluid is clear and strikingly similar to the ejaculate of males who have undergone vasectomy. Women, in other words, supposedly have something quite like the male prostate gland, and it offers the promise of mucho jollies for those who can get past the physical and psychic hangups associated with wetting their pants.

In a way, the Grafenberg spot *is* a throwback to "earlier, less enlightened days," although some think the less enlightened days may have been more enlightened than our current age of upfront sexuality. Sigmund Freud, as you no doubt recall, postulated the existence of two different types of female orgasm, the "immature" clitoral orgasm and the "mature" (and, presumably, more satisfying) vaginal kind. Masters and Johnson killed off the idea when they declared all female orgasms to be clitoral, but the execution may have been a bit hasty. As early as 1950, a German physician named Ernest Grafenberg—who decades before had developed the "Grafenberg ring," a primitive type of IUD—took notice of the urethra and its role in orgasm, but no one paid any attention. Only in the last few years have a determined band of researchers invaded the medical and popular literature with their new discovery of this old phenomenon.

Three of the leaders in this research—nurse Beverly Whipple and psychologists John Perry and Alice Kahn Ladas—published a book in 1982 called *The G-Spot, and Other Recent Discoveries about Human Sexuality*, which tells you, among other things, how to find the Grafenberg spot and what to do with it. Because the spot is so hard to find while you're lying on your back, and because it's so closely associated with the urinary function, they suggest you conduct your initial explorations while seated on a toilet. (This may seem unromantic, but you'll only get out of this what you put into it, so to speak.) After voiding your bladder, poke around the upper front wall of the vagina, from the cervix to the back side of the pubic bone, applying firm presure in the direction of the navel. Eventually you should find an unusually sensitive spot and feel as though you need to urinate again. Go ahead and try. If you were successful in emptying your bladder completely, you won't be able to, but in any case press on. The spot will probably swell and harden, feeling something like a small almond or a lima bean beneath the wall surface, and the sensations you feel may progress from the eliminative to the sexual. Paydirt. You can now experiment with your new toy in much the same way you did when you discovered your clitoris. These instructions are necessarily rudimentary; you can find a more detailed discussion in the aforementioned book.

Now for the bad news. Most other researchers say the G-spot is a myth. Sexual anatomy expert Dr. Kermit Krantz of the University of Kansas Medical Center has been quoted as saying, "I am not a woman and have not read the book, but in all the tissue specimens I have studied, I never found any specific nerve endings in the vagina that can be associated with sexual satisfaction." Other investigators say the vagina is more sensitive than is

70

commonly supposed, but deny that there is any specific love button in there just waiting to be pushed. Perry responds by suggesting that the G-spot nerves are farther below the surface than Dr. Krantz and his colleagues have yet searched.

Cecil, for his part, has been experimenting in this vital area with several persons interested in scientific progress, and he must report that there does seem to be an unusually sensitive spot on the front wall of the vagina that swells up when manipulated. However, I have never noticed anything in the way of a female ejaculation. Pending further study, I suggest the women of this nation incorporate the G-spot into their sexual repertoire if they want to, but let's not get hung up if it doesn't produce explosive results. No sense making sex more of a performance contest than it already is.

When my know-it-all college friend saw my new fish tank he started saying how goldfish are females when they're young and then turn into males later in life, just like that. Ha, I wasn't born yesterday. Cecil, tell this bookbrain to cut the bullshit and pay up on our fish story bet.—G.H., Phoenix.

No dice, junior, although maybe you can call it a draw. Sex reversal is fairly common among some of your lower order critters, the riffraff of the animal world, we might say, fish among them. Changing from female to male is called *protogynous hermaphroditism*, and the other way around is called *protandrous hermaphroditism*. If you've got both male and female appurtenances at the same time you're equipped for *synchronous hermaphroditism*, in which case fertilization takes place by means of mutual copulation, the erotic possibilities of which I leave to the imagination of the reader. Goldfish (*Carassius auratus*) are generally pretty straitlaced, but a Russian researcher some years ago reported he had discovered a protogynous version of *C. auratus gibelio* in a shallow lake on the steppes. I have a shallow lake on my steppes, too, but that is because the downspout is broken (snicker). Most of the fish were born female, but at about the three-year point a small percentage converted to males, thus enabling the species to perpetuate itself. I should point out that the piscine sexual apparatus is not quite so majestic as the human version, and sex reversal is mostly a matter of switching ducts on a sort of all-purpose gonad. There is one character out there, I should mention, who claims that many varieties of goldfish routinely change from male to female at the two-year point, but other researchers believe this to be insupportable bug dung. Just thought you'd want to know.

A three-month trip I'll be making this fall prompts the following question: how do chastity belts work, and how do they interfere (or not interfere) with going to the bathroom? This was not answered in Everything You Always Wanted to Know. . . . *—Henry VIII, Chicago*

They were—are—basically two types of chastity belts, or "girdles of chastity," as they are sometimes called. The first covers only the pudenda (the part in front) with a plate made of metal or bone. The second covers both front and back—or "anterior and posterior regions," as chroniclers of this procedure delicately put it—the two parts being connected by a hinge. Typically, a narrow vertical slot was provided in front to enable the wearer to urinate, and often was fitted out with metal teeth (sometimes spring-loaded) to discourage exploration by so much as a fingertip. In the duplex models, you had a somewhat larger aperture in the back to permit defecation while preventing anal intercourse. Supposedly a woman could wear a belt for extended periods without ill effects, although an examination of the apparatus involved makes it clear that going to the bathroom must have been a pretty messy operation.

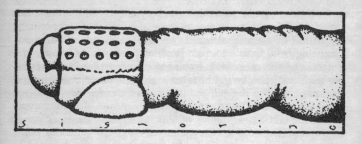

Despite all the tales about European lords locking up their wives before going off to fight the Crusades, it seems likely that the Crusaders did not actually learn about chastity belts until they had traveled around the East for a while picking up interesting local customs. Some Asian and African cultures practiced female infibulation, in which a woman's labia were bound together with rings or wires or whatnot. Compared to this barbaric system, chastity belts must have seemed like the height of civilization.

Knowledge of the belts was widespread during the Renaissance, although they seem to have been most popular in Italy, then as now a highly macho culture. Although chastity belts figure in many ribald tales of the period, it is not known how many were actually used. Several hundred specimens reside in various museums and private collections, but many of these are suspected to have been made just to satisfy the curiosity of some deve collector. There are, however, several instances of women's remains being disinterred with chastity belt still in place.

In any event, the use of chastity belts was not considered a great crime; a woman's body was thought to belong to her husband and he could equip it in any way he wished. Men who did outfit their wives with such devices were targets of ridicule, though. In stories about the belts, the husbands are generally jealous old men married to lusty young wives who remain faithful until the old crock decides to take extreme precautions, whereupon the insulted wife goes out to find a friendly locksmith and some handsome swain to fornicate with.

Chastity belts were advertised as late as the latter part of the 19th century; in 1848, a Scottish doctor advocated their use to limit masturbation. Bondage-and-discipline enthusiasts still use the belts today, although hardly with the idea of ensuring fidelity. In fact, I'd guess there have been more belts manufactured since 1950 than previously existed in the history of the world. The modern sex industry is an awesome thing.

Have chastity belts ever been used on men?—Judy C., Washington, D.C.

We live in an egalitarian age, my sweet. The Pleasure Chest, a New York-based chain of erotic appliance stores, makes and markets a tasteful little item it calls a "Male Chastity Device," which consists of a metal tube that is slipped over the penis and fastened around the testicles with a chain and padlock. As you can imagine, this makes tumescence decidedly unpleasant. But there are earlier, much cruder methods of enforcing male chastity as well. Take male infibulation, for instance, which ranks up there with female circumcision on the list of quack medical procedures once (and in some places, still) practiced in this world. Infibulation basically involves pulling the foreskin down over the tip of the penis (obviously you have to be uncircumcised for this to be feasible,) drilling a couple holes in it, and clamping the whole thing in place with a ring or thread. This prevented sexual activity, and from the sound of it it probably made the more prosaic bodily functions rather problematic as well.

The history of the procedure stretches back some two millennia. Enforcing the celibacy of one's spouse was only an incidental application, although there is a medieval story about a

Frenchman who woke up to find his penis padlocked and his Portuguese mistress in possession of the key. In ancient Rome infibulation was most common among comic actors and musicians, who believed that discouraging erections would help them preserve their voices. In that respect it was certainly an improvement over the alternative, castration, in that it wasn't permanent.

Infibulation fell into disuse until the early 19th century, when it was resurrected by one Karl August Weinhold, a professor of surgery and medicine at the University of Halle. He came up with the notion of rounding up all the poverty-level bachelors between the ages of 14 and 30 and infibulating them with a soldered lead wire, in hopes of keeping the population down. A novel feature of his plan was the proposed addition of a lead seal, which the authorities could inspect from time to time to make sure you hadn't availed yourself of a wirecutter on the sly. Understandably the Weinhold plan did not go over in a big way with the unmarried males of the day, but it later found limited application in the treatment of masturbation, which, among other things, was believed to cause "fatuity." (Maybe they were on to something there.) At any rate, one could read in the medical journals such testimony as the following, written in 1876 by a fearless medical pioneer by the name of D. Yellowlees: "The sensation among the patients was extraordinary. I was struck by the conscience-stricken way in which they submitted to the operation on their penises. I mean to try it on a large scale, and go on wiring all masturbators." It is fortunate, in view of the degenerate moral standards prevalent these days, that there aren't many infibulatable foreskins around anymore, in case some latter-day medical genius gets a similar inspiration.

Is it true that the Vatican has the world's most extensive collection of erotica and pornography locked away where no one who can appreciate it can see it?—M.B., Baltimore

I have not had a chance to personally check this out, M., but I have spoken to others who have tried. Years ago a couple researchers from the Kinsey Institute in Bloomington, Indiana, made an attempt to inspect the Vatican's collections, but church officials refused to permit it. Subsequently, however, it was learned that the Vatican had arranged to have its holdings microfilmed during World War II, when it was feared Rome would be bombed. The film is now stored at St. Louis University in Missouri. The Kinsey folks looked through all the material and found a few mildly erotic art items, but virtually nothing since the Renaissance. From this they concluded that stories about the Vatican's 100,000 books of porn are naught but a myth.

Not everyone buys this, of course; the more conspiracy-minded among us argue that the Vatican wouldn't be dumb enough to microfilm the smut section. One of my correspondents claims the Vatican library has (or had, anyway) thousands of erotic volumes, most of them file copies of works that appeared on the Catholic Church's well-known *Index of Prohibited Books*. This fellow says he spent time in a World War II concentration camp with a Vatican librarian, who gave him a tour of the library in 1945. He says many of the books, "mainly the illustrated volumes," have since disappeared.

Well, maybe. Most researchers, however, doubt that the Vatican has or ever had much genuine smut on the shelves. Gershon Legman, a prominent student of erotica who helped compile a bibliography of porn for Alfred Kinsey, says the Vatican "has no really erotic books," although there are some fairly tame volumes from the classical era. For instance, a copy of Ovid's *The Art of Love* is filed with Latin poetry, and Aristophanes' *Lysistrata* is with Greek drama. The Vatican also has some erotic specimens among its art holdings, including, among other things, some drawings by Michelangelo featuring various phallic fantasies. In addition, there is a famous collection of erotic frescoes designed by Raphael in 1516 and executed by his students in the bathroom of a certain Cardinal Bibbiena. The frescoes, which are badly deteriorated today, consists of scenes involving Venus and Cupid, Cupid and Psyche, and Vulcan and Pallas, and one would be hard put to describe them as even mildly titillating.

This is not to say that hard-core porn is unknown in Rome. A student of Raphael's by the name of Guilio Romano produced some quite explicit erotic art, in particular a series of 20 drawings depicting some rambunctious couplings, which were turned over to an engraver and printed up in book form. Pope Clement VII was outraged and had the engraver heaved into prison, but copies of the book continued to circulate clandestinely in Europe for centuries. Whether the Vatican has a copy today I dunno, but they ought to—most good university art collections do.

As for the *Index of Prohibited Books* (which, by the way, was discontinued in 1966), I've taken a look at it, and you could probably come up with a racier bunch of titles in your average Woolworth's. About 1,500 books and/or authors are listed; of the small percentage alleged to be "obscene" (obscenity was just one of 12 categories of forbidden works, the remainder having to do with heresies and the like), many were written by such famous authors as Honore de Balzac, Alexandre Dumas (both father and son), Emile Zola, Anatole France, and Victor Hugo. None of the erotic "classics" (e.g., *Fanny Hill*, the works of de Sade) were listed, maybe because the Vatican figured they were of such limited circulation they weren't worth worrying about.

In short, I think the legendary Vatican pornography collection is a crock. Most of the stories you hear about it are undoubtedly part of the folklore that surrounds any large, old, secretive institution (the Masons are another case in point). However, there *are* some truly awesome smut depots out there, if you're into that kind of thing. The municipal museum of Naples, for instance, is said to have an amazing collection of erotic artifacts, most of them classical in origin—fornicating satyrs and so forth. The British Museum in London has a famous "Private Case" collection of erotica bequeathed to it by eccentric Victorians that at one time was said to number 20,000 volumes, although theft, vandalism and other causes have reduced it to somewhere between 1,800 and 5,000 volumes, depending on who's counting. In Paris the Bibliotheque Nationale's famous *L'Enfer* ("hell") collection contains 4-5,000 volumes. What may be the largest collection of all is held by the Kinsey Institute (formally known as the Kinsey Institute for Research in Sex, Gender, and Reproduction) on the campus of Indiana University at Bloomington. There are 12,000 books, 50,000 photographs, 25,000 pieces of flat art, 3,700 films, and 1,300 art objects, such as figurines. The collection spans the ages, but much of it is of recent origin. The fact is that color photography, the high-speed offset press, and, more recently, the videocassette have resulted in a profusion of erotica that makes the porn collections of Europe seem positively quaint.

I have a question concerning the practices of sperm banks. How is the sperm collected from the donor?—Ben A., Los Angeles

Meet Five-Fingers Mary, R.N.

Chapter 5

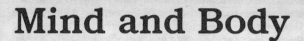

Mind and Body

A couple of years ago, a rumor was going around that Evonne Goolagong, being an Australian aborigine, had a tail. This was plainly absurd, but I do remember reading about a tribe of tailed people living the Philippines. Is this so? If so, where are they?—Roger S., Phoenix

The tailed tribes of the Philippines were the subjects of a famous hoax of the 1900s (these days, the only hoaxes we get are on the order of Jimmy Carter—times have changed, and not necessarily for the better). In the aftermath of the Spanish-American War, the U.S. Army sent exploring parties through the Philippine jungles, looking, no doubt, for vast oil deposits or diamond mines in the territory that the defeated Spaniards had turned over to America. Reports filtered back to the U.S. that the Army teams in the Luzon jungles had stumbled over an Igorot (head-hunting) tribe equipped with four-foot tails. According to the rumor, the tribe was quickly isolated by the government before its members had a chance to slip into the mainstream of Philippines society and pollute the gene pool. A photograph of a tailed tribesman was published, supposedly over the firm protests of the government— genocidal programs, then as now, were Top Secret. The photograph made its way onto postcards that were gleefully hustled to Americano tourists by the Filipino natives.

Eventually, the story got so far out of hand that the United States National Museum decided to open an investigation. The Museum's researchers turned up another copy of the notorious photograph, this one showing the tribesman without his tail. Anthropologists speculated that the original confusion may have resulted from imperfect observation of Igorot rituals: one tribal dance required animal costumes, which were made, of course, complete with tails. After the faked photo was exposed, the rumor died a quiet death.

At one point in his/her life, we note parenthetically, every human being does have a tail. Human embryos have a tail that measures about one-sixth of the size of the embryo itself. As the embryo develops into a fetus, the tail is absorbed by the growing body, but some traces remain even in adults. Occasionally, a child is born with a "soft tail," described by one embryologist as containing "no vertebrae, but blood vessels, muscles, and nerves, of the same consistency as the short tail of the Barbary ape." Modern procedures allow doctors to eliminate the tail at birth, but some children have had to learn to live with them. The longest human tail on record belonged to a twelve-year-old boy living in what was then Indochina; he boasted nine inches, which was probably enough to make him very, very popular.

In my early years, before I knew what a Kleenex was, I always knew the function of those little vertical ridges that run (ha, ha) from the nose to the upper lip. Now that I have grown to the full flower of adulthood, however, I'm curious: what are those ridges really for? And what are they called?—Annie, Dallas

I'm happy to hear your personal hygiene has improved so dramatically since childhood, but those little ridges are still doing the job Mother Nature intended them for—which has nothing to do with keeping your chin clean. The ridges protect a particular sensitive spot in the skull where three bones meet, two from the sides and one from the top (the last being the device that keeps your nostrils separate). Almost every animal has them, all the way down to lizards. In humans, the ridges develop after fourteen weeks of gestation. If they fail to appear, the child is born with an unfortunate condition known as "cleft lip."

The ridges themselves aren't graced with a name, but the depression between them is. It's a cute one: "philtrum," from the Greek "philtron," meaning "love charm." The ancient Greeks, who liked their whimsy as much as the next civilization, thought the lips resembled the shape of Cupid's bow; the philtrum, then, metaphorically represented the grip, the center of Cupid's power. Or so it says here. To me, the philtrum looks more like it ought to be the arrow, but I suppose it's a little late to start criticizing.

How many distinct musical pitches is it possible for the human voice to carry at one time? If two or more are possible, can you explain how the vocal folds are able to carry different vibration patterns simultaneously?—Doug B., Chicago

Voice is produced in the larynx as air passes through a space between the vocal folds. The tension in the folds determines their rate of vibration, and that determines pitch. Since there are two folds, two pitches are possible. Normally, of course, the folds are stretched to the same tension, but it's not uncommon for a growth or obstruction on one of the folds to cause it to vibrate at a different rate than its partner. The result is the voicing of two different pitches simultaneously.

Apparently—and here we get to the interesting part—it's also possible for some people to control their vocal folds to sing two pitches intentionally. A paper presented a few years ago to a national association of ear, nose, and throat doctors (or otolaryngologists, for the more pretentiously inclined) documented the case of a girl who could control the length of her vocal folds to the extent that she could sing with herself in thirds (do-mi, in first-grade musical parlance). Her sister was capable of a similar stunt. I can't tell you exactly how she did this, since not even the doctors are sure, but I can tell you it wasn't considered a pathological case—in other words, the ability wasn't due to any gross physical deformity. I'll bet that babe was a riot on dates.

With all your scatological insight, what exactly is a fart? Is it, as some surmise, a burp gone wrong? Is it a relative of the hiccup? The sneeze? And is it not healthier to vent oneself than to squelch?—Phillip S., Chicago

Your question comes to hand at an opportune moment, Phillip, because it happens I have just been reading up on the subject in the Harvard Medical School Health Letter. Harvard is a veritable

gold mine when it comes to flatulence. Intestinal gas, we learn, is made up mostly of five gases: nitrogen, oxygen, carbon dioxide, hydrogen, and methane. The first two you get from swallowing air during eating, while the last three are generated in the large intestine. From this we may deduce that burps and belches, which emanate from the stomach, consist mostly of air. Hiccups and sneezes, of course, are wholly unrelated.

Hydrogen and carbon dioxide are produced by bacteria nibbling on undigested food in the colon. The noble bean, for instance, contains complex sugars that cannot be broken down by the body's digestive juices. Upon arriving in the colon, these sugars are set upon vigorously by the resident microbes, and the resultant fermentation produces the cheerful calliope effect celebrated in such cinematic masterworks as *Blazing Saddles*. Methane, another digestive byproduct, is responsible for the unique blue flame that has absorbed the attentions of college freshmen for generations. It is recommended, incidentally, that persons contemplating experiments in this line wear fireproof undies when doing so. Unca Cecil speaks from experience. I might further mention that a friend of mine, who has reason to worry, has inquired whether there are any cases on record of persons who have exploded as a result of smoking in bed after a hearty bean barbecue. To date I have not been able to find any. However, internal detonations supposedly have resulted from the incautious use of an electro-cautery device inside the bowel. The eating of beans before surgery, therefore, is definitely contraindicated.

Interestingly, the characteristic fragrance of the fart is produced not by any of the aforementioned gases but by "minute amounts of volatile chemicals formed by bacterial metabolism of residual protein and fat," we read here. Persons whose flatulence is especially memorable in this regard may be suffering from dietary maladjustment. For example, people with lactase deficiency who drink a lot of milk are said to be able to produce a gas of near-lethal impact. My brother, for one, has a toot that could fell sequoias. Other foodstuffs that may produce farts of unusual pungency include broccoli, onions, cauliflower, cabbage, radishes, and raw apples. It seems to me that we have the ideal salad ingredients here for an eventful sorority luncheon. Persons trying it are strongly urged to keep Cecil apprised of the results.

This is a 100 percent serious question, and I want the straight dope. Every night when I'm undressing for bed I stand in front of the mirror and wonder where belly button lint comes from. This is no joke.—John W., Washington, D.C.

What makes you think you have to urge me to be serious, Jojo? Your navel is one of the few places on your body where perspiration has a chance to accumulate before evaporating. Lint from your clothing, cottons especially, adheres to the wet area and remains after the moisture departs.

My high school gym teacher used to tell us that peristalsis was so dandy that a human being could swallow water while standing on his head. He was always going to show us, but never did. Tell me if my gym teacher lied—considering what he told us about sex, I have my doubts.—E.Y., Los Angeles

Peristalsis works just like toothpaste, to wit: circular and longitudinal muscles along the walls of the pharynx (throat), esophagus, stomach, and intestines contract in waves, pushing the food or whatever ahead, much like you squeeze that last smidgen of sex appeal out of the tube. So powerful is the force created by these muscles that food passing through the pharynx is rammed down the line at a speed of about 25 feet per second. Things slow down a tad in the esophagus—here, four to eight inches of muscle contract at a time, and about nine seconds are required for the whole trip from throat to stomach.

Gravity is a secondary consideration, coming into play only when liquids are involved. When you're sitting up, liquids drop straight through the esophagus, then wait nine seconds or so for the peristaltic contractions to catch up and open the gateway to the stomach. If you're standing on your head or bending over, peristalsis does the job just fine, as any giraffe will be happy to attest.

Humanity has been sadly shortchanged in the peristalsis department. Cows and other cud-chewing animals (ruminants) have the ability to reverse the direction of peristalsis when necessary, bringing food up from the stomach to the mouth for a few extra chomps. All we have is Barry Manilow.

What is it, exactly, that goes on when your ears pop? I live in a high-rise building and lately I've become obsessed with the idea that I'm gradually turning my eardrums into swiss cheese every time I take the express elevator. Give me some peace of mind, Cecil.—Harold H., Chicago

Ear-popping is your head's ingenious way of keeping the air pressure balanced on either side of your eardrums. Too much pressure on one side or the other, and the tympanic membrane can't vibrate. A connection called the eustachian tube, beginning on the nether side of the eardrum, is linked to a reservoir of air

81

provided by the cavity located just above the roof of your mouth. When you swallow, the eustachian tube opens and admits enough pressure to equalize the inside and outside pressures. But during the rapid changes in air pressure that occur during an elevator ride or an airplane dive, the eustachian tube remains closed, and it takes some vigorous swallowing to even things out afterward. Or you can try the Valsalva technique, named after the Italian anatomist Antonio Maria Valsalva (1663–1723), who recommended it for clearing pus out of an infected middle ear: cover your mouth and nose and blow out as hard as you can. Daring and original, no? The cracking sound you hear has nothing to do with the eardrum—it's the sound of the air rushing into the tube, rendering everything copacetic.

How many square feet of flesh are there on the human body? I'm thinking of making a coat out of my sister.—Donald H., Dallas

You Teeming Millions have obviously been watching too much sex and violence on TV lately. Try curling up with a good book for a change—the *World Almanac*, for instance. You'd be surprised at how much interesting stuff there is under "Non-Federal Hydroelectric Plants in the U.S."

But back to business. The adult human body, being a noto-

riously variable commodity, comes factory equipped with an average fourteen to eighteen square feet of skin. Not enough for a coat, alas. I'd suggest either putting Sis to work as a macrame wall hanging or letting her stick around until it's time to redo the kitchen chairs.

You have to confirm for me and some friends something I have heard recently about those strange humans, sumo wrestlers. I have been told that they have this peculiar talent of willing their testicles to ascend into their bodies. Is this really true? How do they do it? Just the thought makes me double over.—Gorgeous George II, Chicago

I have probed deeply into this matter, George buddy, and I may say without fear of contradiction that this ascending testicle business is pure unadulterated bird poop. My source on this is a sumo promoter in Hawaii who frequently has occasion to visit the locker rooms of professional sumos in Japan, and I have also checked it out with an experienced amateur sumo. What we have here is one of the great barroom legends. Where it got started nobody knows, but it was greatly popularized some years ago by Ian Fleming, the creator of James Bond, in *You Only Live Twice*, which was set in Japan. In the novel, Bond gets to watch a practice battle by some apprentice commandos, who ferociously kick each other in the cojones without anyone appearing to feel pain. Later, the inscrutable head of the Japanese secret service, Tiger Tanaka, tells Bond that starting at the age of 14, junior sumos are taught that by "assiduously massaging" the appropriate organs, they can eventually cause the testicles to reenter the body via the inguinal canal, from which they originally descended. In the grade school I attended, by way of contrast, we were told that massaging our organs would result in hairy palms and blindness. Just goes to show you the vast cultural gulf that separates us from the Orient. Anyway, Tanaka goes on to say that before a match, sumos retract their testicles and bind them up thoroughly to prevent injury. Afterward in the bath they release them to hang normally.

One hundred percent pure BS, as I say, although that didn't stop *Playboy* from repeating it a while back. The only thing sumo wrestlers do to protect their vitals is bind themselves up tightly with a loincloth. This pushes the testicles just slightly back up the inguinal canal. That's quite enough, though, because the fact is that sumo is not an especially vicious sport. Hitting below the belt is forbidden, as is the use of fists or karate chops. You also can't kick your opponent in the chest or belly. It's illegal even to touch the *mae-tatemitsu*, the portion of the sumo jockstrap that covers the nether regions. The idea in sumo is not to bludgeon the other guy into submission but simply to either (a) make him touch the ground with a part of his body other than his feet, or (b) force him out of the ring. Although the preliminaries can drag on for quite a while, once a match gets underway, it's over in an average of ten seconds.

All this is not to say that willing your testicles to ascend into your body is physiologically impossible. Various of our little four-legged buddies, such as moles, shrews, and hedgehogs, do it routinely. In humans the testes are suspended from the cremasteric muscle, which is controlled by the autonomic (involuntary) nervous system. This muscle raises and lowers the testicles as necessary to keep the temperature-sensitive sperm at a constant simmer. Under certain stimuli, such as a cold shower or, more entertainingly, a gentle stroking on the inside of the upper thigh, the "cremasteric reflex" takes over and the testes are partially retracted into the body. It's been shown that automatic functions such as blood pressure can be consciously controlled through yoga and the like, and presumably the same could be done with the testicles. Not that it'd be all that helpful as a means of protecting yourself—you'd still be vulnerable to a well-placed jolt to the groin, and besides, it's hard to conduct an authentically terrifying fistic offense while in a yoga trance state. Personally, I prefer to repose my trust in certain dependable plastic products made by the Bike company, and if you know what's good for you, you will too.

As a Barry Goldwater fan from way back, I have long been intrigued by the tattoo he sports on the underside of his left hand. It's small but impressive, creating a very subtle effect—macho, yet refined. What's the story behind it? Does Barry wear it only to impress his male constituency, or does it have a deeper meaning? Where did he get one, and can I get one too?—Ronald Reagan, Washington, D.C.

Barry's tattoo is the trademark of the Smoki People, a group that operates out of Prescott, Arizona, and apparently functions as a sort of Boy Scouts for grownups, dedicated to "perpetuating the dances and songs of Southwestern Indians." Clearly, you need not be an Indian to apply. The tattoo consists of a line of four dots capped by a half circle. Naturally, the design is fraught with symbolism. The first two dots are given after the member participates in his first tribal dance; the third and fourth are given after his next two performances. Apparently fearful of turning their members into giant human pincushions, the Smoki People have set an upper limit of four dots per person. The half-circle is given to "chiefs," but since Barry is only an honorary chief, his half circle has been placed on the high end of the row of dots, rather than the lower end, where it belongs.

Goldwater had the first two dots etched on when he was in India during the war (the Big One, that is); the second two were acquired in a Los Angeles tattoo parlor, and the half-circle was applied by the legendary Bruno of Paris. If you really want a set of your own, I'm sure a local needle jockey will be happy to oblige you. Bear in mind, however, that should you tire of your tattoo, getting rid of it won't be easy. A superficial tattoo can be abraded away by a dermatologist, but a big, deep one will have to be cut away, a painful and expensive process. Take my advice and stick with Magic Markers.

After staring steadily out the window for a few minutes and then shifting my gaze to the blank wall across the room, I can still see the ghost image of the window and some objects around it. What's the straight dope on the cause of the negative afterimage?—L.W., Guadalajara, Mexico

Low-quality drugs were usually the problem back when I was a lad, L., but I suppose you kids nowadays don't have to worry about such things. Basically, there are two kinds of after-images—negative afterimages (the kind you noticed), and complementary afterimages (i.e., red becomes green, blue becomes orange, etc.). The latter are the kind you find in intro-to-psych textbooks, where you stare at, say, a green figure for a while, then shift your eyeballs to a blank page, whereupon you see a red ghost image that lasts a few seconds. Related to this are after*effects*, which usually have to do with perception of motion, orientation, and whatnot. For example, next time you're chugging down the highway in the back of somebody's station wagon, stare fixedly at the lane stripes receding in the distance. When the car stops, it'll look as though the stripes are heading toward you—i.e., as if the car were backing up. Similarly, if you stare for several minutes at a set of lines that is tilted out of the vertical, a set of lines that actually *is* vertical will appear to be tilted in the opposite direction.

Psychologists get paid millions to dig up little tidbits like this, but they're not so hot when it comes to explaining what causes them. The best guess is that afterimages are related some-how to nerve fatigue. It's known that if you stare at a brightly colored figure long enough, after a while the color seems much less intense. It's also known that at various points in the eye-to-brain nerve linkage there are things called "opponent process" cells, which fire faster than normal in response to a given color, but slower than normal in response to that color's complement. One scenario has it that if you stare at, say, a red patch long enough, your red-sensitive opponent-process cells get all tuckered out. Then, when you avert your eyes to a neutral color, the fact that these cells are ticking along more slowly than usual is interpreted by the brain to mean you're seeing green.

This sounds plausible until you realize that afterimage is actually an amazingly complex phenomenon. For instance, sometimes (usually after a very brief stimulus) you'll see a *positive* afterimage. Then we have the formidable task of explaining motion aftereffects. If I were you I'd just keep my eyes closed until the whole thing went away.

After enjoying a lazy Sunday-evening game of Trivial Pursuit with my sweetie, I learned that one of her feet had fallen asleep under the coffee table. Wondering aloud what caused this, we decided it was a feedback device for self-protection. However, nobody ever told us if limb snoozing can be dangerous. Can your arms or legs sleep so soundly that damage occurs?—S.Z., Chicago

Trivial Pursuit—let me tell you, there's the story of my life. Anyway, forget that "feedback device for self-protection" stuff. The numbness you're talking about is called *neurapraxia*, and it usually occurs when some major nerve gets compressed between a bone and some other hard object, such as a table or another bone. Nerves that are particularly vulnerable to this include the *ulnar* nerve, which runs through the funny-bone channel in your elbow, and the *peroneal* nerve, which runs through a similar channel at the top of the fibula near the knee. Fortunately, the blood continues to flow normally when your limbs fall asleep, so it's not like you're going to get gangrene or anything. There are two possible dangers, though: first, if you put weight on a numbed-out limb, it may collapse under you, resulting in a sprain or worse. Second, if the compression of the nerve continues for an unusually long time, or if the nerve is pressed against something sharp, like the edge of a desk, a pinched nerve may result, in which case it may take days or weeks to recover normal sensation. So exercise a little caution.

Being a righteous son of the prairies, I never developed a fondness for the Grand Tetons. Perhaps that explains my fondness for the petit tetons, which I fear are swelling into oblivion. It seems to me that since I started taking notice of these things, there has been an upward shift in the range of brassiere sizes advertised. At one time the common range was from AA through B with occasional references to AAA and C. Rarely did one see D listed, and E only in periodicals aimed at older women. Now one commonly sees B and C with occasional listings of A and D, AA and AAA being a rarity. Has there been an increase in the size of women's breasts, or is it that we are entering another period of big is better, causing the average woman untold grief because she isn't?—John F., Evanston, Illinois

I can't claim to have made the detailed study of the fine print in bra ads that you have, John, but the folks at Playtex tell me that the best-selling bra sizes these days are 34B and 36B. The next best-selling sizes, in order, are 36C, 34C, 38B, and 38C. Cecil's informants in the field confirm that women *have* been getting somewhat larger over the last 10 or 15 years; at one point 34B substantially outsold 36B. Students of female architecture will kindly note that this doesn't mean that breasts per se are getting larger (breast size, of course, is indicated by the letter, not the number), but rather that women are getting somewhat, ahh, broader through the chest and back, if you follow me. There are several possible explanations for this: either women are in better physical condition than ever, and thus have better developed (i.e., wider) backs, or women are in *worse* shape than ever, and have become corpulent slabs of lard. (Incidentally, some say that breasts per se *have* gotten larger over the last 15 years due to the use of The Pill, but this apparently hasn't had much impact on bra sales.) As for the disappearance of sizes like AAA, it's not because there aren't any small-breasted women around anymore, but because such women frequently don't bother to wear bras these days.

By the way, what's the largest size bra commercially available on a non-custom job basis?—Z.B., Evanston, Illinois

"By the way," huh? You don't fool me. I know that underneath that urbane offhandedness there lurks a slobbering, nail-biting, red-eyed sex maniac. Fortunately for you, the Straight Dope makes no discrimination on the basis of race, creed, or psychological stability. The largest size I've been able to find on retail shelves (you have no idea how embarrassing this job can be at times) is 48DD. However, one lingerie company I've come across does list a size 52E in its catalog. Staggers the imagination, don't it?

How many heartbeats does the average person have in one year?—
Faustino R., Los Angeles

Your heartbeat, naturally, is by no means constant. The rate can vary from minute to minute, depending on stress and body temperature. In one famous, if rather grisly, experiment, a team of researchers in Utah, in 1939 took an electrocardiogram of a man about to be executed by a firing squad. His heartbeat increased from 72 to 180 just before the shots were fired. Afterward, of course, the rate decreased sharply.

A rate of 72 to 80 beats per minute is generally considered normal for a healthy human being at rest. At birth, the rate is in the neighborhood of 130 beats per minute, with the figure decreasing through adolescence and then showing a slight upswing in old age. Women (and this seems to apply to the females of most species) have a faster heartbeat than men. Clams have the slowest heartbeats of all God's creatures, varying from 2 beats per minute for a clam *en repos* to 20 for a clam in a state of extreme nervous excitement.

Since the solar year consists of 525,948 minutes and 48 seconds, a quick calculation at the rate of 80 BPM gives us a ballpark figure of 42,075,904 beats per year, give or take a couple mill. A reasonable estimate for the number of heartbeats in a lifetime is about three billion.

Is there some specific exercise a concerned citizen can use to get rid of a double chin (his own, that is)? And is it true, as my eighth-grade history teacher used to say, that double chins are caused by sleeping on too many pillows?—Brian H., Chicago

Too many *pillows*? Cripes, they'll let *anybody* teach in the public schools these days. Assuming you're not fat or decrepit with age, we may attribute your double chin principally to one thing: chronic slackness in the muscles of the neck and lower jaw. This in turn is usually caused by lousy posture (particularly in the case of people with flat feet), but occasionally by other things as well. For instance, one of Cecil's woman friends, conclusively beautiful in all other respects, has a double chin because she had a cumbersome set of braces as a child, which caused her to hold her tongue and lower jaw too loosely—which she still does today. Anyway, the cure is simple: stand up straight, don't slouch in chairs, jut your jaw slightly both when speaking and at rest, and (if you have flat feet) make a conscious effort to walk on the outside edges of your soles. At the same time, exercise the neck and jaw muscles by standing up straight, pointing your chin at the ceiling, and stretching, rotating your head slowly as you do. Finally, lay off the Twinkies and try to lose a few pounds. I swear, this job is starting to make me sound like my mother.

You may not think the following question is too cosmic, but let's face it, the topics you address in your column seldom are. How come some belly-buttons are "innies" and some are "outies"?—M.E.L., Los Angeles

Nobody likes a smartass, M. Assuming the attending physician isn't a hopeless bungler, the incidence of "innies" and "outies" appears to be random. The accepted procedure for cutting the umbilical cord, which is usually done a few minutes after birth, is to place two clamps on it near the junction with the kid—an ordinary surgical clamp on the placenta end and a special plastic gizmo on the kid end, a centimeter or two from the abdomen. Then you cut in the middle. Within a week or so the stub becomes necrotic (i.e., dead) and falls off, leaving, ideally, a concave scar. The vagaries of fetal development and the healing process being what they are, however, sometimes you get an "outie," which, apart from any embarrassment it may occasion when you go to the beach, is harmless. If it really bothers you, you can hie yourself to a plastic surgeon. Worse things could happen to you, though. Sometimes the skin of the abdominal wall doesn't reach the base of the cord, and a wide raw area is left that heals slowly. This is called an amniotic navel. Other disorders can result in urine or other bodily fluids leaking through the navel. If things *really* aren't going your way, you may be born with a ghastly deformity called an *omphalocele*, in which the intestines bulge out through the abdominal wall by way of the navel. I am in no hurry to discuss this in detail, and I imagine the reader is not particularly anxious to hear about it either.

Occasionally, just prior to falling asleep, I have experienced a jerk or twitch, as if my body is trying to reverse its inevitable slide into unconscious slumber. How do you account for this peculiar behavior? It's also been known to happen to me when drowsiness overcomes me while listening to a particularly dry lecture.—H.G., Chicago

Why do we itch? I don't mean the specific itches of a mosquito bite, a healing scab, etc; I mean why does an itch suddenly arise on a finger or your back or someplace for no particular reason? It may go away with a light scratch; it may persist for minutes in spite of scratching. Is there a simple physiological explanation for this?—Dawn O., Evanston, Illinois

Nothing is simple by the time I get done with it, Dawn. That is the price the reading public pays for publishers who pay their starving writers by the word. Now then. Unfortunate as it may seem, medical science does not fully understand any of the phenomena described above. However, it has composed majestic polysyllabic names for them anyway, which is the next best thing. Twitches while falling asleep are called *hypnagogic myoclonus*, myoclonus being any sort of involuntary muscle spasm and hypnagogic referring to sleep. The twitches occur during very light sleep as the conscious brain gradually relinquishes control of the motor functions. Often they're accompanied by a sense of falling, or the feeling that something is flowing through the body, and sometimes people will experience vivid dreams or hallucinations. It's not known exactly what causes the twitches, but they appear to be associated (although by no means invariably) with (a) anxiety and (b) some faint stimulus, such as a noise. The twitches have been induced in test subjects who were instructed to push a button whenever they heard a low tone. When, as usually happened, the subjects nodded off after a while—you know how exciting psychology experiments usually are—the tone would often cause a subject to twitch after a lag of a few seconds. It's conjectured that the subjects consciously knew they were supposed to stay awake.

that they fell asleep anyway, and that the tone jarred the semi-conscious brain into trying to scramble itself into action again. That would explain why you experience the twitches during boring lectures. It's thought that at times the stimulus can be purely involuntary, such as a dream.

The general medical terms for itching is *pruritus*, accent on the second syllable. There are all kinds of pruritus; the kind we're talking about here is called *punctate pruritus*, spot itching not triggered by any obvious skin disease or other cause. The operation of the nerve endings in the skin is not clearly understood, but itching appears to be associated with the sense of pain, since persons who can no longer feel pain, for whatever reason, usually don't itch anymore either. In this respect itching is analogous to tickling, which is thought to be related to the sense of pressure. There are numerous "itch points" scattered about the surface of the body, places where it is possible to induce itching simply by touching with a fine metal wire; other areas on the skin usually are relatively insensitive. Itch points appear to be associated with concentrations of fine free nerve endings. It's known that in some cases the nervous system has different mechanisms for conducting sensory impressions of varying intensity, such as light and firm pressure, and there is speculation that itching may be a watered-down sense of pain, designed to detect extremely faint stimuli. Thus if you have dry skin or a stretched hair folicle or some minor localized chemical imbalance, the nerves may multiply it into the sharp irritation that you instinctively scratch. Then again, who knows?

Why do Eskimo people stay there?—David K. and Phil V., Chicago

I will not presume to probe the recesses of the Eskimo psyche, gentlemen. After all, people who are perfectly capable of moving elsewhere spend their winters in Chicago, to whose Januarys the Eskimo climate bears a striking resemblance. However, we may note Artic peoples possess various physiological properties that make them well-suited to life amid the icebergs, and in fact cause them to endure considerable discomfort if transported to a warmer locale.

For one thing, Eskimos are compactly built, which minimizes loss of body heat. The average Eskimo's height is only about 5′2″, but most have massive torsos. The lower portions of their arms and legs are shorter than the upper halves thereof, and their hands and feet are distinctly on the petite side. They have a higher-than-ordinary basal metabolism rate (they burn their food faster), which enables them to keep their blood temperature at a tolerable level despite the cold. Their blood vessels are arranged in such a way that there is increased blood flow to exposed body parts, such as the hands. In addition, blood returning from the hands is warmed before re-entering the heart. In extreme cold, some northern people are capable (via the autonomic nervous system, of course) of shunting blood from one artery to another so that temperature can be reduced in the extremities without affecting more important organs. It has been reported that some Arctic natives could work for considerable periods in subzero temperatures with their bare hands, and would strip to the waist and complain of the heat if the temperature rose above 40 degrees. I don't know that I believe this, but it makes an interesting yarn.

You're going to think this is mundo bizarro, but I need to know a few things about the way a person is buried. First, is the corpse completely dressed? Shoes? Underwear, etc? In the case of a man, is the penis altered in any way? Also, how would the corpse look after six months or a year? Would it be shriveled up or purple or what? How would it smell? Finally, how difficult is it to open an exhumed casket?—A Pseudo-necrophiliac, Baltimore

How difficult is it to open an *exhumed casket*? What *is* this shit? Promise to be good and Uncle Cecil will explain things—but remember, pal, I'm watching you. The average American corpse nowadays is buried fully dressed, including shoes and sometimes even undies, notwithstanding the fact that clothes are of no use to the deceased and that much of the apparel is never seen by anybody other than the mortician who dresses the body. The principal reason for this is that it gives the funeral director an excuse to tack more charges onto the bill. A mortician does not do anything to the deceased in the way of surgical tinkering other than what is required for appearances and for the draining of blood and abdominal fluids. The cosmetic part includes such niceties as gluing the eyelids shut. If an autopsy has been performed, the mortician may be required to sew the body back together, but generally he does not experiment with his client's components, including their privy members, if they have one. I would urge readers to repress their deviant fantasies in this regard.

The speed with which a body will decompose is unpredictable. It is possible to preserve a corpse for extended periods, as in the case of a medical cadaver, but this requires a strong solution of embalming fluid, which results in a leathery, decidedly unlifelike appearance. Since the purpose of modern embalming—which is not required by law, incidentally—is simply to keep the body looking presentable for the wake, a dilute solution is used. This postpones decomposition for only a short time.

Under the most favorable circumstances, a body after six months in the grave would simply be discolored and possibly covered with mold. If the body has had the misfortune to have been sealed in an airtight metal casket, though, anaerobic bacteria—that is, those that thrive in an airless environment—will have had a chance to get to work, and the body will have putrefied, meaning it will be partially liquefied. The smell in such cases is indescribable. Simple wooden caskets, believe it or not, often result in more gradual decomposition.

Getting into a wooden casket, which rots readily, is no big deal, but the situation is different with one of those impregnable metal sarcophagi that most people seem to be buried in nowadays. There you may have an inner liner that is bolted shut, an outer liner sealed with cement, and the whole thing placed inside a massive concrete burial vault. Getting all this open ain't easy. I feel obliged to point out, moreover, that the robbing of graves is generally regarded as a form of criminal trespass and is punishable by fine and/or imprisonment, in case anybody is tempted into it by the appetizing details presented above. You can never be too careful in this business.

As I understand it, the appendix at one time assisted in our digestion. Today it is useless. Our wisdom teeth, I have learned, helped our ancestors chew tough herbs and raw meat. Today they are a nuisance. But there is a third biological mystery for which I have no answer. So please explain, Cece: why do males have nipples?—Susan L., Los Angeles

To tell you the truth, nobody really knows. The best explanation I've been able to find (and frankly it doesn't explain very much) is that nipples are not a sex-linked characteristic. In other words, nipples are just one of those sexually neutral pieces of equipment, like arms or brains, that humans get regardless of sex. As you may know, every human being gets a unique set of 23 pairs of chromosomes at conception. These fall into two categories. One pair of chromosomes determines sex—the XX combination means you become female, the XY combination means you become male. The other 22 pairs, the non-sex chromosomes (they're called the autosomes), supply what we might call the "standard equipment" that all humans get. These 22 pairs constitute an all-purpose genetic blueprint that in effect is programmed for either maleness or femaleness by the sex chromosomes. This programming is done by means of the hormones secreted by the sex glands. Thus, for example, the autosomes will give you a voice box, and the sex hormones will determine whether it's going to be a deep male voice or a high female voice. Similarly, we may presume that the autosomes give you nipples, and the sex hormones determine whether said nipples are going to be functioning (in females) or not (in males).

One interesting consequence of the development set-up just described is that during the very early stages of fetal life, before the sex hormones have had a chance to get cooking, all humans are basically bisexual. Among other things, you have two sets of primitive plumbing—one male, one female. Only one set develops into a mature urogenital system, but you retain vestiges of the other. It's tempting, therefore, to say that male nipples are yet another vestige of your carefree bisexual youth. Trouble is, male nipples are hardly vestigial. They're full-sized and fully equipped with blood vessels, nerves, and all the usual appurtenances of functioning organs. Why this should be so nobody knows—in some other mammals, such as rats and mice, male nipple development is completely suppressed by the male sex hormones. (Incidentally, don't start thinking that at one time our human male ancestors must have suckled their young. So far as anybody knows, male lactation has never developed in any mammalian species.)

Human nipples appear in the third or fourth week of development, well before the sex characteristics. (The sex hormones start to assert themselves at seven weeks.) As many as seven pairs of nipples are arranged along either side of a so-called "milk line," a ridge of skin that runs from the upper chest to the navel. Needless to say, all except the top pair of nipples do not amount to much, although on about one baby in a hundred you can detect some vestige of the other ones, usually on the order of a freckle. There are cases on record of women who have ended up with an extra breast. In the 19th century, before corrective surgery was developed, such people were sideshow items. Humanoids can be real classy sometimes. Anyway, both male and female babies are born with the main milk ducts intact—the gland that produces milk is there in the male, but it remains undeveloped unless stimulated by the female hormone, estrogen. Occasionally, a male baby is born with enough of his mother's estrogen in his body to produce a bizarre phenomenon known as "witches' milk," with the milk glands, suitably stimulated, pumping away at the moment of birth. In the adult male, the dormant glands can still be revived by a sufficient dose of estrogen. Actual lactation is rare—only a couple cases have ever been recorded. But at least one writer (Daly, 1978) has suggested that the "physiological impediments to the evolution of male lactation do not seem individually surmountable." Meaning we may yet see the dawn of the truly liberated household.

I've gone through life wondering about a childhood discovery that I must resolve before I slip into chronic adult paranoia. Lying in bed with a winter cold, I noticed that when I coughed, I sparked— but only when my eyes were closed. What does this mean? Am I all right? Need we be concerned about the power drain? It would be a shame to short out before my time. Should I avoid coughing in the tub? In the rain?—Sparky, Washington, D.C.

Don't worry, goofball, you're not going to electrocute your-self. The sparks are an optical illusion. In the first stage of a cough, pressure is built up in the lungs, and for a split second that pressure inhibits the flow of blood through them. This causes a momentary imbalance in the circulatory system, forcing more blood to the head, and, naturally, the eyes. The eyeball is entwined in a network of blood vessels—you've seen the Visine commer-cials—that we normally see right through. But when these vessels are slightly overloaded, thanks to the pressure in the lungs, they become a little harder to get around. At the moment of the cough, when the lung pressure is released, a final wave of pressure travels to the head, and the combined effect of the bloated vessels and this final burst creates enough pressure to stimulate the photore-ceptor cells. The sparks you see are the outline of the veins. Usually, the sparks are concentrated at the periphery of the eye, where the network of blood vessels is densest.

Interestingly, children spark more than adults—as you get older, you get bigger and less susceptible to subtle changes in pressure. But you can recapture the bliss of childhood by closing your eyes, looking all the way to the right, and touching the left side of your eyelid. Sparks are less likely than a dull glow, but the principle is the same: pressure on the eye creates an illusion of light.

Is it true that women have two more ribs than men do? If so, could this be the origin of the biblical story about how Eve was made from Adam's rib? And while we're on the subject, what does the word "spare" refer to in "spare ribs"?—Bobby V., Chicago

All God's chillun got twelve ribs, Bob. The origin of the Adam's rib story isn't known for sure, but some think it may stem from a Sumerian joke. Here's the dope: the Sumerians had a myth about a consortium of gods who were busily turning the land of Dilmun into a paradise when one of their number, Enki the water-god, committed a breach of etiquette by nibbling on a newly-created plant. Ninhursag, the earth-goddess, put a curse on Enki, and he fell ill as eight of his vital organs failed. Ninhursag was eventually persuaded to relent, but to cure Enki she had to create eight different new deities to cure each one of Enki's ailing organs. The story obviously bears some resemblance to the Hebrew myth: the creation, the eating of the forbidden fruit, etc. But here's where it gets really interesting: the Hebrew name "Eve" means, approximately, "she who makes live." In Sumerian, the word for "make live" is *ti*—which, by some strange coincidence, is also the Sumerian word for "rib." Thus, the name of the goddess created to cure Enki's aching rib, "Nin-Ti," becomes a Sumerian pun, meaning both "The Lady of the Rib" and "The Lady Who Makes Live." The pun was lost when the story—itself much altered—entered the Hebrew tradition, leaving only the enigmatic association of Eve and Adam's rib. Neat, huh?

As for spare ribs—known as "sparribs" in the relatively terse seventeenth and eighteenth centuries—they take their name from the Middle Low German word "rippspeer," which eventually became "ribbesper." It was the custom of the Middle Low Germans (and a hardy race they were) to sit around their fires roasting pig ribs on a spit or, as they preferred to call it, a "sper" (a word that survives in English as "spar," as in the rib supports of a ship). Somewhere in the sixteenth century, the two elements of the German word became transposed as it entered English—"ribbesper" became "sparrib." As time marched on, the excessively literal English insisted on disconnecting the "spar," thinking it came from the adjective "spare." Thus another boneheaded blunder becomes part of the English language, confusing you and keeping guys like me in business.

How high do classical dance performers jump? When I saw Baryshnikov dance in "The Turning Point," it seemed like he got pretty far off the ground. Also, do men jump higher than women (that is, ballet dancers)? Or are they just given more chances to show off their jumping abilities?—Willa C., Dallas

Your average male dancer is expected to be able to leap somewhere between four and five feet off the ground. Baryshnikov, though, is an exception: on a good day, with a good wind, he can reach six feet. Not bad for a little fella (he stands 5'8" in his leotard feet), especially considering the world's record for the high jump, which was in the neighborhood of eight feet, last time we looked.

Male dancers do leap higher than their female counterparts, but while this has something to do with the advantages of height and muscular development, it's also a consequence of the prejudices built into classical choreography and training. A leap has long been considered a more "masculine" movement (for reasons which elude this casual observer,) and training, consequently, has tended to emphasize the development of this ability in the male. So next time you start disparaging some danseur's manliness, make sure you're out of range.

Why don't male ballet dancers dance on their toes? Is it something in the anatomy of the male foot, or possibly a weight distribution problem? The only answer I've received, "because no choreographer wrote a ballet calling for male toe-dancers," seems to be begging the question. Certainly Baryshnikov on his toes would have novelty value, if nothing else.—Hilda S., Washington, D.C.

I recognize that the following explanation lacks something in the way of *je ne sais quoi*, sweetie, but the fact is that male dancers don't dance *en pointe* (or "on point," as we children of the streets more commonly put it) basically because no choreographer ever wrote a ballet calling for male toe-dancers. From a physical standpoint males are perfectly capable of the maneuver. The idea in toe-dancing, which first appeared in the 1820s, was to portray women as ethereal, sylphlike creatures, rather than as the lumbering hippopotamuses that had been the predominant female characterization up to that time. Just about the only time you'll see men on their toes is in certain Russian folk dances. I have, however, had occasion to see a unique ensemble called Les Ballets Trockadero de Monte Carlo, which specializes in—I am not making this up—all-male drag ballet, wherein one may see not only men dancing *en pointe*, but a host of other extraordinary sights besides. Don't miss 'em next time they come through town.

I know that body hair only grows to a certain length and then stops. But how does hair know it's been cut? For instance, if I cut some arm or leg hair off, how does it know this, and grow back? Do you understand?—Mary B., Dallas

I do, but you don't, and therein lies the crux of our problem, unless I am sadly mistaken. Hair doesn't know it's been cut, and being dead tissue, doesn't much care. The fact is that body hair will grow if you cut it, and it will grow if you *don't* cut it—it is, in short, *always* growing (or at least, at any given time, a substantial portion of it is). You just don't realize it, since in aggregate it never seems to get any longer. That's because the longest hairs fall out, having been pushed out of their sockets by newer hairs working up from beneath.

The difference between body hair and scalp hair (and, in, males, chin and mustache hair) is that the latter grows continuously, whereas the former alternates regular periods of growth and dormancy. During the growth portion of the cycle, body hair follicles are long and bulbous, and the hair advances outward at about a third of a millimeter per day. Eventually, growth stops (at which point, needless to say, the hair is as long as it is going to get). The follicle shrinks, and the root of the hair rigidifies. Following a period of dormancy, another growth cycle starts, and eventually a new hair pushes the old one out of the follicle.

Naturally, the process doesn't occur simultaneously all over the body, or you would be shedding like a cocker spaniel. Whenever you happen to shave your legs you'll be mowing some long, nongrowing hairs, as well as some shorter, still-growing ones. And you'll miss some tiny new hairs, which haven't yet protruded above the skin surface. The stubble you feel a day or two later is evidence that growth continues unimpeded.

OK, you say, but *why* does head hair grow to great length, whereas body hair doesn't? Nobody knows exactly, but some anthropologists believe the purpose of long head hair is to give you something to tie ribbons in. No shit. Quoth one, "the functional significance of long head hair is almost certainly adornment, providing for the 'sexual selection' that Darwin correctly argued was a potent factor in the evolutionary process." In other words, by using the fine products of the Clairol company, we are helping to advance the species.

I seem to remember reading sometime in my childhood (but I can't remember where . . . I bet you get a lot of letters like this) that given the present rate of interracial births, somewhere in the future—say, several hundred years—the entire human race will be the same color. Is this true? If it is, approximately what color will our descendants be? Will the makers of flesh-colored Band Aids finally be able to settle on a shade that makes everybody happy? Most important of all, will we have to come up with a new reason for hating each other?—Absalom C., Phoenix

Cecil is always happy to answer questions on racial topics which give him the opportunity to alienate vast new segments o

98

his already disgruntled readership. The likelihood is that widespread interracial humping would result in rapid (i.e., within several generations) lightening of skin tone among that portion of the population we now inaccurately call black. Cecil bases this statement on his anthropological researches in Brazil, where he conducted a combination field trip and all-night beach party several years ago. Racial mixing in Brazil is very common, and in fact has come to be a point of national pride there. This apparently traces back to the rabbitlike sexual proclivites of the original male Portuguese settlers, who were accustomed to assembling vast hierarchies of wives, mistresses, and concubines, with whom they cheerfully begat children by the cartload. The story is told of one Correa (called by the Indians Caramuru, "man who makes lightning"), a European who may have been a castoff from one of the original exploring parties. He supposedly fathered an entire village full of people in the present-day state of Bahia, over which he presided as chief.

The current population of Brazil exhibits an amazing variety of racial characteristics in every conceivable combination, including such novelties as the blond Afro. Skin tones range from very dark to very light. The belief among Brazilians, however, is that the population is "bleaching," and in fact the percentage of inhabitants who describe themselves as white has been steadily increasing during Brazil's history, even though a large percentage of such persons actually is of mixed ancestry. (Admittedly there has also been substantial immigration from Europe.) But this is not to say that Brazil is necessarily headed toward some sort of national average, skin-tone-wise. While overt racial hostility is virtually unknown in the country, there is a widely shared feeling that a light skin is more desirable than a dark skin. For this reason, dark-skinned people make an effort to mate with lighter-skinned folks, with the result that the percentage of persons of pure-blooded African descent is small and in all likelihood steadily decreasing. On the other hand, the number of pure-blooded Europeans is sizable and likely to remain so. The upshot of all this, some think, is that eventually Brazil will probably have a fair number of pink people, a whole passel of brown people, and not very many black people. Cecil regrets to report that he failed to investigate the impact of this development on the Brazilian Band-Aid industry, but he promises to do so at the earliest opportunity.

Though I recently completed a course in physical anthropology, there is something that I still don't know. How come there seems to be a greater range of variation in the hair color and texture and eye color of Caucasians than in the other three or four races? Caucasian hair goes from practically white to black; eye color, too, can vary from pale blue to black. There aren't as many Caucasians as some of the other races, and they seem to be plenty close together, geography-wise. I know this sounds an awful lot like "all those people look alike," but I'm curious.—Rosa, Seattle

I'm glad you have disavowed any unworthy motives in asking this question, Rosa, because we are dealing here with a highly touchy subject. Nobody knows for sure why Caucasians exhibit a wider range of physical traits than other races, but there are a number of theories, some of them more dubious than others. But let's clarify a few things first. For one thing, Caucasians don't all live "plenty close together, geography-wise." Even in precolonial times, ethnic groups now classified as Caucasian were spread across Europe, North Africa, the present-day Soviet Union west of the Urals, the Middle East, and the Indian subcontinent. Given the enormous distances involved, you'd expect considerable variation. Second, Caucasians don't show the widest variation in *all* traits, just certain superficial ones—hair color and texture and eye color, as you point out, along with skin color, which varies from very light to almost black. When it comes to something like height, on the other hand, Caucasians lose out to Africans, whose average stature ranges from 4'8" for adult male pygmies to 5'10" for adult male Batutsis. Similarly, other races show greater variation in nose configuration, distribution of body fat, and so on.

Finally, whatever may be said for Caucasians, *all* major races show substantial variation in coloration, largely because of adaptation to local conditions. For instance, it's generally conceded that skin pigmentation acts as a filter for the sun's ultraviolet rays, and it's possible to plot out a sort of gradient called a "cline" showing that the closer you get to the equator, whether it's in Africa, Europe, or Asia, the darker the characteristic skin color of the locals. Something similar may conceivably apply to eye or hair color.

Still, that doesn't explain why there are no blond, blue-eyed Eskimos. Here's where the theories come in. The least controversial is that Caucasians are the most thoroughly "hybridized" of the major races—that is, they've had the most additions to their gene pool as a result of invasions, migration, slave trade, and so on. Caucasian "territory," if you want to call it that, spans three continents; it has been repeatedly overrun by Asian tribes such as the Mongols and the Huns. The Romans imported Nubian slaves, and the Moors, with a significant percentage of Negro blood, invaded during the Middle Ages. One might plausibly argue that Negroid and Mongoloid peoples, by contrast, either (a) suffered fewer invasions and other such traumas, or (b) totally annihilated anybody who did try to invade. The trouble with this line of thinking is that it's extremely difficult to document tribal migrations, especially in prehistoric times.

The other theory, which is widely regarded as racist, is that Caucasians show more variation in color because they're the furthest removed from mankind's hominid ancestors, who (some think) were all heavily pigmented. To put it another way, Caucasians are most "advanced," Mongoloids slightly less so, and Negroids least of all. The most elaborate expression of this theory was given by an anthropologist named Carleton Coon in the mid-60s. Coon's idea was that there originally were five basic races that evolved separately, in widely differing times and places, from our *homo erectus* forebears—Caucasians, predictably, being the first. Coon, I should point out, was not a crackpot, and there is a certain amount of fossil evidence to support his view. But there are some major objections to it as well, the most obvious being that one would expect races that had evolved separately to be unable to interbreed, as all humans today clearly can. In addition, there's nothing to indicate that our ape grandparents were necessarily all dark-skinned—after all, under their hair, modern chimps are often relatively fair-skinned. And Caucasians are generally hairier than other races, which you would think would be a more primitive trait. Besides, Coon's theory does not account for such noted Caucasians as Ted Turner. Now *there's* an evolutionary retard.

Is there any reason why we read from left to right? That is, is there something about the mechanisms of brain perception that make it more natural to go in that direction?—S.G., Chicago

Obviously not—witness Chinese and Hebrew. It's just a matter of habit. In fact, I once knew a proofreader who read everything upside down, being either too lazy or too drunk to turn the page over once the typesetter tossed it at him.

Professional busybodies have often suggested that every other line of type on a page should be printed "backwards," so the eye could quietly drop from the end of one line to the beginning of another without having to go zipping back and forth across the column. Actually, it's surprisingly easy to get used to—a couple hours of practice seem to be enough. Maybe we can get to work on this once we're through with the great Metric Conversion.

Chapter 6

History

Recently, the "I, Claudius" series on public television had an episode where Claudius gains the popularity of the masses by building a harbor to bring more corn to Rome. The Encyclopedia Britannica also refers to this. But wasn't corn domesticated in the Americas? And weren't American plants in short supply in B.C. (Before Columbus) Rome? And wouldn't it be fun to embarrass PBS and EB by pointing out that in Rome there was no corn?— J.T., Baltimore

There's nothing I'd enjoy more than humiliating the two overrated institutions you mention, but I'm afraid you're the only target in range at the moment. "Corn" comes from the Latin word for grain (*granum*), and through the ages it's been used indiscriminately for whatever grain happens to predominate in a particular region. In England, for example, corn is the word the natives apply to wheat. Up country a bit, in Scotland, the locals say "corn" when they really mean "oats." Naturally, when our British forebears jumped off the *Mayflower* and found the welcoming committee brandishing long green stalks with funny yellow things pointing out of them, "corn" was the first word that came to mind, and the name stuck in American English. "Indian corn," as the plant is called now and then, is a more logical and precise name (at least if you're willing to be tolerant about the "Indian" part). Better yet is "maize," the term used by thinking botanists and by English-speaking peoples outside the Americas, where the word "corn" is already spoken for.

Maize is, of course, a product of the New World. No historical evidence suggests that any European had encountered it before Christopher Columbus landed in Cuba. According to Columbus's journal for that fateful day, November 5, 1492, two

Spanish scouts he had sent to explore the interior of the island came back with wild tales of "a sort of grain . . . which was well tasted, baked, dried, and made into flour." The natives, in their Taino dialect, called it *mahiz*, which Columbus promptly corrupted into *maiz* or maize.

So, getting back to Claudius, he was really expanding the harbor to accommodate more wheat, thus upping the pasta supply. Claudius would have called it *granum*, and the BBC scriptwriters' rendering, "corn," becomes confusing when the program is shipped over for American consumption. An even more confusing episode occurs in the Masterpiece Theater debasement of *Anna Karenina*: two characters are standing in the middle of what is manifestly a wheat field, making casual references to the sea of "corn" that surrounds them. If PBS is going to insist on importing all their blockbusters from England, maybe they ought to consider adding subtitles.

Why do men keep the bottom button of their vests unbuttoned? I asked a male companion and he said, "just in case." Just in case what?—Sylvia D., Oak Park, Illinois

There are certain jokes of such ineffable stupidity that they will not bear explanation, Sylvia, and this is one. In the fullness of time I'm sure it will come clear to you. Several explanations have been offered for the custom of leaving bottom vest buttons undone, all partaking of a certain degree of ridiculousness. Preem-

Proper
Button
Usage

inent among these is the story that a member of the British royal family once appeared at some public function with his bottom button carelessly left unbuttoned. Thinking that some bold new direction in fashion was thereby being decreed, all of the gentlemen present promptly unbuttoned their own buttons. Thus was custom born. This hypothesis requires a certain credulity, I think.

Theory number two traces back to the days when dandys wore two waistcoats, each of some luxuriant material. In order to show off the undercoat (as it were), each dude would reveal it by unbuttoning his bottom button.

Finally, there is the explanation that old-time waistcoats were so tight that it was impossible to sit down unless you unbuttoned the bottom button. This one has a certain nuts-and-bolts plausibility to it. However, you can take your pick.

For years I have seen films and TV shows and have read magazines and books on the subject of the Alamo. And I can only seem to find the Texans' version of the attack. Since there was only one survivor (Ms. Dickinson, wife of the slain captain), how is it that so much detail from her story could work its way into the many other stories surrounding the battle? What do the Mexicans say about it? Did they have heroes equal to the legends of Bowie or Crockett in their ranks? Find that out, bub!—V.A., Washington, D.C.

Show some respect, pipsqueak, or I'll squash you like an insect. Let's straighten out a few facts here first. There was not just one Texan survivor at the Alamo, but six: three women, two children, and a black male servant. In addition, sympathizers from the town of San Antonio across the river from the Alamo were sneaking in and out of the fort more or less continuously during the siege preceding the massacre, so there was no lack of American witnesses to the whole affair. Still, the most detailed reports of the battle itself come from Mexican soldiers. It turns out that the stirring stories of heroic deeds so cherished by Texans were arrived at mostly by that creative process we call "making it up," the basis of much American history.

One of the longest and possibly most objective accounts of the Alamo's last stand was written by one Jose Enrique de la Pena, a lieutenant colonel with the forces of the Mexican president-general Santa Anna. He was critical of the leadership on both sides, particularly his own. For instance, when Mexican forces first arrived at San Antonio on February 23, 1836, the Texans were sleeping it off from a rousing party the night before, and the

Alamo (a converted mission) was guarded by only ten men. Rather than move swiftly, though, the Mexican commander dawdled, permitting the Texans to raise the alarm and scramble their forces into position. As it happened, the defenders were about as disorganized as the Mexicans. They had a clumsy system of dual leadership, with the regular forces commanded by William Travis while the volunteers answered only to Jim Bowie. The Texans had not bothered to store much food or ammunition, and they had nowhere near enough men to defend their fort, a large, irregularly shaped compound whose walls were crumbling in places.

The Mexican troops, for their part, were poorly paid, ill-fed, and haphazardly trained, and had been exhausted by a grueling march over the desert. Even so, morale was reasonably high. The Mexicans with some justice regarded the Texans as murderous barbarians. Indeed, one of the reasons the Texans were so determined to win independence from Mexico in the first place was that the Mexican constitution outlawed slavery, which the Texans favored.

Having lost the advantage of surprise, Santa Anna could have done two things: simply bypass the Alamo altogether, since it was of little strategic value, or wait until his artillery arrived, which would simplify breaching the fort's defenses. He did neither, opting instead for a rash attack on March 6—according to rumor, says de la Pena, because Santa Anna had heard that Travis and company were on the verge of surrendering, and he didn't want to win without some battlefield heroics first.

The assault was a nightmare. Advancing on the fort, the Mexicans were ordered to commence firing while still out of range, with the result that they had to reload under the Texans' guns. Scaling ladders were inadequate, and the Mexican soldiers were forced to scrabble over the walls on the backs of their fellows. Once the Mexicans were inside, the battle degenerated into a melee, with soldiers shooting at their comrades as often as at the enemy. When it was all over, seven captured defenders, including Davy Crockett, were brought before Santa Anna. He ordered them killed, and they were hacked to death with sabres. American losses are variously given as 182, 188, and 253, while the Mexicans lost more than 300, de la Pena says. All in all, it was not a heroic effort for anyone concerned.

In 1858 Abraham Lincoln and Stephen A. Douglas traipsed back and forth across the state of Illinois conducting the famous "Lincoln-Douglas debates," supposedly in a campaign for election to the U.S. Senate. However, the constitutional provision in effect at the time provided that U.S. senators were to be elected by state legislatures. Not until passage of the 17th amendment in 1913 were senators elected by popular vote. So why were Lincoln and Douglas wasting their time and money traveling around speaking to voters when they could have more profitably occupied themselves offering bribes to members of the Illinois legislature?—Charles T., Chicago

You have asked a serious question, Chuck, and you are going to get a serious answer, by gum. Pull up that chair and make yourself comfortable. It's true that prior to 1913 U.S. senators were elected by state legislatures. But the members of those legislatures were themselves up for election every two or four years. In theory, therefore, a candidate for U.S. Senate might attempt to affect the outcome of the vote in the legislature by (a) securing his party's nomination, and then (b) convincing the public to elect his party's candidates to seats in the state house and senate. In practice, however, it wasn't done. It was considered presumptuous for a party to nominate a senatorial candidate before obtaining the legislative majority necessary to get its man the job. It was also considered pretty pointless, at least from the party's standpoint. Under normal circumstances, the question of whom the legislature might choose for U.S. Senate was a minor issue, and nobody would vote for a party's candidates just because they promised to send so-and-so to Washington. Even if the party did decide to nominate somebody ahead of time, getting the guy elected was bound to be a long shot. In Illinois, only a portion of the state senate was up for election at any given time, and the chances of significantly altering the legislature's balance of power at one crack were slim.

For these reasons, Stephen Douglas's first senatorial "campaign," in 1846, consisted of traveling around the state buttering up the local party sachems in hopes they'd nominate him after the general election, which in fact they did. 1858, though, was a special case. The Republicans, a relatively new party, were moving into a power vacuum at a time when sectional differences—chiefly over slavery—had submerged most purely local concerns. They were up against Douglas, a Democrat of national prominence who had made many enemies during his attempts to work out a solution to the slavery question. In Lincoln the Republicans knew they had an able spokesman for the emerging notion that the union could not remain indefinitely half slave and half free. With Lincoln as their standard-bearer, focusing on national concerns in public debate, the Republicans had an opportunity to increase their strength at all levels. In essence, they'd be making the local elections a referendum on slavery and other national issues. It was an opportunity they lost no time in exploiting. On June 16, 1858, five months before the general election, they nominated Lincoln as their candidate for U.S. Senate.

It was a bold, unprecedented strategy, but in the short run it didn't work. The Republicans didn't get enough of their people elected to the state legislature, and Douglas won reelection to the Senate 54–46 in a joint session of the General Assembly held January 6, 1859. Had senators been elected by direct popular vote, Lincoln might well have won; in one of the few statewide contests, Republicans took the state treasurer's post by 4,000 votes. In any event, the setback was only temporary. The groundwork had been laid for the Republican presidential victory of 1860, and, not incidentally, the Civil War.

Where can I join the Millard Fillmore Society?—W.E.B., Baltimore

The last address I have for the Millard Fillmore Society is out-of-date and we must face the distressing possibility that the group is no more. Too bad. The society sponsored many activities, all dedicated to the honor of the thirteenth President, including an annual birthday party (January 7), a national essay contest on the theme "What would American be today if there had been no Millard Fillmore?", and the publication of a magazine, *Milestones With Millard*. No doubt the surge of interest in Fillmore in recent years is due to several uncanny parallels between Millard's career and recent occupants of the White House. Fillmore, who had the forethought to be born in a log cabin (thus ensuring that one day he would become president), was a political nonentity when he was chosen as the Whig Party's vice-presidential candidate in 1848, sharing the ticket with Zachary Taylor. Fillmore was selected to give the ticket balance—not, in this case, geographic, but aesthetic. Taylor, a Mexican War hero, was short, fat, grubby, and crude. Millard was athletic, handsome, and polite.

Taylor won the election by taking advantage of a squabble between the Democrats and the "Free Soil" Party over the slavery question. He refused to say anything about the issues at all, anticipating the technique of modern politics by over one hundred years. But sadly, Taylor died in office after eating too many strawberries on a warm day. This left the ship of state in Millard Fillmore's trembling hands. Millard faced up to the responsibilities of his new office by doing, as far as anyone could tell, nothing at all. But every dog has his day, and Fillmore's *Mayaguez* came when he settled an historic dispute between American businessmen and the Peruvian government over the exploitation of Peru's guano resources. (Guano, mined from the mountains of dried sea-gull droppings along the Peruvian coast, made an excellent fertilizer.) A relieved America showed Fillmore its gratitude.

Fillmore prepared to run for another term, but his party passed him over in favor of another Mexican War hero, Winfield Scott. A disappointed Fillmore died in 1874. His last words, on being given a spoon of soup by his doctor, were the legendary "The nourishment is palatable." His greatness, obviously, was with him to the end.

Many people today believe that Fillmore's greatest accomplishment while in office was the installation of the first bathtub in the White House. Alas, this turns out to have been a cruel hoax, perpetrated by newspaperman H.L. Mencken. On December 28, 1917, he included the Fillmore yarn in a column he wrote for the *New York Evening Mail*. So many people believed the column, a bogus history of plumbed bathtubs, that Mencken was forced to write a second and third column denying the first one. Unfortunately, people preferred the hoax to the truth, and to this day trivia books and even a few encyclopedias perpetuate the error. Cecil is glad to set the record straight here. The Fillmore legend has no need of exaggeration.

There comes a time in every upwardly mobile young man's life when he has to face up to buying a suit. While doing so recently I noticed, as if for the first time, the buttons sewn on the bottom side of the coat sleeves. They had always been there, I suppose, but never before had they seemed so conspicuously useless. The salesman couldn't tell me why the buttons were there; neither could the tailor. Now I'm becoming obsessed. What's the scoop, Cecil?—M.P., Los Angeles

I don't guarantee that the following is true, M., but it makes a good story, which is about all you can ask in this wicked world. At one time, supposedly, coat sleeve buttons had an eminently practical function. It seems that Frederick the Great, ruler of Prussia from 1740 to 1786, used to enjoy nothing more than the spectacle of his troops decked out in natty uniforms and lined up in rows. Only one thing spoiled the scene: the soldiers insisted on sweating, getting dirty, catching diseases, and bleeding profusely. Since no one had the foresight to provide the troops with Kleenex with which to mop their brows, the soldiers made do as best they could with their coat sleeves. After a hard day's skirmishing, said sleeves would be covered with unsightly blots and blemishes, and perhaps a vital organ or two.

Naturally, this was unacceptable. Frederick pondered long and hard on what to do. Finally, the solution (or "der zolution," as he more likely put it) dawned: sew buttons on the top sides of the sleeves, and the soldiers would scratch their faces open every time they tried to use their coats for handkerchiefs. Thus was the snappy appearance of Frederick's army preserved. B. F. Skinner would have been proud.

As the army uniforms metamorphosed into civilian dress, the sleeve buttons gradually migrated to the lower side. By this time, presumably, manners among the masses had improved enough that the threat of physical pain was no longer needed to encourage public decency.

Can you tell me if the rumor is true concerning Catherine the Great, her unusual interest in horses, and her resulting death?— C.S., Baltimore

I knew if we waited around long enough somebody was sure to ask this question, C., and I and the entire Straight Dope staff wish to thank you for coming through for us. The simple answer to your question is no, the rumor is not true. However, this will not stop us from repeating the rumor, to wit: that Catherine the Great, empress of Russia in the latter part of the 18th century, was crushed to death when attendants lost their grip on the ropes supporting a horse that was being lowered on her for, ahh, sexual

purposes. This is without doubt the most outrageous story I heard during my entire college career, which is when you usually come across these little historical sidelights.

The boring truth is this: Catherine the Great died of a stroke while sitting on the commode in the palace at St. Petersburg. Another less commonly circulated rumor has it that Catherine was so grossly fat (true in itself) that she broke the commode and died of blood loss from resultant injuries, but this is regarded as a fabrication also.

The story about Catherine's alleged yen for horses probably has its roots in the fact that she had an active and unusually public sex life. She had numerous lovers throughout her long reign, one of whom, Grigori Potemkin, procured young men for her after their own relationship cooled. The lucky stud would be "tested" by one of Catherine's ladies-in-waiting, and if he showed class he would be appointed adjutant general, or something along those lines, and spend a couple soft years performing as required. Catherine developed an extremely colorful reputation among the courts of Europe on account of this system. She had lots of enemies, any of whom might have embellished on the already randy truth and come up with the horse story. There is some thought that Polish emigrés might have invented it after her death to discredit her and the Russians in general, Poland having fared badly at the hands of Russian armies during her reign.

Why was it popular in the 18th century to occasionally substitute the letter f (or a reasonable facsimile) for s? What were the rules of grammar concerning this usage? Was it Noah Webster who finally put an end to this absurd practice?—Nina G., Chicago

At last, a chance to show off my encyclopedic knowledge of paleography, the study of ancient writing. You have no idea how seldom this topic comes up in casual conversation.

What you take to be an *f* is actually the so-called long *s*, also known as the medial *s*, to be differentiated from the terminal or short or round *s*, which we regard today as the conventional form. Throughout its history, the long *s* has always looked suspiciously like the lowercase *f*, even to the extent of having a little nubbin vaguely reminiscent of a crossbar appended to its middle sometimes. But the two letters are not otherwise related. As one might deduce from the nomenclature, the long/medial *s* was supposed to be used in the middle of a word, while the terminal *s* was used to finish one off. (In practice this rule was somewhat haphazardly adhered to.) The two versions were phonetically equivalent, and derived from the same Roman letterform. Why folks in those days figured they needed two varieties when they could have scraped by with one is beyond my power to say, but we might note that having terminal and middle letterforms is not inherently any dumber than having every sentence start with a capital letter, a comparatively recent invention.

The use of two types of *s* dates back at least to the Middle Ages. The long *s* became especially popular during the Italian Renaissance, with the development of the various "humanistic" scripts that gave rise to our present English script. The Italians often used the long *s* even when they should have used a short one, because letters with long expressive strokes in them made for an artier-looking manuscript. Unfortunately, they also made for a manuscript that was damned near impossible to read, and it is probably for that reason as much as any other that the use of the long *s* finally died out in the 19th century. The form survived in the formal German script Fraktur until Fraktur itself bit the dust after World War II. Some of the amateur calligraphers who correspond with this column from time to time still use the long *s*, producing missives whose beauty is equaled only by their impenetrability. That is the price we pay for art, I guess.

Many of my Irish friends have suggested that certain Irish surnames, such as Costello, Moore, and Spain, originated at the time of the Spanish Armada, what with all the seagoing Spaniards swimming ashore and becoming enchanted with the fair colleens. Some have even gone so far as to suggest that the names Murray and Murphy originated this way (apparently they mean something like "from the sea"). Is this blarney, or do I see some blue Spanish eyes when Irish eyes are smiling?—Andrzej Kowalczyk, Chicago

Good to hear from somebody with a nice Irish name like Kowalczyk, Andrzej. However, I would have known you were a son of the auld sod even if you hadn't signed your letter, mainly because like all the Irish you like to lay it on real thick. I mean, come on now—*Murphy* a Spanish surname? Murphy is the most common name in all of Ireland. Those Spaniards would have to have been humping like bedbugs to populate the whole damn island.

In fact, it seems likely that very few, if any, survivors of the Armada took up residence in Ireland. For one thing, there weren't many survivors. Perhaps as many as 17 Spanish ships ran aground or sank off the Irish coast in the fall of 1588, as the crippled Armada made its roundabout way home after its defeat in the

English Channel. The records of the period are incomplete, but it's possible that as many as 6,000 Spanish soldiers and sailors were dumped into the sea. Of these, 2,000 or more simply drowned. One contemporary account claimed that 1,100 bodies washed up on a five-mile stretch of beach. Between 3,000 and 3,500 of the remainder were killed or captured by the English or their Irish minions. The English had fewer than 2,000 troops to maintain their hold on all of Ireland, so they resorted to the simple expedient of not taking any prisoners. In one instance, several hundred Spaniards were induced to surrender with the promise of honorable treatment, only to be methodically butchered the next morning. The richest or most prominent of the survivors were held for ransom, or for public spectacle (the English always were a class act). Only a few hundred of the castaways managed to make it to Scotland and to the Continent with the help of sympathetic Irishmen, themselves no great lovers of the English, who at the time were attempting to consolidate their grip on their miserable neighbor.

Frankly, there was little to induce the shipwrecked soldiers and sailors to stay. The Spanish considered the Irish to be savages—evidently they'd been to a few Notre Dame games—and they thought the island was a cold and forbidding place. One Captain Francisco de Cuellar, who managed to make it to Spanish-held Antwerp, relates in a letter how an Irish chieftain, impressed by de Cuellar's bravery, offered him his daughter's hand in marriage. The Spaniard's response was to sneak away in the middle of the night, which doesn't say much for the fair colleens you mention.

A few Spaniards stuck around for a while, of course; several were on hand to help a combined force of Scotch and Irish defeat an English army at Ballyshannon in northwest Ireland in 1597. But the Armada's castoffs did not make much of a dent on the ethnic makeup of the country.

This is not to say that Spaniards in general never settled in Ireland. Spanish merchants did a brisk commerce in Irish ports for hundreds of years before and after the Armada; some took up residence there. More interestingly, there was a tradition among the Gaels, Ireland's original inhabitants, that they had originally migrated from Spain. This tradition did not find its way into writing until nearly a thousand years after the supposed event, though, and the evidence from other sources is inconclusive. Basically, the story is that three sons of Mileadh (Mil, in some versions; the sons were Heremon, Heber, and Ir) came to Ireland from Spain about the time of Alexander the Great. The consensus among scholars is that the Gaels *could* have come from Spain (although some say France), but there's no way of knowing for sure.

The Spaniards-in-Ireland myth has many weird permutations. One of the Teeming Millions wrote in a while back with the curious claim that there have been several Spanish-surnamed Sephardic Jews involved in Ireland over the years, notably the patriot Eamon de Valera. She also says that the Gallego culture in northwestern Spain has many similarities to the Gaelic culture of Ireland, and further says that the Gaels were a green-eyed people, as many Irish, Gallegos, and Sephardic Jews supposedly are today. Most of this is rubbish, of course. There have been Jews in Ireland for generations—you probably recall the story about the Irish being one or more of the Ten Lost Tribes of Israel— and for all I know some of them were Sephardic, but Eamon de Valera certainly wasn't one of them. He was a Catholic, as were his parents. He had a Spanish surname because his father was a Spaniard who had emigrated to the United States and met and married De Valera's Irish mother in New York. As for the Gaels, it's generally thought they were a *blue*-eyed people, although obviously they didn't keep the best records on this kind of thing back in those days.

A somewhat more promising line of inquiry is offered by another correspondent, who wonders whether Irish redheads can trace their ancestry to randy Vikings who had their way with the somewhat put-upon colleens. I have studied this matter for a while, and my considered opinion is: I dunno. A fair number of Norsemen invaded Ireland's coastal regions around the turn of the millenium and eventually settled there, but they didn't differ dramatically from the natives in appearance, at least as far as hair color went. Persons with some Norse-Irish surname like Harold, however, are free to conjecture about the studly nature of their ancestors.

A couple last points: Murray and Murphy are old Gaelic sept (clan) names; Moore is an anglicization of another such name, and Costello is a name adopted by certain of the Normans who invaded Ireland in 1171. Spain, as near as I can make out, is an English surname also of Norman origin. So much for pop genealogy.

My late father worked in Chicago's Loop for many years. He told the story that one day during the 20s a truck driver approached him and asked him if he would like to shake hands with the man who shot Lincoln. Dad said he would so he entered the truck and shook the hand of the cadaver inside. Was this teamster putting Dad on, or was the body of the assassin ever brought to Chicago?—Wondering, Chicago

There've been a lot of famous corpses in Chicago over the years, but John Wilkes Booth probably wasn't one of them. You do bring up an interesting topic, though. The circumstances surrounding the death of John Wilkes Booth are hazy—hazy enough, in fact, to have kept a rumor in circulation for some years after his death (or "death," if you prefer) that J.W. was alive and kicking. According to the history books, Booth died on the night of April 26, 1865. Heading south from Washington after the assassination, he reached the rolling Rappahannock River in Virginia on the twelfth night of his flight, and took refuge, along with one of his co-conspirators, in a tobacco barn belonging to the farm of one Richard Garrett. Federal troops in the area were tipped off, and the barn was surrounded and set on fire at about three in the morning. The troops had been instructed to take Booth alive, but he was found inside the burning building with a fatal bullet wound, an apparent suicide. A sergeant named Boston Corbett later took credit for the shooting, claiming that "Providence directed me" to disobey the order, but the point was never settled. Booth lived for some hours after the shooting, muttering the words "useless, useless," according to a popular account. The badly burned body was taken to Washington, where it was identified by some of Booth's friends, but the corpse had been damaged severely enough to make a positive identification impossible. The body, whoever it was, was secretly buried in the floor of a Washington warehouse to keep it safe from molestation. Four years later, the corpse was exhumed and taken to the Booth family plot in Baltimore, where as far as anybody knows or cares, it has remained ever since.

Famous corpses were a hot item in carnivals well into the 20th century; one enterprising showman even exhibited what he claimed were the bodies of Nicholas and Alexandra, hand delivered to the U.S. by the Bolsheviks. Most of these charming entertainments were frauds, of course, and it seems unlikely that if Booth had survived the night of April 26 he would have been indiscreet enough to leave his remains to a sideshow after shuffling off this mortal coil once and for all.

Chapter 7

Science

Remember MDA, the miracle drug of the early 70s? Well, I do. It used to turn me into a blissed-out motormouth, and I can remember more than once strolling along the beach watching the sun come up after an all-night gabfest. My question is, what was in that stuff, anyway? I remember being told it was a combination of speed and acid, but this now strikes me as chemically improbable. It also occurs to me, now that my Puritan impulses have reasserted themselves with age, that something that felt that good had to be bad for you. Was it? In terms of value for the money, I always thought MDA beat the hell out of Yuppie drugs like cocaine.—Former flower-child, Los Angeles

Waxing nostalgic about the great chemicals of old strikes me as a bit weird, F., but I guess we have to expect this from Age of Aquarius alumni. MDA was chemical shorthand for 3,4-methylenedioxyamphetamine—maybe now you know why they told you it stood for Miracle Drops of Acid instead. The stuff was in fact chemically related to both speed (amphetamines) and hallucinogens like LSD. Dope lore had it that MDA induced a sense of confidence and a feeling of warmth and empathy toward other people (hence the appellation "the love drug"). In small doses, say about 60 mg (the average street dose was 120 mg), it acted mostly as a stimulant and could also cause some visual distortions. In larger doses, its hallucinogenic properties started to take effect, and combined with the stimulant effects—heavy breathing, rapid heartbeat, etc.—things could get pretty unpleasant for the user. But maybe you've forgotten that part. The drug produced a tolerance in the body with use, so that it took progressively larger doses to produce the desired effect each time.

MDA was relatively safe as drugs go, which of course isn't

115

saying much. It's difficult to OD on stimulants, and MDA wouldn't kill you except in massive doses. It may interest you to know, however, that a rather simple mistake in the MDA drug synthesizing process could produce a toxic drug called PMA, which made deadly poisoning a serious possibility. As far as long-term effects go, I haven't come across anything particularly horrifying, but you can be assured all that speeding didn't do your ticker any good. Cecil has never been one to get sentimental about his youthful vices.

I have observed that traveling at high speeds causes strange things to occur (e.g., the Charger's hubcaps in Bullitt *regenerated twice during the high speed chase scene). If I traveled down Austin Avenue at a speed exceeding Mach 1 (the speed of sound) would noises made by the people on the streets be distorted or totally inaudible to me? While cruising at this speed, if I blasted my car radio, would the people on the streets hear it as I would, or would I be traveling faster than radio waves, causing my radio to die? What phenomenon would occur if I shifted into second around North Avenue and my Buick exceeded the speed of light? This information will be helpful when I rush my wife to the hospital sometime in January to deliver our baby.—Life in the Fast Lane, Chicago*

I think it's splendid that a young person such as yourself is trying to get these crucial preparations out of the way before the big day arrives. So many of today's youth have their heads full of bizarre ideas instead.

Dealing with the easy parts of your question first: At the speed of sound you won't hear sounds happening behind you, because the sound waves won't be able to catch up with you. You'll hear sounds occurring in front of you, but they'll be increased in pitch about an octave due to the well-known Doppler effect—i.e., as you move toward a sound source, you crowd up on the oncoming sound waves, which increases their frequency relative to you. By the same token, people on the street won't hear you coming, but they'll hear you (and a sonic boom) after you've passed—with the pitch decreased about an octave.

What was more interesting to the team of research physicists we employ here was what *you* would hear if you turned on your car radio at the speed of sound. If you keep the windows closed there's no problem, because you, the radio, and the air will all be stationary relative to one another. With the windows open, however, you wouldn't hear the rear deck speakers at all—the air carrying the sound waves would be blown backward too quickly. However, you'd hear the dashboard speaker normally (or as normally as you'd hear anything at 700 MPH)—the twin Doppler effects of source to air and air to observer would cancel out.

Finally, regarding your last question, the velocity of light is the speed limit of the universe and as such is rigidly enforced by the FBI. Any attempt to exceed it would defy one of the fundamental principles of creation, and would likely result in your getting a ticket.

I yearn for practical scientific knowledge. Unfortunately, I have come upon no practical scientists, so I turn to you, Cece. What makes Scotch tape stick? Also, why can't you light a match on sandpaper, but you can on the strip of flint provided on the matchbook?—Robert W., Baltimore

Unfortunately, R., it seems that nobody quite knows what makes tape—or any other sort of adhesive—stick. Most tapes are made with synthetic elastomers, which are very long molecule chains (polymers) that have certain elastic properties. Up until the 1960s, it was assumed that sticking was either a mechanical operation, involving the dovetailing or interlocking of molecular structures, or a chemical change that formed new chemical bonds. Now there is a theory of adsorption that postulates adhesion to be a result of the universal property of attraction that holds all matter together. Presumably, if this hypothesis is correct (and it appears to be enjoying some popularity), than *any* two materials will adhere if jammed close enough together.

As for your second question, one of the combustion elements that sets safety matches off is red phosphorus, which is contained not in the match, but in the "strip of flint." Without the red phosphorus, it takes more friction that most mortals can produce to get a rise out of the match head, which characteristically contains antimony sulfide, an oxidizing agent such as potassium chlorate, and sulfur or charcoal. In most wooden matches, by contrast, which usually you *can* light on sandpaper, everything you need to get things cooking is contained in the matchhead.

In these winter months when I go to open the car door and sit on the vinyl seats, I can feel the cold right down to my bones. Yet when I grab the wooden-handled snow shovel or sit on velour seats it's not so cold. When touched against the skin, why do metal objects feel colder than wooden objects of the same temperature?—L.F., Guadalajara, Mexico

117

You've got your nerve writing Cecil a question like this from Guadalajara, turkey. Get your caboose up here and freeze with the rest of us. What you're asking about has to do with *conductance*. Metals generally are much better conductors of heat than wood is—that is, they carry heat away from your body much more quickly, meaning your tootsies freeze faster and you feel colder. These things are easier to figure out when your head isn't fogged by jungle vapors.

I have a bet with my roommate about why wool is the only kind of material which still keeps you warm when it is wet. I say it's because even when wool is seemingly saturated with water, some dead air space still remains and provides insulation. She says (the dummy) that only wool dries from the inside (skin side) out. I don't know what that has to do with keeping you warm. Who is right?—Matthew N., Chicago

You're both wrong, so I guess I win the bet. I would prefer a cashier's check.

Each wool fiber (measuring about a thousandth of an inch in diameter, depending on the grade) consists of a bundle of corticle cells, made up of polypeptide chains arranged in coils. These corticle cells are wrapped up in a scaly outer layer called a cuticle, which in turn is covered by a filmy skin called an epicuticle. The epicuticle actually sheds drops of water. In addition, raindrops are less likely to break upon the surface of wool and seep through than with other fabrics, since the fuzziness of the fibers cushions the fall. So in a light rain, much of the water runs right off, the fabric hardly getting damp at all.

But the real genius of the wool fiber lies in its ability to cope with the high humidity that you may get during rainstorms or at other times. The sheep (they make look stupid, but it's all an act) have cleverly equipped the epicuticle with tiny pores that allow water vapor to pass through to the core, where it's chemically absorbed. A single fiber can slurp up to 30 percent of its own weight in moisture without feeling wet.

It may comfort you to know that you have not made a complete fool of yourself, in that wool does have a natural insulating property, thanks to its built-in crimp. The fibers repel each other, keeping a bit of dead air in between them. But it's the epicuticle that really counts.

Help, Cecil! We've been having a ferocious argument for the last hour, and if you don't come to our rescue, tragic violence will

118

surely result. My cute but mentally retarded girlfriend insists that if I want to make the six-pack of Budweiser that I just bought cool off faster, I should put it in the freezer rather than the regular part of the refrigerator. I calmly replied that this is bullshit, things cool off at the same rate whether you put them in the freezer or not (I'm sure I read this somewhere). But she doesn't believe me! She thinks I'm nuts! Cecil, I love this woman dearly, and I cannot bear to see her crushed by this burden of ignorance. Please explain to her that I am right and she is wrong (as usual), and restore peace to our once-happy household.—Daniel C., Los Angeles

Sorry, chump, but your girlfriend's opinion of your sanity is depressingly accurate, as the following lesson in heavy-duty physics will make clear. The mechanics of heat transfer are a bit complicated, so to simplify things we'll just concentrate on the heat that's transferred through the aluminum sides of the beer cans (I know you asked about cold, not heat, but think about it like this: when heat is transferred *out*, cold is transferred *in*). The process involved here is conductance, and it's governed by the following ineluctable equation, known as Fourier's Law (yes, *the* Fourier):

$$Q = \frac{KA\Delta T}{L}$$

To translate this into English, Q is the amount of heat transferred per second; K is the conductivity of aluminum (heat travels

119

through aluminum pretty fast, in case you're interested); A is the surface area of the can: $\triangle T$ is the difference between the fridge temperature and the beer temperature; and L is the thickness of the sides of each beer can. No doubt you find this baffling, Daniel, but I want you to concentrate your mental powers upon it until it becomes clear to you. Now, in studying Fourier's Law, we are led to one inescapable conclusion—the bigger the difference between the beer temperature and the fridge temperature, the more heat is transferred per second. The more heat is transferred per second, the faster the beer gets cold. Therefore it makes sense to put the beer in the coldest part of the fridge, namely the freezer. Hand the little lady a brew and apologize.

OK, no bullshit now. I got a simple question, I want a simple answer: how come you can see through glass?—Daniel C., Washington, D.C.

Not to beat around the bush or anything, Dan, but the reason you can see through glass basically is that there is no reason for you *not* to be able to see through it. Despite its appearance, glass is really a highly viscous liquid rather than a solid, and you can see through it for the same reasons that you can see through water. Having supplied that admirably simple answer, permit me to elaborate. Conventional liquids, when cooled, have a freezing point at which they suddenly become solid. Liquid glass, by contrast, simply gets gradually stiffer as it cools. At room temperature its rate of flow is so slow that it would take billions of years to ooze out of shape, and for most practical purposes it may be treated as a solid. Its internal structure, though, is not the regular crystalline latticework of your standard solid but rather is essentially random, like the typical liquid. As with many liquids, the rather loosely spaced molecules in glass are simply not big enough to obstruct the passage of light particles. Furthermore, (a) there are no footloose electrons in glass to *reflect* light, as with metals; (b) the energy levels of the individual atoms in glass are not such that they *absorb* light in the visible spectrum, although they will absorb infrared and ultraviolet; and (c) there are no internal boundaries or discontinuities in glass as there are in ordinary crystal solids to *refract* light, which would cause some light to be lost to internal reflection. (Glass reflects light only at its *external* boundaries— that is, the boundary between the glass and the surrounding air, or whatever. This permits refraction to be precisely controlled, which is what makes eyeglasses, and optics in general, possible.) In short, the reason you can see through glass is that there is no reason for you not to be able to see through it. QED.

120

I have recently experienced a phenomenon that a friend of mine declares has also happened to her. It's rather ghastly. I covered a meatloaf with a ketchup glaze and stored the thing in the refrigerator covered with aluminum foil. Where the foil touched the meat I found that it was eaten away, dissolved somehow, leaving a gray aluminum puddle deposit on the glaze. Thinking it was a fluke I re-covered the meat loaf with another piece of foil and the same thing happened. What happened?—Ms. T., Dallas

Aluminum has what we scientists call a "highly negative standard reduction potential," which means, if I may be permitted to bowdlerize a few pertinent scientific concepts, that it readily loses electrons and oxidizes. Ketchup, on the other hand, is highly acidic, having a pH of 3.85 (7.0 is neutral), and like all acids likes to oxidize obliging metals. The result, therefore, of a conjunction of foil and ketchup is, as you can attest, a grayish-black mush of aluminum oxide. Incidentally, I note here on my list of food acid levels that Coca-Cola, the all-American beverage, has a pH of 2.7, which leads me to conclude that with a couple of adroitly placed eight-packs during the late Falklands Islands war, the Argentine air force could have reduced Britain's tinfoil navy to jelly.

But this is no time for idle speculation. Standard reduction potentials also explain why it's painful for people with silver tooth fillings to chew aluminum spitballs. Silver, it turns out, has a highly *positive* standard reduction potential, which means it has an unnatural need for electrons. In the presence of an appropriate catalyst, such as your mildly acidic saliva, we have what amounts to a crude electric battery, in which electrons flow from the aluminum to the silver. This current is transmitted to the nerves of your teeth, producing the unpleasant sensation familiar to all.

People often talk about dominant and recessive traits, but does anyone really understand what that means? I know, for example, that genetically speaking, brown hair is supposed to be dominant, blond hair recessive. But by what process does one gene (or chromosome) dominate? Does it involve leather? Whips and chains? Or is the word "dominant" just a shorthand way of expressing the statistical predominance of one of the outcomes when brown-haired people and blond-haired people mate?—William H., Chicago

Admit it, Will, people do not "often" talk about dominant and recessive traits. I can't remember the last time I heard a good dominant and recessive traits story. Be that as it may, I can assure you that, as a general rule, the concepts of dominance and recessiveness refer to real chemical functions, not simply statistical correlations.

To illustrate with the example you've offered—brown hair versus blond—let's imagine a dominant gene, *B*, for brownness, and its recessive counterpart, *W*, for whiteness. (We are simplifying the real world a bit here, but hey, that's what journalism is all about.) *B* produces an enzyme that is needed for the synthesis of melanin, the brown pigment that most people possess to one degree or another. *W* produces no such enzyme, or a defective brand that can't do the trick. Finally—this is the important part—*B* produces, all by itself, enough of this enzyme to supply a whole normal body with all the melanin it needs. So the gene pair *BB* produces sufficient melanin to color the hair brown; so does the pair *BW*; only the poor sap who draws a pair of *W*'s ends up with white (i.e., blond) hair.

Cecil, you're my final hope
Of finding out the true Straight Dope
For I have been reading of Schrödinger's cat
But none of my cats are at all like that.
This unusual animal (so it is said)
Is simultaneously live and dead!
What I don't understand is just why he
Can't be one or the other, unquestionably.
My future now hangs in between eigenstates.
In one I'm enlightened, the other I ain't.
If you understand, Cecil, then show me the way
And rescue my psyche from quantum decay.
But if this queer thing has perplexed even you,
Then I will and won't see you in Schrödinger's zoo.
                                        —*Randy F., Chicago*

Schrödinger, Erwin! Professor of physics!
Wrote daring equations! Confounded his critics!
(Not bad, eh? Don't worry. This part of the verse
Starts off pretty good, but it gets a lot worse.)
Win saw that the theory that Newton'd invented
By Einstein's discov'ries had been badly dented.
What now? wailed his colleagues. Said Erwin, "Don't panic,
No grease monkey I, but a quantum mechanic.
Consider electrons. Now, these teeny articles
Are sometimes like waves, and then sometimes like particles.
If that's not confusing, the nuclear dance
Of electrons and suchlike is governed by chance!

No sweat, though—my theory permits us to judge
Where some of 'em is and the rest of 'em was."
Not everyone bought this. It threatened to wreck
The comforting linkage of cause and effect.
E'en Einstein had doubts, and so Schrödinger tried
To tell him what quantum mechanics implied.
Said Win to Al, "Brother, suppose we've a cat,
And inside a tube we have put that cat at—
Along with a solitaire deck and some Fritos,
A bottle of Night Train, a couple mosquitoes
(Or something else rhyming) and, oh, if you got 'em,
One vial prussic acid, one decaying ottom
Or atom—whatever—but when it emits,
A trigger device blasts the vial into bits
Which snuffs our poor kitty. The odds of this crime
Are 50 to 50 per hour each time.
The cylinder's sealed. The hour's passed away. Is
Our pussy still purring—or pushing up daisies?
Now, *you*'d say the cat either lives or it don't
But quantum mechanics is stubborn and won't.
Statistically speaking, the cat (goes the joke),
Is half a cat breathing and half a cat croaked.
To some this may seem a ridiculous split,
But quantum mechanics must answer, 'Tough shit.
We may not know much, but one thing's fo,sho':
There's things in the cosmos that we cannot know.
Shine light on electrons—you'll cause them to swerve.
The act of observing disturbs the observed—
Which ruins your test. But then if there's no testing
To see if a particle's moving or resting
Why try to conjecture? Pure useless endeavor!
We know probability—certainty, never.'
The effect of this notion? I very much fear
'Twill make doubtful all things that were formerly clear.
Till soon the cat doctors will say in reports,
'We've just flipped a coin and we've learned he's a corpse.'"
So said Herr Erwin. Quoth Albert, "You're nuts.
God doesn't play dice with the universe, putz.
I'll prove it!" he said, and the Lord knows he tried—
In vain—until fin'ly he more or less died.
Win spoke at the funeral: "Listen, dear friends,
Sweet Al was my buddy. I must make amends.
Though he doubted my theory, I'll say of this saint:
Ten-to-one he's in heaven—but five bucks says he ain't."

It must be these uncertain times, but once again I find myself coming to you to find the solution to a tantalizing enigma. In banks and other places that want to give that continental effect, one sees rows of clocks showing the time in various locales—New York, Paris, London—you know what I mean, being a man of the world. Anyway, the hour hand varies, but the minute hand is always the same—except for Bombay! It's always half an hour off. Or is the rest of the world half an hour off? I'm very concerned about this. Please explain so if I ever go to Bombay I can set my watch correctly.—Garnet J., Seattle

Bombay, and India generally, isn't the only place chronometrically out of step with the rest of the world. Lots of countries, particularly in Asia, are a half-hour out of sync, including Burma, Sri Lanka, and Afghanistan. Some have even stranger quirks. If my handy time-zone map here is to be believed—I am a little dubious about some of it, frankly—Nepal is 40 minutes off the mark. Saudi Arabia, ever the trailblazer, has some bizarre system in which clocks are supposedly reset to midnight every day at sunset. Keeping one's watch properly attuned aboard the Riyadh-Rangoon express must be an exhausting experience.

All of this traces back to the haphazard system of time-keeping prevalent before the 1884 Washington conference that established Greenwich Mean Time (GMT) as the international reference point and divided the world into 24 zones, the time in each of which was to differ by a whole number of hours from GMT. Prior to this, people made use of "local mean time," i.e., they figured out approximately when the sun was directly overhead, called that noon, and went from there. City A's time would thus differ by some odd number of minutes from that of cities B and C to the east and west. For instance, in 1880, England established two time zones for the British Isles—GMT for England, and Dublin Mean Time, 25 minutes earlier (or later, depending on how you look at it), for Ireland. After the standardization conference, most countries "rounded off" their local time, as it were, so that it differed by a whole hour(s) from GMT and from adjoining time zones. But some, for reasons of geography or politics, rounded off to the half-hour. Newfoundland, for example, was (I think) three hours, 35 minutes, and some seconds behind GMT before standardization, and elected to round off to three hours, 30 minutes—owing, I suppose, to the native perversity of its inhabitants, who delighted in being out of sync with the rest of Canada. India, as it happens, straddles two time zones, but for obvious reasons preferred to have one uniform time throughout the country. Rather than choose between GMT + 5 and GMT + 6 (which would make dawn and dusk in the far reaches of the country either unusually early or unusually late), the government apparently decided to split the difference. Don't ask me to explain Saudi Arabia.

My question arises from the fact that my kitchen happens to have both a boldly appointed digital clock and an old noisy analog thing my grandmother bought around 1940. I was delighted to discover quite by accident one bloodshot night that I could read the time on granny's clock from a far greater distance, and with much less light, than I could its digital counterpart. However, it occurred to me that were it to have been divided into eight equal sections, like a compass, reading it would be even less ambiguous. There is an obvious length to our day, but pray tell where is it written that it have 24 divisions called hours?—P.P., Chicago

Personally, I could always rely on finding it in the back of the *Growth in Arithmetic* book, along with 16½ feet to the rod, but maybe you have the abridged edition. In any case, we have the Babylonians to thank for our present system of timekeeping. The number 12 held mystical significance for the ancients, owing to the fact that there were generally 12 full moons a year, and so they divided day and night into 12 parts each. The number 60, apart from being a multiple of 12, is evenly divisible by more integers than any lesser number, and thus was useful for dividing hours into minutes and seconds, since you could readily noodle out your fractions. The Babylonian calendar had 12 months of 30 days; since this left five days unaccounted for each year, every sixth year they repeated the month of Adar. The Romans, of course, introduced the present cockeyed system of 28-, 30-, and 31-day months.

While the Babylo-Roman method possesses a certain primeval charm, it does not make for ease of calculation, and there have been several attempts over the years to devise a more rational system. Perhaps the most famous of these was the social experiment conducted during the French Revolution. In 1793, in an effort to sweep away the superstitious associations of the old method of timekeeping (you know how revolutionaries are), the French National Convention established a new calendar with 12 months of 30 days each, followed by five (six in leap years) "complementary days," which belonged to no month. Each month was divided into three 10-day "decades," and each day into two sections of 10 hours each. The hour was further divided into 100 "decimal minutes," which were in turn divided into 100 "decimal seconds." The year began on the autumnal equinox, which happened to be the anniversary of the foundation of the Republic. Each month was given a descriptive name, e.g., Thermidor, July 19–August 17, "month of heat." Each day was also given its own name, although owing to the magnitude of the task at hand some of the names were necessarily less inspired than others, including such dubious appellations as Eggplant, Manure, Shovel, Gypsum, Billy Goat, Spinach, and Tunny Fish. I don't see that any of these represented a significant advance over old faves like Maundy Thursday, but perhaps I am not taking a sufficiently Gallic view of the situation.

At any rate, the French public made a valiant effort to implement the new system, going so far as to manufacture watches with concentric 10- and 12-hour dials, but ultimately the task proved to be beyond them. In 1806, after 13 baffling years of missed dentist appointments and overdue library books, they abandoned the revolutionary calendar. This was the only known defeat of Progress in the modern era prior to the establishment of the Illinois General Assembly. Gives you pause, when you think about it.

How is it determined which date Easter Sunday will fall on each year?—Tim F., Washington, D.C.

Easter falls on the first Sunday subsequent to the first full moon after the vernal equinox (March 21). Thus, it can occur as early as March 22 and as late as April 25. (If the full moon after the equinox falls on Sunday, Easter follows a week later.)

Originally Easter was celebrated on the same day as the Jewish Passover. Since the Jewish calendar is lunar, Passover can fall on any day of the week, and some church fathers were distressed that the Lenten fast should end on any day other than a Sunday. They argued about it until the 8th century, when the church officially adopted the procedure we have now.

I heard that the four-color map problem was solved recently . . . by a computer! What's the straight dope on this, Cecil? Is this only a "limited" solution?—G.B.C., Van Nuys, California

I don't know that I would call 1976 "recently," G., but yes, the four-color map problem was solved (more or less) using a computer by two prairie geniuses at the University of Illinois at Champaign-Urbana, Wolfgang Haken and Kenneth Appel. The four-color map problem, as all mathematically hip personages know, s to determine whether there is any map that requires the use of more than four different colors if you want to avoid having adjacent regions be the same color. A matter of no great consequence, you might think, but this is the sort of thing that fascinates math aficionados—in this case for well over a century. Haken and Appel proved that (as was widely suspected) four colors are all you ever need.

Cecil would be greatly pleased to reproduce H&A's proof here, except that it took 1,200 computer hours and 6 zillion cubic yards of printout paper to do, so you're just going to have to take my word for it. Basically what the computer did was check out all the possible map combinations by trial and error. There are those who complain that this process does not constitute a mathematical proof, as that term is usually understood, but rather falls more into the category of an experiment, understandably something of a novelty in the field of abstract mathematics. Some suggest that a simpler and more elegant proof may yet be found. But most experts regard the H&A proof as quite sufficient in the meantime.

If cold is simply the absence of heat, i.e., the absence of rapidly moving molecules of water or air, then how come vacuum-packed canned food doesn't come out frozen, or at least very cold? And then if you walked a hundred feet out of your spaceship with a glass of water, would the water freeze because of the vacuum, or would it boil since there's no air pressure or barometric pressure to overcome?—Barry H., Chicago

Christ Almighty, Barry, you're asking for a short course in thermodynamics. Don't you guys want to know about Neil Sedaka anymore?

Let's clear up a couple misconceptions to start with. First, your idea that cold is "the absence of rapidly moving molecules of water or air" is a bit confused. Cold refers to *very slow-moving* molecules of anything, whether water, air, or Eskimo Pies. If you have no molecules at all, the concept of temperature is meaningless. That's why it's technically incorrect to speak of the "cold of outer space"—strictly speaking, space has no temperature, period. (On the other hand, space will make objects that are floating around in it cold—in some cases, *very* cold. Space is what's known as a "temperature sink," meaning it drains heat out of things. But we'll get back to this in a minute.)

Second, a vacuum never causes water to freeze; it causes water to *boil*. As air pressure decreases, so does boiling point. That's why water boils much faster on a mountaintop than it does at sea level. By the same token, you can make water boil at room temperature in the laboratory by applying a partial vacuum.

Now then. The contents of an earthbound vacuum-packed can do not freeze because they're in contact with the sides thereof—they absorb room heat by conduction. There is no room heat in space, though, so the temperature of a solid object floating in the void consists of the difference between the heat the object absorbs from the sun and the internal heat it radiates away. This temperature is entirely dependent on such things as the reflectance of the object's surface, its shape, mass, orientation toward the sun, and so on. Polished aluminum will absorb sufficient heat to raise its temperature as high as 850 degrees Fahrenheit; certain types of white paint, on the other hand, absorb so little heat that their temperature may not get much above −40 Fahrenheit, even in full sunlight. Parts of the NASA space shuttle get down to −180 to −250 degrees Fahrenheit. Theoretically, in fact, the temperature of an object in space could get down pretty close to absolute zero, −460 degrees Fahrenheit. (This leads one of my correspondents to suggest that the "ambient temperature" of space is 3 degrees Kelvin—that is, 3 degrees above absolute zero. I don't know that I buy this statement, but I offer it here nonetheless, being a liberal-type guy.)

Finally, we have the question of liquids in space. In a vacuum most liquids have such a low boiling point that they vaporize almost instantly. For that reason most substances exist in space in

either the gaseous or the solid state. When the astronauts take a leak while on a mission and expel the result into space, it boils violently. The vapor then passes immediately into the solid state (a process known as *sublimation*), and you end up with a cloud of very fine crystals of frozen tinkle. It is by such humble demonstrations as this that great scientific truths are conveyed.

During a lull at one of our recent staff meetings, I questioned my boss, brother, and dentist (one and the same, although not necessarily in that order of importance) about the mysterious properties of Life Savers candy. I'd heard that the wintergreen and peppermint varieties, if crunched smartly between the teeth, will emit a cloud of blue sparks. My brother verified this phenomenon, based on his own childhood experiences, but was at a loss to explain just how and why it occurs. Any ideas?—Dona S., Mesa, Arizona

It is all very well for a layman to take her brother's word on things like this, Dona, but professionals such as myself insist on checking out the situation firsthand. Accordingly, I have conducted a rigorous program of experiments, aided by the Straight Dope Kamikaze Research ("we laugh at death") & Display Advertising Battalion, which will do anything if it will get them out of actually having to work for an hour. Having completed our labors, we have arrived at the following conclusions: (1) wintergreen Life Savers will indeed produce spectacular if somewhat pint-sized clouds of blue flame when mashed vigorously between the molars. However, (2) peppermints don't do shit. Our failure in the latter department may perhaps be attributed to the fact that the peppermint Life Savers we had on hand were unbelievably ancient, and had consequently absorbed considerable moisture, which is said to inhibit sparking. However, theoretical considerations lead us to believe that even under the most favorable conditions the sparks from the peppermints would not be very bright.

Most students of the modern Life Saver classify sparking as a type of *triboluminescence*, which occurs when something is crushed or torn, the something in this case being the hard crystalline sugar that Life Savers contain. (Another example of TL is the spark you get when you tear the piece of tape off the end of a roll of photographic film.) Wintergreen sparking, it's believed, is actually a three-step process. *Step One:* When you shatter the sugar crystals with your teeth, electrons (which are negatively charged) break free. As a result, the atoms in which the electrons were formerly embedded become positively charged. In what amounts to a subatomic game of musical chairs, the free electrons dash around madly trying to find a new home. *Step Two:* Meanwhile, as the sugar crystals disintegrate, nitrogen molecules from the air attach themselves to the fractured surfaces. When the free electrons strike the nitrogen molecules, they cause the latter to emit invisible ultraviolet radiation, along with a faint visible glow. *Step Three:* The UV radiation is absorbed by the wintergreen flavoring, methyl salicylate. This then emits the fairly bright blue light you see. Pretty complicated, I admit. Ma Nature and Rube Goldberg have a lot in common.

I should point out that even without the wintergreen flavoring, virtually all crystal sugar candy, including peppermint Life Savers, will emit *some* visible light when crushed, although it's usually pretty faint. The effect was first described in 17th-century Italy, and since then it's been discussed in numerous papers and articles. Some of these are more imaginative than others. For instance, I have here an unpublished paper by researcher Patricia Nakache that is somewhat grandly entitled, "The Life Saver: A New Energy Source?" It contains the fascinating news that if you connect a Life Saver to a neon tube with wires and bash it (the Life Saver) with a hammer, *the neon tube will flash*. We can thus envision that when the next energy crunch comes, an adequate supply of Life Savers will be as important to survival as MasterCard is today. Better hustle on down to the store toot sweet.

Will the 21st century begin at twelve midnight of December 31, 1999, or 12:00:01 (midnight and one second) of January 1, 2000? Moreover, is midnight AM or PM? Does it belong to the day before or to the day to come? When is the first time that AM is used during the day? Or the last time that PM is used? Is the meridian referred to in AM and PM only at midnight, or is it at noon? Or both? Dave is really involved in this, so if you could hurry . . .—Susan A., Roz Z., Dave Z., Paula L., Chicago

Tell Dave I said he ought to get himself a hobby.

The 21st century will start neither at midnight nor at 12:01 AM January 1, 2000. It will start on January 1, 2001. Our calendar starts with the year 1 (there is no zero); thus, the 1st century expired at the end of the year 100, and the 2nd century began at the start of 101. Similarly, the 21st century will begin at the start of 2001.

Strictly speaking, midnight belongs neither to the day before nor the day after, and it is not proper to designate midnight as either AM or PM. Midnight is the dividing line *between* days, in the same sense that the present is the dividing line between the future and the past (think about this for a while). Midnight is defined in terms of noon—i.e., it's exactly 12 hours after noon. Noon, in turn (also called the meridian) is that instant at which the sun is at its highest point in the sky. (This, of course, depends on where you're standing. Because of time-zone standardization, when the clock strikes noon in most places the sun is usually a little ahead of or behind the meridian.) The highest point in the sky is precisely that—a point; hence, it has no dimension, and the time that the sun is there has no duration. So "noon" is that unmeasurable instant during which the sun is neither ascending nor descending in the sky. (The ascension and descension are apparent, of course. You can never be too careful in this business.) The first second of the conventional day comes after midnight— 12:00:01, and is thus properly designated AM. Of course, if you like, you can divide time up into smaller units than seconds, in which case you could say, "1 nanosecond after 12, AM." I trust you see the importance of the comma between "12" and "AM" in this expression.

Part of the confusion you folks are having about time designations stems from our somewhat perverse system of using 12 numerals to count 24 hours. In 24-hour time systems, in which the last minute of the day begins at 2359, there is no real need for terms like noon, midnight, AM, or PM. Astronomers use such a system with noon as the beginning of the day, or 0000; in the more familiar military system, noon is 1200. Which neatly illustrates (I hope) an important point about the way we designate time—namely, that it's pretty arbitrary. If we were to decide on December 31, 2000, at 1 nanosecond before midnight, that we'd prefer to call the coming century "the 22nd century" instead of "the 21st," we would change nothing but our own terminology. The calendar men might be upset, and the historians of millennia to come might be a little turned around, but the universe would hum on.

I come to you, the great bet settler and bubble physicist, for the final decision on an argument. What would happen to the bubbles in a beer mug if the mug fell off the top of the Empire State Building? Would the bubbles shoot to the top of the glass, the bottom, or stay motionless?—L.T., Los Angeles

The bubbles would remain motionless relative to the mug, since gravity would act uniformly on the fluid surrounding the bubbles—meaning, in short, that there would be no sloshing. You, on the other hand, would be thrown forthwith into the penitentiary for dropping beer mugs off of office buildings. Leave the daredevil scientific experiments to me, buddy.

Chapter 8

Politics, Law and Government

What would happen if a president-elect and his running mate both left this vale of tears before they were sworn in? Since they wouldn't have selected a cabinet yet, would captaincy of the ship of state go to the new speaker of the house? Would we get to vote again? Also, is Ronald Reagan the oldest man ever elected to a first-term presidency? Is he the least educated man of this century to be elected president?—Al L., Baltimore

Since I have a hard time dealing with abstractions, let's use as an example the demise of Ronald Reagan and George Bush. Heh-heh. Now then. If the president-elect, the veep-elect, or both die *before* the electoral college meets, there's no problem, because

the college is theoretically an independent body that can vote for anybody it wants to. In fact, something like this situation has already come up. In 1872 the Democratic presidential nominee,

Horace Greeley, died between the popular vote and the meeting of the electoral college. The Democratic electors thus had nobody to vote for, and since nobody really cared because Greeley had lost the election anyway, they got to vote for whomever they wanted. Consequently their votes were split among four now-forgotten politicians. (Three Georgia electors tried to vote for Greeley—Georgians are used to voting for stiffs—but Congress refused to count their ballots.) What would probably have happened if Reagan had died would be that the Republican National Committee would have gotten together and nominated a new candidate, whom the electors, being mostly loyal party functionaries, would likely then elect without further ado.

If Ronnie had passed into the Great Void *after* the electoral college vote, but George didn't, still no problem. The 20th Amendment provides that the vice-president assumes the office. If both lads had joined the choir, though, we'd have had trouble. The 20th Amendment says "Congress may by law provide for the case wherein neither a President elect nor a Vice President shall have qualified" (one of the qualifications for office presumably being that you're still breathing when you take the oath), but as far as I can tell Congress has never gotten around to so providing. Under ordinary circumstances—your run-of-the-mill emergencies, as it were—the succession passes from president to vice-president to speaker of the house to president pro tempore of the Senate. So some believe that when Carter's term had expired at noon on January 20th, the presidency would rightfully have gone to Tip O'Neill (O'Neill's term, according to the Constitution, began on January 3). Others, pointing out that O'Neill is a Democrat and that the will of the people would thus have been thwarted, suggest that it would have been time for an uncharacteristic display of statesmanship on the part of the nation's leaders, who probably would have cooked up some scheme to permit another Republican to be chosen. In view of the delicacy of the situation, it's unlikely anyone would want to go to the trouble of holding another presidential election. Some may think improvisations of this sort are a pretty casual way to run a country, but equally strange things have happened before. History buffs will undoubtedly recall the case of David Rice Atchison, who may or may not have been the 12th president of the United States for a total of one day. At midnight on Saturday, March 3, 1849, outgoing president James Polk's term expired, but incoming president Zachary Taylor refused to be sworn in on the Sabbath, and put the ceremony off until Monday, March 5—which meant nobody was president on Sunday, at least officially. Atchison was president pro tempore of the Senate then, and under the law in force at the time the succession would have devolved upon him, but he wasn't sworn in, he didn't do anything presidential (I believe he took a nap), and nobody to this day is really sure if he was president or not. It is this kind of thing that makes you wonder how the country has gotten this far without somebody conspiring to sell it to the gypsies.

As it turned out, of course, Reagan did survive until January 20, 1981 (and well beyond, God help us), and was in fact the oldest president inaugurated for a first term. He's not the least educated president of the century, though. President Truman, for one, had only a couple years of night courses at Kansas City Law School, while Reagan received a bachelor's degree at Eureka College.

Ronald Reagan was elected by what was referred to at the time as an "avalanche." However, given the declining percentage of the population that bothers to vote nowadays, I suspect Mr. Reagan's victory really isn't all that impressive. What was the percentage of eligible voters who supported him? Was it really such a landslide? How does the percentage compare with that of other presidents? Did Reagan even make it into the top ten?—Curious in Sunland, California

If Reagan's 1980 victory was an avalanche, I'm Wilt Chamberlain. Ron got 50.7 percent of the popular vote, which is nothing compared to the landslide champs: LBJ in 1964 (61.0 percent), FDR in 1936 (60.8 percent), and Nixon in 1972 (60.7 percent). Since only 53.9 percent of the voting-age population actually voted in 1980 (the lowest percentage since 1948), Ron got a scant 27.3 percent of the eligible vote, which is pretty terrible. Of the 40 elections held since 1824 (popular vote totals prior to that time are unavailable), Ron comes in 34th in percentage of eligible vote received, beating out only Carter, Nixon (in 1968), Truman, Coolidge, Wilson, and John Quincy Adams (who had an unbelievably crappy 8.2 percent in 1824—but more on this anon).

The leader in the eligible-vote rankings isn't exactly who you'd expect—it's William Henry Harrison in 1840, with 42.5 percent. (Harrison lasted only 31 days in office; some guys just can't cope with success.) The next two are Grant in 1868 (41.1 percent) and Lincoln in 1864 (40.6 percent). The reason these guys did so well was that voter turnout in the period 1840-1900 was amazingly high—it fell below 70 percent only once, and it topped 80 percent three times. (Of course, you have to remember that "eligible voters" prior to 1920 meant only males, and prior to 1868 meant only white males. After the turn of the century, voter turnout declined sharply for various reasons. Among other things, the South systematically disenfranchised blacks—and since the Democratic party had virtually no competition in the South, there wasn't much incentive to vote anyway. In addition, many states implemented tough voter-registration laws to curb ballot-box stuffing by corrupt big city machines. The low point in this century came in 1924, when only 48.9 percent of those eligible voted.

But back to Ron. If you look at *margin of victory* in the popular vote, he does a little better, but not much. He beat Carter by 9.7 percent, which ranks him around 12th or so on the landslide list, way behind the leaders: Harding in 1920 (26.4 percent), Coolidge in 1924 (25.2 percent), and FDR in 1936 (24.3 percent). When we get to *electoral college* vote, though, things start picking up. Reagan got 90.9 percent of the electoral votes cast, good enough for 7th behind George Washington's two elections (100 percent each time), Monroe in 1820 (99.6 percent), FDR in 1936 (98.5 percent), Nixon in 1972 (96.6 percent), and Jefferson in 1804 (92.0 percent).

OK, so who had the all-time *worst* eligible-vote performance? Good question, and it gives Cecil an opportunity to tell a little story of the sort he dearly loves. The worst turnout since 1824 occurred, interestingly enough, in 1824, when only 26.9 percent of eligible voters cast ballots (which is why John Quincy Adams looked so bad). Property-owning requirements for voters were common in those days, and besides, in some states the electors who chose the president were elected by the legislature with no popular vote at all. Still, 1824 may not be the all-time low. Vote totals from earlier elections aren't known with certainty, but some historians believe the absolute pits vote-wise was achieved in 1820, when James Monroe ran virtually unopposed for a second term. The election was such a yawn that probably *fewer than 1 percent* of the voters turned out. Nonetheless, Monroe got all but one of the electoral votes cast. (A legend grew up that the lone dissenting vote, by William Plumer of New Hampshire, was cast so that Washington would be the only top guy ever elected by unanimous vote of the electoral college. BS, at it turns out; Plumer just thought Monroe was a jerk.) Said one observer, it was "the unanimity of indifference, and not of approbation." And you thought things *now* were bad.

A while back this item appeared in Playboy's *"After Hours" column: "Better check the mirror before venturing out in Chicago, because, according to a city Ugliness Ordinance, 'No person who is diseased, maimed, mutilated or in any way deformed so as to be an unsightly or disgusting object, or an improper person to be allowed in or on the public ways or other public places in this city, shall therein or thereon expose himself to public view, under a penalty of not less than one dollar nor more than $50 for each offense.' Is this for real, and what's it all about?—Josh B., Chicago*

It's no joke, Josh. The ordinance (it's since been repealed) dates back to 1881. Originally certain extenuating circumstances were provided for. "On the conviction of any person for a violation of this section, if it shall seem proper and just, the fine provided for may be suspended, and such person detained at the police station, where he shall be well cared for, until he can be committed to the county poor house." The enlightenment of the twentieth century (which, according to some historians, reached Chicago *circa* 1930) led to the deletion of this clause.

The alleged purpose of the statute was not, as you might think, to rid the public ways of unsavory characters, but to protect the pitiful creatures from being exploited for profit—in other words, not to punish the deformed, but to protect them. Perfectly clear? An earlier ordinance had given the City Council the power to "regulate, license, suppress, and prohibit . . . exhibitions of natural or artificial curiosities," but apparently that legislation was too much to the point to be useful.

Of late, I have become interested in becoming the Prince of Wales. However, I am not an English citizen and cannot inherit the throne. I can resort to marrying one of the royal family, though. Would you please tell me who I would have to marry to attain this coveted position?—Vance L., Washington, D.C.

It pains me to have to crush your dreams, Vance, but the only way to become the Prince of Wales is to have very highly placed relatives. And even if you'd been blessed with the charming and graceful Queen Elizabeth for a mother, your princehood wouldn't come automatically. The Sovereign's eldest son acquires a few titles at birth—in the English peerage, he becomes the Duke of Cornwall; in the more effusive Scottish hierarchy, he's the Duke of Rothesay, the Earl of Carrick, the Baron of Renfrew, and all-'round Lord of the Isles and Prince and Great Steward of Scotland—but he only becomes the Prince of Wales (and simulta-

137

neously the Earl of Chester) at his parent's behest. Not that there's a whole lot of suspense—only one British ruler, Edward III, has taken the throne without the title since Edward I acquired it for the English royal family by killing the last *Welsh* Prince of Wales in 1282. Prince Charles was granted his title in 1958 when he was ten years old, his sterling leadership capacities being apparent even at that early age. When Charles turned 21 in 1969, he was formally presented to the Welsh people at the princely estate in Wales, Caernarvon Castle, where he actually managed to utter a few words in the native language. The Teeming Welsh Millions looked him over and decided to keep him, as if they had a choice or even cared very much.

Marrying into the royal family won't do you a whole lot of good. The wives of princes are automatically royal, but the husbands of princesses can only hope to receive a courtesy title. Just before Prince Philip married the then-Princess Elizabeth in 1947, the late King George was kind enough to make him Duke of Edinburgh, Earl of Merioneth, and Baron Greenwich. In 1957, Queen Elizabeth finally condescended to grant the poor guy "the style and dignity" of a Prince of the United Kingdom.

So far, though, Captain Mark Phillips, Princess Anne's soulmate, hasn't seen so much as a crummy barony—the pits of the peerage. In fact, Princess Anne has been shortshrifted herself: as Queen Elizabeth's eldest daughter, she's entitled to become the Princess Royal (the female equivalent, more or less, of the Prince of Wales), but the old lady hasn't gotten around to it yet. For Anne, however, the title would only be a small comfort—she can only become Queen if she eliminates her two younger brothers, the Princes Andrew and Edward, along with Charles, which isn't going to be easy. They only *look* stupid.

Why is it that leases frequently are made for 99 years instead of 100, or some other more manageable figure? The idea, obviously, is that the person who takes the lease will be dead by the time it comes up for renewal, but how was this particular number arrived at? It all seems very strange to me.—Leonard S., Chicago

The 99-year lease is apparently a by-product of an old English custom, dating back at least to feudal times. In the Middles Ages, extended leases were made for a period of 1,000 years, but as the Renaissance approached, the figure was reduced to 999 for reasons that today aren't entirely clear. In *Henry IV, Part II*, Shakespeare bends a metaphor around the thousand-year lease—"Now I am so hungry, that if I might have a lease of my life for a thousand years, I could stay no longer"—so the practice must have survived into the 17th century. But a contemporary of Shakespeare's, Sir Edward Coke, is already speculating on the origin of the 999-year lease. The thousand-year lease, he thinks, might have at one time been ruled fraudulent by the English courts—a lease that long was really a sale. If such a law existed, the landowners would avoid it by setting a term of 999 years, the loophole hardly being a modern invention. But no record of any such ruling exists.

The 99-year lease was largely an American invention, the hubba-hubba colonists apparently having no patience for the long-term view, and was probably worked out by analogy to the traditional 999 year figure. But not all of the experts agree. John Bouvier, writing in his 1839 *Law Dictionary*, the first legal reference book published in the United States, offers a different explanation: "The limit of 99 years would seem to be connected with a somewhat arbitrary estimate of 100 years as the probable estimate of a man's life. Leases for years are in their attributes, evolution, and history, a sort of a middle term between estates-for-life and a tenant-at-will. For this reason a period little short of the duration of the life of man was devised so that the lessee might reasonably build or lay out money for the property." Other speculation ranges from the cabalistic, focusing on 9 as a mystic number, to the hierarchical, 99 years being the approximate period covered by three generations. The hard-nosed approach suggests that the government once levied a higher tax on leases of 100 years or more, but there is no concrete evidence of this.

You are perfectly free—this being the land of the same—to draw up a lease for whatever term you wish, a millennium or twenty minutes. The 99 year figure has certain obvious advantages, being a nice, solid number to satisfy the bankers, but still being wide open for all practical purposes.

In reading I have come across a reference to "felo-de-se," which seems from the context to mean "suicide"—but I'm not sure. Can you help?—D. C., Los Angeles

"Felo-de-se" is a Latin phrase meaning "evildoer upon himself," or, simply, a suicide. In England before 1870 a distinction was made between a suicide, which was the name given to an act of self-destruction committed by a person of unsound mind, and a felo-de-se, which was committed by a sane person. If a self-destruction was judged a felo-de-se, the deceased's estate was generally forfeited to the crown.

England has had a few interesting suicide laws. Before 1961, persons who survived suicide attempts were subject to criminal prosecution and penalty. (My dip brother used to claim that the penalty was death. He also said the penalty for successful suicide was life imprisonment. My brother is a very funny guy.) Up until 1823 the genteel British would drive a stake through the body of a suicide before burying him at the side of a road.

Would you briefly summarize George Harrison's dilemma with his song, "My Sweet Lord," the tune to which he supposedly plagiarized? I find it hard to believe that any well-known artist would intentionally lift a song.—L.H., Baltimore

Actually, Richard Owen, the U.S. District Court judge who convicted Harrison of copyright infringement in September of 1976, also found it hard to believe that a well-known artist would lift a song (particularly that one). While allowing an uncanny resemblance between "My Sweet Lord" and the 1963 Chiffons hit, "He's So Fine" (written by the group's manager, Ronald Mack), Judge Owen—apparently gifted with psychic powers—delved deeply into the mysteries of Harrison's mind to conclude that the theft had been inadvertent: "His subconscious knew that song had worked out," Owen said, "but his conscious mind did not remember." Ordered to pay $587,000, Harrison remarked, "It's a pain in the neck," adding, with Wildean wit, that the lawyer who brought suit against him was "a sneak, who saw money pouring out of the sky." Proof once again that being rich is a bitch.

From time to time there is talk that Congress will soon reinstate the draft, perhaps including mandatory service on the part of all 18-year-olds. This brings to mind a question: why isn't the draft considered "involuntary servitude," and forbidden by the 13th Amendment? Has this ever been tested by the courts? If so, what was the outcome?—Tom G., Dallas

There are a couple promising legal strategies you might avail yourself of in attempting to elude the draft, but the 13th Amendment dodge isn't one of them. A couple chumps tried it during the Vietnam era and were pretty much laughed out of court and into the ranks. The amendment was meant to prohibit slavery and has never been successfully applied to military service.

On the other hand, you could make a plausible case that the Constitution forbids Congress to send conscripts off to fight an undeclared war, or to conduct a peacetime draft. The theory here is that while Article I, Section 8 of the Constitution empowers Congress to "provide for the common defense" and "raise and support armies," the framers simply meant to establish a professional army, composed of volunteers. This is not as off the wall as it sounds. You will recall that early Americans found the British Navy's practice of forcibly inducting men into service pretty obnoxious, and it is unlikely they would turn around and authorize a draft.

The Constitution does permit the separate states (or "the several states," as we legal beagles like to put it) to organize militias for home defense (note the Second Amendment), and in the broadest sense the militia in colonial times consisted of every male 18 and over who was healthy enough to carry a gun. So (in this view, anyway), while the federal government can't draft people, the states can.

What enables the federal government to conduct the draft is clause 15 of Article I, Section 8, which permits Congress to call out the militia to "execute the laws of the Union, suppress insurrections and repel invasion." This means that Congress can send draftees off to foreign countries after a declaration of war, which has the force of law. But it doesn't include undeclared conflicts like Vietnam. And presumably it wouldn't include a peacetime draft.

A number of inductees pursued this notion during the Vietnam period, with mixed success. The government's case was shaky, but the judiciary was reluctant to declare Uncle Sam's military experiments illegal, mostly for political reasons. So the cases tended to drag out. On a number of occasions the Selective Service people found excuses to reject potential draftees when it appeared they might have a good chance of winning a court fight. There is at least one case on record of a man whom the Army honorably discharged before the end of his term, simply to avoid the possibility of an embarrassing court ruling.

At any rate, nothing was ever settled and no precedent was ever set. But the issue might come up again if a peacetime draft is ever reinstated. We await developments.

I am a young fellow who has not registered for the government's current nondraft, thus violating the law of the land. I haven't exactly been spending sleepless nights awaiting a knock on the door from the authorities, but any information I can glean on the subject does interest me. Specifically, I heard someone saying that a treaty between the U.S. and Canadian governments, put into effect since the Vietnam era, allows authorized agents to remove nonregistrants and draft evaders from Canada against their will.

What he actually said was, "They can haul your ass back from there now." Is this true? If so, where can poor fools like me go in the event the nondraft turns into a real draft, and getting killed in some faraway land sounds no more appealing to us than it did to our predecessors?—Not-signed-because-you-never-know-who's-reading-this, Phoenix

Not to cast aspersions on your moral fiber or anything, N., but personally I have always regarded sneaking off to Canada to avoid the draft as an act of craven puppyhood. It seems to me that if you're going to resist, the only proper thing to do is to *resist*, by either going the conscientious objector route or going to jail. Admittedly this is a lot less fun than cavorting with the baby seals north of the 49th parallel, but that's the breaks. Now, getting down to your question: there is no treaty between the U.S. and Canada that permits U.S. authorities to haul your ass, or any other portion of your anatomy, back down here for draft evasion. The existing treaties, which antedate the Vietnam era by a considerable stretch, permit extradition only for offenses that are *recognized as crimes in Canada*. Since Canada has no draft, it has no such thing as draft evasion. On the other hand, you *can* be extradited for desertion once you've actually been inducted into the military.

Treaty or no treaty, emigrating to Canada to avoid the draft nowadays is much more difficult than it was 15 years ago, owing to the fact that Canadian immigration policies are stricter. Assuming you don't want to spend your entire time in Canada as an illegal alien (a way of life that truly sucks, let me assure you), what you want is "landed immigrant" status, the equivalent of "permanent resident" status in the U.S. (no, "landed immigrant"

doesn't mean you have to own any land). In the early 70s the Canadian government implemented a point system to determine if you qualified for landed immigrant status, which gave you credit for things like knowledge of English and/or French, close Canadian relatives, or a job offer in Canada. However, there are also a lot of discretionary points that can be awarded depending on whether the investigating officer thinks you'd be a worthwhile addition to the Canadian polity. Such determinations are heavily influenced by Canadian public opinion, the amount of grief Canada is getting from the U.S. for harboring draft dodgers, and so on. Ever since the Canadian economy began to go sour in the mid-70s, there's been resentment of U.S. citizens taking Canadian jobs, and I'm told that at present the chances of a well-educated young male getting landed immigrant status are extremely small. In any event, the process is extremely time-consuming.

Finally, I should point out that while emigrating to Canada was one of the most publicized methods of draft evasion during the Vietnam era, in reality it was not all that heavily used. Estimates of the number of persons who actually fled to Canada vary from 20,000 to 200,000, of whom maybe half were illegals. Most would-be draft evaders simply stayed put in the U.S. As a practical matter—not saying I approve of this, you understand, but it's one of the options—the easiest thing may be just to stay where you are, don't register, and keep your yap shut. The government may never find you. On the other hand, if they *do* find you, it's one of the easiest things to get a conviction on. Accordingly, before you do anything drastic, I strongly recommend contacting one of the draft counseling services established in most major cities.

What happened to the men who tried to steal Elvis Presley's body from Forest Hills Cemetery in 1977? Did they go to jail? It is very important for me to know this.—Barbara G., Evanston, Illinois

I shudder to think what you may be contemplating, but I'm afraid the Elvis kidnapping case doesn't offer a very strong deterrent against body snatching. The charges against the three men who allegedly tried to swipe Presley's body were dropped by the Memphis prosecutor when the chief witness and accuser (legalese for "rat"), one Ronnie Lee Adkins, demonstrated his "unreliability" by getting himself arrested for fraud. Adkins apparently had checked into Memphis's Doctor's Hospital posing as a policeman in order to claim that he was covered by the city's insurance plan.

Following the attempted theft, Elvis's body was moved

beyond the reach of would-be defilers and into a corner of his Graceland estate, which Vernon Presley, Elvis's father, christened a high-security "Meditation Garden." In addition to plots for Elvis and his mother, the senior Presley thoughtfully laid aside space for Elvis's grandmother, two uncles, and himself. Vernon died in 1979 at the age of 63, and I presume he's now keeping company with his son.

I listen to the radio a lot and, frankly, I'm confused. Every few years a song comes along with a title identical to that of an earlier song ("Truckin'," "One Man Band," and "Pillow Talk" are a few of the examples that come to mind). How does this happen? Obviously I couldn't go out and write a book called Valley of the Dolls *or make a movie entitled* Porky's *(not that I would want to, but you get my drift). Aren't there such things as copyright laws? Please answer posthaste as I'm in the midst of writing a rock opera with the tentative title* How to Stuff a Wild Bikini.*—V.N., Phoenix*

You may be surprised to learn this, V., but the team of ace legal piranhas on retainer here at Straight Dope World HQ informs me that titles, whether of songs, newspapers, or what have you, *cannot be copyrighted.* Ditto for short phrases. Titles and so on come under the general heading of *trademarks*—which is to say, signs used by companies to distinguish their products from those of other firms. In other words, we move from the realm of creative genius (i.e., stuff covered by copyright) to the world of grubby commericalism. If someone steals your title or trademark, you can sue them for unfair competition, but your chances of winning are by no means guaranteed. Besides, a first-class trademark suit could cost you $30-$100,000, so it's not something you undertake lightly. When someone steals the title of a song that's several years old, usually there's not enough money involved to make a lawsuit an attractive proposition. With movies and some books, however, there's a lot more at stake. Wherefore, bag the bikini business, bucko, and pick on somebody who can't afford to fight back.

How much right does a person have to his own name? For instance, here in duh Great City of Chicaguh, we have a well-known high-rise haven called Sandburg Village. Did Carl Sandburg or his estate have to give their permission to have this named after him? Could Sandburg have vetoed the idea? Could I name, and then advertise, an apartment complex as the Cecil Adams Estates? —Mother Cabrini, Chicago

Personally I think it's about time they named something after me, being the acknowledged cultural monument that I am, but I take it you are using this purely as a hypothetical example. As it happens, the law never specifically deals with a person's right to his name; rather, the subject is covered under the general heading of the right to privacy. But "privacy" means different things in different contexts. A public figure, according to several rulings, has far less of a right to privacy than your ordinary schlub. It boils down to a question of proving damages: if someone uses your name against your will and in such a way as to substantially injure your reputation, the judge in your case might decide that your existence has been impoverished to the tune of x dollars. Then again, he may not: damage rulings, particularly those involving such intangibles as name and reputation, are notoriously capricious.

As an individual, you have no proprietary right to your name—no "copyright," so to speak. Names are in the public domain; you can name your kid whatever you want to. However, when it comes to naming a building, a company, or any other enterprise that smacks of commercial exploitation, we enter a very murky area of the kind so beloved by hustling lawyers.

In the case of Sandburg Village, the developers obtained the formal consent of Sandburg's widow before using his name. But that may not have been strictly necessary: it could be argued that Carl Sandburg had achieved such an extraordinary degree of fame that his name was no longer "his"—that, in effect, he had no more privacy left to be invaded, and so could suffer no damage (being dead, anyway) from the use of his moniker. It's also difficult to imagine what injury you might suffer from having a high-class housing project like Sandburg Village named after you. On the other hand, Mother Cabrini, I don't suppose having one of the country's most notorious public housing projects named after you has done much to burnish your reputation. If I were you I'd sue the bastards.

I recently saw a movie that featured a trial scene at the end, and I noticed how heavily the court played on the witnesses' belief in God, the Bible, etc., as they were sworn in. I began to wonder: what if an atheist or an agnostic were an important witness to a crime—how would that person be sworn in?—Barbara T., Los Angeles

When a witness refuses to swear to God, the court accepts an "affirmation" instead. In a jury trial, the smart lawyer will

145

arrange for this ahead of time in the judge's chambers, so the witness won't look unduly obstreperous or morally deficient in open court. The judge may then instruct the jury that the funny oath they are about to hear should be considered legally valid. In U.S. District Court (to take the most widespread example), the standard oath is amended to: "You do affirm that all the testimony you are about to give in the case now before the court will be the truth, the whole truth, and nothing but the truth; this you do affirm under the pains and penalties of perjury?" After the witness replies, "You got it, Jack," or whatever godless heathens say in such situations, eveyone sits back and pretends that the "pains and penalties of perjury" are every bit as intimidating as the wrath of a vengeful Almighty. It's not an ideal situation, if you want my opinion, but I suppose it's the best the judges can do under the circumstances.

While sitting here at my boring desk job, I periodically contemplate the criminal life. Excitement. Danger. Easy money. But before I change careers, I need to know the answer to this question: there are state cops, county cops, city cops, suburb cops, and the almighty FBI. Who has got superiority over whom? Who has authority where? Can a city cop nail me for speeding in the suburbs? If state, county, and city cops nab me in the city, who gets first crack, since they're all within their proper jurisdictions? Does a private gumshoe, security guard, or even a citizen have the power of arrest?—F.L., Chicago

Cecil is always happy to help the Teeming Millions achieve personal fulfillment, so long as they give him a cut of the swag. I prefer small bills in an unmarked envelope. As far as city, county, and state cops go, nobody has superiority from a legal standpoint. All derive their authority in equal measure from the state constitution, and no matter who arrests you or what the crime (assuming it's not a federal crime, which we'll discuss in a moment), the state's attorney's office (the title may vary in different states) will handle the prosecution. A city cop can pull you over for speeding anywhere in the state, and so can county or state cops.

Ordinarily, of course, cops from different jurisdictions coordinate their efforts—city cops handle everything that normally comes up within the bounds of their municipalities, county cops patrol unincorporated areas, and state cops cruise the highways. If you conclude a crime spree with a chase involving city, county, and state cops, the question of who actually gets to bring you in is mostly a matter of expedience: who laid hands on you first, who feels like filling out the paperwork, and so on. City cops or county cops may on occasion be instructed to defer to, say, state law enforcement officials who are conducting an investigation, but this is a matter of management, not law.

Things get more complicated if we bring in cops from other states, or the federal authorities. Although Illinois cops, for instance, can chase you all over the Land of Lincoln, they can't pursue you into adjoining states. They have to radio ahead to alert the cops in the state you're trying to escape into. Later Illinois officials will have to arrange to have you extradited back here for trial. Usually this is a formality, but there have been several well-publicized instances where one state refused to surrender a prisoner to another.

As far as the feds go, Article VI of the U.S. Constitution declares that document to be the supreme law of the land, so if you're accused of a variety of federal and state offenses, Uncle Sam gets first dibs, strictly speaking. As a practical matter, though, all local and federal agencies subscribe to the notion of "comity of jurisdictions," meaning they try to cooperate. Normally you'll be turned over to the authority that's after you for the most serious offense.

Every citizen possesses the common-law power of arrest, which means that you have a legal right to detain someone if (a) you catch them red-handed in the act of committing (b) a genuine crime. Bear in mind that you can be sued for false arrest if you screw up. Private guards and the like have no more right to arrest than the ordinary schmoe, but they are permitted to carry guns and wear uniforms and badges. Having faced the wrong end of a six-shooter in my day (no joke), I must say they confer considerable powers of persuasion.

I was idly reading a Grape-Nuts package the other day and was struck by the fact that the ingredients seem to have nothing to do with either grapes or nuts. Reading the fine print, I see that it's really "grape nuts brand natural wheat & barley cereal," etc., but the type sizes jump around madly and any normally myopic person would just see the "grape nuts." So here are my questions: (1) Can I market my "100% Lean Beef brand desiccated corn husks" without getting in trouble with the consumer protection people, the FTC, et. al.? (I assume anything I do will get me in trouble with Ralph Nader.) (2) If I can't, how can the Post division of General Foods? (3) In any case, how did they come to call them Grape-Nuts?—Winfield S., Chicago

Your corn husk scheme shows a certain evil ingenuity, Win—I have come to expect this kind of thing from the Teeming Millions—but unfortunately you can't market it, because the Federal Trade Commission would promptly slap you with a cease-and-desist order for promulgating advertising with a "tendency to deceive." (Although you never know. The way things have been going lately, they might give you an award and appoint you commissioner.) In the early years of the FTC, an equally ingenious predecessor of yours tried to sell Ice Cream brand bars that did not, in fact, contain any ice cream, but he was shot down forthwith.

So how does Post get away with it? Here we must delve into the mysteries of history (rhymes, doesn't it?) Grape-Nuts was introduced in 1898 by Charles W. Post, founder of the company that was later to become a division of General Foods and inventor of such other gustatory delights as Post Toasties. C.W., as he was known, was given to devising extravagant names for his products, with advertising claims to match. Post Toasties, for instance, was originally known as Elijah's Manna, although Elijah had not actually endorsed it, having expired several thousand years earlier. In touting the advantages of Postum Cereal Food Coffee over conventional coffee, Post accused the latter of containing "poisonous alkaloids" that caused rheumatism, "coffee heart" (true enough, I guess), and other disabilities. A diet of Postum and Grape-Nuts, coupled with abstention from coffee and "poor foods," presumably meaning those made by Post's competitors, would cure "any known disease." The brand name Grape-Nuts was conceived in a similar spirit.

Nonetheless, there was a rationale, however thin, for the name. The product contained maltose, known at the time as "grape sugar," and it did have a nutty flavor. Moreover, bearing in mind that the name is properly spelled "Grape-Nuts" and not "Grape Nuts," one might argue that while there were generic commodities known as grapes and nuts, there was nothing called grape-nuts, in the sense that there were cashew nuts, and thus the name could have no tendency to deceive. A fine distinction, I suppose, but that is what we have lawyers for. Anyway, the 1906 Pure Food and Drug Act specifically excluded "fanciful" (as opposed to deceitful) trade names from prosecution, and when the FTC set up shop in 1914 it showed no inclination to get persnickety about things. We might finally note, Winfield, that while you and I are insignificant insects, General Foods is a multinational megacorporation. However, I am sure that this had no bearing on the matter.

From time to time the media use the terms "court-authorized burglary" or "black-bag job." My research in front of the TV tells me that the authorities are free to search the following, without a warrant or the occupant's permission: (1) rented quarters, residential or business, where the landlord allows entry, or (2) a hotel room or train compartment. In addition, however, is there such a thing as a "court-authorized burglary" of a privately owned residence or office? Is this constitutional? Has anyone ever claimed, "Hey, guys, the judge said it was cool," and got officially let off? If one of these guys gets blown away by a citizen defending himself against an apparent intruder, is it "tough noogies, Justice Department," or is the citizen in trouble?—Phil C., Washington, D.C.

Before we get into this, Phil, let me pass along a handy rule of thumb that we print journalists find useful in assessing the work of our electronic brethren: *absolutely everything you hear on TV is wrong.* This (along with genetic drift) is what accounts for your present state of mind. Contrary to what you may have heard on the tube, the cops can*not* search your apartment, hotel room, or train compartment just because the landlord (or whoever) says so. They have to get either a warrant or your permission first. There are some exceptions to this, such as if you go out and kill somebody and somewhat stupidly hotfoot it back to your apartment with the police right behind you. However, this does not exactly qualify as a black-bag job. (Landlords themselves, I might point out, generally have the right of "reasonable access" to your place for purposes of maintenance, showing the joint to prospective tenants, and so on—but that's as far as it goes.) Having said all this, I must admit that there *does* appear to be at least one instance in which a so-called black-bag job is permissible: when the authorities have to get into your house to install an authorized wiretap. We learn this from the 1979 U.S. Supreme Court ruling in *Dalia* v. *U.S.* (Uncle Cecil loves to read all this ancient legal rubbish). Lawrence Dalia was an evil being from New Jersey (where else?) who conspired to transport a truckload of stolen cloth. In hopes of proving this, the feds got a court order allowing them to bug Dalia's office. Unfortunately, the order didn't say anything about "covert entry,"as we masters of deceit like to refer to it. For that matter, the Omnibus Crime Control and Safe Streets Act, which legalized wiretapping in the first place, never mentions covert entry, although it seems pretty obvious you can't just go knocking on somebody's door and ask if it's OK to put a tap on the phone. At any rate, the feds went ahead and sneaked into Dalia's office, installed the bug, and used the evidence obtained thereby to convict him. Dalia petitioned to have the evidence thrown out on the grounds that black-bag jobs were illegal, but the judge basically said that permission to sneak in was implicit in the warrant authorizing the wiretap. The Supreme Court upheld this ruling. Note that the coppers *still have to get a warrant of some sort,* and also that they can't just go in and steal stuff, the latter field of endeavor being restricted to the Internal Revenue Service.

We must further note that the court left unanswered the tantalizing question of what would happen if a citizen offed a G-man who was sneaking onto the premises one night with authorized wiretap in hand. However, Phil, you seem like the adventurous sort, and you may well have an opportunity someday to deal with this issue at first hand. Be sure to let Cecil know how things work out.

Tradition states that when a president or former president goes to that big White House in the Sky, the American public responds

150

by going into mourning for thirty days. Among other things, Richard Nixon qualifies as an ex-president. Has anybody given any thought to what will happen when he dies? Will flags automatically be lowered to half staff, or will we have a big brouhaha while people argue about the appropriate procedure for mourning disgraced public leaders?—Veda Ann B., Chicago

This particular hot potato will be dropped into the lap of the man lucky enough to be president when Nixon kicks. It's not "tradition," but a presidential proclamation that establishes the customary 30 days' public mourning. Conceivably, whoever's in charge could declare a national 30-day period of embarrassed throat-clearing, or choose to ignore the whole thing.

The flags that fly on the east and west ends of the Capitol building traditionally set the style for the rest of the country, and they're automatically lowered to half staff only when a sitting member of Congress dies. Otherwise, it takes a tete-a-tete between the speaker of the House and the vice-president (acting as the president of the Senate) to decide on the merits of each individual case. Thus, the flags could be lowered when Buffalo Bob Smith passes on, which arguably would have deeper meaning for the nation than RMN's demise.

At a recent rock concert I was subjected to more than the typical cursory check for cans and bottles when I entered the theater. The promoter had security people keep ticket holders in line for over an hour as they conducted what can only be described as a search-and-seize mission at the door. Concertgoers were permitted to enter single file, doormen spent several minutes per person rooting through purses and pockets (they even checked one guy's hair looking for who knows what) and relieved people of pipes, papers, bags of grass, wineskins, and other assorted spirits. Do promoters have the right to conduct such a shakedown? A friend of mine was parted from a small pouch of excellent Colombian which was found in his pants pocket—a rather frightening experience. Legally, do these private security people have the right to confiscate drugs? Is the concertgoer subject to a possession charge if he's caught holding? Am I within my rights to refuse to submit to a search, or to demand a warrant? Can I be prevented from entering if I refuse to be searched? As for somebody patting me down, it seems to me that they'd be open to an assault charge. Could you spell out the law on this issue?—Susan, Los Angeles

Sure, but you're not going to like what you hear. The constitutional safeguards against search and seizure apply only to the

151

government, not to private parties. This is not to say that a concert promoter can search you with impunity. When you buy a concert ticket, you're essentially entering into a contract: the party of the first part (the promoter) agrees to allow the party of the second part (you) to attend his concert as long as you agree to play by his rules, which may include submitting to a search. Basic contract law permits private parties to extract such conditions so long as they do not violate public policy—e.g., the promoter can't force you to commit a crime. You are within your rights, of course, to refuse to be searched, but the promoter can then refuse to admit you. (As a general rule he's also obliged to give you your money back, and in fact promoters are almost always willing to do so.) Note that there must always be an element of free choice involved in searches. If you're allowed into a concert and halfway through two of the promoter's goons take it into their pebble-sized minds to forcibly search you again, you could have them charged with assault. On the other hand, if you commence trashing the joint, it's perfectly all right for the goons to give their all in defending the boss's property (again, within reason—lawyers have made millions arguing about what exactly constitutes "within reason").

The question is somewhat complicated by the fact that the "private security people" employed by concert promoters are often off-duty coppers. An off-duty police officer has the right—nay, the duty—to make an arrest when he or she witnesses a crime. This means that your friend—the one with the Colombian—*could* have been charged with possession and carted off to the slammer. Fortunately, most promoters adhere to a policy of either ignoring drugs or simply confiscating them. All this may sound unfair to you, but next time you're at a show where some 13-year-old music lover decides it's time for a a fireworks display, maybe you'll see the sense of it.

I recently completed a photography course at a local college, where our instructor told us we could not get into any legal trouble photographing people in public places, and that we did not have to get their permission to take a picture. So far I have been verbally threatened (although not yet beaten up) by people who did not take kindly to the idea of having themselves immortalized on film. Is the law really on my side?—Maria, Baltimore

I'm sure your heart's in the right place, snugglebuns, but I'm not sure I can say the same for your mind. Taking pictures in public is indeed legal, but that's not likely to impress some toad who's determined to tapdance on your cranium. What you need is a plan involving subterfuge and deviltry, which Cecil shall shortly provide. First, however, be assured that you do not need to get the permission of your subjects before you take their pictures. If you make a real nuisance of yourself, after the manner of Jackie Onassis's nemesis, Ron Galella, you could conceivably be sued or charged with disturbing the peace, but that's a separate issue. You can even publish your pictures, subject to certain restrictions.

As I say, though, what you've got is more a practical problem than a legal one. Your best bet is to get your mitts on an old Rolleiflex or some camera of similar design, where you sling the thing over your neck and look into the viewfinder from above (be forewarned—these cameras ain't cheap). This makes possible the following stratagem. Suppose you want to take a picture to the east of you. You face north. You point the lightshield on the viewfinder of your Rollei so it looks like you're actually *shooting* north. Surreptitiously, however, you *swivel the cubical camera body so the lens is facing east*, and click away (if you don't follow this, have somebody at the camera store show you what I mean). We journalists are nothing if not devious.

A friend of mine and I have had a little running joke for many years. He says he saves every letter he gets from me so that when I become a rich and famous writer, he can publish them and make a ton of money. This doesn't seem quite fair to me, since, after all, I wrote them, and I deserve as much of the take as he does. He points out that letters from famous people are hot collectors' items, and that nobody asks Richard Nixon, say, if it's all right with him if they sell his letters. Obviously, only Cecil Adams can settle an important legal issue like this one.—Karen L.,Dallas

A little running joke, eh? Boy, you two do have a lot of fun, don't you?

Collecting and publishing are two very different things. As a material possession—like a pair of socks or a souvenir paperweight—a letter is yours if someone sends it to you, and you can sell it if you like. But as a literary composition, a letter belongs to its author, and only s/he has the right to publish it. If you acquired the original manuscript of *A Farewell to Arms*, for instance, you'd have no right to run off a few copies (or, technically, even put it on display—that's considered "publication," too) without the author's permission. The same rules apply to letters as to novels, plays, poems, or whatever.

But I'll think I'll hang on to this one anyway, just in case.

My social security card says that my social security number is not to be used for identification, yet the state requires it for driver's licenses and the city needs it for voter's registration. Do they have any federal authority to do this or did this practice just start?—John C., Evanston, Illinois

John, you lovable peat-brain, they didn't mean your social security *number* couldn't be used for identification purposes, just that the *card itself* couldn't be presented as proof of identity. I trust you understand the distinction. The reason for the warning was that prior to 1972 having a social security card didn't prove much of anything, certainly not your identity. Obtaining a card was ridiculously easy—all you had to do was stroll into any local social security office, fill out a form or two, and they'd assign you a number there and then. Certain of my low-life high school classmates took advantage of this lax procedure to obtain cards under several names. When social security numbers were first issued in 1936, such shenanigans didn't matter much, because the only thing you were supposed to do with the number was submit it to your employer when you started a new job. In later years, however, the social security number evolved into an unofficial identity number (although the feds hate to admit this). In 1943, a presidential executive order directed the military and other government agencies to use the number for identification purposes, and in 1961 the Internal Revenue Service began using the number for taxpayer identification. Eventually states began requesting the number on driver's license applications and the like.

Finally in 1972 Congress realized that the government's casual card-issuance procedures were an invitation to abuse, and it decided to tighten things up. Applicants over age 18 now have to present proof of birth and proof of identity, and they also have to apply in person. Other equally stringent regulations apply to minors and aliens. Cards and numbers are no longer issued directly at the local office, but have to be cleared through a central office in Baltimore, a process that takes about ten days. Among other things this prevents an applicant from being issued more than one number. As a result of all these changes, the "not to be used for identification" line was dropped from the cards. Uncle Sam still wishes the cards weren't used as proof of identity, but seems resigned to the fact that they will be nonetheless. Accordingly, the cards being issued these days employ a tamper-resistant printing process like that used on U.S. currency. It is by such means as these that we form a more perfect union.

Chapter 9

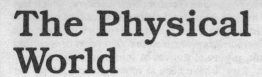

The Physical World

I hope you can answer a question that has plagued me since childhood. If every man, woman, and child in China each stood on a chair, and everyone jumped off their chair at exactly the same time, would the earth be thrown off its axis? Also, if prior to jumping, they all yelled at the top of their lungs, would we hear it here in the United States, and how much of a time delay would there be?—Robert P., Los Angeles

Amazing as it may seem to the general public, I am actually going to answer this incredibly retarded question. But first Uncle Cecil wishes to have a word with his devoted readers. As you can imagine, I possess phenomenal scholarly resources. I have converted the spare bedroom in my house into a research library containing 16 million volumes, which are dusted twice a day by a team of robed acolytes holding candles. I have instant access

155

via my Apple 380S GT to all the world's data banks. Why, right here on my writing table next to the box of spare quills I have a dog-eared copy of *16,000 Unbelievably Complicated Physics Experiments for the Home and Garden, With Answers*, which has helped me out of many a jam. But despite this wealth of scientific knowledge, the Teeming Millions routinely write in with questions that *not one sane person has ever asked in 6,000 years of recorded history*. As a result, my usual sources of information are useless.

Nonetheless, I try. I have been in repeated contact with the Peking government all week in an effort to persuade them to get all 1,027,000,000 Chinese (1980 estimate) to jump off chairs. I have pleaded with them that this will significantly advance the cause of science. However, they have not been cooperative. They point out that China is a poor country, and lacks a sufficient quantity of chairs. Moreover, many of the chairs that *are* available are of nonuniform height, meaning that even if all the Chinese jumped off at the same time, they would hit the ground at different times, thus throwing off the results. Finally, they point out that discipline among the Chinese people has become notoriously lax since the Cultural Revolution, and many of the participants in the project could be expected to be fooling around when they were supposed to be jumping. The Chinese government suggests that instead of having the entire nation jump off chairs, I should get one representative citizen to jump and multiply the results by 1,027,000,000. I have, needless to say, rejected this solution as grotesquely inadequate.

The possibility of an actual test thus being remote, I have been forced to rely on my considerable powers of inductive logic, to wit: given the principle that every action has an equal and opposite reaction, when the Chinese got up on their chairs, they would essentially be *pushing the earth down* in the process of elevating themselves. Then, when they jumped off, the earth would *simultaneously spring back*, attracted by the gravitational mass of one billion airborne Chinamen, with the result that the Chinese and the earth would meet somewhere in the middle, if you follow me. The upshot of this is that action and reaction would cancel each other out and the earth would remain securely in orbit.

Just for fun, however—after you've been doing this job for a while you get a pretty bizarre notion of what constitutes a good time—suppose 1,000,000,000 Chinese, give or take 27,000,000, were somehow to materialize atop chairs without their having to elevate themselves thereto. And suppose they jumped off. Having performed astonishing feats of mathematical acrobatics (requiring

156

the entire afternoon, I might note—sometimes I can't believe the crap I spend my time on), I calculate that the resultant thud in aggregate would be the equivalent of 500 tons of TNT. Not bad, but nowhere near enough to dislocate the earth, which weighs 6 sextillion, 588 quintillion tons. I refuse to even discuss what would happen if all the Chinese yelled at the top of their lungs.

Cecil, can you predict when California will fall into the sea?— Mary Ann With the Shaky Hands, Los Angeles

Yes, but I don't want to be held responsible for causing a panic, so I'll just tell you what the geologists say.

It all depends on what you mean by "fall into the sea." If you mean "when will California break off the continent and sink to the ocean floor," the answer is "never." The sea, you see, is only about two miles deep. California is about twenty miles thick.

Perhaps you mean "when will there be a major earthquake?" (An earthquake centered at the San Andreas Fault could involve a lot of vertical slip, which could conceivably put some California coastline underwater.) In that case the answer is "any day now, maybe." Some geologists believe that the strain built up around the San Andreas Fault is already reaching the level that caused the great San Francisco earthquake of 1906. Others say the big day could be 100 years away. This is the sort of razor-edge precision you come to expect from rock jockeys.

If you simply mean "when will California slide away to oblivion?" the answer is about 50 million years. The Pacific "plate," which carries the western sliver of California, is sliding past North America at the dizzy rate of about two inches per year. Someday, Los Angeles will slide under the earth's crust near the Aleutian Islands, but this is no time to worry about it—I'll let you know when it's time to start packing.

A man of average height stands on an open plain and looks out to the very edge of the horizon. How far away is that horizon when (part I) he is standing on the earth, and (part II) when he is standing on the moon? (For the earth you may assume he's at sea level; for the moon, that his feet are at the mean distance of the surface of the moon from the center thereof.) You might want to give the result in both miles and kilometers (that is, if you don't cop out by consulting some kind of survey) just in case the country converts to the metric system in the time it takes you to figure this one out.—H.C.E., Phoenix

This one was so tough that I took the liberty of assuming

that the eyes of our "average man" stand exactly 5 feet above the ground. In that case, his distance from the horizon is about 2.3 statute miles (3.68 kilometers) on earth, and 1.4 miles (2.24 kilometers) on the moon.

We were discussing weather the other day—specifically, crappy weather, and what causes it. I seem to recall reading somewhere that big cities were a major cause of climatic wretchedness, due to pollution and the like—and I don't mean just smog, I mean clouds and rain and stuff like that. Is this true? Is there any scientific proof?—Sandy N., Baltimore

Big cities do have a major impact on the weather, although the effect isn't uniformly dismal. For one thing, big cities tend to be warmer, which is obviously useful in the winter. But they also seed the skies with a lot more dust, which gives rise to a lot more rain. One of the most striking scientific demonstrations of this was a study of the so-called "La Porte weather anomaly" conducted by Stanley Changnon, an atmospheric scientist. La Porte is a town in northwest Indiana just east of Chicago that has notoriously bad weather—this in a region that is not exactly known for its balmy clime to begin with. Changnon's study surveyed weather conditions in La Porte from 1901-65 and showed a dramatic increase in unpleasant weather conditions starting around 1925, roughly corresponding with the growth in productivity of the Chicago-Gary iron and steel industry. In 1920, for example, La Porte had about 175 inches of precipitation; in 1945, that figure had increased to about 290 inches, and fell to 245 inches in 1960. There was no correspondingly dramatic increase in rainfall for other areas near La Porte—statistically, at least, the "anomaly" appears to be fact. Other weather conditions that have been similarly affected are hail and thunderstorms.

The industrial activities on the south side of Chicago spill a lot of heat, water vapor, and various kinds of dust into the air. The heat can cause rising and expansion of air, thus cloud formation and precipitation. Dust provides nuclei for the condensation of water vapor. (Water vapor needs a surface to condense on—in the air, these surfaces are provided by particles called cloud nuclei, and an increase in them can stimulate rainfall. This is the basis for the practice of cloud seeding.) The influence of Lake Michigan on the general atmospheric circulation of the area seems to play some part in limiting the effect to La Porte.

Is there really such a thing as quicksand or is it just a make-believe sand trap found in Tarzan movies? If it does exist, where is it usually found, can it actually pull you down and under, and how can a person escape from it?—Barbara R., Normal, Illinois

It's real, all right. "Quicksand" is the name given to a mass of sand particles that are supported by circulating water rather than by each other. It can be found wherever sand and water can be found—especially near streams, beaches, and the mouths of rivers. Quicksand *cannot* suck you down and under—its density is greater than the density of most things, including human bodies; in other words, you can float in it. If you struggle, you'll only succeed in digging yourself deeper in.

If one of your fun excursions around Normal is interrupted by quicksand, keep yourself still until you stop sinking (you will). Use slow swimming motions to get yourself into a horizontal position and then roll yourself to terra firma.

The other day I got into an argument with a friend who's a Christian and he claimed it can be proved the moon is only 12,000 years old (thus bolstering creationist claims about evolution) by the amount of meteoric dust on its surface. He said that some scientists have calculated that if the moon were really billions of years old it would have five feet of dust surrounding its surface features. However, when Neil Armstrong stepped on the moon in 1969, there was only one inch of dust! What's the scoop?—George W., Baltimore

There's a lot more than one inch of dust on the moon; Armstrong only *sank in* one inch, which is a different matter entirely. After all, you only sink into loose beach sand about an inch, although it's certainly a lot deeper. The surface of the moon is composed primarily of debris called "regolith," which is from 35 to 60 feet deep and consists of boulders of varying size intermixed with dust. Most of the material is made up of lunar rock shattered by meteorites; the remaining 1-2½ percent is the pulverized remnants of the meteorites themselves. Much of the dust is in the form of tiny glass spheres created in the heat of the meteorite impact. Dating of lunar samples has established the age of the moon at about 4.6 billion years. None of this will make the slightest difference to your friend, of course. Creationists have a powerful affection for the ridiculous.

Several years ago there was a story going around that all the planets were going to line up on a certain date and the combined gravitational effect was going to wreak havoc on the earth, and for all I know send us crashing into the sun. As far as I know none of this ever happened, although, come to think of it, I was inexplicably depressed in 1981. What's the story on this?—Mary S., Baltimore

I believe you're referring to the "Jupiter Effect," a scenario put forth, in a book of the same name, by a couple jokers named J.R. Gribbin and S.H. Plagemann. Their treatise, first published back in 1974, predicted that a "superconjunction" of planets due on March 10, 1982, would exert extraordinary tidal forces on the sun and ultimately trigger massive earthquakes here on Mother Earth. The theory, which involves sunspots, climatic change, and all sorts of other unsupportable hokum, was roundly debunked in various quarters, most notably by Belgian astronomer Jean Meeus, who pointed out that during the alleged "superconjunction," the planets would actually be spread out over a sun-centered arc of some 95 degrees. If, for the sake of convenience, we ignore the effect of Pluto (an eminently ignorable planet, it has always seemed to me), we see that the planets have occupied far smaller sections of sky before—for example, 83 degrees in 1817, and 46 degrees in 1307—without apparent ill effect. Mr. Gribbin, for his part, was moved to state publicly that maybe he made a little mistake, an admission that seems to have been amply borne out by reality.

What is sea level? Where is "zero feet sea level"? Who decided that a particular place was to be considered zero, instead of some other place, such as Lake Titicaca? And what time of day can "zero" be read at the designated place (you know, what with tides and all)? How can zero be plotted around the globe, to, say, the Rocky Mountains, where there are no zero locations, with any accuracy? And what difference does it make, anyway?—Bob B., Dallas

There isn't any particular place at which sea level (mean sea level, to be more accurate about it) is measured; it's a purely metaphysical concept. It's based on the assumption that because all the oceans are interconnected and water tends to find its own level, the ocean surface around the world forms an ellipsoid (or flattened sphere, which is what shape the earth is) of more or less uniform geometry, once you average out the tides and seasonal variations over a long period, typically 19 years. That makes sea level a useful reference point in calculating elevation, which makes a big difference in climate. In fact there are some permanent differentials in ocean level amounting to about a meter or so due to currents and whatnot, but we may conveniently ignore them.

Because the ocean surface forms a floor for the atmosphere

and because atmospheric pressure decreases predictably with height, you can use a barometer to establish the elevation of any inland landmark, once you've corrected for local climatic variations.

My sources tell me that water, when it spirals out of a drain, flows in one direction only in the Northern Hemisphere and in the opposite direction in the Southern Hemisphere. Is this so? Why? Is the spiral especially pronounced at the poles? Subdued at the equator? If I carried a drain across the equator would the spiral reverse directions? How do drains work in outer space? I know this probably seems like a lot of questions, but I have an unquenchable thirst for learning.—Victor C., Chicago

Well, son, you've come to the right place. The erroneous bit of folk wisdom you refer to says that water always drains in a clockwise direction in the Southern Hemisphere, and in a counterclockwise direction in the Northern Hemisphere. The supposed reason for this "fact" is the Coriolis effect, which has to do with the effect of the earth's rotation on moving objects.

Now, there *is* such a thing as the Coriolis effect; it explains why macroevents such as hurricanes rotate in a clockwise direction in the Southern Hemisphere and counterclockwise in the Northern Hemisphere. However, when you get down to itty-bitty phenomena such as the water draining out of your bathtub, the Coriolis effect is insignificant, amounting to roughly three ten-millionths of the force of gravity (in Boston, at least, which is where they happened to do the measuring). The boring truth is that water drains every which way no matter what hemisphere you're in, for reasons which have to do mostly with the shape of the drain, the way you poured in the water in the first place, and so on.

All this was demonstrated way back in 1962 by one Ascher Shapiro, a researcher at the Massachusetts Institute of Technology. Shapiro filled a circular tank six feet in diameter and six inches high in such a way that the water swirled in a clockwise direction. (Remember, now, that Coriolis forces in the Northern Hemisphere act in a *counter*clockwise direction.) Shapiro then covered the tank with a plastic sheet, kept the temperature constant, and sat down to read comic books for a spell. When he pulled the plug after an hour or two, the water went down the drain clockwise, presumably because it still retained some clockwise motion from filling. On the other hand, if Shapiro pulled the plug after waiting a full 24 hours, the draining water spiraled counterclockwise, indicating that the motion from filling had subsided enough for the Coriolis effect to take over. When the plug was pulled after four to five hours, the water started draining clockwise, then gradually slowed down and finally started swirling in the opposite direction. Needless to say, unless you are a consummate slob, you do not wait 24 hours (or even 4-5 hours) to drain your bathtub. Hence the influence of the Coriolis effect may be safely described as slight. But I'm sure the myth of the bathtub spirals will endure. Most people prefer entertaining nonsense to unexciting reality.

Here's a poser ... what device or instrument does the Weather Service (it used to be "bureau" but they changed it for show business reasons) use to measure the exact depth of a snowfall? A cup and rule? A graduated window ledge? A demarcated fireplug?—E.W., Baltimore

Snowfall is measured with a hand-held linear device that provides a visual readout comparing the depth of snow to a universally understood unit of measure. This device is called a ruler. What the meteorologist does is, he takes his ruler out to a pile of snow and sticks it in. Generally the snow is piled on what is called a "snow board" (ain't science complex?), which is wiped clean after every measurement. In high wind conditions the meteorologist may decide to abandon his snow board and stick his ruler instead into many piles of snow at various spots on what is known as "the ground" to get a reliable figure. If things are really bad he may also opt to stay inside and calculate the snowfall from a graph hooked up to his precipitation gauge, which melts the snow (with anti-freeze), weighs it, and reads out in inches of water. The density of snow varies, but in general an inch of water is equal to about 10 inches of snow. In the Southern Hemisphere, 10 inches of snow are equal to about an inch of water.

Can you tell me the best time of the year to see the aurora borealis? Also, can I see it from, say, northern Wisconsin, or do I have to go to northwest Canada or Alaska?—Peter T., Chicago

The auroras are the result of collisions between atoms in the thin upper atmosphere and fast-moving protons and electrons that come from—or are energized by—the sun. They are generally not visible at latitudes below 60 degrees, although intense solar flare activity can and does make them visible at lower latitudes on occasion. (Chicago, by way of reference point, is about 42 degrees north.) There's no way to predict these solar flare-ups, and they follow no seasonal routine; however, when they are intense enough to cause auroral activity around your area, your friendly TV weatherman will usually say so.

Your chance of seeing the aurora borealis increases as you move north, but until you get up into Alaska and Greenland you get no guarantees. Wherever you are, you have a much better chance of seeing something if you're way out in the wilderness somewhere where it's very dark. You can expect more auroral activity as the sun reaches the peak of its 11-year sunspot cycle. Unfortunately, that won't happen again until 1990 or so. Until around 1986, if I read my astronomical manual correctly, we'll be sliding down to a sunspot minimum, so it looks like you'll have to head to Canada.

Sitting here on the sun deck, we've been involved in a heated debate for the past several weeks. It seems these midwesterners and New Yorkers have some distorted perceptions about the capacities of the sun's rays. Those of us from the south and southeast, having far more experience and innate wisdom, know better. You see, they insist that absolutely no ultraviolet rays can pass through the plain clear glass of a car window. I have apparently hallucinated the tan or burn I've noticed after driving across the desert. And, according to them, sun lamps either don't give off ultraviolet rays or the bulb is not glass. Please enlighten my poor misguided friends. In return, I'll be happy to share with you the lunch I win from this wager—Alice, Los Angeles

Good thing I'm on a diet this week, Alice, because you lose. For what it's worth, those other bozos don't know what they're talking about, either. To summarize briefly: *some* ultraviolet rays can pass through car window glass, although most of the burning (as opposed to tanning) rays can't. On the other hand, most sunlamps *aren't* made of ordinary glass—they're made of quartz or special UV-transparent glass.

Having thus confronted our ignorance, let us humbly endeavor to learn. Ultraviolet light, which causes both erythema (sunburn) and tanning, ranges in wavelength from 4,000 angstrom units (A) down to about 100 A. (Light with wavelength greater then 4,000 A lies in the visible spectrum.) The most potent rays for burning and tanning lie in the 2,900-3,050-A range, with radiation of 2,967 A supposedly being most effective of all. Ordinary window glass, however, is pretty much opaque to wavelengths below 3,000 A. From this we deduce that the intervention of a window will significantly reduce but not halt the burning/tanning process. In addition, UV rays above 3,200 A will cause tanning (but usually not burning) if administered in sufficiently massive doses, such as you get when you're driving across the desert. Your tan, therefore, was no hallucination. This business about your innate wisdom I'm not so sure about.

Every winter my mind drifts to thoughts of the balmy shores of Rio. But do we really need to go so far for relief? My friend says that at the top of tall buildings it's a lot warmer. Is this true?

When it's blizzarding down below can I go up to the top of the Sears Tower in Chicago or the World Trade Center in New York with a bottle of Coppertone and a beach towel?—Connie V., Chicago

If you would take the time to think for about two seconds, Connie, you would realize that the temperature generally decreases with height, rather than the other way around. This is why we see snow-covered peaks in the Rockies in the summertime (or at least until late in the spring). As a general rule the temperature drops about 3½ degrees Fahrenheit for every 1,000 feet of elevation, which means that at the top of 1,454-foot-tall Sears Tower it's about five degrees cooler than it is at ground level, barring unforeseen meteorological aberrations. There are several reasons for this phenomenon. For one thing, the lower portion of the atmosphere (the troposphere) is mostly warmed by heat radiating from the earth, so that up to a point the farther you get away from the earth the cooler you get. There is also the matter of "adiabatic cooling," but Yahweh Himself could not render this concept intelligible, so there is precious little reason to think that I can. Just take my word for it.

You may recall that Alice wondered about how deep the tube was while she was falling down the rabbit hole into Wonderland. If such a frictionless tube actually did exist, and went from the North Pole to the South Pole, and you or I accidentally stumbled into one of its open ends, exactly what would happen to us?—Larry W., Baltimore

Whenever this job starts to get boring, I know I can count on one of you screwballs out there in Baltimore to come up with something. You guys are a national asset.

What we are dealing with here is essentially a cosmic pendulum. But let me explain a few basic concepts first. For one thing, we are going to disregard the problem of the earth's molten interior. We do not want to contaminate this discussion with the facts if we can avoid it.

Next, you must force yourself to accept the following notion: if you were somehow teleported to a cave in the center of the earth, you would find that you were weightless. This is because you would have approximately equal amounts of mass on all sides of you, which would cancel each other out.

Now then. If you jumped into a frictionless (and consequently airless) interpolar tube, you'd fall, obviously, picking up momentum as you went. As you approached the center of the earth

165

the pull of gravity would decline and eventually (at the center) cease, but inertia would keep you going. Once past center, though, the pull of the earth's mass *behind* you would begin to slow you down, at exactly the opposite rate that you'd accelerated. You'd come to a complete stop just at the brink of the Antarctic end of the tube, where you'd have an opportunity to wave gaily to the bunny rabbits or whatever they have out there before beginning to fall back in the opposite direction. This process would continue forever.

Once we start figuring for the effects of atmospheric friction, of course, the situation changes. After a certain point in the course of falling you'd reach a top speed called "terminal velocity," where air resistance would counteract the accelerating effects of gravity. With less momentum, you'd only fall a relatively short distance past the center of the earth before you stopped and started heading in the other direction. Eventually you'd reach equilibrium at the earth's center. I was going to calculate how long this would take, but I have numbers all over the pad here and still can't make anything out of it, so forget it. Anyway, watch where you're going.

Why do Europe and Asia count as separate continents, when any fool with a map can see they're parts of the same landmass? I expect the answer has something to do with the historical fact that ancient people in, say, China and France would have no way of knowing they were on the same continent, but surely this excuse should not stand today. After all, people on the opposite ends of any of the other three continents would have said the same thing, but we don't let them get away with it.—Terry McC., Dallas

Not to be picky, Terry, but there are *five* other continents, not three. You're right about Europe and Asia being parts of one continent, though. What we have here is a carryover from the ancient Greeks, who used the terms Asia, Europe, and Africa to designate *regions*, rather than continents. (The term continent, in the sense of "a major landmass mostly surrounded by water," originated in 17th-century England.) Nowadays, persons in the know refer to Europe as "the western peninsular appendage of the Eurasian landmass," which has the added advantage of sounding like a description of Yul Brynner's wazoo. I trust you will find this helpful.

I remember hearing somewhere about being able to tell from the static on your television set whether a tornado is coming. Is this true, Cecil? If so, how and why?—Auntie Em, Kansas

Tornados create an electrical disturbance somewhere in the 55 megahertz range, close to the frequency band assigned to channel 2. With this phenomenon in mind, Newton Weller, an electronics technician, has devised the following method for using your TV set as a tornado warning device: tune to channel 13 and turn the brightness control down to the point where the image is nearly—not completely—black. Then turn to channel 2. Lightning will register as horizontal streaks on the screen. When the picture becomes bright enough to be seen, or when the screen glows with an even light, there's a tornado within 20 miles, and it's time to find that twit Dorothy and head for the basement.

A guy in a bar tried to bet me that Illinois doesn't really lie east of the Mississippi. This sounded like an obvious trick to me so I didn't bet him. But my curiosity is aroused, Cecil. What's the gag?—Robert P., Chicago

You are clearly a very prudent young man, Robert. I predict a bright future for you in investment counseling.

Not *all* of Illinois lies east of the Mississippi. Kaskaskia township, an area of about 27 square miles in downstate Illinois, slops over onto the west bank of the river. During a flood in April 1881, the Mississippi—which serves, for most purposes, as the state's legal western border—lost its self-control and cut over into the small Kaskaskia River, forming a new channel about four miles east of its old course. The people of Kaskaskia, alarmed at finding themselves in Missouri, insisted that the border between the states adhere to the old outlines of the river.

Would you give me the straight dope on the rumor I once heard that the northern and southern horizons are not equidistant from the observer? And also that they are not equidistant to the eastern and western horizons? (This assumes that the observer is standing on a perfectly flat surface.)—T.C., Washington, D.C.

I don't know that this is exactly what I would consider to be a "rumor," L., but let's ignore your terminological idiosyncrasies and get right down to the heart of the matter. In the Northern Hemisphere (except near the North Pole) the northern horizon is slightly farther away from you than the southern horizon, owing to the fact that the earth is not perfectly spherical, but ellipsoidal, i.e., fatter around the equator than it is around a meridian (a circumference that includes both poles). You may want to get an egg out of the refrigerator and think about this; otherwise just trust me. The eastern and western horizons are equidistant from an

167

observer, but they are closer than the northern horizon and farther away than the southern horizon. (Got that?) Having performed the usual round of superhuman calculations, I am prepared to state for the record that for a person five feet tall standing on a raft in calm waters at 45 degrees latitude in the Northern Hemisphere, the distance to the northern horizon exceeds that to the southern horizon by a total of . . . four inches. Large charge. Still, it is with just such minutiae that we impress the babes at the boathouse.

Cecil, my world view has been severely altered, and I need your help. While on a recent trip to the wilds of Arizona, I had the opportunity to witness—and indeed, participate in—a demonstration of "wishing," which is the location of underground water through a divining rod, or "wish stick." I had always thought this practice was an old wives' tale, but the natives use it routinely to determine where to dig their wells. If a stick of wood is used, it bends toward the ground; if a coat-hanger wire or thin brass rods are used, one is held in each hand, and they cross over each other when water is found. The only explanation the local experts could provide is that moving water creates a magnetic field, but this doesn't account for its effect on wood. I swear on a stack of Straight Dopes that I speak not with forked tongue. Illuminate me, Cecil.—Cooper B., Chicago

Listen, Slick, if you let a bunch of rustics from Arizona fool you with an old dodge like dowsing for water, you need more help than I can give you. You don't describe what your "participation" consisted of, but let me guess: you watched some old geek with a divining rod (typically a forked stick held in a peculiar grip with both hands, but sometimes just an ordinary single stick) wander around the desert for a while with an expression of concentration on his face. By and by the stick began to quiver, and suddenly plunged sharply downward, whereupon he exclaimed something to the effect of, "Dig here, you'll find water." Then he said, "You try it, sonny, it'll work for you, too." And gosharoonie, he gave you the stick and showed you how to hold it and lo and behold, when you got to the spot where the stick had plunged down for the old coot, it did the same thing for you—just like some mysto force had grabbed onto it. Naturally, since water in Arizona is typically found 175 to 200 feet below the surface, you didn't actually dig a well to test the accuracy of the rod, but assumed that *since it worked for you*, it must be legit.

Congratulations, sucker. You've fallen victim to the classic Skeptical Young Guppy Becomes a True Believer syndrome, described in great detail in a study of dowsing (as wishing is sometimes called) published by two University of Chicago researchers in 1959. "Wishing," incidentally, is a corruption of "witching," as in "water witching," the most common American expression for dowsing, AKA rhabdomancy and divination. Although divining has been around in various forms for millennia, the well-known forked stick method appears to have been devised in the mining districts of Germany (you can supposedly find minerals with a dowsing rod, too) in the late 15th or early 16th century. It was first formally described in an essay in 1556, and since then has been spread around the world by European colonists. In the past 400 years, more than a thousand essays, books, and pamphlets have been published on the subject.

Needless to say, dowsing is entirely a fraud, although often an unconscious one. Innumerable experiments, beginning in 1641—that's right, 1641—have demonstrated that (a) the presence of water has no discernible effect on a rod held above it, whether the rod is made of wood, metal, or anything else; (b) the success rate for diviners is about the same as that for people who use the hit-and-miss method when looking for water, and (c) geologists trained to recognize telltale surface clues (certain kinds of rocks and plants, various topographical features) will invariably far outdo dowsers in predicting where water will be found, and at what depth.

Nevertheless, belief in dowsing has persisted, partly because most people secretly want to believe in magic, partly because water is fairly easy to find in most parts of the inhabitable world, and partly because the plunging-stick phenomenon seems so convincing to untutored observers. It is worth noting that in many parts of the eastern U.S. it is virtually impossible to dig a hole and *not* find water. You don't mention where you went witching in Arizona, but I lived in Tucson for a spell and they had gotten well-digging down to such a science that the success rate approached 100 percent. Even over complex hydrological formations, the success rate by the hit-and-miss method is often as high as 75 percent.

The plunging-stick phenomenon is caused by a well-documented psychological effect known as "ideomotor action," first described in the 1800s and clinically demonstrated in the 1930s. What happens is that conscious thought gives rise to involuntary, usually imperceptible muscle movements. If I strapped you to a table in a lab and loaded you up with sensors and told you to just think about raising your arm—but not to actually do so—the sensors would probably detect some slight upward motion in that arm, which you'd be completely unconscious of. Ouija boards and several other seance-type tricks make use of this principle.

In forked-stick dowsing, the two ends of the stick are held in a rather uncomfortable grip in such a way that the stick is under considerable tension—coiled up like a spring, as it were. Any of four minor muscle movements will result in the stick taking a sudden lurch downward (you can try this in the backyard some-time). An experienced dowser, who has often picked up a fair bit of practical geological knowledge, particularly if he has worked in the same geographical area for many years, often develops a good instinct for judging where water might be just by looking at the terrain. When he walks around doing his number with the stick his mind unconsciously transmits this knowledge to his arm mus-cles, with predictable results. You, the young sap, don't know anything about geology, but you do know where the stick pointed the first time, and unconsciously you want to duplicate that feat. If either you or the dowser is blindfolded, though, you won't even get close to the spot twice. Besides forked sticks you can use barbed wire, a fork and spoon, coat hangers, welding rods, even a bunch of keys hanging by a chain from a Bible. If you want more information on this ridiculous art, most libraries have lots of books on the subject—right next to the section on tarot cards.

For a long time I have been debating this point with friends: I say there is no such thing as heat lightning. I say it is just lightning occurring far off in the sky, and all we see is the glow from the bolt. Who's right?—Ed. E., Chicago

You are, as long as you're not getting your heat lighting mixed up with your sheet lightning. "Heat lightning," the sudden reddish glow you sometimes see on warm summer nights, looks the way it does (and sounds the way it does, i.e., silent) because of its distance from you, the observer. At its source, it looks like regular old blue-white lightning; what makes it appear reddish from a distance is the atmosphere's propensity for scattering light on the blue end of the spectrum, the same phenomenon that pro-duces red sunsets. Much more common than heat lightning, how-ever, is "sheet lightning," which is produced by a discharge within a cloud rather than one from cloud to ground. Here the electrical channel is obscured by a cloud, and all you see is a huge "sheet" of illuminated cotton, or whatever it is they're making clouds out of these days.

In making plans for a trip to Ireland this spring, I checked into weather conditions there to know what kind of clothes to pack.

Imagine my surprise to find that summer starts there on May 1! How is this possible? I always thought the seasons were regulated by when the sun crosses the equator and the longest and shortest days of the year. Is this just an American interpretation? What about other European countries, especially Great Britain? I am enclosing a copy of the page from the tourist information booklet provided by the Irish Tourist Board, just so you won't think I'm making this up in my overly optimistic hopes for a sunny vacation.—Mary Z., Oak Park, Illinois

There is a widespread misconception in this country—which extends, I might note, to the makers of most calendars, dictionaries, and encyclopedias—that summer "officially" starts on the day of the summer solstice, June 21 or 22, which is the longest day of the year. Americans also believe (1) that there is some valid scientific reason for doing it that way, and (2) that everybody in the Northern Hemisphere does it that way, and always has.

None of these things is true. So far as I have been able to discover, no scientific or governmental body has ever formally declared that summer starts on the solstice. Certainly there is no good scientific reason for doing so. In the Northern Hemisphere the period of maximum daylight falls roughly between May 7 and August 7—in other words, the six weeks before and after the solstice. The period of maximum temperature, on the other hand, is June 4 through September 3. (The period of max temperature in the mid-latitudes always lags about 25 to 30 days behind the period of max daylight, due to the fact that the earth heats up and cools off relatively slowly.) "It isn't really clear how the astronomical definition [i.e., summer starts on the solstice] got started," says Kevin Trenberth, a climate researcher at the University of Illinois in Urbana. "Although the sun-earth geometry is clearly the origin of the seasons on earth, it has nothing directly to do with temperature or weather." He notes that meteorologists define summer simply as June, July, and August. "For practical purposes, the meteorological definition is the best one, being very close to the [weather] statistics," he says.

In fact, it appears that June 1 was accepted as the beginning of summer in the United States until relatively recently. According to many older reference books, ranging from *The American Cyclopedia* (1883) to *Webster's Third New International Dictionary* (1966), a summer in the U.S. comprises the months of June, July, and August. Seasons in Britain, for no particularly good reason, start a month earlier. The *Oxford English Dictionary*, somewhat confusingly, says that spring in Britain (and evidently in Ireland) runs from February through April, but that summer runs from mid-

171

May to mid-August. This leaves the first two weeks in May mysteriously unaccounted for, by my reckoning, but that is England for you. The Irish appear to have opted for May 1 as the starting date of their summer, but it was not always thus. I have here an old Irish guidebook (1938) that says summer begins the day after the third Saturday in April (Sunday, presumably) and ends the day after the first Saturday in October. The present system may strike Americans as odd, but compared to what went before it must certainly be regarded as improvement.

I should emphasize that just because our Irish friends start their summer earlier does not mean Ireland gets *warmer* earlier. The cruel truth is that it *never* gets warm in Ireland, which has one of the most dismal climates on earth. A July day in which the temperature reaches 72 is considered a scorcher. For the most part, the weather is damp and cloudy (although May and June are fairly sunny), with frequent rain—an average of 180 days a year in the southeast, and over 250 days a year in the west. The humidity averages around 85 percent and seldom drops below 75 percent. On the plus side, it never gets that cold—the annual mean temperature variation in Dublin is only 18 degrees Fahrenheit. And the weather is extremely variable, which means the sun breaks out pretty frequently. Usually, however, the only effect of this is to convince you that better days are coming, which, for the most part, they ain't. Enjoy your trip, sweetums.

There's an old cliche about things that happen "once in a blue moon." Has there ever been a blue moon, or is this just a variation on hell freezing over? If blue moons have happened before, when will the next one be?—Alma N. Phoenix

A blue moon is an optical illusion produced by a cloud of sulfur particles floating in the upper atmosphere. The moons looks bluish when it's seen from the right angle through the chemical haze. It takes a good-sized conflagration to shoot enough sulfur into the air, though—usually, nothing this side of a volcanic eruption or a major forest fire will do it. Happily for us, natural disasters on that scale are few and far between. Hence the saying. The most recent blue moon that I know of appeared on September 26, 1950, when a forest fire in northern British Columbia sent up enough sulfur to make the moon seem bluish when seen from England. The very next day, Andy Rooney wrote a good column.

172

Chapter 10

I, Consumer

Being typical college students, my friends and I were sitting in my room this Friday discussing our favorite childhood toothpaste brands. One of us recalled Stripe toothpaste, which was characterized by its incredibly straight red lines. We started joking about cans of polka dot paint and the like when it suddenly occurred to us that we had no idea how the lines came out so straight. Cecil, could you tell us how this seemingly impossible feat was accomplished?—Tom G., Evanston, Illinois

There is little, it seems, that the mind of man can't accomplish once it sets itself to a task. Striped toothpaste is only a beginning.

The stripes were created by a special device that was fitted to the nozzle end of the tube: a tube within the tube, if you will,

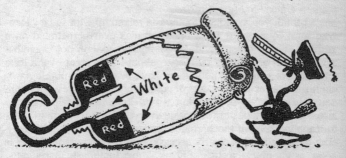

about one inch in length and perforated with a ring of small holes around the top. Toothpaste tubes are normally filled from the flat

173

end, which is then folded over and sealed. In the case of Stripe, a red toothpaste was first filled around the special fitting; the white toothpaste, filled second, held the red toothpaste in place at the top of the tube. When the tube was squeezed, the white toothpaste would run through the special inner tube, while the pressure of the squeeze simultaneously forced the red toothpaste through the tiny orifices at the end. With the flow of red matched to the flow of white, the toothpaste emerged from the nozzle perfectly striped.

For years those sugarless gum commercials have said, "Sugarless gum is recommended by four out of five dentists for their patients who chew gum." What does that fifth dentist recommend? Gum with sugar?—Elizabeth E., Towson, Maryland

As it turns out, the fifth dentist usually recommended no gum at all, but this is not advice that a chewing-gum company is anxious to convey to its prospective customers. The Warner-Lambert Company, makers of Trident sugarless gum, commissioned a market research firm to undertake the study under discussion in July 1976. By some arcane means the survey people came up with a list of 1,200 dentists who were supposed to represent a cross-section of their profession. These were then asked what they recommended to their gun-chewing patients, the choices being sugared gum, sugarless gum, or no gum at all. Sugarless gum won with 85 percent. Nobody seems to remember exactly how many votes sugared gum got, but there's bound to have been a couple— even dentists have a sense of humor.

I understand some brands of toothpaste contain sugar. Would you be a consumer advocate and list those that do so I can avoid them?—Cheryl S., Los Angeles

I think you've gotten toothpaste mixed up with sugary Dentyne gum, one of the most brazen frauds ever perpetrated on a gullible public. Most brands of toothpaste contain not sugar but a very small amount of saccharin, about 0.2 percent of the total volume. As you may know, there have been reports linking saccharin to cancer in laboratory rats, but industry spokesmen claim that a healthy 150-pound adult would have to eat 606 standard size 5.5 ounce tubes of toothpaste every day for 50 years in order to reach the level of saccharin that caused the rat tumors. A sweetener of some kind is clearly necessary; unsweetened toothpaste is about as yummy as a stick of chalk. Other toothpaste ingredients, while we're on the subject, include natural flavoring such as spearmint or peppermint, beefed up by emulsifiers, preservatives, and artificial flavors. These also are thought to be harmless, but you never know. Personally I am oblivious to considerations of personal safety, but if you would rather not risk it you might want to get yourself a box of baking soda and brush with that. For flavor you can throw in a little cinnamon. Sounds pretty weird, I know, but hey, it's organic.

It never occurred to me until one of Levi's competitors started running ads for "plain pocket" jeans, but that stitching on the back pockets of Levis is certainly very distinctive. So distinctive, in fact, that it looks downright frivolous. Whatever motivated the manufacturers of the world's most purely functional clothing to indulge in this flight of fancy? As near as I can tell, the extra stitches play no practical role at all. Are they symbolic, perhaps? Or did some high-minded artistic type manage to insinuate himself among the stern pragmatists on the Levis Strauss staff at a crucial moment in jeans history?—Albert D., Evanston, Illinois

The pocket stitches were the brainchild of the man who virtually invented the Levi's jean, a Russian immigrant by the name of Jacob Davis. Working as a tailor in Reno, Nevada, Davis hit upon the crucial concept of the riveted seam—a dramatic advance in work clothes technology that doubled the durability of the product. In 1870, Davis approached the wholesale company that sold him his denim, offering to sell the west coast rights to his riveted jeans in exchange for the cost of securing a patent—a matter, in those days, of $68. The wholesaler was Levi Strauss, and the rest is history. Davis joined the company in 1873, presiding over the final design of the product. His two primary contributions were the orange thread used in all stitching (to match the copper rivets) and the inimitable curved stitches (known as "arcuate" in the trade) on the back pockets. Originally, the pocket flourishes had a practical function: early Levis featured cotton-lined back pockets, and the stitches were intended to keep the lining from buckling. Although the lining was soon dropped, the stitches lived on, so distinctive a part of the Levis look that the company was able to register them as a trademark in 1942. Their survival was threatened only once, during the material shortage of World War II. As their contribution to the national emergency, Levi Strauss decided to stop wasting valuable thread on idle aesthetics. For the duration, the design was not sewn, but carefully painted on every pair of Levi's jeans.

Since I gave up smoking cigarettes three years ago, cigars, joints, and women have been surrogates for my oral fixation. However, I find the substitute that spends the most time in my mouth is toothpicks. This intimacy has stirred my curiosity as to their origin. It's hard to imagine a crew of minimum-wage craftsmen whittling perfect little javelins from tree branches, so I assume they have some sort of processed wood product that they press into forms. But how do they maintain the grain? I rest my dilemma in your hands, Cecil—and while you're at it, find out what family of tree it is that regularly lies twixt cheek and gum.—Todd F., Dallas

I don't know that I would go around resting my dilemma in other people's hands if I were you, Todd; you could get arrested. Try to control yourself in the future. Toothpick makers manage to get wood grain into their toothpicks by the simple expedient of not taking it out in the first place. Remarkable as it may seem in this synthetic age, the modern toothpick is made out of unreconstituted virgin white birch, just as its predecessors have been since after the Civil War, when one Charles Forster invented the automatic toothpick-making machine.

Toothpick manufacturers (most of them are in Maine) steam birch logs to make them easier to cut, then "veneer" them, which means they peel each log into a thin sheet, sort of like unrolling a roll of paper towels. Flat toothpicks are simply stamped out of the sheets, while round toothpicks are first cut into oversized blanks, then fed into a milling machine called a "rounder," which grinds them down to little javelins, as you so poetically put it. No reconstituted toothpick has ever been made that matches birch for strength and low cost. You see plastic toothpicks occasionally, but they are hard on the gums and periodontists discourage their use— as do the makers of wooden toothpicks, not surprisingly.

Scott tissue, in its advertisements, used to claim that each roll of its paper was 1,000 sheets, 500 sheets longer than any other brand. Yet it claimed that the additional 500 sheets made it last 28 percent longer. How did the Scott people arrive at the 28 percent figure? If there are 100 percent more sheets in one of its rolls, shouldn't it last 100 percent longer, not 28 percent?—Anonymous, Phoenix

You'd think so, all right. However, we are dealing here not with the crisp elegance of mathematics, but the fetid swamp of human nature. We ought to point out, first of all, that in a Scott roll you're getting 1,000 one-ply sheets, while in some brands you get 500 two-ply sheets. The total volume of paper

176

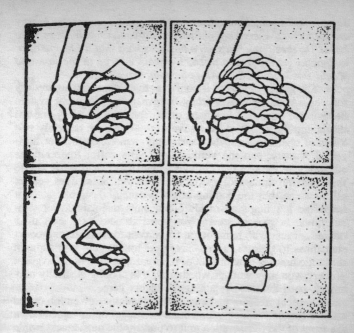

involved is not vastly different. What does vary is how people use the stuff. The penetrating eye of science has found that there are all kinds of toilet-paper techniques in this world. There are wadders; there are folders; there are people who would probably go to jail if it was known what they did with their toilet paper. Some people use, say, five sheets per pass (note ingenious euphemism) no matter what brand they encounter, while others use enough to make an acceptable handful, which means they'd use more of a thinner tissue. The fact that you get more linear feet of TP in a Scott roll does tend to make it last longer, but exactly how much longer depends on the individual user. Scott's dedicated research team learned that on the average a Scott roll would last 30-35 percent longer than other rolls, a figure they trimmed down to 28 percent for safety's sake.

Notwithstanding the fact that I am a college graduate, I consider myself fairly intelligent. I even think I'm capable of mastering the intricate motor skills involved in opening a freezer door. Why then do the grocery stores keep all their frozen and refrigerated foods

*in open racks, which would seemingly require a far greater energy
outlay to keep everything chilled than if coolers with doors were
used? Do they think I'm such a hopeless klutz that if I had to open
a door to get my frozen pizza, I wouldn't be up to the task and
would starve to death?—Allan S., Chicago*

The grocery industry is confident that doors hold no mystery
for you, Allan. However, they believe that the present system
better serves the dual functions of (a) conserving energy and (b)
displaying the goods to best advantage. There are basically two
kinds of open freezers: the charmingly-named "coffin," or horizontal, variety, and the vertical kind. The coffin freezer takes
advantage of the fact that cold air weighs more than warm air, so
that relatively little escapes out the open top. Some does get out
all the same, but the cooling effect is usually desirable, since it
helps the building's air-conditioning units maintain lower temperatures. In grocery stores, you generally shoot for around 75
degrees or less with humidity at 55 percent for maximum product
shelf life. To be sure, if you have ever fought your way through
the arctic breezes howling out of the freezer section of the average
grocery, you may wonder whether all this cooling is strictly necessary, but I am just explaining the theory here.

Vertical freezers make use of an ingenious invention called
an "air curtain," which is essentially a stream of air forced down
the front of the refrigeration unit to prevent the outside and inside
air from mixing. The rapidly moving air, blown by fans at the top
of the freezer,, maintains a sharp temperature differential between
shelf and aisle areas. In recent years the air curtains have been
supplemented by transparent plastic curtains which look sort of
like vertical Venetian blinds. Air curtains are also used in front
of the meat-cutting area, which you want to keep cooler than the
rest of the store.

The problem with door-type freezers, apart from any diffi-
culties they may cause persons with inadequate motor skills, is
that they spill air out every time you open them, which can get
pretty wasteful if people are taking things out frequently. Door
freezers are used chiefly for low-traffic items.

*What's the truth about protein shampoo? Is there any scientific
basis for the claims made about the stuff? What do real experts
say you should wash your hair with?—C.L., Baltimore*

All shampoos—regular old supermarket brands, home-
formulated concoctions, and groovy lemon-protein-herb products—have one thing in common: they end up on the far side of

your bathtub drain. It's simply not possible for a shampoo to take stuff *out* of your hair (dirt and oil) and put stuff *in* your hair (protein and conditioners) at the same time. The fancy products may leave a nice smell, but that's all they leave. Even a protein conditioner—which you leave on your head—will help little more than any other type of conditioner. Your hair is made up of *dead* tissue, and no amount of protein, vitamins, minerals, or seasonings is going to make it live again. In addition, the protein derivative (not a protein at all, you see) used in shampoos bears no resemblance to the protein (keratin) that made your hair.

So what do you do? Use a shampoo that contains the right amount of detergent for you. (Concentrations vary from about 5 to 20 percent; of course, the labels don't say, so you'll have to experiment.) And before you get too upset with the advertising people for trying to lead you astray, remember that it's people like them who made our country what it is today.

I'm getting a lot of junk mail these days, and I notice that on many of the computer labels there is the same series of symbols, in my case CAR-RT PRESORT**CR37. At first, I thought it was a code the junk mail places were using to determine my marketing profile or something. But when I noticed the same code on my IRS label, I wasn't so sure. What is the meaning of this code? Can you give me a letter-perfect answer and stamp out my ignorance? If you can you'll be my male #1.—Eugene S., Evanston, Illinois

Frankly, Eugene, I have no desire whatever to be your male #1. But don't think I don't appreciate the thought. "CAR-RT" means "carrier route," and "carrier route presort" means pretty much what it sounds like. The bulk (i.e., junk) mailers sort out their letters into separate stacks for each mail carrier before turning them over to the Postal Service. In return for this kindly act they get a 30 percent lower rate. The USPS, needless to say, supplies the mailers a list of what addresses each carrier route serves. The result is the ever-burgeoning collection of trash you find in your mailbox every day.

I can't plug anything in anymore! This is crazy. The space heater I bought last year is all right, but my new blow dryer, my new clamp light, and the TV I got for joining the health club all have plugs with one prong wider than the other. The instructions to each suggest some unspecified safety factor and tell me to call an electrician on the outside chance I should ever want to use any of these appliances. It seems all my outlets and extensions are now obsolete. What a boon for the electrical supply industry, and what a doggle for the rest of us! Who is responsible—the same person who came up with swine flu vaccine? Is there a significant safety improvement, beyond the fact that nothing is working right now?—Richard L., Chicago

You sound like a good fellow, Richard, but you are too excitable. The electrical manufacturers of America are selflessly trying to prevent you from accidentally murdering yourself with your reading lamp, and if that means you have to rewire your entire house and throw away every extension cord you ever owned, well, that's Progress, buddy. We are dealing here with what's called a "polarizing" plug, which can only be inserted into an outlet one way. In your basic household outlet, you have a "hot" side and a "neutral" side. To illustrate the importance of this distinction, find a small, odious child and place him in a bathtub full of water. Say you are going to play a fun new game called "shaking hands with Jesus." Plug a pair of bare wires into a nearby outlet and grasp the one that is connected to the "neutral" side (the wide slot). If the outlet is correctly wired, nothing happens. Then hand the wires to the odious child, surreptitiously substituting the "hot" wire for the "neutral" one. Big laffs! Similarly, suppose you were reading with your new clamp light while taking a shower, when suddenly you were stricken with the desire to embrace the metal collar that is usually visible around the base of the bulb. If the lamp did not have a polarizing plug and the collar was consequently "hot," you would be instantly annihilated, and unable to purchase additional appliances. Realizing this, Underwriters Laboratories a few years ago began to require polarizing plugs on many electrical devices. Show some gratitude.

We've seen all those clever "Do you know me?" American Express ads ad nauseam. But who the heck is C.F. Frost, the other guy Amex features on the sample cards in its ads?—Frank F., Dallas

Charles Frost—or Chuck, as we like to call him—is a real person, believe it or not. He was an account executive for the advertising firm of Ogilvy & Mather, which put together the original "Do you know me?"ads for American Express. Ogilvy and Amex thought it would be convenient to use Frost's name on the sample ads rather than some phony moniker, which would probably turn out to be the real name of some joker in Pocatello who would later sue for privacy infringement. Luckily for Chuck, the number on the credit card is not his real American Express card number. Mr. Frost has since left Ogilvy & Mather to establish his own ad agency in Manhattan, but he continues to be buddies with the folks at American Express. He was an honored guest a while back at a party Amex threw to kick off the fund-raising effort for the restoration of the Statue of Liberty. Predictably, he was featured in a "Do you know me?" skit in the course of said party. Chuck says hello, and says to give his regards to the wife and kids.

Forget the dumb questions and answer one of real *importance. Why are ketchup bottles tall and thin, while mustard bottles are short and fat? The Freudian implications are obvious, but what's the real reason?—David F., Chicago*

Your letter has restored my faith, David; I was starting to think the Teeming Millions were obsessed with trivia. We start by noting that the crucial difference between ketchup and mustard bottles isn't so much the shape of the container as the size of the

mouth. After years of scientific study, condiment researchers discovered that most people delicately daub mustard on with a knife, whereas ketchup they brutally slobber over everything straight out

181

of the bottle. That's because mustard is a highly pungent substance that can induce convulsions or death if used to excess, while ketchup is more benign. The bottle mouths are designed to accommodate the differences in usage. Interestingly, the H.J. Heinz company did put a wide-mouthed ketchup bottle on the market in 1966, for people who wanted to use ketchup by the spoonful in recipes. This daring innovation promptly bombed monstrously (although it is still sold in a few places), apparently because Heinz had overlooked the fact that for the most part there *aren't* any recipes that call for ketchup, except as a glaze—most people use tomato sauce instead. In contrast, quite a few recipes for sauces and dressings and whatnot require mustard. At any rate, French's does make a mustard bottle with a narrow mouth for use in restaurants, where you want to discourage people from poking their grubby cutlery into the condiments.

Is it possible you can answer a 20-year-old concern? My high school chemistry teacher told us that Airwick worked by deadening one's olfactory nerves with some mild anesthetic, thereby "eliminating" unpleasant odors, and presumably every other odor, pleasant or not. I notice on the Lysol can that it "actually eliminates odors by neutralizing them." Could this be corporate advertising jargon for "kills your olfactory nerves"? Was my high school chemistry teacher (gasp) right?—Chuck C., Chicago

You got it, Bub. There are three basic ways of getting rid of undesirable odors: masking them with stronger scents, such as the ubiquitous lemon and pine fragrances; chemically dissolving or absorbing them, as with activated charcoal or silica gel; and numbing out your nose, so you can't smell a damn thing. In the old days the air-freshener folks used to make products in the last category using formaldehyde (or its solid version, paraformaldehyde), which, as you may know, is both poisonous and carcinogenic. In 1976, the Monsanto company came up with a somewhat less murderous nasal anesthetic (the precise formulation of which, needless to say, is secret), which has since been incorporated into some air-fresheners along with the usual masking fragrances.

Airwick Industries denies that it makes use of a nasal anesthetic, saying that its products employ a combination of masking fragrances and "odor counteractants" instead. Curiously, however, the similar-sounding term "malodor counteractant," as used in the scientific journals, is usually a code word for nasal anesthetic, so you can draw your own conclusions. The numbing effect is temporary and not thought to be harmful in itself, but who knows. Lysol spray disinfectant supposedly works by killing airborne microorganisms that cause odor as well as by masking, although it's debatable how effective the disinfecting part is. If you want my advice, open the window, or else learn to live with a little stench. Never killed anybody.

Certain razor blade companies have been making claims to the effect that "two blades are better than one blade," and show an animation on their TV commercials to demonstrate the "twin-blade effect." Personally, I can't tell the difference when I shave with a razor that has one or two blades. My question is, is the "twin-blade effect" for real, or just so much advertising bullshit? Also, how many shaves is the average disposable razor good for? I read somewhere that all the razor blade companies use the same steel source for their blades. Is this true? If so, shouldn't all razor blades be of equal sharpness, and hold their edges for an equal number of shaves?—Mark H., Scottsdale, Arizona

Personally I think the twin-blade effect—technically known as "hysteresis"—is bullshit, but you can judge for yourself. Twin blades were first incorporated into Gillette's Trac II "razor system" in 1971 (ah, for the days when you could buy a razor blade or a bookshelf without having to get some cockamamy "system" along with it). What you get is two parallel blades placed 0.06 inch apart. When you run the razor over your face, the first blade slides through each whisker and in the process pulls it slightly out of the follicle. Before the whisker can retract, the second blade comes along and slices it off even shorter. Eventually (so the theory goes), the whisker retracts below the skin surface, giving you an exceptionally close, long-lasting shave.

Gillette claims to have done slow-motion microphotography that shows hysteresis actually works, and, in an *Esquire* magazine article on this subject some years ago, a spokesman for Bic, one of Gillette's chief competitors, admitted his firm couldn't prove hysteresis *didn't* work. Nonetheless, years of testing by consumer magazines and by the razor blade companies themselves have never demonstrated any clear superiority for twin blades—at times, quite the contrary. In 1974, *Consumers' Research* magazines tested four cartridge razors and found the best to be Wilkinson's, the only one of the bunch that did *not* use twin blades. (The Wilkinson blade was good for 40 shaves, compared with 7-10 for Gillette, Schick, and Personna; also, the twin blades tended to get clogged up with gunk pretty fast.) A follow-up report in 1977 found the situation unchanged. *(Consumers' Research,* incidentally, claimed the average throwaway razor was good for 10 shaves in a 1978 report, but for only 4 shaves in 1981—a discrepancy it let pass without comment. Gillette and Schick refuse to disclose how many shaves you're supposed to get, saying the matter is too "subjective.")

Shave quality, it's generally agreed, is mainly a function of blade sharpness, beard preparation (whether you get your whiskers wet enough), and how catatonic you are when you do your shaving. Razor construction (number of blades, swivel head versus non-swivel, etc.) appears to be a relatively trivial factor. Still, "two blades are better than one blade" does make a pretty catchy slogan, you gotta admit, even if it is basically jive.

As for what the blades are made of, Cecil must confess he was too lazy to find out exactly where all the steel comes from,

but it's true that blades from most of the major manufacturers are pretty much identical—a Gillette executive admitted as much in the *Esquire* article. On the other hand, there *are* differences in some cases—certain Wilkinson blades, as noted, are better, and some low-price house brands are a lot worse. There are also technical differences between, say, carbon-steel and stainless-steel blades, although as far as the consumer is concerned these may not amount to much. In any case, the remarkable fact is that most razor blades today perform pretty much as advertised and don't cost very much. There are few consumer products about which a similar claim might be made.

In the 70s Canadian Club whiskey had a print advertising campaign that challenged devoted drinkers, or anyone else, to go to great lengths to find hidden cases of the stuff. Allegedly these cases were placed in places like Manhattan (for the urban adventurer) and the North Pole. The ads gave clues and coordinates to help treasure hunters. I'm curious to know if anyone ever seriously accepted the challenge and whether any of the cases turned up.— Kevin G., Chicago

Amazing as it may seem to upright personages such as ourselves, Kevin, there are people among us who lead lives of such uproarious decadence that they have nothing better to do than look for cases of booze. This is a sorry commentary on the declining moral character of the nation, if you want my opinion. As a matter of fact, most of the hidden cases of C.C. were found.

The Hiram Walker company, which distributes Canadian Club, has always pursued the macho line in its promotion of the brand. You may recall the ads of a couple decades ago, in which various desperadoes would perform (or claim to perform) some act of suicidal bravery, such as wrestling with a shark, after which they would retire to the lounge for a soothing jolt of Canadian Club. By such means, Canadian Club was associated in the public mind with the notion of deranged recklessness. This was thought to sell whiskey, in some unaccountable manner.

The treasure hunt campaign was an extension of this line of thinking. When the project was first launched in 1967, the cases were planted in exotic locales like Mt. Kilimanjaro in Tanzania and Angel Falls in Venezuela. In the beginning Hiram Walker did not seriously expect anyone to actually go and look for the stuff. The Mt. Kilimanjaro case, in fact, was not discovered until the mid-70s, when a Danish journalist stumbled over it while on an expedition searching for lost children, or some such thing.

However, it swiftly became clear that there were any number of well-to-do guppies out there who were willing to frivol away their fortunes looking for a crate of hootch. The case buried near Angel Falls, for example, was found by a young hero on his honeymoon. The little lady had the idea they were going to go to Acapulco until they got on board the plane, when she learned otherwise. I am sure the idea of gamboling through the swamps being eaten by jungle vermin greatly appealed to her sense of romance.

The original promotion concluded in 1971, but was resurrected in 1975, or thereabouts. In the second version it was intended that most of the cases would be found eventually, so they were generally hidden somewhat closer to hand, e.g., near the reputed site of the Lost Dutchman Mine in Arizona, in Death Valley, and so forth. The depositing of the case was coupled with heavy regional advertising to stir up the interest of the locals. Consequently most of the cases didn't stay hidden very long. The box in Arizona was found in about a week; a case hidden atop a New York skyscraper eluded searchers for 13 weeks.

Still, some of the whiskey will probably never be found. A case dumped off in the Arctic is thought to have passed forever beyond the ken of man, what with blizzards and ice movements and what-not.

The Hiram Walker people finally tired of the "Hide-A-Case" campaign, and retired it in 1981. In all, 22 cases were hidden during the period 1967-1981; six have yet to be found. The current promotional effort for Canadian Club centers around the slogan, "Be A Part Of It," which is supposed to suggest "mystery and romance," according to the Hiram Walker people. You bet, guys. Bring back the hidden cases.

I was recently told that McDonald's serves about 600 million burgers every year. Out of idle, perhaps morbid, curiosity, I wonder just how many unfortunate cows must die each year to fill this incredible demand.—Michael J., Los Angeles

There are a lot of variables in this question, so the answer isn't going to be very exact, but here goes: your average cow (as opposed to my average cow) weighs somewhere in the neighborhood of 1,000 to 1,200 pounds when it's ready for slaughter. Once it's been butchered, about 700 to 800 edible pounds remain. Depending on how the carcass is divided up, some 12 to 15 percent of that total weight becomes hamburger meat—which means roughly (very roughly) that one cow is good for some 100 pounds of burger meat.

You were probably floored when you heard that McDonald's pushes 600 million burgers a year, right? Well, sit down and put your head between your knees, chum—the real figure is more like five billion burgers every 16 months. That's through the entire worldwide McDonald's system, of course, not just in the United States. So—not to stretch credulity too much—let's say that three billion hamburgers pass through the Golden Arches every year. Unfortunately, since McDonald's operates on a franchise (individual ownership) basis, there's no way of knowing how many of those three billion burgers were Big Macs, how many Quarter Pounders, and how many were those wretched little numbers at the bottom of the line. Quarter Pounders, the best seller, weigh in at 4 ounces (hey, truth in advertising!), while the small burgers are ten to the pound, or 1.6 ounces each. Therefore we must make a completely arbitrary determination that the average burger weighs—oh, let's make it three ounces. Employing awesome computational skill, we discover that McDonald's moves about 560,000,000 pounds of hamburger per annum. At 100 pounds per cow, that means that the company sends some 5,600,000 of the gentle creatures to their doom every year, along with an indeterminate number of kangaroos. The meat that McDonald's buys amounts to a staggering 1 percent of the entire American beef market. Anybody for an Egg McMuffin?

Do you know anything about "subliminal advertising"? Supposedly, they can flash a message, like "Buy right now!", real quickly in a commericial, so we viewers don't know it, but it registers in our subconscious and we do what we're told. Is this technique really used? Does it work?—J.C., Phoenix

On September 12, 1957, a market researcher named James M. Vicary called a press conference to announce the formation of a new corporation, the Subliminal Projection Company, formed to exploit what Vicary called a major breakthrough in advertising: subliminal stimuli. Vicary described the results of a six-week test conducted in a New Jersey movie theater, in which a high speed projector was used to flash the slogans "drink Coke" and "eat popcorn" over the film for 1/3,000 of a second at five-second intervals. According to Vicary, popcorn sales went up 57.5 percent over the six weeks; Coke sales were up 18.1 percent.

Vicary's announcement immediately touched off something like a national hysteria. Outraged editorials appeared in major magazines and newspapers; outraged congressmen drafted laws and made themselves available for outraged interviews. This was the year of Vance Packard's best-selling expose of the advertising industry, *The Hidden Persuaders,* and the public was apparently willing to believe anything about Madison Avenue—1984 was just around the corner.

Overlooked in all the hullaballoo were Vicary's own relatively modest claims for his invention. It was useful only as a reminder, he said, and couldn't persuade anyone to do what they didn't want to do in the first place. But even he was probably overstating the case. While Vicary steadfastly refused to release any of his data (or even the location of the theater where the tests were conducted), psychologists who had performed similar experiments gleefully contradicted his results. A weak stimulus, they said, produced a weak impression; the subliminal "message" was no more hypnotic than a slogan on a billboard glimpsed out of the corner of the eye. Moreover, Vicary's ideas were hardly new. A subliminal projector called a tachistoscope had been used during World War II in training soldiers to recognize enemy aircraft, while a book published in 1898 *(The New Psychology* by E.W. Scripture) laid out most of the principles of subliminal response.

Still, the panic over subliminal "brainwashing" continued. In January of 1958, Vicary agreed to conduct a publicly announced test over the Canadian Broadcasting Company stations. The message "telephone now" was flashed 352 times during a half-hour show, but there was no noticeable increase in telephone use during or after the program. Instead, the CBC received thousands of letters reporting unaccountable urges to get up and get a can of beer, to go to the bathroom, to change the channel—not a single viewer correctly guessed the message. Since the technique apparently wasn't working, the advertising industry felt free to denounce it (and help repair some of the image problems brought on by Packard's book). Subliminal ads were banned by the American networks and by the National Association of Broadcasters in June of 1958. A proclamation that subliminal ads were "confused, ambiguous, and not as effective as traditional advertising" issued by the American Psychological Association finally laid the controversy to rest, one year almost to the day after Vicary's historic press conference.

In 1962 Vicary granted an interview to *Advertising Age* in which he called his invention a "gimmick"—the Subliminal Projection Company had been dissolved, and he was working in happy obscurity for Dunn and Bradstreet. Eleven years later, though, the subliminal pitch made an unexpected comeback. A commercial for a game called "Husker-Do" was found to contain the phrase "get it" flashed four times (one frame each) during its 60 seconds. The manufacturer, the Pican Corporation of Los Angeles, expressed horror and surprise, withdrawing the ads (which, of course, violated the NAB code) and writing the whole thing off to an overzealous copywriter in Cincinnati. But the company's scruples apparently didn't extend to countries where there were no regulations against subliminal ads: in 1974, the spots appeared on Canadian television. More outrage followed, and subliminal ads were quickly (if pointlessly) outlawed in Canada.

You probably saw the ads on TV for the Oldsmobile Cutlass Ciera. The foreign language department of the public library tells me the name Ciera is not in any of their dictionaries for Romance languages. What does it mean?—Fred E., Chicago

As you might have guessed, it doesn't mean anything. The name was chosen, if you can believe the folks at Oldsmobile, after a two-year search in which hundreds of other names were considered, most of them equally meaningless. Ciera was chosen on the basis of its alleged "appeal," which I guess means that it sounds vaguely Spanish in a watered-down, Californiaesque sort of way. In a similar vein GM has also given us Toronado, Catalina, Seville, Silverado, and so on (although admittedly some of these actually do signify something). The ultimate expression of this line of development, to my mind, is Ricardo Montalban, the premier example of a marketing concept made flesh. Exotic but accessible. Dangerous but cuddly. If he were a car they'd sell a million of him.

Where the trend toward meaningless car names got started nobody knows, but it seems to have gotten a big boost in 1964 when Pontiac came out with the GTO. Pontiac pilfered the name from a race car made by Ferrari; the letters originally stood for *Gran Turismo Omologazione*, which loosely translates from the Italian as "approved grand touring car." *Omologazione*, though, is not a word that can readily be fitted into an advertising jingle, so after some hesitation Pontiac decided not to bother explaining to its American customers what the letters really meant. As it turned out, most people didn't really care. This has given rise to the present situation, in which car makers and oil companies alike feel perfectly free to flood the nation with gobs of total gibberish. The advantage, of course, is that you can create a brand name that has no secondary meanings that might distract from its impact. For this purpose foreign words are often as useful as nonsense words. Pontiac, for example, came out with a car for the 1984 model year called Fiero, which supposedly means "very proud" in Italian. The only problem, it seems to me, is that the name is uncomfortably close to Ciera, not to mention Fiesta, the name of a Ford product. And GM already makes a line of trucks called Sierra. Clearly there is a certain poverty of imagination in an industry that cannot think up another letter pair besides "ie" to put in its product names. No wonder the Japanese are killing us.

I would like to know why condensed milk is packaged in those foolish little cans without any lip, making them nearly impossible to open.—D.T., Wilmette, Illinois

It's cheaper, mainly. The can in question is the three-piece lead-solder "venthole" can; the milk is inserted through a hole in the top, which is subsequently sealed with a solder plug. At one time all canned goods were packed in soldered cans of one kind or another. Such cans were quite well suited to liquid, since they could be completely fabricated before filling, but bulkier commodities required the whole lid to be soldered on afterward, a tedious process. Thus when the modern "sanitary" can came along, in which the lid is crimped on in one swift motion, most canners converted—except for evaporated milk producers, who found that for their product soldered cans were still cheaper.

Over the last few years the Food and Drug Administration has been trying to get the industry to convert to unsoldered cans to reduce dangerous lead levels, but the Evaporated Milk Association doesn't want to, saying its members will go broke if they do. Use of evaporated milk has declined markedly since World War II, due to the general availability of refrigeration and competition from other products; sales have dropped 25 percent just since 1973. The association says converting would add almost a penny to the cost of each can and kill off all the smaller and some of the larger producers. I am disposed to have some doubts about this, but I would never say so in print. I am sworn to scrupulous objectivity.

My friend, Nick O'Teen, has admitted that even if cigarettes were to go up to a $1.50 a pack, he would probably still buy them. I suspect many others would, too. But it occurs to me that even though a pack of puffers may vary in price from place to place, virtually every vendor uniformly prices the selection he carries (barring the differences between kings and 100s). Because of state cigarette taxes, federal subsidies, and parities, are these prices *controlled by the government? Or is this some kind of smoke screen surrounding a major price-fixing condition? It seems to me that an enterprising tobacco company could blow rings around the competition by lowering prices designed to reach the consumer. Can you clear the air?—Duke of Marlboro, Tobacco Road*

Ah, innocence. We clearly have need here of a basic economics lesson. In the cigarette biz, as in many other American industries, we have what is known as an oligopoly, where a few large firms dominate the market and by various more or less legal means contrive to keep the prices for all brands uniform. Demand for cigarettes in general is thought to be highly inelastic, meaning that people will buy about the same number no matter what the price is; but demand for individual brands is highly elastic— people are fickle, and will readily switch to another brand if it's priced significantly lower. What this means is that if one manufacturer cuts his prices, he'll sell a lot more cigarettes, but mainly at the expense of his competitors. Knowing this, the competitors would immediately have to drop their own prices, and the upshot is that everybody ends up selling about as many cigarettes as before, only at a lower profit margin. For this reason the manufacturers try to avoid price competition if at all possible. What usually happens is that one of the biggest companies emerges as the "price leader" (for many years it was R.J. Reynolds) and the others follow along with whatever price changes it decrees.

The Federal Trade Commission complains about such practices from time to time (or it used to, anyway), but to little effect. Most manufacturers of consumer products compete on price only when (a) introducing a new product, or (b) trying to drive a competitor out of business. In the cigarette racket, for example, predatory price-cutting was common around the turn of the century, when the Tobacco Trust, composed of the American Tobacco Company and several allied firms, cornered 95 percent of the market, typically by selling its products at a loss in a given area until local competitors went bankrupt or sold out. In 1911 the Supreme Court ordered the trust broken up into 16 successor companies (many of which are still around today). Since then the companies have mostly been content to compete on the basis of largely imaginary differences in quality, which they promote through extensive advertising. National ad campaigns are quite expensive, of course, which discourages new firms from entering the market, and as a result the existing manufacturers have the field pretty much to themselves.

This all sounds pretty snaky, I suppose, but it's worth pointing out that oligopolies can't just set any old price they want to. In 1931, for instance, all the major tobacco companies followed Reynolds's lead in raising cigarette prices, despite the fact that the price of tobacco leaf had fallen to a 25-year low. This stupid move permitted several small manufacturers to introduce 10-cent brands to compete with existing brands, which were going for 13 cents a pack. By 1932, the 10-cent brands accounted for 23 percent of the market, setting off a price war in which wholesale prices were slashed 20 percent. Despite this, several relatively small companies, such as Philip Morris, were able to gain a foothold in the market and eventually overtook some of their previously impregnable competitors. Restores your faith in free enterprise, almost.

In every city I can ever recall being in, the major taxi company, or one of the major taxi companies, is the Yellow Cab company. I know Star Trek *postulated theories of parallel development, but there must be some other reason for yellow being the color for taxicabs. Please satisfy my curiosity on this bit of arcane Americana.—D.C., Washington, D.C.*

It does seem a little suspicious, especially when you consider that at one point there were 1,300 North American cities or towns with Yellow Cabs. We owe it all to one John Hertz, a Chicago entrepreneur whose name is most commonly associated today with rental cars. An Austrian immigrant, Hertz spent his early years engaged in such Horatio Alger-type occupations as hawking newspapers and driving delivery wagons, all the while looking out for the Main Chance. He found it in 1905 in the person of Walden W. Shaw, a wealthy young gentleman who needed a partner to help save his foundering auto dealership. Hertz served admirably in this role, and restored the company to prosperity—so much so that Hertz and Shaw soon found themselves with a surplus of traded-in cars. Hertz hit on the idea of using them to establish a taxicab service, like those already in operation in New York. He decided that the secret to success in the cab biz was high visibility, so he commissioned a local university to "scientifically ascertain which color would stand out strongest at a distance," as his biographer notes. Yellow, needless to say, won, and thus was born what eventually became the Chicago Yellow Cab Company. After enduring the usual travails, Hertz succeeded in building the company up into the largest of its kind in the world, operating some 2,000 cabs.

After a few years, Hertz decided that the vehicles then generally available were not durable enough for efficient taxi service, so he designed his own, the first of which began operating on Chicago streets in 1915. The Model J, as it was called, proved extremely successful and gained nationwide recognition. Orders from around the country began pouring in to the Yellow Cab Manufacturing Company, a Hertz subsidiary also located in Chicago. Hertz shrewdly decided that he would not simply sell Yellow Cabs but rather Yellow Cab franchises, complete with what he believed to be his guaranteed success formula. The Hertz system proved to be quite successful indeed—supposedly less than 1 percent of the franchises failed. Ultimately the various Yellow Cab companies (which were independently owned, for the most part) came to dominate the nation's taxi business so completely that "Yellow" and "taxi" became virtually synonymous. Hertz, for his part, was widely known as "America's taxi king."

Over the years Hertz expanded into such fields as bus manufacturing and auto rentals. In 1925, having made his pile, he sold controlling interest in many of his companies, including what was by then known as the Yellow Truck and Coach Manufacturing Company, to General Motors. GM merged Yellow Truck with its own truck division and moved the plant to Michigan.

Although Hertz's original franchises seem to have been set up more or less on the square, the subsequent history of American cab-company operation is filled with tales of graft and corruption, the leading examples of which, as one might expect, are provided by the Chicago taxi companies, Yellow among them. In the 40s the Justice Department tried, with mixed success, to break up a cartel that controlled all or most of the taxis in Chicago, Minneapolis, and Pittsburgh, as well as a substantial number of those in New York. Even today Chicago's Yellow and Checker cab companies are linked by a murky arrangement of interlocking directorships and mutual stock ownership, and periodically there have been scandals involving such things as approval of fare increases by the City Council. It is on such unshakable foundations as these that Chicago has built its enduring reputation as scumball capital of the universe.

I'd like to know the difference between Diet Coke and Tab. I always thought Tab was diet Coca-Cola. What are these guys trying to pull, anyway? P.S.: I love your column. Better than the World Book.—*Swill Swallower in Santa Monica, California*

What do you mean, better than the *World Book*? That's like telling me I'm better in bed than Don Knotts. I'll thank you to come up with a slightly more pungent comparison in the future, if you don't mind.

For all practical purposes, the difference between Tab and Diet Coke is that they come in different-colored cans. While the two products are somewhat different in taste (Diet Coke is marginally less odious, to my way of thinking), both are basically low-calorie colas. They are also, needless to say, both made by the Coca-Cola company. We thus have the spectacle of a multi-billion-dollar corporation selling two virtually identical products that in effect *compete with each other*. A monumental blunder, you say? Not according to the Coke folks. What we're dealing with here, you see, is the twilight science of marketing, where the normal rules of common sense are out the window. Permit me to explain.

Most consumer products companies make use of a dubious practice known as "line extension," in which you take a successful brand and spin off innumerable variations—so that Budweiser, for example, begets Budweiser Light. The idea, naturally, is that you achieve instant recognition in the marketplace without having to go to all the trouble of developing a whole new brand identity. Until recently, however, the Coca-Cola company refused to play the line-extension game, on the unassailable grounds that slapping the name "Coke" on some rank-tasting diet drink would only serve to muck up the brand's otherwise excellent image. That's why Coke decided to develop an entirely separate brand, Tab, when it got into the diet cola biz years ago.

Unfortunately, a new generation of managers took over at Coke several years ago and with the rashness of youth decided to abandon the noble policies of their forebears. Partly this was because archrival Pepsi was enjoying considerable success with its own line extensions, such as Diet Pepsi and Pepsi Free, and partly because Coke wanted to broaden the diet-beverage market, which up till now has been predominantly female. Woman drink 60 percent of all diet soft drinks, and the percentage for Tab is even higher. In view of the fact that Tab advertising in the last few years has consisted largely of shots of pretty girls in bikinis, this is not surprising, and one would have thought an obvious solution to the problem would have been to start putting pictures of guys in the ads on occasion. But Coke execs evidently regarded such notions as needlessly easy and inexpensive. Instead they spent $50 million to introduce a "new" product in July 1982 called Diet Coke, with the announced intention of attracting a 50-50 male-female consumer mix. The diff twixt Diet Coke and Tab? According to *Advertising Age*, "Diet Coke will be promoted as a great-tasting cola that happens to be low in calories, while Tab will continue to be positioned specifically as a low-cal product." A fine distinction, you may think, but that's what marketing is all about.

By June of 1983, Coke honchos were crowing that Diet Coke has surpassed Tab to become the nation's top-selling diet soft drink—which means, if you think about it, that Coca-Cola spent 50 million bucks to shoot its own foot off. Nonetheless, to hear the boys in Atlanta tell it, the whole thing has been a smashing success. Only 35 percent of Diet Coke sales were "cannibalized"—that is, consisted of customers who had switched from other Coke products. A 50 percent cannibalization rate had been expected. Moreover, research indicates that many women remain intensely loyal—one might even say addicted—to Tab's bizarre petro-chemical taste. So it appears Coke will be selling both products for years to come.

I have always wondered why Heinz ketchup bottles all say "57 varieties," even though I have never seen but one type, whether it be on grocery shelves or in restaurants. What gives? Where's the other 56 kinds?—R.B., Dallas

Fifty-seven varieties doesn't mean 57 varieties of *ketchup*, you dope, it means 57 varieties of food products in general. There are only two varieties of Heinz ketchup, hot and regular, but there are far more than 57 varieties of Heinz pickles, Heinz sauces, Heinz soups, and Heinz God-knows-what-else. In fact, if you count everything Heinz and all its divisions and subsidiaries make, there are something like 1,300 varieties, including 108 varieties of baby food, 60 kinds of pickles, and so on.

The number 57 has mystical significance to the Heinz company, but it has never had much to do with reality. The slogan was invented by the company's founder, Henry J. Heinz, in 1892 while he was cruising around on the elevated in New York one day. Whilst reading the car cards on the ceiling, his eye alighted on the slogan "21 styles of shoes." To pedestrian minds such as our own, R.B., this probably does not sound like a real killer of an advertising motto, but that is why we are not millioinaire ketchup barons. Heinz, on the other hand, could recognize genius when he saw it. Cogitating briefly, he soon conceived the immortal words "57 varieties," whereupon he got off the train and set about plastering the nation with the now-famous pickle-plus-number logo. The one problem with this scheme was that at the time the company was manufacturing more than 60 varieties. However, Heinz stuck with 57, for what his biographer describes as "occult reasons."

Heinz, as may already be evident, was something of a character. He started off bottling horseradish in a little town near Pittsburgh in 1869 (ketchup did not arrive on the scene until 1876). He made a major selling point of the fact that he put his product in clear glass bottles, thus demonstrating that he did not adulterate his sauce with turnips or other false vegetables, as his competitors did.

Once Heinz hit on the notion of "57 varieties," he constructed a number of hideous advertising signs at various strategic locales around the country. One, which was six stories high, was located at 23rd and 5th Avenue in New York City and dazzled tourists with a 40-foot-long electrified pickle. Heinz also built an exhibition hall in Atlantic City on a pier that extended 900 feet out into the ocean; another monstrous pickle, this one 70 feet tall, perched heroically on the end.

After a few more demonstrations of this style of architecture, the citizenry became alarmed lest Heinz encumber every landmark in the Republic with giant pickles. When a rumor (unfounded, it appears) got out that he had purchased Lookout Mountain near Chattanooga, Tennessee, in order to scrape off the side and sculpt a pickle of unprecedented proportions in the native granite, or whatever it is they have out there, there was a general uproar, with one partisan threatening to pickle Heinz 57 ways if he tried it.

The Heinz people are still quite attached to the number 57. The phone number at corporate headquarters in Pittsburgh is 237-5757, and the address is P.O. Box 57. One of their salesmen was a player for the Pittsburgh Steelers at one time, and you'll never guess what his number was. It is enough to make you want to swear off ketchup forever.

AMAZING DISCLOSURES FROM THE TEEMING
MILLIONS REGARDING THE INSIDIOUS NATURE OF
HITHERTO UNSUSPECTED KETCHUP MANUFACTURERS
Thank you for the leg work. In case you're not aware, you've uncovered another Illuminati agent in Henry J. Heinz. Let me expand briefly. The Illuminati are an extremely secret sect, and have been among mankind practically from the beginning, originating, it is believed, in the Lost Continent, Atlantis. Being a secret, powerful, occult sect, the Illuminati gathered great mystical power from their use of the number 5. Five is an extremely

strong number, still used in the worship of Satan, the power of our military, the logic of our digits, the points of our extremities, our senses, and a great many other things rooted in our collective psyche. Also important, and perhaps more powerful, is the combination of the numbers 2 and 3, equalling 5, of course. Two is the symbol for symmetry, and three, the divinity and others. It is a blatant game that the Illuminati are extremely fond of, flaunting their symbols to each other—the more bizarre the better, the more flagrant the waste of money, the better yet. Keeping this in mind, think again of the giant pickles, the man whose "mysterious" number is 57. (Remember, 7 is simply the repeating $2+3$ cycle, i.e., $2+3=5+2=7+3=10$ or 5×2.) Now observe the phone number—237-5757. Ergo, buying Heinz products finances the Illuminati.—Daniel K., Baltimore

P.S.: Notice how many letters in his first and last names.

Very shrewd, Dan, and just the sort of thing we expect from the sly inhabitants of your native city. I should point out, by way of addendum, that by using the digits 2 and 3 in appropriate combinations, you can generate *every conceivable integer* except 1. Thus we learn that the very foundations of mathematics are mortally infected with Illuminism. Man, those guys are *everywhere*.

Why do the 16-ounce money-back bottles of Coke have names molded into their bottoms like BERLIN, PA; BATON ROUGE, LA; GLASGOW, MONT; MOUNT PLEASANT, MICH, and THOMASVILLE, GA? Do those names tell where the bottles are made? How come they're so far from home?—Larry H., Los Angeles

Obviously you were never a Cub Scout, Larry. In the Cub Scouts we learned that the name stamped on the bottom of the bottle signified where it had first been filled. When you went on field trips to the bottling plant and got a free Coke at the end, the kid whose bottle had migrated from farthest away got a prize. This was supposed to imbue us impressionable youths with a sense of romance and adventure, which (it was hoped) we would thenceforth associate with the Coca-Cola company and its fine products. Indeed, to this day I cannot gaze upon a Coke bottle without feeling a surge of inexpressible longing. For that reason it pains me to report the following dismal fact: the name on the bottle no longer necessarily indicates the place of origin. It seems that in 1955 Coke HQ in Atlanta decided that making separate quantities of bottles for each individual bottler was too expensive and that the use of the marks ought to be discontinued. Legions of nostalgic former Cub Scouts, however, raised a hue and cry, and in 1963 Coke decided that bottlers could again have the name of their city stamped on their bottles if they were willing to pay a little extra per bottle. Apparently quite a number were in fact willing to do so. The velocity of modern commerce being what it is, though, bottle manufacturers, who naturally make glassware for bottlers all across the country, frequently find that they have, say, a rush order from Los Angeles without enough Los Angeles-stamped bottles on hand to fill it. So they throw in whatever other bottles they happen to have sitting around the warehouse. Thus eight-year-olds are forced to contend with the disquieting possibility that a bottle stamped with the name of some exotic locale like Thomasville, Georgia, may in fact be an unconscionable fraud, having spent its entire working life within shouting distance of the Pacific. Yet another cancer at the heart of the nation's moral fiber, if you ask me.

How many ants are there in America? How many aunts? Is there about the same number of uncles? Does Armand Hammer have anything to do with Arm & Hammer baking soda?—Larry C., Baltimore

Baltimore again. It never stops. We will attempt to ignore your first three questions, Larry, and confine our attentions to the fourth. Armand Hammer, of course, is the well-known head of Occidental Petroleum Corporation, one of the nation's largest oil companies. Among other things, it owns Hooker Chemical Company, onetime proprietor of the notorious Love Canal toxic waste dump. I mention this purely as a matter of idle gossip. There are several versions of how Hammer came by his name. The most widely circulated is that his father, a radical who apparently also had a weakness for weird puns, named him after the arm-and-hammer insignia of the Socialist Labor Party in 1898. Explanation number two, which is perhaps even dumber, is that Armand was indeed named after Arm & Hammer baking soda. Hammer's mother, Mama Rose, described by her son as "a remarkably intuitive individual, a person with an enormous judgment about things," is said to have "had a simple solution for every problem—bicarbonate of soda and a good enema." Given the alternative, I guess Armand should be grateful he was named after the soda. Hammer himself has long maintained that he was named after a character in *Camille*, one of his father's favorite plays. Whatever the truth of the matter, Hammer once painted an arm-and-hammer emblem on his yacht, giving rise to persistent speculation that he either was (a) the owner of Church & Dwight, makers of A&H baking soda, or (b) a Commie. Tired of explaining otherwise, Hammer has toyed with the idea of buying Church, but hasn't to date. We await further developments.

Chapter 11

≈≈≈≈≈≈≈≈≈≈≈≈≈≈≈≈≈≈≈≈≈≈

Death Threats

Please, Cecil, answer my questions and put my mind to rest. (1) What would happen theoretically if the earth was swallowed by a black hole? (2) How would we, i.e., mere mortals, experience this? Would we know it was coming in advance or would it just zap us? Please, our very lives might depend on this! —K.C., Los Angeles.

Tranquilize yourself, laddie. Most black holes are thought to arise from the collapse of very large stars—at least ten times larger than the sun. What happens, as you may recall, is that the star, having begun to run out of gas, expands to red-giant size and then explodes as a supernova. Whatever's left over then collapses into a very small, very dense core. If by the time you get down to neutron-star stage (very *very* dense) you find your mass is still three times that of the sun, then you continue to collapse into a black hole, where the pull of gravity is so great that even light cannot escape.

This will not happen to our sun, but that is no cause for comfort; Life As we Know It will be extinguished during the red-giant stage (if not sooner), which most stars go through sooner or later.

However, suppose you are just tootling around the galaxy in your cosmic Cadillac and you happen to trip over a black hole that's already there. What happens? Basically you are sucked irresistibly into the black hole's "accretion disc," a whirlpoollike mass of gas and dust surrounding the hole. As you get closer and closer to ground zero, the temperature gets higher and higher. At 100 miles away you're heated up to 2,000,000 degrees Kelvin, which is, needless to say, Snuff City as far as your caboose is concerned.

But let us suppose further that you have brought the all-time mother air conditioner along with you—then what? Here we must enter the murky swamps of conjecture. In your classic black hole, all matter eventually contracts to a single point called a "singularity," where density and pressure are infinite and space and time have no meaning. Some think that as you were drawn into this point both time *and* space would contract for you (i.e., you would go slower and slower), so that as far as you were concerned, you

would never arrive at the bottom of the well—you would fall forever. Possibility number two is that the black hole would so warp the space-time continuum that something called a "wormhole" or an "Einstein-Rosen bridge" would be formed. You would be sucked into this wormhole and spat out the other side, in a different place in space and time. Say, Mattoon, Illinois, last Tuesday night. Hardly worth all the trouble, to my way of thinking. Possibility number three (you may want to sit down for this) is as follows: for reasons that I confess are not entirely clear to me, when a black hole grows to enormous mass, it becomes *less* dense. If our entire galaxy collapsed into an ebony aperture (I am getting tired of typing black hole), said BH would be about ten billion light years across, with the average density of a thin gas. If we take this to its logical conclusion, it is possible that the known universe is *itself* a black hole, with us living in it. Wherefore, it seems to me, the obvious question is: *how the hell do we get out of here?* The casual attitude of our public officials toward this baleful possibility is nothing short of scandalous.

What are the chances of a huge meteor hurtling through space and smashing us flat? What precautions should I, as a concerned citizen, take? What are the authorities doing about it? Answer quickly—I'm worried. —Larry W., Chicago

This is the price we pay for 15 years of mediocre Mexican weed—we've got a nation of frothing paranoiacs on our hands. In the first place, meteors don't smash anything, flat or otherwise. By definition, a meteor is a meteor only when it's burning itself up. Before it enters the Earth's atmosphere, the particle is called a meteoröid; ripping through the upper atmosphere at about 40 miles a second, it vaporizes and becomes visible as a meteor, known in the vulgar tongue as a "shooting star." From any one vantage point, five to ten meteors are visible every morning, adding up to about 200,000 visible meteors worldwide each day. The vaporized matter that passes through the atmosphere adds about ten tons daily to the weight of the Earth; "micrometeors"—particles about the size of a grain of salt and too small to be seen—account for another 100 tons of acquired mass every day.

So far, no sweat. But every year, about 150 meteors are hardy enough to survive the friction of passing through the atmosphere and actually strike the ground. At that point, they become "meteorites." Most of them are small and do no damage whatsoever—the Earth is a fairly good-sized planet, after all, and the chances of a meteorite landing in a populated area are comfortably remote. It's estimated that a meteor strike causing 100 or more fatalities could only occur once in 100,000 years, a strike causing more than 1,000 deaths once in every million years.

The largest meteorite ever found checked in at 132,000 pounds; happily, it struck a remote region of southwest Africa in prehistoric times. The biggest meteor crater in the U.S. is near Canyon Diablo in Arizona, measuring about one mile across and 500 feet deep. The Chubb Crater in northern Quebec, now a lake, has a circumference of seven and a half miles, still narrow enough to spare the suburbs had it landed in, say, downtown Chicago. I regret to report that not one city in a thousand (except maybe in California) has an adequately staffed Office of Meteorite Preparedness. Chicago, however, appears to have things well in hand. "After the Blizzards of 1979, we're pretty much used to the idea of horrible things falling from the skies," one alderman told me.

"All we're arguing about now is who'll get the paving contract for the pothole."

A few years ago there was a story in the papers about a TV crew that accidentally discovered a dead body inside a "mummy" in a Long Beach amusement park fun house. But I never saw anything more about it. Did they ever figure out how the body got in there, or who killed the guy? Was anybody ever brought to justice? — Milo T., Los Angeles

The mysterious Long Beach Mummy turned out to be the earthly remains of one Elmer J. McCurdy, an Oklahoma outlaw who was killed in a train robbery in 1911. In those blissful pre-television days, it seems, looking at dead felons was a popular form of amusement, and a celebrated cadaver was always in demand. Poor Elmer was duly embalmed and sold to a traveling carnival, in which he entertained thousands of fun seekers through the South and Southwest. Due to the nature of his business, Elmer's posthumous movements are difficult to trace, but apparently he enjoyed his greatest success in the 1930s under the management of Louis Sonney, a one-time Washington sheriff who acquired Elmer for his wild west show as collateral on a $500 loan to an impoverished showman. When the bottom fell out of the corpse business (the American public having turned to more sophisticated amusements like *Amos 'n' Andy*), Elmer was shuttled from bankruptcy to bankruptcy, eventually ending up as an anonymous attraction in a California carnival. When that concern folded, Elmer was sold along with the rest of the show's assets to his present employers at the Long Beach amusement park, another sad victim of the fickleness of mass taste.

Like most people my age, I've seen thousands of dramatized murders on TV and in the movies. My question is, what mechanism in real life causes a person to die after a bullet is shot into them or a knife is stuck into them? Is it loss of blood, or shock, or organ damage, or what? How does that alien piece of metal kill a person? —Jordan S., Baltimore

It depends (in the case of bullets) on how big the bullet is, how fast it's going, and where it hits you. Speed (muzzle velocity) is the most important factor; we learn from physics that kinetic energy, i.e., destructive power, increases arithmetically with mass, but geometrically with velocity. Thus you have more to fear from a rifle than from a handgun. Slow, small caliber bullets, and knives, too, for that matter, rarely kill anybody immediately, unless they sever a major artery or pierce the brain, and even then death often takes several minutes. In most such cases, death results from blood loss, brain damage, or (in the long drawn-out cases) from infections such as gangrene resulting from contaminants borne into the body by the bullet or knife. An abdominal wound can result in mortal infection from fecal matter seeping out of the intestines.

Large bullets, and small bullets that travel very fast, such as those from an M-16 rifle, can kill almost instantly, mainly by reducing the region of impact literally to hamburger. They also generate something known as "hydrostatic shock." The body is composed largely of water and as such may be viewed as a hydraulic system. Liquids being noncompressible, the shock caused by the high-velocity entry of a large projectile (I love all this techno-babble) is transmitted throughout the body, causing widespread organ damage and general disruption of nervous functions. Even a wound to an arm or leg can be fatal in some instances.

There are numerous variations on the above, most of which are undoubtedly familiar to readers of detective stories. Hollow-nosed bullets, for instance, flatten on impact and bulldoze their way through the body, making death almost certain, since the massive damage they cause is virtually irreparable. I could go on, but I'm sure you get the basic idea.

Could you explain why all the wrist slashers of popular literature, television, and film make a practice of running water (bath, shower) during their exits? Is it intended to keep the hemoglobin from coagulating, or is it merely some kind of embellishment from art forms whose true origin has been lost to the mists of time? — H.C.E., Washington, D.C.

The idea is that very hot or very cold water will, to a small extent, anesthetize the area to be carved. Cold water discourages bleeding, and hot water promotes it, and the suicide may use either according to his or her preference. Although the running water bit is almost standard procedure in Hollywood, it is apparently not overwhelmingly popular among suicides in real life. (Ha!) The movie men have no doubt latched onto it because it is a convenient form of cinematic shorthand—depressed person brandishes razor, turns on water, sticks arms into sink, and you think suicide without ever having to see any of the gory details. One other common detail of movie suicides is quite accurate, however (at least as depicted in movies of the last several years, such as *Ordinary People*): if you're serious about self-destruction, slash your wrists parallel to the arm, not at right angles. A right angle slash can be stanched and sewn up much more easily than a longitudinal slash. Another helpful hint from your friends at the Straight Dope.

By the way, less than 2 percent of U.S. suicides use cutting or piercing devices to do themselves in. Firearms and explosives are the 'in' means these days, accounting for more than half of all male suicides and almost a quarter of the females.

Being a frequent traveler in elevators, I have had occasion to ponder various unpleasant scenarios, such as being trapped inside with a car plunging me to almost certain death many floors below. I have always wondered, however, whether I might be able to save myself in such a predicament by jumping into the air at the moment of impact, thus offsetting the force of gravity. Would it work? I await your supreme knowledge. —B.J., Los Angeles

Sorry, kiddo. The only thing you can do if you get stuck in a falling elevator is tuck your head between your knees and kiss your ass good-bye. It's a simple matter of physics. Let's say, for purposes of illustration, that your falling elevator reaches a terminal velocity of 100 feet per second. Even if you manage a leap of Nureyevian proportions, you'll only reach a speed of maybe 5-10 feet per second (for purposes of comparison, a sprinter doing 40 yards in five seconds is moving at 24 feet per second—horizontally, of course, and with room to work up a little velocity). That leaves you with a net downward velocity of 90-95 feet per second. In short, Pancake City.

I am a member of a small group who meet Sunday afternoons to read aloud the novels of Charles Dickens. Last week we reached chapter 32 of Bleak House. In this chapter, a rather low character by the name of Krook dies by—get this—spontaneous combustion. All that remains of him is a small heap of cinder and ash. I was delighted, but since then I have been looked at rather pathetically by everyone I've reported it to. No one believes it to be possible. Well, Cecil, if it is an actual phenomenon, then why hasn't anyone heard of it? If it isn't, how did the notion start and how was our dear Mr. Dickens led astray? —Scott E., Chicago

Spontaneous human combustion (SHC for short) is one of those bizarre phenomena that people tend to lump with ectoplasm and telekinesis, and discussion accordingly has been confined mostly to the nutball journals. Nonetheless, a considerable body of evidence suggests that something like SHC actually does occur. Over the past 300 years, there have been more than 200 reports of persons burning to a crisp for no apparent reason. The victims are discovered as piles of ashes and oily residue, completely consumed except for an occasional unburnt arm or leg. Although temperatures of about 3,000 degrees Fahrenheit are normally required to char a body so thoroughly (crematoria, which usually operate in the neighborhood of 2,000 degrees, leave bone fragments which must be ground up by hand), frequently little or nothing around the victim is damaged, except perhaps the exact spot where the deceased ignited. SHC victims have burnt up in bed without the sheets catching fire, clothing worn is often barely singed, and flammable materials only inches away remain untouched.

According to researcher Larry Arnold, the first medical report of SHC appeared in *Acta Medica & Philosophica Hafniensia* in 1673. A hard-drinking Parisian was found reduced to ashes in his straw bed, leaving just his skull and finger bones. The straw matting was only lightly damaged. Since then many other occurrences have been noted. Charles Dickens, in doing research for *Bleak House*, found 30 cases on record. The following are typical of the genre:

• On April 9, 1744, Grace Pett, 60, an alcoholic residing in Ipswich, England, was found on the floor by her daughter like "a log of wood consumed by a fire, without apparent flame." Nearby clothing was undamaged.

• On May 18, 1957, Anna Martin, 68, of West Philadelphia, Pennsylvania, was found incinerated, leaving only her shoes and a portion of her torso. The medical examiner estimated that temperatures must have reached 1,700 to 2,000 degrees, yet newspapers two feet away were found intact.

• On December 5, 1966, the ashes of Dr. J. Irving Bentley, 92, of Coudersport, Pennsylvania, were discovered by a meter reader. Dr. Bentley's body apparently ignited while he was in the bathroom and burned a 2½-by-3-foot hole through the flooring, with only a portion of one leg remaining intact. Nearby paint was unscorched.

Perhaps the most famous case occurred in St. Petersburg, Florida. Mary Hardy Reeser, a 67-year-old widow, spontaneously combusted while sitting in her easy chair on July 1, 1951. The next morning, her next door neighbor tried the doorknob, found it hot to the touch and went for help. She returned to find Mrs. Reeser, or what was left of her, in a blackened circle four feet in diameter. All that remained of the 175-pound woman and her chair was a few blackened seat springs, a section of her backbone, a shrunken skull the size of a baseball, and one foot encased in a black satin slipper just beyond the four-foot circle. Plus about 10 pounds of ashes. The police report declared that Mrs. Reeser went up in smoke when her highly flammable rayon-acetate nightgown caught fire, perhaps because of a dropped cigarette. But one medical observer declared that the 3,000-degree heat required to destroy the body should have destroyed the apartment as well. In fact, damage was minimal—the ceiling and upper walls were covered with soot. No chemical accelerants, incidentally, were found.

No satisfactory explanation of SHC has ever been offered. Many SHC victims have been alcoholics, and at one time it was thought that alcohol or its derivatives in the body simply ignited. But experiments in the 19th century demonstrated that flesh impregnated with alcohol will not burn with the intense heat associated with SHC. Other theories involve deposits of flammable body fat—many victims have been overweight. But others have been skinny. One school of thought blames phosphorus. One of the Teeming Millions explains: "SHC is thought to be the result of an error in phosphorus metabolism. As you may recall from your college biochemistry, living creatures store accessible energy in phospho-diester bonds. Under certain conditions, improperly manufactured polyphosphorus compounds in all the body cells can undergo an autocatalytic reaction. Water will not stop SHC. To get an idea of what's happening, have a chemist drop polyphosphoric acid in water." If nothing else, my correspondent here has a good grasp of the jargon. Unfortunately, I have scoured the recent scientific literature in vain for any discussion along these lines, and biochemists I have spoken to reject the idea out of hand. So the question remains open. At least nobody's claiming that UFOs or the spirit world are involved. You may rely on Uncle Cecil to keep you abreast of future developments.

Recently my girlfriend has been obsessed with tickling me. I hate it. I'm very ticklish and find it to be real torture. She on the other hand enjoys being tickled and says it even turns her on. My questions are: (a) Why are some people ticklish and others not? (b) Is it true the Chinese used tickling as torture? (c) Can you actually tickle someone to death? (d) If so, how would death result? — W.L.M., Chicago

Precious little serious research has been done on this topic, W., meaning that the following column is going to consist (as usual) of about 1 part fact to 20 parts harebrained speculation. However, so what. For the record, the physical mechanism of tickling is not well understood (it's thought to be associated with the sense of pressure in some indeterminate way). Nor is it known why some people are more ticklish than others. Nonetheless, it's clear that tickling is no mere idle diversion, but rather a profoundly ambiguous act fraught with numerous mundo bizarro pyschosexual implications. No jive. Consider, for instance, that you *cannot tickle yourself*. According to Darwin, this is because "the precise point to be tickled must not be known," lest some sort of mental tickle-canceling mechanism be automatically invoked. From this we deduce not only that it takes two to tickle, but that the tickling sensation is associated with *a loss of control over the relationship*. Furthermore, consider the fine line between pleasure and pain that tickling entails. You entertain babies by tickling them, but your girlfriend is making you suffer by causing you to enjoy yourself (i.e., laugh) too much.

But can you literally be tickled to death? Well, maybe. According to researcher Joost Meerloo, who wrote a monograph on laughter some years ago, it is indeed possible to *laugh* yourself to death. Epidemics of laughing, mostly due to mass hysteria, have been noted since the Middle Ages, and similar episodes are occasionally reported in the medical literature today—for instance, 1,000 people in Tanganyika suffered a mass laughing fit lasting several days in 1963. Most of the victims of such afflictions recover, but some die from a combination of exhaustion and starvation, the latter arising from the fact that it's impossible to eat while laughing. As for being tickled to death, Meerloo offers a possibly bogus story about a sadistic method of torture devised by the Romans (and for all I know, used by the Chinese as well). The victim is strapped to a scaffold and his feet are dipped in a salt solution. Then a goat, attracted by the salt, licks the victim's feet with its raspy tongue, driving the poor sap nuts with laughter and gradually abrading away the skin at the same time.. The feet are then recoated with salt and the process resumes until the victim, having suffered unimaginable agonies, dies horribly.

However, according to Meerloo, the more important meaning of being "tickled to death" is not *real* death but *metaphorical* death—i.e., sexual surrender. Sez he, "In a deeper sense, being tickled to death means taking part in sexual orgasm and experiencing the *sterbe und werde* feelings (to die and to be resurrected) provoked by deep ecstatic sexual satisfaction. . . . The clitoris . . . is in other languages called the organ of being tickled and titillated (in Dutch: *kitelaar*). All these words are also related to itch, the old English *yicchen*: a combination of restless hankering and irritation, of ambivalent yearning after fun and the taboo against giving in to the yearning. . . . 'I'm being tickled to death' means . . . that the pleasure is nearly too much for me." This may strike some as a bit far-fetched, but hey, that's the way shrinks talk.

So what does this signify for you, W.? God only knows. On the one hand, your excessive ticklishness may mean you're a putrid swamp of repressed psychopathic compulsions. On the other hand, maybe you're just . . . well, ticklish. Listen, you can't expect me to figure out *everything*.

Can man live by bread alone? If so, how long? —Irving Butternut, Los Angeles

Long enough to wish it were shorter, Irv. What we are about to discuss here is the massive breakdown of the human body. It will be a slow death and a messy one, but before we proceed let me say that science hopes you will step forward. Not until some selfless volunteer such as yourself eats bread and dies will your question receive the precise answer it deserves.

First the good news. You may assume that you would die of thirst. That's not necessarily true—*if* you take certain precautions. Bread is about 35 percent water, but most breads also contain so much salt that a greater amount of water than is contained in a loaf is needed to rinse that loaf's sodium out of your body. If you were to try to live on ordinary bread, you would become hypernatremic (too much sodium in the blood—for a fine word like that you should pay me), you would vanish into a coma and in about ten days you would vanish forever out of it.

So . . . if drinking water is out, as I assume from your question it is . . . find yourself a low-salt bread that doesn't resort to potassium chloride or some other hazardous (in your case) ingredient as a substitute (salt keeps bread from rising too quickly and then collapsing, in case you were wondering). Then find yourself a nice room somewhere with a steady temperature of 65 degrees and relative humidity of 60 percent (optimal conditions for avoiding the disastrous loss of precious bodily fluids by sweating) and start to eat. And eat. Yes, a lot of eating is ahead of you, Irving, because to extract the two pounds of water you need each day you will have to eat nearly six one-pound loaves a day. Easy does it—you can't afford to upchuck.

So in theory at least, we've licked the thirst problem. The next one's tougher. Bread is great for carbohydrates but it isn't exactly a teeming hotbed of proteins and vitamins. If you were a rat you'd be sitting pretty, because rats manufacture their own vitamin C. But humans must consume vitamin C in their diets, and bread, alas, doesn't have any. (Not even raisin bread, and I am not going to sully this discussion by considering wacky, hypothetical "breads" like lemon-peel loaf.) So there doesn't seem to be any way you can avoid getting scurvy.

Scurvy is the reason many of the seamen of old didn't live to become old seamen. After about six weeks on a bread-only diet the level of ascorbic acid, or vitamin C, in your body will drop to zero. The early signs of scurvy are fatigue, loss of appetite (you're going to have to force those six loaves down), and aching bones and joints. Then your gums will begin to bleed and your teeth start to wiggle. Without ascorbic acid, a protein called collagen that holds the body together will stop doing its job. Look for hemorrhaging under the skin, with anemia resulting. Your hair will begin to split and coil and bury itself in its follicles. The nice thing about scurvy is that vitamin C can reverse it at any point, but we're not going to allow any backsliding here. The preterminal signs are vomiting and swooning blood pressure. You will be weak by now, collapsing on so many fronts and so open to infection that it might be hard to pinpoint the exact cause of death.

Breads in general also won't give you enough of vitamins A and D and some of the B vitamins. This deprivation will contribute to your general deterioration, but not as swiftly or as critically as the lack of vitamin C. Doing without vitamin A, for example, will eventually cause you to go blind, and your corneas will fall out, but you have a two-year supply of vitamin A stored up in your liver, and before it's gone you'll probably already have croaked of other causes.

So how long would you last? Judging from the experiences of old sea dogs and pilgrims with scurvy, it's possible you could live two years, especially if you allow yourself to drink water. (Purists such as myself regard this as cheating, but I know how it is with you kids these days.) With water you can eat less bread and not worry about your sodium intake—either the perilous excess or, conversely, a deficiency of sodium, which would also mean a hastier death. But if you don't drink water, and consequently try to shove six loaves down your throat day in and day out—and that means consuming about 8,000 calories a day, four times what a 160-pound man needs when he's moderately active (and you won't be)—you'll be lacing your urine with glucose and wildly overtaxing your kidneys. Which means you should be happy to be alive six months later—that is, if you don't wish you were dead.

Several times I've heard people say that a drowning victim actually drowned when he "went down for the third time." I know I've seen this same situation depicted in animated cartoons, too. Is there any truth to the belief that people drown once they've gone down for the third time? And how could scientists study something like this without letting people drown? —Bill H., Chicago

Scientists study drowning the same way they study everything else—by administering slow death to kitty cats, guinea pigs, and whatever else is handy. (They do not, incidentally, watch the cartoons, which are not normally regarded as a source of reliable medical insight.) At any rate, it's not true that you go down three

times before drowning. In fact, in some cases, notably those involving alcohol (thought to play a role in 25 percent or more of adult drownings), the victim does not struggle at all, and consequently goes down just once. However, it's true that in most cases of drowning there is a fairly predictable predeath scenario, to wit: (1) panic, violent struggle; (2) attempts at swimming; (3) apnea, or breath-holding, during which time the victim often swallows large amounts of water; (4) vomiting, gasping, and inhaling (as opposed to swallowing) of water; (5) convulsions; and finally (6) death. To the extent that "going down three times" is a crude folk attempt to describe the preceding process, there's a germ of truth in it, but it's not literally accurate.

Interestingly, there are several distinct ways of drowning. In perhaps 10 percent of all cases, the victim does not actually breathe in any water, but instead dies of asphyxiation due to laryngospasm, or reflex closing of the vocal cords (this may be what causes drunks to drown, although others suggest the cause is actually sudden heart stoppage.) There's also a big difference between drowning in fresh water and drowning in salt water. In a freshwater drowning, the inhaled water is quickly absorbed out of the lungs and into the bloodstream. Unfortunately, the water washes away the wetting agent (the surfactant) in the lung air sacs (the alveoli) that helps keeps the sacs inflated. As a consequence, the air sacs collapse, oxygen can't get into the bloodstream, and the victim expires. In a saltwater drowning, on the other hand, the inhaled salt water draws blood plasma *out* of the bloodstream and *into* the lungs. The subsequent fluid buildup in the air sacs prevents oxygen from reaching the blood, resulting in death. In other words, in salt water you basically *drown in your own juices*. (Other things besides lack of oxygen contribute to drowning, but they're generally of secondary importance.) A couple other points while we're on the subject: hypoxia, or tissue oxygen starvation, can persist long after you get a near-drowning victim out of the water—in some cases for days or weeks. So don't assume the danger is over just because the victim looks like he's recovering. Second, hypoxia is worse with salt water than with fresh, and saltwater near-drowning victims are more resistant to certain forms of treatment than freshwater victims. In short, if you're going to get in trouble in the water, have the sense to do it in the fresh stuff, not the ocean.

I'm afraid for my life. All these years I've been eating the seeds of fruit, such as apples, oranges, apricots, peaches, plums, etc. I started when I began living with my grandfather, a dentist, about 10 years ago. He said they were good for the teeth because of the minerals they contained. Over the years I've cultivated a taste for them, and was extremely delighted when I found I could buy them in quantities of a pound or more at health food stores. Recently, however, a friend told me that all fruit seeds contained cyanide, and that he had read an item in a newspaper once about someone who had died from eating apple seeds! I am especially concerned about apricot kernels, my favorite. What's a lethal dose? Can any be eaten safely? If so, about how many? I really like them and would be loath to give them up, but on the other hand I really don't want to be slowly poisoning myself and my guests and roommates.—John T., Phoenix

You've got good reason to be afraid pal. Fruits of the rose family—including cherries, apples, plums, almonds, peaches, apricots, and crabapples—contain in their seeds substances known as cyanogenetic glycosides, which on ingestion release hydrogen cyanide gas through an enzymatic reaction. They can almost certainly do you in. Since 1957, Turkey—a big apricot country— has reported nine cases of lethal poisoning from apricot seeds. Unfortunately, victims of such poisonings have a habit of kicking the bucket before doctors have a chance to ask them how many seeds they've eaten; in addition, the amount of amygdalin—the most important cyanogenetic glycoside—varies from species to species, and since the poisoning does not involve a direct transfer of cyanide from one place to another, "lethal dosages" of these various seeds are hard to pin down. Use the following as guidelines: (1) Bitter almonds contain by far the greatest amount of amygdalin, and it takes 50-70 of them to kill an adult, 7-10 to kill a child. (2) Ingestion of about a cupful of any of the above seeds is pushing things a bit.

If you've been munching on seeds for years and have never felt any ill effects, you can safely continue to eat them in similar quantities without worrying. Keep in mind, however, that one gluttonous binge will put you away forever. Sub-lethal doses of cyanide gas are detoxified and passed out of the body rapidly, so it's impossible to slowly poison yourself over a period of time. Symptoms of cyanide poisoning are excitement, convulsions, respiratory distress, and spasms. Another warning sign is death, which can occur without any of the other symptoms.

All of this, by the way, applies only to fresh seeds. Roasting the seeds will destroy the enzymes needed to produce the lethal reaction without appreciably affecting the mineral content of your munchies. Note to shocked almond freaks; regular old almonds contain far less amygdalin than the bitter variety.

Periodically, there are stories about a baby-sitter who was tripping on LSD and cooked the baby in the microwave oven. Did this ever actually happen? Also, what would happen to a baby if it were cooked in a microwave? —Kenneth S., Dallas

I figured this question was bound to come up sooner or later, Ken—the only thing that puzzles me is how you Teeming Millions managed to restrain your curiosity so long. What we have here is one of those ubiquitous yarns that have come to be known as "urban legends." There are so many of these, and they're so widely repeated, that they were collected recently in a book by Jan Brunvand called *The Vanishing Hitchhiker: American Urban Legends and Their Meanings*. From this exemplary volume we learn that there are two main versions of the microwave story: in one, some smog-brain, typically an old lady or a little kid, washes or at least splashes the family pet (usually a dog or cat, but sometimes a turtle), and puts it into the microwave to dry, whereupon the pet either "cooks from the inside out," or "explodes." The story may have evolved from an older, low-tech version that cropped up some 20 years ago, in which the pet crawls into a gas oven or a clothes dryer for a nap, only to get roasted next time the appliance is used. (Dryers actually have been known to be lethal on occasion. One of my correspondents says a kitten of her acquaintance died of a broken neck in one.) In one particularly grotesque variant of the microwave story, someone who's just washed his (or her) hair sticks his head into the oven, having somehow defeated all the safety devices, and promptly does an instant Nagasaki.

The second main version of the story, namely the baby-in-the-oven yarn, was first officially recorded in 1971. What happens usually is that a couple hires a hippie baby-sitter who proceeds to get stoned on acid, marijuana, or sometimes even scotch. Later in the evening the mother calls up to see how things are going, and the baby-sitter says everything's fine, she just stuffed the turkey and put it in the oven. The mother hangs up, then suddenly thinks, "What turkey?" (The mother in these stories are always incredibly stupid.) Both parents rush home and find the kid's been cooked, while the baby-sitter watches with a spaced-out smile. (In some versions the baby-sitter has set the table with crystal and candles and says, "Look, I fixed a special dinner for you.") Older versions of this story, in which the kid is entrusted to someone who cooks it but without the microwave-and-LSD trappings, have been noted in South American and African folklore.

As you can imagine, tracking down whether something of this sort "actually happened" is next to impossible, even for somebody with my legendary investigative abilities. The microwave manufacturers, of course, stoutly deny that any child has ever been incinerated in their products. However, they do privately concede that, given the number of bent arrows walking the streets these days, there have probably been a few irradiated pussy-cats over the years. Cecil has also heard tell of several lawsuits involving people who claim to have been burned by microwave ovens, but to date nothing definite has turned up.

A number of the Teeming Millions have written to inform me of a movie called *No Deposit, No Return* whose disgusting

214

climax featured a baby in an oven (conventional, not microwave) and a stoned man. The flick, which I'm told starred Groucho Marx's daughter Melinda, was made by a couple would-be film moguls in Ohio and shown there on several occasions around 1972 or so. It failed to get national distribution (deservedly so, in the opinion of several viewers), and the title was eventually appropriated for an innocuous 1976 Walt Disney release.

As for what would *really* happen if you microwaved a kid—well, the Straight Dope Medical Research Board isn't exactly sure, but we do note that any sealed vessel containing water, such as an egg, potato, or plastic cooking pouch, can explode due to steam buildup if placed in a microwave without being punctured first. We also note that the eyeball . . . uh, you get the picture. Boiling blood might also produce interesting results. Look, buddy, *you* asked the question.

FLASH UPDATE ON THE MICROWAVE BABY CAPER

It appears that after years of apocryphal stories we now have evidence of a child actually having been burned by a microwave oven. According to a pile of clippings I have here from the *Grand Rapids Press*, Claudia Raynes of Caledonia, Michigan, is accused of child neglect in the microwave burning of her infant daughter, Tracy. Details of the incident, which occurred on October 31, 1982, when the child was one month old, are not clear. Ms. Raynes says she placed the infant on an ironing board about 18 inches from her microwave oven, put some formula in the oven to warm up, and then left the room briefly. When she returned she found the child badly burned. The infant was taken to a hospital and treated for third-degree burns on her left hand, right foot, and over her abdomen. The burns required partial amputation of Tracy's left hand and right foot and removal of part of the abdomen, according to police. Doctors said the burns were caused by radiation; for one thing, the child's clothing was not damaged. The child has since recovered.

Experts who examined the oven and the ironing board found nothing wrong with either. However, police were unable to find evidence that the baby had actually been placed inside the microwave. The charges against the mother accordingly place the emphasis on negligence: she's charged with failing to provide "necessary food, clothing or shelter, to wit: protection from microwave radiation." As we went to press (July 1984), the case had not gone to trial, but was expected to do so shortly.

What's the straight dope on the aluminum-senility link? Is it true that deodorants and/or antiperspirants cause brain damage if they get in your bloodstream?—Very Nervous, Baltimore

Funny you should bring this up, V., because I just happen to have clipped an article on the subject out of *American Health*, a magazine that no self-respecting health paranoid should be without. Aluminum, it seems, is suspected of playing a role in Alzheimer's disease, a form of degenerative senile dementia thought to afflict 5-10 percent of all persons over 65. Victims of Alzheimer's have been found to have four times the normal concentration of aluminum in their brain cells. Furthermore, studies have shown that aluminum can cause brain cell damage in lab animals. A similar cause-and-effect link has not yet been conclusively demonstrated in humans, but research is continuing. However that may turn out, it's obvious aluminum isn't the *sole* cause of Alzheimer's disease, since many people don't contract it, even in environments where they're exposed to high amounts of aluminum. In fact, there's some indication that a predisposition to the disease may be hereditary. Thus if one of your forebears had Alzheimer's you may have inherited some genetic kink that makes you especially vulnerable to aluminum poisoning. (To be fair about it, some think that the high levels of aluminum found in Alzheimer's victims are simply the by-product of some other as-yet unknown pathological process. In other words, the aluminum may be the *effect* of the disease, not the cause.)

In any case, aluminum isn't easy to avoid. You can probably dump your aluminum cookware without too much trouble, but you'll find aluminum is also contained in many common antacids and antiperspirants. I note, for example, that my friendly bottle of Ban Basic here contains aluminum chloride and aluminum chlorhydrate. Even more insidious, aluminum is added to many municipal water supplies to help remove floating debris. Aluminum is also found in household baking powder, self-rising flour, cake mix, pancake batter, and frozen dough (as sodium aluminum phosphate, a leavening agent); in nondairy creamers, table salt, and other powdered foods (as an anticaking ingredient); in processed cheese (as an emulsifier); and in hemorrhoid preparations (up to 50 percent aluminum hydroxide). The known human *requirement* for aluminum, you may be interested to know, is absolutely zero. Have a nice day, kids.

What is Herod's Evil? In the book I, Claudius, *Herod succumbed to a disease that had symptoms described as "putrescent stomach,*

*corpse-like breath, maggots breeding in the privy member, and a
constant watery flow from the bowels causing inflamed madness."
Is this disease confined to the Herods, or shall I live in fear that
I'll catch it?—Linda Z., Calumet City, Illinois*

Unless you have had your original equipment modified
somewhat since installation, Linda, you are not going to have to
sweat the problem of maggots breeding in your privy member.
Come on up to the office sometime and I'll show you what I mean.

Modern science is not exactly sure what Herod had, because
modern science was not there at the time, but (like me) it is
perfectly willing to take a guess all the same. The majority view
is that Herod had arteriosclerosis. This is a little disappointing, I
realize; you would think a tyrant like Mr. H. would go in for
something a little more grandiose, like syphilis. Some people just
have no sense of theater. Be that as it may, it is felt that arteriosclerosis, when accompanied by deterioration of the heart and kidneys, would result in the symptoms described. Bodily poisons
would not be excreted properly and would accumulate in the blood,
causing general itching, sharp, constant abdominal pain, diarrhea,
and possible ulceration of the bowels. In extreme cases, which is
plainly what we are dealing with here, the scrotum could become
distended and gangrenous, at which point a lesion might well
become infested with maggots, personal hygiene not being a prior-
ity item back in the old days.

The minority view—there is always a minority view, and if
I do not mention it, its scrofulous adherents are going to write me
insulting letters—holds that Herod succumbed to a combination
of cirrhosis of the liver, hypertension, and diabetes. Needless to
say, all of these things you could personally fall prey to, if you
put your back into it. Let me know what happens.

*I think I may be dying—more quickly, that is, than is strictly
necessary. I'm trying to eliminate most salt from my diet, including
the salt in processed foods. The problem is that commercially
produced salt, as I understand it, is the only source of that elusive
mineral, iodine. If I cut out the salt altogether, will some distant
cousin of kwashiorkor cripple my as yet youthful physique? Set
my mind at rest, won't you please?—Reid B., Evanston, Illinois*

Nothing personal, Reid, but it sounds like your mind's already
at rest, which is precisely the problem. You don't want to *totally
eliminate* salt from your diet, or you would expire horribly. You
just want to cut down some—to between three and eight grams
a day, according to the National Academy of Sciences (a teaspoon

of salt is five grams). To avoid goiter, the thyroid condition associated with lack of iodine, you need about 150 micrograms of iodine per day, which you get from roughly one-third teaspoon of iodized salt. It's estimated that the average American consumes 10-15 grams of salt per day, and since excessive sodium intake has been linked with high blood pressure, cutting back is probably a good idea. But don't overdo it.

For those few of us who actually like liver, and for those many others who live with mama and are force-fed the stuff, should we eat it or not? I presume mothers aren't lying when they say it's a good source of iron. On the the other hand, wouldn't liver be full of pesticides? Have we been poisoning ourselves all these years while getting "healthy"? Are mothers killing their children? Or is iron-rich blood more important that poison-free internal organs? Or is the whole problem a myth perpetuated by the liver-haters? I'm relying on you to give an unbiased answer, even if you're not a liver lover.—Alice B., Phoenix

If you want to know the truth, Alice, I kinda like liver, and always have, although I realize for most people this is akin to saying you have a taste for bondage and discipline. Come on over sometime and we'll split a slab.

You don't have much to fear from liver as far as pesticides go, but there are a few other things in it worth worrying about. Pesticides in general have a fondness for the lipids (fats) and thus tend to wind up in the adipose tissue, or body fat. They can also be found in high concentration in milk, which has a substantial fat content. If you want to avoid pesticides, therefore, stick to lean meat and ice water.

Liver does contain other types of nastiness, though, as do kidneys, whether the beef variety or otherwise. Mostly that's because the two organs play an important role in eliminating toxins from the body. Some of the contaminants can be kept to a minimum through careful management. Government regulations, for instance, require that ranchers wait a specified period after administering certain medications to their livestock before shipping them off to market, in order to give the drugs time to be metabolized and/or excreted.

But other toxins are harder to control. In 1980, for example, the Canadian federal health and welfare department found traces of certain forms of dioxin, one of the most poisonous substances known, in chicken livers from a town in Ontario. Dioxin is produced in the course of a number of common industrial processes and can get into the food chain by many routes; the source in the Ontario case was poultry bedding that had been treated with pentaclorophenol (PCP), a preservative in which dioxins are often found. Officials claimed the chicken livers posed no health hazard, but the fact is little is known about what effect minute amounts of dioxin might have on humans over long periods. A study published by two Michigan State University researchers in 1980 indicated that some forms of dioxin tended to concentrate in beef liver, although cooking reduced the level a good deal. The study warned that careless use of PCP on farms could make beef liver positively dangerous.

Still, it should be noted that for the most part dioxin is a *potential* problem rather than a current threat. A more pressing issue is the high concentration of trace metals often found in liver and kidneys. Some trace metals, notably iron, are good for you, but others, such as lead, mercury, and cadmium, are poisonous. Cadmium in particular is worth watching out for. The World Health Organization recommends a maximum daily intake of 70 micrograms; the typical daily intake in the U.S. and Canada is 50 to 100 micrograms. The concentration of cadmium in beef liver is two and a half times that in beef muscle tissue, and in kidneys nearly seven times as high. Accordingly, some researchers have suggested the two foods be avoided. While you're at it, you may as well knock off the oysters, too (no problem for Cecil, I might note), which have the highest concentration of cadmium of any commonly available food, some 35 to 50 times the concentration in beef muscle tissue. I realize that such warnings do not do much to enhance the total dining experience, but shit, man, I ain't Betty Crocker. Happy eating.

I have a fear of, yet a morbid curiosity about, execution by electrocution. How does one get to see an execution? What preparations go on before an execution? What happens to the prisoner before and after? What physically happens to the prisoner during an electrocution? Has anyone ever been strapped in, then taken out? Are there tours of Death Houses at prisons? Please try to be as detailed as possible.—Scared Stiff in the Chair, Chicago

Great. Another nut case. Ordinarily I try to avoid inquiries from the mentally unbalanced, but in the present instance I am going to make an exception, in hopes of stamping out any incipient enthusiasm for the barbaric practice alluded to above. The squeamish are advised to avert their eyes.

Now then, clown, suppose we wish to electrocute somebody.

Suppose it is yourself. Around midnight (this schedule for purpose of illustration only; times vary from state to state) we transfer you from Death Row to a cell next to the death chamber. At 5 AM or so we shave the top of your head and the calf of one of your legs, so as to permit better contact with the electrodes. A couple hours later we read you the death warrant. A few hours after that we take you into the electrocution chamber and strap you into the chair at the wrists, waist, and ankles, in the presence of witnesses. (Again, the exact number varies from state to state. Sometimes the witnesses view the proceedings from behind a one-way window.) Electrodes are clamped to head and leg.

At the designated hour, an electrician throws a switch and a high-voltage alternating current surges through your body for two or three minutes—typically starting at 2,000 volts at 5 amps, with the voltage varied periodically. Your muscles will instantly contract to a state of absolute rigidity, causing your heart and lungs to stop immediately. Some medical observers go so far as to say your blood will boil. If the guards have been careless and bolted you in too loosely, an arc may jump from the electrode to your body, searing your flesh. If you're lucky, you die promptly. If not, you get another jolt. Nobody, to my knowledge, has ever survived this process. By and by the doctors examine your remains and certify your decease.

Many years of scientific experiment have gone into making electrocution the refined art it is today. First suggested in the 1880s as a humane alternative to hanging, the practice figured prominently in the dispute between Thomas Edison and George Westinghouse over the merits of direct vs. alternating current. Claiming the latter was too dangerous, Edison thought to prove his point graphically by equipping Sing Sing's new electric chair with one of the competition's AC generators, an application for which it proved to be admirably suited. Unfortunately, upon being presented with their first prospective victim, one William Kemmler (he had murdered his girlfriend), the executioners seriously underestimated the amount of juice required. They burned him for a mere 17 seconds, at the conclusion of which Kemmler was still twitching slightly. The current was thereupon reapplied for another 70 seconds, causing one of the electrodes to smoke. Westinghouse later commented, "They could have done better with an ax." Still, Kemmler could safely be said to have expired, and a new era was born.

Offhand I can't think of anybody who was strapped in only to be taken out later, although I do know of a prisoner in California who had been placed in the gas chamber when a reprieve was phoned in—too late, as it turned out. I am not aware of any tours, and I am not particularly interested in learning of any. Witnesses, incidentally, are usually reporters, officials, and the like; persons who are assholes, such as yourself, are not permitted to participate.

A character in the movie Wolfen *said that during the days of the French guillotine, some decapitated heads actually were cognizant of their plight. Since the brain can live over a minute without oxygen, could some of the heads have seen their headless bodies and realized what a predicament they were in? —Anonymous, Phoenix*

You've been watching too many cheap horror movies—although to be frank about it, this kind of thing isn't confined to the silver screen. My somewhat credulous mother used to tell us a story about a Catholic martyr who, after decapitation, *picked up his head and kissed it*. Not being dummies, we pointed out to her that there were practical problems involved in a headless body kissing anything. Anyway, the fatal blow in a beheading induces immediate unconsciousness, even though the brain may not actually expire for several minutes. Even if the head were somehow miraculously reattached to the body, a phenomenon known as "retrograde amnesia," common in accident victims, would most likely prevent the subject from remembering anything about the event.

Remember the rumors that circulated when Goldfinger *first came out? Well, we do, and we'd like to know if they have any basis in fact: if your skin is covered with gold paint (or any other color paint, for that matter), will you die as a direct or indirect result? Why?—Columbia, Jackson Park, Chicago*

As I recall, the consensus at the time the movie appeared was that you would die of asphyxiation, somehow. There was a notion abroad in those days that you breathed through your skin. Well, science—or at least the popular understanding of it—has made mighty strides since those early years, and it is now known that you do not breathe through your skin. You breathe through your mouth and nose. So much for the asphyxiation theory.

Nonetheless it's true that if someone gilded you, you would very likely die. However, death would result from what amounts to an extreme case of heat stroke. Paint would clog the pores, thus preventing perspiration and ruining the body's principal means of heat regulation. You'd develop a high fever, and after a few days of unbearable suffering, you would expire. Lead or other toxic substances in the paint might contribute to your demise.

I might mention that anyone contemplating a homicide of this type should take care to coat the subject as completely as possible, since partial coverage will result only in an increased rate of perspiration across the unoccluded surfaces. Particular attention should be paid to the palms, armpits, and the soles of the feet, which contain a great number of sweat glands. Personally I think it'd be easier just to hit the guy over the head with a rock, but you know me.

Can a person get lead poisoning from eating tuna fish packaged in lead-soldered cans?—C.M., Washington, D.C.

We enter here into the shadowy world of microbiology, where all bets are hedged, so if the following answer seems a bit on the wimpy side, don't blame me. You will probably not get lead poisoning from the lead in tuna cans alone, or so at least one study claims. On the other hand, lead is one of those heavy metals that remain in the body for a long time, and the *cumulative* effect of a lifetime's exposure to such things as tuna-can solder and lead-laden auto exhaust could mean trouble. It's thought that the average joe has 10-20 micrograms of lead floating around in every 100 milliliters of blood, with about 3.5 percent of the population having more than 30 micrograms. 40-60 is considered the danger level, so there are some people who really have to watch it. Mild cases of lead poisoning are difficult for the average general practitioner to diagnose, since you may just feel run down, but even at an early stage you may start to get chromosomal abnormalities. For that reason pregnant women are urged to minimize exposure to lead. Further, since young children are particularly susceptible to lead-induced ailments (it's suspected of causing anemia, kidney trouble, accelerated cellular aging, and various other things), the Food and Drug Administration is trying to get the baby-food industry to eliminate lead-soldered cans in favor of seamless containers.

Are there any known instances of winos, derelicts, and others possessing unreliable bladders meeting their Maker while peeing on the third ("hot") rail from a subway or elevated train platform?—Impatient on the Howard line, Chicago

Not in Chicago, but I did turn up one instance in New York City, ever the pacesetter in this regard. Marshall Houta's *Where Death Delights* contains the sad story of one Joseph Patrick O'Malley, a man with two unfortunate habits; heavy drinking and wandering through subway tunnels. One morning, O'Malley's mangled body was found in a tunnel 50 yards from the nearest station; he had apparently been struck and killed by a train. But an autopsy turned up another cause: "The burns on the head of the penis and on the thumb and forefinger were obviously electrical burns. . . . The stream of urine had come into contact with the 600 volts of the third rail. The current had coursed up the stream to cause the burns on his body as the electricity entered it. In all probability, he was dead from electrocution before the train ever hit his body."

Others have their doubts, however. The combination of water and electricity is notoriously volatile—so much so that there might be a built-in safety factor—i.e., the shock would be great enough to knock you down, thus spoiling your aim and cutting off the current before the electricity could do its lethal work on your heart muscles. In any case the experience would not be pleasant. So take a tip from your Uncle Cecil: play it cool, stay in school, and watch where you're spreading those vital fluids.

Why is "propylene glycol alginate" found in salad dressings? It sounds suspiciously similar to a famous antifreeze.—Gary K., Phoenix

Propylene glycol alginate is used as a thickener and stabilizer in such products as ice cream and candy as well as salad dressing. Originally derived from brown algae and since mixed with a few other goodies, the chemical has been used for almost a century in one form or another. It's on the government's GRAS (generally recognized as safe) list, but that just means it's been around for a long time and hasn't killed a conspicuous number of people. As with many additives, little long-term testing has been done. PGA does not accumulate in the body, which is mildly reassuring, but there is some evidence that it inhibits the absorption of whatever nutrients happen to be in the food product it's mixed in with. On the positive side, it also inhibits the absorption of strontium, one of the more toxic components of nuclear fallout. A helpful hint for your Day After menu planning.

You're probably familiar with those grills for backyard barbecuing that run on crumpled newsprint, and can probably explain whether the lead in printer's ink gets in the food being cooked, right?—N.M., Baltimore

Right. The Food and Drug Administration, which approved the grills after a series of tests at the Hazelton Laboratories in Virginia in the 60s, claims that no toxic substances, lead or otherwise, are transferred from the newspaper to the meat. The only problem they found was with one of the chemical additives in green ink which creeps into the meat and makes it taste mighty funny, but stops short of making you sick (if that's any comfort). Actually, the real genius of the newspaper grill is that the newsprint itself isn't the main fuel source. Following the ancient design of the Zulus, the grills capture the fat dripping from the meat, which burns as it runs over the paper.

A long time ago, before cigarette ads were banned from television, I can remember seeing cigarette commercials that pictured doctors and nurses happily puffing away on their cancer sticks, with the strong implication that the product was being endorsed by the medical profession. My father says that when he was young the cigarette ads were even more outrageous, complete with testimonials from doctors claiming that cigarette smoking was actually good for you—helps relieve nervous tension, helps you get to sleep at night, and so on. One slogan he remembers is "Not a cough in a carload"—a claim that seems patently untrue. All of this looks to me like a conscious policy of false advertising. If it doesn't lie outright, it sure seems to bend the truth about as far as it can go. My question is this: can a cancer victim sue the tobacco company, if he can prove that the company's advertising willingly misled him into thinking that smoking posed no threat to his health? It certainly seems that the tobacco companies must bear some kind of responsibility, particularly if they knew what they were doing when they downplayed the risks in their campaigns.—Bruce S., Park Ridge, Illinois

In the 50s and 60s, a number of suits were filed against the tobacco companies making more or less the claims you describe. The Surgeon General's famous 1964 Report on Smoking and Health, with its conclusion that smoking was "a health hazard of sufficient importance in the United States to warrant appropriate legal action," seemed to provide a strong legal footing for arguments that the manufacturers had behaved irresponsibly at best, and maliciously at worst. But as things turned out, not one of the suits (most were filed by relatives of cancer patients) was decided in favor of the victims. Although the claims seem cut and dried on the surface, no one could prove that the cigarette companies had genuinely acted with gross negligence or malicious intent. Nor was it easy to demonstrate that the victim's decision to smoke was based solely on the information put forth in the manufacturer's advertising, and not on other factors—the notorious "peer group pressure," for one.

Ironically, the 1970 Public Health Smoking Act, which required all cigarettes and all cigarette advertisements to carry warnings, has actually worked in favor of the manufacturers on this point. It now seems impossible to prove that the smoker—having been warned at least twice, in the ads and on the package—made his decision to smoke without being aware of the risks. The cigarette companies are covered, while the ads continue to express symbolically the healthy, clean pleasure of a good smoke.

I have this friend and he isn't playing with a full deck, if you know what I mean, and he said if you drop a penny from the top of the Empire State Building and it happened to hit someone in the head it would go through just like that; and also if even the tiniest pebble was inadvertently sucked into the engine of a jet airplane the whole thing would blow up. What I need to know is, are these things true?—Joe D., Towson, Maryland

The Teeming Millions have lately demonstrated an unhealthy fascination with throwing things off tall buildings, which we cannot but regard as ominous. However, we will assume your interest in such matters is purely academic. Given that the Empire State Building is 1,250 feet tall and ignoring such factors as wind resistance for the moment, a penny dropped from the top would hit the ground in approximately 8.8 seconds, having reached a speed of roughly 280 feet per second. This is not particularly fast. A low-powered .22 or .25 caliber bullet, to which a penny is vaguely comparable in terms of mass, typically has a muzzle velocity of 800 to 1,100 FPS, with maybe 75 foot-pounds of energy. On top of this we must consider that the penny would probably tumble

225

while falling, and that the Empire State Building, like all tall buildings, is surrounded by strong updrafts, which would slow descent considerably. Thus, while you might conceivably inflict a fractured skull on some hapless New Yorker (or, more likely, some cretinous tourist from Towson), the penny would certainly not "go through just like that," as you so theatrically put it. For the record, the Empire State folks claim no one has ever dropped anything off their building. The youth of New York being what they are, I have my doubts about this, but we won't get into that. Your friend's speculation on jet engines, I need hardly add, are as daft as his other ideas.

A few years ago, a powerful bomb exploded at the University of Maryland computer center and killed a visiting scholar from the People's Republic of China. The year before that, the home of a prominent Baltimore physician who was also a Zionist was twice fire-bombed. A couple of years before that (according to an official account), an ex CIA agent ate his lunch, rowed himself into the middle of the Chesapeake, hog-tied himself, donned cement over-shoes, and, again according to official reports, pushed himself overboard. My Italian literature teacher, who is visiting from the University of Bologna, tells me that there are 2,000 terrorist incidents a year in the U.S.—twice as many as there are in Italy. Is he right?—Chris L., Baltimore

No. There is no such thing as uniform reporting of terrorist incidents—for one thing, nobody can agree on a definition of terrorism—but such studies as there are suggest that terrorist violence is far worse in Italy than in the U.S. A book published in 1979 by two researchers for Stanford University's Hoover Institute totes up roughly 140 bombings in the U.S. since 1969 by such groups as the Weather Underground, the New World Liberation Front, and the Puerto Rican FALN. A considerably more thorough tally put together by CIA analyst Edward Mickolus lists 288 incidents in the U.S. during the period 1967-1977, ranging from antinuke bomb threats to the Patty Hearst kidnapping. By contrast, the Stanford folks note that Italy reported more than 2,000 incidents during the height of Red Brigades terror in the period 1977-1978.

Then again, it's all a matter of definition. At least 300 incidents involving the Ku Klux Klan were reported in 1981, for instance, including one aborted attempt by a handful of Klansmen and Nazis to invade the predominantly black Caribbean island of Dominica. And we ought to point out that when it comes to international terror, the U.S. seems to provide an inordinate number of victims—1,471 during 1968-1977, according to Mickolus, compared to 108 Italians. Keep your heads down, kids.

Chapter 12

Nukes

If the Russians ever nuked Chicago, how big a hole would it make? Would I be safe in the suburbs? This is a matter of genuine and serious concern to me.—H.B., Schaumburg, Illinois

Since the Russians aren't telling how big their bombs are these days (and the CIA has been no help—even Cecil Adam's influence has to stop somewhere), this is a hard question to answer exactly. The last we heard—when Nikita Krushchev announced it to a cheering throng of East Berliners on January 16, 1963— the Russians were packing a 100 megaton warhead. One megaton has the explosive power of one million tons of TNT (hence, megaton), so, as you can see, this sucker is pretty big.

However, this might be mere Commie Rat propaganda. The biggest bomb that the Russkies have actually exploded (on October 30, 1961) amounted to a mere 57 megatons, by their own admission. Some scientists, though, have estimated the power of that blast to be more in the 60 to 90 megaton range, so maybe we should take the Reds at their word, for once. A 100 megaton bomb would make a crater about 19 miles in diameter, which would let Schaumburg off the hook (initially) in the unlikely event that it struck downtown Chicago dead center. The devastating fire storms that follow in the wake of the explosion, though, would reduce Schaumburg to a rubble of melting McDonald's stands in a matter of hours. To escape the fire storms, you'd have to move another ten or twenty miles out. Then, all you'd have to worry about would be the radiation, which will get you sooner or later, no matter what. Sweet dreams.

During the Falkland Islands naval battles a few years ago I got to thinking about what might happen if one of Britain's nuclear subs was destroyed and its nuclear reactor breached. Would calamitous China Syndrome (or Poseidon Syndrome) effects necessarily result? Would there be massive fish die-offs? An end to life as we know it?—Robert B., Dallas

Funny you should mention it, Bertie, because I just happened to be reading up on this subject in one of my evironmental journals, which I rely on to keep me abreast of the latest threats to civilization. The real danger nowadays, it seems, isn't so much from ship-borne nuclear pollution of the oceans (although this situation could change—more below), but rather from the space-borne variety—specifically, from falling satellites with nuclear reactors aboard. Twice in the last half-dozen years, atom-powered Russian reconnaissance satellites have tumbled earthward. One disintegrated over the South Atlantic (apparently harmlessly, although you never know about these things), while the reactor from the other crashed into a frozen lake in northern Canada. Authorities successfully retrieved the 143-pound chunk of lethal debris in the latter case, but if I were you I would eye any Canadian lake trout I might be presented with in the next 6,000 years with grave suspicion. The nuclear power pack from a U.S. weather satellite fell into the Santa Barbara Channel off California in 1968, whence authorities managed to recover it, but another power pack was lost for good in the Pacific north of New Zealand in 1970. Fortunately, its heavy shielding supposedly won't disintegrate for some 860 years.

But back to ships. You may recall there's been some talk of the U.S. Navy disposing of its obsolete nuclear submarines by the straightforward method of scuttling them in mid-ocean somewhere. The nuclear fuel would be removed first, but opponents say enough radioactive junk would remain on board to pose a significant pollution hazard. As for what will happen on that inevitable day when a nuclear reactor actually breaks open in the ocean—well, I dunno, and neither does anybody else. Certainly the China Syndrome (i.e., a massive meltdown) will not occur, due to the cooling effect of the seawater. The pollution, however, could be disastrous. No doubt we'll find out soon enough.

USA Today *once quoted President Reagan as follows: "All the wastes for a year from a nuclear-power plant could be stored under a desk"—but I won't believe him until old Cecil says he's right. Be my guide.—Perplexed, Los Angeles*

You did right to come to me, P., since Ron was once again indulging his penchant for politically convenient oversimplification. We note in the president's quote the weaselly presence of the word "could." What he was saying was that if the spent fuel from a nuclear power plant were *reprocessed* (i.e., if the reusable portions were separated out from the unsalvageable trash), you'd conceivably end up with just a few cubic feet of waste. This would indeed fit under a desk, and I might add that if Ron were to sit down at that desk, the whole country might be a lot better off. Unfortunately, for a variety of economic and political reasons (see following question), no commercial reprocessing is presently being done in the U.S., and none is contemplated. What happens is that the utility simply removes the spent fuel rods from each reactor periodically and stores them in a big swimming pool at the plant site, until such time as some genius comes up with (a) an economical way to reprocess them, or (b) a nice, geologically stable hole in the ground where they can safely be stored for the next 200,000 years, which is roughly how long they're dangerous (you begin to get an idea of the dimensions of the problem here, I think). The friendly folks from the Nuclear Regulatory Commission and the power company and I have been doing jolly numbers all morning (and getting mighty tired of it, too—can't you people ever come up with some nonmathematical questions?), and the way we figure it, from a typical 1,00-megawatt unit you'd get maybe 8,000-10,000 spent fuel rods per year, which works out to about 130-165 cubic feet of unreprocessed high-level waste. Needless to say, it would take one helluva desk to have all this fit under it. In addition, you also have anywhere from 2,400 to 22,000 cubic feet of *low-level* waste per unit per year, which consists of contaminated clothing, filters, sludge, and stuff like that. This waste is usually shipped out in drums and buried. The upshot of all this is that Regan's statement consists of 1 part fact to about 99 parts jive—about what you'd expect from a guy who once claimed pollution was caused by trees.

Certain legislators are looking to pass laws stating that my state (Illinois) will not take nuclear waste from states that don't take our nuclear waste. Being a lover of life and long-term existence (read that: antinuclear, pro-solar and wind, on principle), why does anybody's waste have to be sent anywhere? Why don't we keep ours and they keep theirs? Is it just to create jobs for people who could otherwise be employed in recycling facilities, hospitals, teaching, etc.?—Robyn M., Chicago

We must attempt to clear our heads of mush when discussing these matters, Robyn. The nation's nuclear waste dumps (there are currently three) were hardly intended as make-work projects. The reason every state doesn't have its own disposal site is mostly a matter of economics.

But let's clarify a few matters first. What we're talking about here is *low-level* radioactive waste, which consists of things like contaminated gloves and tools, the residue from medical tests and experiments, and so on. We distinguish this from *high-level* waste, which results from the processing of spent fuel from nuclear power plants. Originally spent fuel was supposed to be reprocessed so that it could be used over again. Unfortunately, reprocessing necessarily involves the production of plutonium, a principal ingredient in the manufacture of nuclear weapons, and reprocessing plants and associated vehicles thus would be a prime target for theft attempts by terrorists. The Carter administration accordingly put a hold on the construction of any such plants pending further study. In the meantime spent fuel is piling up in temporary storage facilities at most nuclear power plants, permitting us to postpone for the moment the inevitable question of what to do with high-level waste.

The disposal of low-level waste (hereinafter LLW) is another matter. LLW is usually packed into 55-gallon drums and buried under five to ten feet of earth in trenches at privately operated sites near Hanford, Washington; Beatty, Nevada; and Barnwell, South Carolina. Although not as lethal as high-level waste, LLW is still nasty stuff, and most states—including Washington, Nevada, and South Carolina—would rather dump theirs on somebody else. To force the states to take some responsibility, Congress in 1980 passed the Low-Level Radioactive Waste Policy Act, which declared that each state would be held responsible for the disposal of low-level waste generated within its borders. That means each state has to either build its own waste dump or enter into a regional compact with nearby states to establish a joint waste disposal site. The federal government prefers the latter strategy, partly because it's easier to police a few large sites than many small ones, but also because of the implacable economics of what we business school jockos call "waste management." Waste dumps are high-fixed-cost operations—i.e., costs don't fluctuate much with volume—and consequently per-unit costs are much higher at small dumps than big ones. Many states, as it happens, do not generate much waste at all—in 1979 quantities ranged from less than 1 cubic meter for Alaska to 9,570 cubic meters for New York. A study conducted for the Department of Energy in 1980 found that over a 20-year-period overall disposal costs per cubic foot of waste would be roughly five and a half times as high at a small intrastate facility as at a large multistate unit. Regional dumps are thus supposed to save everybody money. Just in case any state fails to see the wisdom of this, though, the Radioactive Waste Policy Act further provides that dumps operated by compact states have the right to refuse wastes from non-compact states after January 1, 1986. Since Illinois is the fourth-largest producer of LLW in the country (6,760 cubic meters in 1979), one assumes state officials will pursue the regional option with some zeal.

The disclosures about the Pentagon's plans for a protracted nuclear war, as if dioxin, killer bees, and the failure of the social security system weren't enough, make me feel like it's time to relocate. If you were considering an alternative nation that would be least physically affected by nuclear war, where would it be? It would have to be a decent place to live, self-sufficient in energy and foodstuffs but not sizable enough to attract predators, free from its own internal abuses politically, and civilized enough to suggest gainful employment and a constructive culture. South America, Africa, and Asia would seem to be out, but what about Ireland, Costa Rica, Australia/New Zealand, Canada, some Pacific island, or northern Great Britain? The Falklands might've sounded peaceful enough a few years ago, but what's a safe bet for the next 40 years—including dependable medical care and coin-operated photocopy machines?—Fred N., Washington, D.C.

If you want to know the truth, Freddie, you sound like the kind of guy who would complain that there weren't any seat cushions on the lifeboat. We're talking about dodging nuclear holocaust here, not taking a goddamn vacation. In any case, there is no place on earth that meets your goofball specifications. Some years ago an editor at *The Bulletin of the Atomic Scientists* used wind data and a list of probable targets to calculate that Tierra del Fuego would be the last place on earth to be affected by radioactive fallout. Tierra del Fuego happens to be a godforsaken rockpile just off the southern tip of South America. I make no claims as to the availability of photocopiers.

If you really want to pursue this rather pointless line of inquiry, you might want to buy one of those survivalist magazines and check out the small ads in the back. The other day I noticed one from an outfit in Chicago that was offering "complete computerized analysis" of the effects of a nuclear attack on any given location, at $5 a crack. Given the editorial company they keep, these people are probably a little squirrelly, but what the heck, it might be good for a few laughs.

232

Upon inspecting the smoke detector in my apartment recently, I discovered a sticker warning that it contains radioactive material. It also states that for repair or disposal said unit should be returned to the manufacturer. Not meaning to sound like an alarmist, but just how much radioactive material does this innocent-looking white dish contain? I've been living with this thing for two years—how much longer till my hair starts falling out?—John Z., Chicago

Your hair may well fall out one of these days, John, but if it does you'll have naught to blame but Ma Nature and your balding forebears. The additional exposure you receive from a smoke detector is considerably less than the normal background radiation in most parts of the country. Most detectors make use of about two microcuries of americium-241, which is used to make the air in the detector's so-called ionization chamber electrically conductive. If smoke enters the chamber, it inhibits the flow of electricity, which causes the alarm to sound. At a distance of one foot—which, needless to say, is much closer than you normally get—you'd receive a radiation dosage of about a half-microrem per hour. Normal background radiation in Chicago is about two millirems (i.e., a whole lot more than a half-microrem) per hour. One consumer organization estimates that if ionization-type smoke detectors were placed in every U.S. home, they'd result in one additional cancer death every seven years. On the other hand, they'd conceivably save the lives of 4,500 of the 7,000 people who die in fires every year. From the cost-benefit point of view, that's a pretty good trade-off.

While we're on the subject, I might mention that when your smoke detector begins to beep every few seconds, it means it's time to *change the battery*, for Chrissake. Not one of the vaporheads in my apartment building seems to have figured this out yet.

THE TEEMING MILLIONS BEG TO DIFFER, PART ONE

I know you're not in the habit of admitting you were wrong, but for the sake of your reader's health and safety you should at least publish all the facts on an issue. Ionizing smoke detectors are indeed dangerous—the Health Research Group, a unit of Ralph Nader's Public Citizen organization, said so in 1976. The detectors are so radioactive that defective or "used" detectors are supposed to be shipped to the NRC. However, nobody does this so the darn things get crushed and burnt in city incinerators. Even if they did it wouldn't matter because in reality the NRC has no disposal plan. The thin foil surrounding the americium is able to be punctured and detectors can be destroyed by fire or vandalism while

233

still in their boxes or in use. Imagine a whole shelf full of them destroyed in a hardware store fire or roof collapse, and leaking radioactivity into the environment. What's more, safe detectors are available. Any Sears store can order the photoelectric type, which is no more costly than the radioactive type—and they are very effective. I know because several friends of mine were saved by one in their apartment last winter.—C.A.S., Baltimore

I am not in the habit of admitting I am wrong for the simple reason that it isn't often I *am* wrong. The Ralph Nader charges you refer to were examined by Consumers Union, a widely respected research organization not known for its proindustry bias, and found to be largely without merit. CU's full report appeared in the January 1977 issue of *Consumer Reports*, which I suggest you read. For the present I'll simply respond to the claims you make in your letter.

It is generally recommended that used detectors be returned

not the the NRC but to their manufacturers, which are required to dispose of them at approved low-level waste facilities, of which the U.S. has three. Americium-241, the substance used in smoke detectors, mainly emits alpha and gamma particles. The principal danger comes from the alpha particles, which are indeed toxic, but only within a range of a few centimeters. Moreover, the particles are readily blocked by almost any material. The tiny quantities of americium used in smoke detectors would become a hazard

234

only if they became lodged in the body, where they would be able to irradiate tissue for an extended period of time. Experiments indicate that the chances of this happening as a result of fire, vandalism, or general carelessness are remote. The NRC tested various scenarios and calculated that only in the most extreme— firemen fighting a blaze in a warehouse containing 25,000 smoke detectors under numerous unfavorable conditions—would there be a significant radiation danger.

Photoelectric alarms are *not* as effective as the ionizing kind for detecting certain kinds of fires, notably fast-burning, smokeless ones, although they are better for smoky blazes. To provide double protection, some smoke alarms use both kinds of detector. There is unquestionably some risk involved in the use of a radioactive substance, but it is small compared to the risk of fire deaths that ionizing detectors are meant to prevent. It would be a great comfort to me if the Teeming Millions could learn to think rationally about such things.

At work I have occasion to use the Xerox machine. Since I am copying from books, I sometimes have to hold them in position while the light flashes and end up Xeroxing my hand. My question is this: do copying machines emit radiation? If so, what kind?— Office Worker, Los Angeles

Xerox machines absolutely ooze radiation—but it's radiation of a friendly and fairly harmless sort known as "light." No X-rays, or anything of that kind, are involved; it's a simple photographic process, not that much different from what happens in your Brownie.

No office is complete without the joker who likes to stick his face in the Xerox machine and reel off dozens of hysterically funny poses. Likewise, no office is complete without the stern secretary who continually warns said joker that by persisting in this quaint pursuit he will "ruin his eyes" by exposing them to deadly rays. Alas, this is not true. The most violent visual reaction that a Xerox machine can produce is an afterimage like that of a flashbulb. Even so, the Xerox Corporation, in its infinite vision, has put a joker-thwarting interlock device on its high-speed copiers, which use an extremely bright light. The flash won't flash unless the lid is closed. Once again man is saved from his baser instincts by corporate conscience.

Dentists, physicians, and certain industrial workers are considered "occupationally exposed" to radiation. Given the fact that an average cross-country flight in an airplane is bombarded with the same amount of radiation one might receive from an average series of dental X-rays, are airline pilots considered "occupationally exposed" too? The airlines seem to be keeping this a secret.—*Michael K., Baltimore*

Over the past decade or so the Federal Aviation Administration and the National Aeronautics and Space Administration have conducted various studies of the radiation hazard you describe, but to date airline workers have not been classified as occupationally exposed, and probably won't be in the near future. The radiation hazard arises from cosmic rays, chiefly high-speed protons and helium ions, as well as from solar radiation, which can get extremely intense during solar flares. In 1968 an English researcher estimated that a pilot flying a very heavy schedule (160 trips) might absorb 1,300 millirems per year, well above the maximum permissible dose of 500 millirems for the general public, but below the 5,000 millirem limit for radiation workers. Most subsequent studies, though, have found much lower average annual doses. A 1978 survey estimated the annual dose for flight crews to be around 160 millirems per year, which is not excessive.

Cosmic rays get more intense at higher altitudes as well as at higher latitudes, due to the shape of the earth's magnetic field. For that reason it was conjectured that supersonic transport flights over the polar regions (such as on the Paris-Washington route) might get a little hairy. The British-French SST, the Concorde, was equipped with radiation detectors that signaled the pilots when the 10-millirem-per-hour level was reached (during a solar flare, for instance). At 50 millirems per hour, the pilots were required to descend to a safer altitude. A report issued by the British government after a year of Concorde operation indicated that none of the alarms had ever gone off. Concorde pilots are limited to 500 hours' flying time per year (as opposed to 1,000 hours for crews on conventional aircraft), so that, given an average dose of 0.9 millirems per hour while flying at SST altitudes, their average annual exposure remains within recommended limits. On the other hand, it should be noted, flying time for cabin crews (stewards and stewardesses) is not so strictly governed, so their potential exposure may be greater.

THE TEEMING MILLIONS BEG TO DIFFER, PART TWO

You missed the boat entirely in your discussion of the occupational radiation exposure of airline flight crews. You note the results of a 1978 study which estimated the annual radiation dose to be around 160 millirems per year. You then conclude that this level of exposure is "not excessive."

You have evidently swallowed hook, line, and sinker the myth that there is some "safe" level of radiation exposure below which one will not experience any ill effects. The nuclear industry and the federal government have been hard at work brainwashing us to this effect for several decades. You need only read the 1980 Encyclopedia Britannica article "Hazards of Low Level Radiation" to learn that all exposure to ionizing radiation is harmful, that there is no dose so low that it may be considered safe, and that low doses may be even more harmful, per unit of exposure, than higher doses. It is well documented that radiation causes cancer, genetic diseases, and birth defects. Radiation also has been linked to an increased infant mortality rate, increased aging, and stroke.

The point is not that we shoould have an unreasoning fear of radiation. We've always lived with—and suffered from—a certain amount of "natural" radiation. Rather, we should try to minimize our radiation exposure from "unnatural sources"— radiation exposure which is the result of our human activities, and about which we can do something. Radiation is obviously of great benefit in many situations: medical X-rays, for example. But we should always be sure that the benefits of an increased radiation exposure outweigh the risks.

With regard to the increased radiation exposure incurred by airline flight crews, you'd have done better to inquire if there isn't some simple way of reducing this radiation exposure, e.g., by providing a thin layer of lead shielding in the upper part of the aircraft fuselage. Here there is an obvious, major benefit, fast air travel, and the risks may not be all that great. The risk should be minimized, but it cannot be done away with without eliminating jet planes.

With regard to the increased exposure we all get from nuclear power plants, the situation is different. Here the benefit is electricity, but there are several alternative ways of obtaining electricity which are much safer, more economical, and which expose us either to no radiation—e.g., conservation, wind power, and solar power—or to greatly reduced radiation—e.g., drastically cleaned-up coal plants. There is no need to incur the risks posed by the radiation exposure resulting from radioactive releases from nuclear power plants.—Edward G., Evanston, Illinois

I am going to be patient with you, Ed, because you seem reasonably intelligent, and thus may profit from instruction. Therefore, listen up. (1) When we are talking about the price of mangoes in Sumatra, I am not interested in having you drag in your opinions on the temperature of spit in Wichita. We were talking about the effect of cosmic rays on airline pilots, not nuclear power plants. (2) Make no blithe assumptions about what "boats" I may or may not have "missed," since they will usually be erroneous. I am well aware that there is no known dose threshold beneath which ionizing radiation can be said to be "safe." The mechanism of carcinogenesis is not well understood, but some believe that a single high-speed particle striking a cell nucleus in the right way can produce the biological event necessary to trigger cancer. (3) Do not lecture me on the obvious. Risk-benefit analysis has been a fundamental tool of both pro- and anti-nuke scientists since the dawn of the atomic age. It is a cold-blooded business. When I say that a certain radiation level is "not excessive," I do not mean that it is harmless; I mean that it will kill or maim a relatively small number of people. In the 1978 study, it was estimated that the biological effects of air travel on the U.S. population would be so small as not to be directly observable, but that purely from a statistical point of view it was likely that there would be 3 to 75 cases of disability due to genetic defects and 9 to 47 early cancer deaths over a period of years. Out of a population of 225 million, this was not thought to be significant. Some years ago, the possibility of outfitting jetliners with lead shielding was considered but rejected after it was calculated that carrying capacity would be substantially reduced in doing so.

Whether a risk is justifiable has more to do with ethics and politics than it does with biology. For the present a radiation dose limit of 500 millirems per year has been somewhat arbitrarily set for the general public. At this level, it is believed, only a few people will die before their time. Others are paid to subject themselves to higher risks. Radiation workers in the U.S., who presumably know what they're getting into, can be subjected to up to 5,000 millirems per year by their employers. One hopes that every conceivable precaution is taken, but nonetheless it is certain that a substantially higher percentage of these people will die as a result of their jobs than is true of the general public. In Europe there is an intermediate category of 1,500 millirems per year for workers who are incidentally exposed to radiation in the course of their jobs but who derive no direct economic benefit therefrom. This would include airline pilots, who could do their jobs just as well without cosmic rays, but excludes workers in nuclear power plants, who would be out of a job if there were no such thing as uranium-235. Readers may find discussions of this sort heartless, but essentially the same sort of calculation goes into estimates of death from coal dust.

What's the gig with these radiation-nullifying pills I've heard about? They supposedly build up the body's defense mechanisms against plutonium particles and the like. After seeing both The Day After *and* Testament *I am quite depressed and would rather munch pills than don a lead rain jacket. Do the pills work? If so, where could I score a bag?—C.F., Los Angeles*

Amazingly enough, antinuke pills are one of those screwball survivalist gimmicks that may actually help. Nuclear fallout, you see, contains radioactive iodine, which the body mistakes for ordinary iodine and absorbs into the thyroid, where it hangs around long enough to poison you. To prevent this, you can take a dose of a benign chemical called potassium iodide *before* a nuclear attack. This swamps your thyroid with good iodine, preventing the evil radioactive version from being absorbed. The Food and Drug Administration says potassium iodide is safe and effective and recommends that civil defense officials include it in their emergency planning. Note that PI will not cure radiation poisoning, nor will it prevent radiation injury from sources other than radioactive iodine. In a survivalist magazine the other day (no, I don't spend *all* my time reading survivalist magazines), I saw an ad offering a "doublepack" of PI (supposedly enough for two adults) for $10 plus $2 shipping. Twelve dollars strikes me as a little steep; I'd shop around if I were you. If we're going to have a nuclear holocaust, we might as well be thrifty about it.

How does the president of the United States "push the button"? What exactly happens? Can anybody do it?—Zvi F., Chicago

The popular expression notwithstanding, Zvi, when the prez wishes to obliterate mankind, he doesn't actually press any buttons. He uses the telephone. A bit banal, I suppose, but that is the nature of the 20th century. The president is accompanied at all times by an Air Force warrant officer carrying a thin black satchel containing the Emergency War Order (EWO) authentication codes. To launch a nuclear attack, the president calls up CINCSAC (commander in chief, Strategic Air Command, Omaha, Nebraska), uses the codes to establish that he is indeed the president, and gives his orders. The president's codes, it should be noted, are not "enabling" codes—that is, you don't actually have to punch them into the computers to initiate the firing sequence.

This is an important distinction, as we shall see.

CINCSAC, an Air Force general, sits on a Captain Kirk-like command chair on a balcony overlooking SAC's Underground Command Post. If the post were to be destroyed, command would automatically shift to a specially equipped E-4B jet, one of which is kept in the air at all times, or to one of several dozen other auxiliary command posts.

Having verified the president's orders—presumably several officers are involved in this for safety's sake, but the details are not clear—CINCSAC activates the Single Integrated Operational Plan, a command sequencing computer that electronically issues EWOs to the pertinent parties. Again, details are a little vague, but apparently two sorts of command are sent. The first is a message to bomber and missile crews containing instructions and a verification code, which the recipients are required to check against their own code books. The second command is purely electronic in nature, and arms each launch device via something called a Permissive Action Link, which is sort of a safety catch.

After each land-based missile command center confirms its orders, two crew members must simultaneously turn brass keys at control consoles some distance apart, casting one "launch vote." The crew in another command center some miles away does the same thing, and the two votes together launch 10-50 ICBMs. On submarines, two officers dial combinations into a special safe, do the same thing on another safe inside the first, get the brass key, and give it to the captain, who arms the missiles. Then four officers located in various parts of the vessel press buttons or turn still more keys to initiate launch. On bombers, two or three officers have to cooperate to arm the bombs.

How much of all this equipment will actually work is open to debate. Questions have been raised as to the reliability of the Worldwide Military Command and Control System, by which all orders are transmitted, and most of the land-based missile sites have never test-fired a missile. However, one assumes that a fair amount of destruction will occur.

Nobody outside the government really knows if anybody but the president can launch a nuclear strike. Pentagon officials have told congressional committees that the president is the only person so authorized, and that the legal line of succession would have to be followed were the president incapacitated. But the code system makes it physically possible for the military to fire missiles on its own, and nobody really believes that SAC would spend a lot of time hunting around for the vice-president if disaster were imminent. By the same token, it's not certain if anybody can overrule the president either. You may recall that in the final days of the Nixon administration then-Secretary of Defense James Schlesinger instructed commanders to report any "unusual" presidential orders to him before taking action, evidently out of a suspicion that Dick might decide to torch the planet out of pique. I cannot say that the situation fills me with confidence.

What is the Emergency Broadcast System? Does it tell me what to do when there's a flood, fire, pestilence, or hurricane, or is it used only just before we all get cooked? Why do they use that horrible noise?—Bill B., Los Angeles

The Emergency Broadcast System is a carryover from the Cold War days. Back in the 50s, the system was known as CONELRAD, and it was part of an anti-missile defense program. Supposedly, the Russkies had missiles that followed radio waves to their targets (see, Murray the K really *was* a threat to the nation's well-being), and CONELRAD told the stations to get off the air. The Russians now have much more sophisticated homing devices, and CONELRAD has accordingly been transmogrified. Today the Emergency Broadcast System is a sort of giant chain letter, intended to pass word of an impending disaster (nuclear, natural, or otherwise) as quickly as possible. It's run by a division of the Federal Communications Commission with the help of the Civil Defense people and the voluntary cooperation of all but two or three hundred of the nation's 9,000 radio and TV stations. When the governor of each state is notified of an impending disaster by the proper "authority"—the White House, the Department of Defense, or whatever—he calls a few key stations, which immediately broadcast the tone signal. Other stations, assigned to continuously monitor the key station, immediately broadcast their own signal, which is in turn picked up by still other stations assigned to monitor

241

them, and so on down the line. The entire state, supposedly, can be alerted in a matter of minutes.

The signal actually consists of two tones, chosen, for a variety of boring technical reasons, to trigger the electronic monitoring devices in each station. One tone isn't enough—imagine what would happen if Van Halen unknowingly released a single containing 20 seconds of the magic note (and they're just the ones to do it). National panic! On the other hand, the chances of Van Halen hitting on both notes simultaneously—hell, the chances of everybody in Van Halen even being in the *same key* simultaneously—are comfortingly remote.

Last night as I was putting my keys in my pocket, I was stricken with fear—is this glow-in-the-dark key ring doing harm by its proximity to several vital organs? As a child I demanded that disgusting varieties of cereal be purchased so that I could obtain a skull ring that, when taken into a closet, glowed an eerie green. Was the cereal contaminated? What is that stuff, and how does it work? Should I change to a rabbit's foot to hold my keys?—Joyce K., Oregon

The rabbit has more to worry about than you do. The phosphorescent pigments used in making glow-in-the-dark items do emit X-rays, but at such a low level that they're barely detectable. Phosphors absorb energy from visible light, ultraviolet light, and X-rays and for the most part return that energy in kind. All in all, they're not nearly as harmful as that flood of electromagnetic radiation we call sunlight.

The phosphor generally used in pigment is calcium sulfide, "activated" by bismuth, with additional traces of copper, silver, or lead. When light energy strikes the phosphor's atoms, some electrons are kicked up into high-energy orbits (I hope you remember your high school physics). Later, these electrons fall back down into their regular orbits, releasing some eletromagnetic radiation in the process, mainly in the form of visible light. Hence, phosphors work as a sort of energy storage system, gathering up light and slowly releasing it as the stimulated electrons return to normal.

As far as the phosphorescent trinkets in your cereal are concerned, the FDA has found no reason to classify them as anything different from the other giveaways that are packaged with food. Since they come in contact with the food surface, and generally have not been produced under health guidelines, the gimmicks must be packaged in an FDA-approved plastic or film. The problem is sanitation, not fallout.

242

Some phosphors, used mainly in watch dials, are genuinely radioactive. Instead of being activated by light, zinc sulfide crystals are stimulated by alpha rays, supplied by trace amounts of radium—no more than two parts per million—mixed into the pigment compounds. Again, the best information available at the moment finds no real threat in this low level radiation, and the amount of radium used is strictly controlled by no less an authority than the Nuclear Regulatory Commission. Still, radiation is a funny thing (ain't it?), and the scientific community is a long way from understanding all its effects. There's always the outside chance that your children will be born with softly glowing letters spelling "TIMEX" across their stomachs.

Chapter 13

〰〰〰〰〰〰〰〰〰〰〰〰〰〰〰

Technology

A friend of mine, impressed that in the past you have deigned to answer a few of my humble queries, has requested that I seek an audience with you for a mystery. His question is this: how do so-called odor-eating socks work? Now realize I would never ask such a question (I suspect deodorant or fraud). But this dear friend of mine is involved in the field of medicine; perhaps he feels ashamed not to know the answer to this one. Won't you please have pity and illuminate him?—Joyce K., Seattle

It's always a pleasure to hear from you, Joyce, because you have True Grit, unlike certain toads I could name. Also I appreciate your thoughtful enclosure of a double sawbuck, an excellent attention-getting device that I heartily commend to this column's loyal readers. But on to the socks. As you know, for countless eons mankind has been plagued by the problem of stinky feet. My father, for one, has a pair of pods that ought to be outlawed by the Geneva Convention. Fortunately, awesome scientific resources have been brought to bear on this matter in recent years, and the result is the High-Tech Sock, of which the Burlington Bioguard Sock is a representative example. In primitive low-tech socks, sweat from the soles of the feet collects next to the skin, providing a fertile breeding ground for the noxious bacteria that cause odor. Burlington Bioguard Socks, however, are made with a couple of synthetic inner layers and a cotton outer layer. The nonabsorbent synthetic layers convey moisture to the absorbent outer layer via capillary action, so that the feet remain relatively dry. In addition, the socks are treated with a potent antimicrobial agent made by Dow Corning, a sister company of the firm that once manufactured napalm. In other words, we ain't fooling around here, folks. The antimicrobial agent consists of a polymer known as silicone quaternary amine, which mercilessly annihilates offending bacteria (or more accurately, keeps them from breeding), thus preventing odor and prolonging the life of the sock. The stuff is relatively immune to the abrasive effects of laundering; Burlington claims it will last the life of the sock.

I have not yet had an opportunity to experiment on my father with Bioguard socks, and my mother is frankly of the opinion that in his case using deodrant socks is like fighting a forest fire with a squirt gun. However, persons with a less cynical outlook (or less pestilential feet) are cordially invited to give the aforementioned product a try.

Three questions occasioned by a recent plane trip to Denver: (1) How does a person with a steel plate in his head get through the airport security systems and onto his plane? You are allowed to fly if you have a metal plate in your head, aren't you? (2) At what altitude would a can of beer explode if it weren't in a pressurized airplane cabin? (3) Flying over western Iowa and eastern Nebraska, I saw for the first time in my life large circular patches of ground colored differently than the surrounding land—like the familiar rectangular patchwork patterns on farms, only round. What are they?—P.C., Washington, D.C.

(1) The walk-through metal-detection gates are only the first line of the airport security process. They beep or flash or whatever they do to warn a human security guard that the passenger just passed is carrying some heavy metal. The security guard then checks to satisfy him/herself that the metal detected is not of a dangerous sort; for this purpose, he/she is often equipped with a hand-held scanner, as well as eyes, fingers, and (presumably) a brain, with which he/she should be able to handle unusual and perplexing circumstances such as the one you describe.

(2) Conventional beer cans begin to fail at pressures of about 100 pounds per square inch during the pasteurization process, when the contents are heated to about 140 degrees Fahrenheit. Since atmospheric pressure is approximately 15 PSI at sea level, we deduce that a pressure differential of about 85 PSI is needed to induce rupture. The absolute pressure of the typical beer can's contents at room temperature is about 50 PSI, which means the greatest possible differential (achievable in a perfect vacuum, where atmospheric pressure is zero) is also 50 PSI. In other words, if you keep your beer at room temperature or below, you can get as high as you want without worrying.

(3) The curious round patches you've seen result from an

irrigation device known as a self-propelled boom, which is like a very large and elaborate lawn sprinkler. The boom is anchored in the center and, as you can plainly see, spreads water in a circular pattern, covering about 180 acres at a shot. The boom is usually only used in the Corn Belt during a season of poor rainfall.

The other night I went to see John Water's movie Polyester, *filmed in Odorama, which enables you to smell certain, ah, unique fragrances periodically via a "scratch-n-sniff" card. I was hoping you might be able to explain to me the principles of "scratch-n-sniff." How does it work and how can I make my own? I have some interesting Christmas card ideas.—Patrick W., Milwaukee*

Yeah, I'll bet you do, you deve. The basic S&S process, called Micro-Fragrance Coatings, was invented a decade or so ago by the 3M Company, and is intended for the transmission of cheerful fragrances such as daffodils and buttercups, and not some

disgusting reek such as you and your weirdo friends are likely to come up with. Smell, to begin with the basics, is a matter of molecules dislodging themselves from a substance's surface and finding their way into your nose. To get something's smell on paper, its molecules, or a lab-bred facsimile of same, must be distilled into a sort of perfume (i.e., a highly volatile liquid) that is insoluble in water. Then 3M emulsifies the liquid, which essentially means they dump it into a giant Waring blender and whomp the bejeebers out of it. Since oil and water don't mix, we end up with millions of tiny bubbles of essence suspended in liquid. By means of a magical proprietary process that 3M has sworn me never to reveal, the bubbles are then conveyed into a plastic goo, which can then be used like ink and printed onto (preferably) some sort of stiff card stock with a modified printing press. When the plastic carrier dries, the bubbles of liquid are trapped inside until you scratch (the card, I mean), whereupon they break open and become smellable. A similar process is used to make carbonless copy paper, only the bubbles are filled with a special chemical instead of a fragrance. When you press down your pen, the chemical is released from the back of the top copy and reacts with another chemical coated on the front of the second copy (got that?), producing the inky stuff that makes the copy. The bubbles, you may be interested to know, are something like half a thousandth of an inch in diameter and there are roughly 50 million to the square inch, so this is not something you can whip up in the kitchen. 3M will be pleased to knock some out for you, though, as long as you don't mind buying enough for 50,000 copies or so.

Why are manhole covers round? P.S.: This is no joke.—Barry L., Glendale, Arizona

Hey, man, the Straight Dope is always serious—it's *reality* that's a joke. The solemn truth is that manhole covers are round so some moron from Streets and Sanitation, or whatever it is they have out there in Glendale, won't be able to drop them accidentally into the manhole. Honest. Take squares, for instance. A square cover you can tip up on edge and drop through the hole on the diagonal, if you follow me. Similarly with ovals. A circular hole, however, will defy the most determined efforts in this regard, as a moment's thought will make plain. (Bear in mind that there's a lip around the inside of the manhole that the cover rests on; this effectively makes the diameter of the manhole about an inch less than that of the cover.) Manholes are thus one of the few things in the universe that are absolutely goofproof. Kinda reassuring, isn't it?

Typing is one skill I've never been able to master, but whenever I get hung up, I think of what the poor Chinese must have to go through with all the thousands of characters in their written language. Is there such a thing as a Chinese typewriter? If so, what's the point?—E.F., Phoenix

The Chinese have been manufacturing typewriters for decades, the standard model offering in the neighborhood of 1,500 selected characters. In 1962, the new improved *Hoang* model hit the market, packing a mind-numbing 5,850 characters on a keyboard that measured two feet by seventeen inches. A Chinese typist is considered excellent if he/she can handle eleven words a minute (at last, a job for Elizabeth Ray), which is still, apparently, somewhat faster than drawing the characters by hand.

Among the alphabetic languages, Cambodian poses the biggest threat to the typist with 74 letters. If you lived on sun-drenched Bougainville Island in the South Pacific, though, the secretarial life would be a blissful one. The native language, Rotokas, uses only eleven letters, a,b,e,g,i,k,o,p,r,t, and u. No problem.

I recently started a job that requires lots of work at a typewriter-style keyboard, and being of a logical bent, I am struck by how little sense the arrangement of letters on the keyboard makes. A common complaint. But last night, when I mentioned the matter to my wife after a long hard day at the office, she casually mentioned that she "read somewhere" (and of course does not remember where) that the keyboard was deliberately designed to put the most-used letters in the worst places. Could this be true? Is this the ultimate expression of man's inhumanity to man?—T.P., Wilmette, Illinois

If you ask me, T., Cocoa Puffs are the ultimate expression of man's inhumanity to man, but I suppose there will always be

differences of opinion on this point. As for the typewriter keyboard, your spouse's story is not far from the painful truth. The "qwerty" keyboard, so called for the top row of letters on its left-hand side, was devised to make things easy for the typewriter, not the typist. In what is generally considered the first "practical" typewriter—designed by an American inventor named Christopher Sholes and a group of cohorts in the late 1860s—the type, arranged in a sort of circular basket under the carriage, was prone to frequent jamming at typing speeds in excess of hunt-and-peck. (Another problem, by the way, was that type met paper on the underside of the cylinder, so the typist couldn't read the fruits of his or her labors without lifting up the carriage.) To solve the jamming problem, Sholes and company, who had originally arranged their keyboard in alphabetical order, decided to put the most commonly used letters (or what they thought were the most commonly used letters) as far apart as possible in the machine's innards. The next year, 1873, they turned their invention over to the Remington gun company of New York State, and their keyboard has been standard ever since, despite the fact that succeeding improvements in typewriter design quickly rendered it ridiculous.

Of course, a superior system exists. It's called the Dvorak Simplified Keyboard, or DSK, after inventor August Dvorak, who developed it while a professor at the University of Washington in Seattle. Among other improvements, the DSK puts all vowels in the "home row" of keys—the second row from the bottom—and favors the right hand slightly. Numerous studies have proved that it can be learned quite easily even by experienced typists, and that it makes for faster, less fatiguing, and more accurate typing than the conventional system. But habit, apparently, dies hard in the typing biz—the DSK was patented in 1932.

Living with a future ecologist is driving me crazy. She'll shut off the water while I'm brushing my teeth or turn off the lights while I'm in a five-minute shower. Isn't it harder on the generator to shut off a light for five minutes and then turn it back on than just leaving it on? Also, isn't it true that it takes more electricity to turn the lights on and off frequently than just to leave them on? Any info is welcome, as I am . . .—Infuriated, Chicago

Junior eco-buffs are a curse. I had a friend once who used to make me feel like I was squandering the nation's resources every time I spent more than 20 minutes in the shower, which was almost all the time, since I am an irrepressible shower aficionado. The only good way to deal with these people is chloroform. Use it liberally.

Now then: we will not discuss the water situation here, since it varies too much from time to time and from region to region to make generalizations possible. Electricity, however, is another matter. Humbling as it may seem, it doesn't make any appreciable difference to the generator what you do with your lights, since several hundred thousand consumers are on the same line as you are. Where it does make a difference is in (a) your electric bill and (b) your light bulb bill, particularly for fluorescent lights. At one time, manufacturers strongly advised against switching your fluorescent fixtures on and off frequently, because you could reduce tube life as much as 20 percent. You may recall that some downtown office buildings used to leave their lights on all night on the theory that it was cheaper to burn the extra juice than to send a maintenance worker around every few months to change the tubes. However, the 70s saw the introduction of longer-lasting, rapid-start tubes that last 20,000 hours, as opposed to 10-12,000 with the old ones, and these you can flick on and off with greater abandon, since you'll only be reducing tube life from 5 to 10 percent. But don't make an obsession out of it. The rule of thumb is that if you're going to be out of the room for more than 15 minutes, you'll save money by turning out the lights. Thus you may brazenly leave the lights going for the five minutes it takes you to get through with your shower. Frankly, taking a shower in the dark seems like a pretty daredevil proposition to me. Your woman may have motives other than conservation on her mind.

If you've got incandescent bulbs, you needn't sweat the possibility of burning them out or wasting electricity by diddling the switch too much. It does take a slight extra shot of electricity—called the "inrush current"—to boost the tungsten filament of a bulb up to operating temperature, but the amount involved is less than it would take to burn the bulb continously even for only a second or two. On the other hand, if you do go to all the trouble of shutting off your 100-watt bathroom light for an extra five minutes every morning, you'll save all of about three kilowatt hours per year—where I live, less than 50 cents' worth. Whoopee.

The effective way to conserve power is by replacing wasteful incandescent bulbs with cooler fluorescents and, more importantly, by buying more energy-efficient appliances, since it's the big items that consume 90 percent of your electricity.

We're always fascinated by reports of ancient cultures like the Incas who performed great feats of civilization despite the fact that the wheel was unknown to them. But how could a halfway with-it civilization not invent the wheel? Rocks roll. Lighting knocks down trees and the trunks roll. Skulls roll. It must have been the axle, specifically, that they didn't invent, but it shouldn't take Isaac Newton to think of an axle. Was there some cultural commitment to dragging litters and hoisting loads on beasts of burden (and slaves) that inoculated these civilizations against the concept of wheels?—Eddie Yuhas and Al Brazle, Chicago

Yuhas and Brazle, huh? Boy, we don't get too many retired Cardinals pitchers writing in to the Straight Dope. Glad to see you guys are still keeping your minds occupied.

Now, then: let's not be too critical of the Incas. First of all, we must take note of a peculiar pattern here: it wasn't just the Incas who failed to invent the wheel; every other civilization in the New World (with one exception, which we will discuss by

and by) managed to overlook it as well. For that matter, the ancient Americans also had to struggle along without the true arch, the cart, the plow, the potter's wheel, the bellows, glass, iron, and stringed instruments. But it's unfair to attribute this pathetic technological record to either an excess of stupidity or (as far as the wheel was concerned) an infatuation with transport via brute strength. The fact is that most civilizations in the Old World didn't invent the wheel either—instead, they borrowed it from some other culture. The wheel appears to have been first used in Sumer in the Middle East around 3500 BC, whence it spread across Europe, Asia, and North Africa. It didn't arrive in Britain until 500 BC. This orderly diffusion pattern makes it conceivable that all the wheels in use today are directly descended from the invention of a single gifted individual—an individual, however, who was such a chump that he failed to sign his name on the patent application, thus assuring his (or her) eternal anonymity. We might therefore attribute Inca wheellessness to the absence of a pre-Columbian Thomas Edison.

But there are other factors involved. The principle of rotary motion, as you point out, is pretty obvious, and was well known throughout the New World as well as the Old. The Incas, for instance, are thought to have used wooden rollers to haul the giant stones they used to build their cities. Unfortunately, the New World suffered from a conspicuous lack of draft animals. The only beast of burden known in the Americas was the llama, a delicate critter restricted to certain parts of the Andes, which was used solely as a pack animal. Without draft animals you cannot do extensive hauling with sledges, and without sledges it will never occur to you that the wheel would be a handy thing to have around. When the Incas had to transport heavy objects, they relied on manpower, often to the considerable sorrow of the men doing the powering (some 3,000 of 20,000 workers died dragging one particularly massive stone, according to chronicles). Consequently heavy hauling in the New World was restricted to the occasional special project. The Sumerians, on the other hand, had considerable experience with what we might call regularly scheduled sledge service, and even so it took them 2,000 years of fumbling around before the idea of the wheel finally dawned on them. Not that it just popped out of the blue. The general sequence of friction-reducing inventions is thought to have been runners, rollers, rollers held in place by guides, rollers held in place by guides and thickened on the ends to make them roll straighter, the wheel and axle, and finally the Chevy Impala.

It is interesting to note, by way of conclusion, that the wheel evidently *was* familiar to the ancient Mexicans, the only known instance of its having been invented independently of the Sumerian version. Unfortunately, it apparently never occurred to anyone at the time that wheels had any practical application, and their use was confined to little clay gadgets that are thought to be either toys or cult objects. Another example of good technology gone to waste. Reminds me of Pac-Man.

Something has puzzled me for years. Suppose I worked on the 110th floor of the Sears Tower. Nature has reminded me it's time to relieve myself of last evening's supper. Now, I can't imagine the pileup of poop that would splatter all over the Wacker Drive sewer system if the stuff went straight down the tube. Do they have some kind of diversionary piping system, or does it indeed drop 1,450 feet to street level?—T.J. Crapper, Chicago

Modern architecture is supposed to remind us of the glories of civilization, T., not toilets. Let's try to get our minds out of the gutter in the future. As for your question, the answer is no, the stuff doesn't drop in a straight shot from the top floors. There are offsets in the soil pipes every so often where the water runs horizontally for a short distance and then down again. Some of these were included just as a matter of convenience—the pipes were in the way of something else—and others were put in for the express purpose of slowing down the water.

The problem with water running downhill and picking up a lot of momentum is not as severe as it might seem at first thought. For one thing, flowing water tends to adhere to a surface, such as the inside of a pipe, and the friction slows things down a good deal. There's also a phenomenon known as "terminal velocity," which skydivers are familiar with: after you fall through the air for a certain period, you reach a maximum speed. For water inside a pipe, this usally comes out to around 10 to 20 feet per second, depending on the diameter of the pipe and whatnot.

The more serious difficulty in a drain system of any kind (not just Sears's) is venting. Bathroom waste releases a lot of gases, which have to escape somewhere. Additionally, when you have a large volume of water falling down a stack, the air beneath has to get out of the way without creating a lot of turbulence—the glug effect, to put it in technical terms. To alleviate both problems, vent pipes are cut into the soil stacks at regular intervals to help relieve the pressure.

Waste water runs into a catch basin below street level and thence into the city sewer system. Toilets on the basement levels drain into a sump at the very bottom of the building, the contents of which are pumped up to sewer level from time to time.

The real challenge in Sears Tower was not so much getting the water down—after all, gravity does most of the work—as getting it up there in the first place. Street pressure is only good for the first four or five floors in an ordinary building. Sears has a series of pumps and tanks located in the basement, the 31st floor, the 64th floor, and the 88th floor. Water is pumped up under high pressure from one tank to the next, and then drains to the faucets in bathrooms and other facilities below. A few fixtures operate directly off the high-pressure line by means of pressure-relief valves.

Plumbing is a fascinating topic, no doubt about it. Come on up to the office sometime and I'll explain about male and female pipe fittings.

I have a theory that, as a nation, we could save about 10 percent of our gasoline consumption by the simple expedient of making

253

sure our tires are fully inflated. My questions are: (1) What is the relationship between underinflation and gas mileage deterioration (e.g., 20 percent underinflation reduces mileage 10 percent, etc.)? (2) What is the trade-off between tire inflation and tire life? (3) Do the auto manufacturers in fact specify too low an inflation level for tires in order to soften the ride?—Dirk V., Evanston, Illinois

The trick in proper tire inflation is to pump in as much air as is safely possible without reducing the traction necessary for acceleration, braking, and handling. Too little air causes your tires to flatten out under load, and the resulting distortion means increased "rolling resistance" (drag) and decreased gas mileage. Too little air also means your tires will be getting an uneven grip on the road, which will cause some portions (typically the outside edges) to wear more quickly than usual, shortening tire life.

A typical tire with a maximum recommended pressure of 32 pounds per square inch has a safe pressure range of 24-32 PSI. Variations within that range won't affect traction that much, but they will affect your gas mileage, ride quality, and tire life. At 24 PSI you'll get a softer ride but lower mileage and faster tread wear, while at 32 PSI you'll get a rougher ride but higher mileage and longer tire life. Not surprisingly, in pre-energy crisis days auto makers recommended 24 PSI, but nowadays a lot of them recommend 30 or 32.

In recent years the relentless march of technology has enabled manufacturers to significantly improve the gas mileage you can get with their products. Radial tires, for instance, will give you about 4 percent better mileage than bias-ply tires because their more rigid construction makes them less likely to flatten out under load. In addition, many of the current generation of tires—the so-called P-metrics—are designed to be inflated to as much as 35 PSI, increasing their resistance to distortion. Goodyear makes several lines of all-season radials (Arriva came out in the late '70s, and Vector was introduced during the winter of 1984) which can be inflated to 35 PSI and which also use an unusually rigid, nonsticky rubber compound to reduce drag even more. Such tires give you about 2-5 percent better mileage than conventional radials, and about 7-9 percent better than bias-ply tires. Other manufacturers have similar products.

The relation between air pressure and mileage goes something like this: 10 percent underinflation (with 24 PSI being the norm), 5 percent mileage loss; 20 percent under, 15 percent loss; 25 percent under, 20 percent loss. As for pressure/tread life, 15 percent underinflation means 10 percent loss of tread life; 25 percent under, 20 percent loss; 50 percent under, 40 percent loss. These figures are meant to give you the basic idea and are subject to considerable fluctuation depending on individual conditions.

By the same token, if you *increase* pressure from 24 to 30 PSI, you'll increase your gas mileage about 3-4 percent (more in some cases) and your tire life maybe 3-6 percent. As a general rule, the best thing to do is check the maximum safe pressure printed on the side of the tire and maintain inflation at or slightly below that level. (Caution is advised with older tires. For accuracy's sake, make sure you check pressure when the tire is cold, using your own gauge if possible.) The ride may be a tad on the rocky side, but think how patriotic you'll feel.

Lately I've been running into urinals in women's restrooms. I have tried using them in pants and skirts, but the only way I can figure they would work is if the woman were naked or not wearing any underwear. Who invented the infernal contraptions, how are they intended to work, and why are they cropping up more and more?— K.L., Baltimore

Actually, they're not cropping up more and more—you're just frequenting a broader variety of public restrooms. Most major American manufacturers discontinued women's urinals for various reasons 15 or more years ago. They were introduced into this country from Europe in the early 30s (along with the bidet, which is still being made), and were intended as a convenience for women who did not want their delicate flesh coming into contact with verminous public toilet seats. They came in both floor- and wall-mounted models, in the latter manifestation looking very much like men's urinals, and could be used either with stalls or lined up like their male counterparts. Basically the urinals featured a protruding narrow bowl that the user was expected to straddle while facing the wall, having first lowered her panties and hiked up her skirt, whereupon she could unload whatever bodily fluids she had a mind to.

Cecil's experience in this department is regrettably limited, but he cannot imagine that shuffling hither and yon with your undies around your ankles makes for a significantly more satisfactory urinary experience than the conventional potty. Apparently women felt the same way, because the popularity of the fixtures declined significantly in the 60s, resulting in their ultimate demise. One problem may have been that women's underwear manufacturers never managed to come up with an equivalent to the male underpant, which is laden with useful apertures that greatly facilitate the use of urinals. Another likely factor was the increasing popularity of women's pants, which make using a urinal something of a trial. You still see the fixtures around, since proprietors of public lavatories are loath to discard serviceable equipment, but they are gradually being replaced by the ordinary flush toilet.

Why does the post office insist on stamping a little blue "T22" on the picture side of all the postcards I get? Is this some anti-aesthetic postal purge? Make 'em 'fess up, Cecil!—Steve K., Chicago

In Postal Service parlance, those tiny blue numbers are affectionately known as MPLSM marks, which stands for Multi-Position Letter Sorting Machine. Deep in the bowels of the main post office in Anytown, U.S.A. (or at least Any *Big* Town), hundreds of dedicated public servants sit hunched over their MPLSMs, feeding the zip codes on every letter that passes before them into a computer, which makes sure (ideally) that mail is sent to the proper substation. Every time an operator records a zip code, his ID number (T22, L3, B6 or whatever) is stamped on the letter. This allows the post office to trace a letter back to its starting point in the case of foul-ups, so that the perpetrator can be congratulated and/or promoted (joke). If there is no identifying mark on your mail, that means your letter was sorted by hand. Unfortunately, since the address has to face the operator, the machines are designed to stamp the code number on the back side of the mail—which means, in the case of postcards, the picture side. The Postal Service offers it apologies and begs you to realize that progress always has a price.

How did they mass-produce those old-fashioned cylinder records? A conventional molding press, like they use for discs, would leave some sort of line where the two halves met, which would show up as a click or thump when the cylinder was played. How did they make 3-D moldings of such accuracy in the 1890s? Or did the artistes just make the same recording over and over again?— Winfield S., Chicago

Indeed they did, at least at the beginning—and it just about drove them nuts, too. The need for a cheap and easy method of reproduction was one of the first problems the early recording industry faced, and the problem you describe was one of the reasons why cylinders lost out to discs as the principal recording medium.

In the *very* beginning, of course, a little thing like a seam on the recording surface didn't matter too much. On Edison's original phonograph, the ends of the tinfoil sheet that recorded the sound were just tucked into a slot that ran the length of the metal cylinder that the foil was wrapped around. You did get a click this way, but since you also got an indescribable cacophony of burps, wheezes, and rasps, the first recording device being a little on the rustic side, you did not mind the clicks so much. Later, the recording blanks were made of wax, which could be cast in one piece, eliminating the click, if nothing else.

When records first began to be sold commercially, the only way to make additional copies was to have the artistes make the same recording over and over. You would hire, say, a brass band, which you would surround with a phalanx of recording machines loaded with blank discs, and you'd get some guy with a suitably stentorian voice to go around to each machine, flip it on for a second, and holler the title of the piece into the speaking horn. Then you'd turn on all the machines at once, and the band would play as much of any given tune as would conveniently fit onto the cylinders, which was generally about two minutes' worth. Then you changed cylinders and started over. Apart from being stupefyingly monotonous for the performers, this method was very slow.

Eventually somebody hit on the idea of recording additional cylinders of a master cylinder by means of a pantograph, which was an arrangement of levers and wires that transmitted the sound vibrations from the stylus on the master disc to that on the receiving disc. This was faster and less boring, but the masters tended to wear out quickly, and then the band had to go at it again.

Finally, around the turn of the century, Edison's phonograph company developed a reliable method for mass production. They coated the wax master with a thin layer of gold by an electrical process, coated the gold layer with a copper layer for strength, then melted out the original wax. This left a negative metal mold. Then they put a wax blank inside and applied heat and pressure. When the wax was cooled, it shrank a little. In addition, the master and blank were tapered slightly—one end was slightly wider than the other. The combination of shrinkage and taper was enough to let them slip the master off the copy without (a) damaging it, or (b) leaving a seam.

Actually, this method had occurred to Edison and his buddies fairly early on, but the first recording styli gouged out such deep grooves that the shrinkage wasn't enough to enable them to clear.

The development of the sapphire-tip sylus, which made shallower indentations, cleared up this problem.

Unfortunately, by the time they got all this worked out, cylinders were beginning to decline in favor of discs, which were longer playing, among other things. So it was all for nothing, as is often the case in the record business.

Can you tells us stereo freaks what causes the sound on a record which is like a faint pre-echo of the music (if that makes sense) at the very beginning of a song? I have noticed this on more than one record but not all.—Neil M., Los Angeles

Recording engineers call the phenomenon you describe "print-through," and say it originates in the tape recordings that are used to produce records. The coating on recording tape has a magnetic field that penetrates a short distance into space. When the tape is wound up on a reel, it's possible under certain conditions for the field on one layer of tape to imprint a faint duplicate of itself onto the layer next to it. This can occur on both rewind and take-up, but it's most noticeable on rewind because the phantom signal ends up being printed on the blank stretch of tape that precedes every cut, producing what you call "pre-echo." To reduce the problem, most tapes in professional studios are stored "tail-out," meaning the tape must be rewound before playing. To further improve matters, you can adjust the bias on the recorder, use a thicker back-coated tape, record at a lower level, or simply keep the tape away from high temperatures. Some of these remedies cause other problems, such as more noise or poorer high frequency response, so what you shoot for is a happy medium. Eventually the whole thing, "pre-echo" and all, gets transferred from the master tape to the disc. On direct-to-disc recordings, which are made without the intervention of tape, there is no pre-echo. Science marches on.

What's so special about the record speeds 33, 45, and 78 RPM except that 33 plus 45 equals 78? How and why were these speeds chosen?—John L., Dallas

Like many things in this world, John, the various record speeds were determined by chance and compromise, the compromise in this case being between playing time and fidelity. The slower a record revolves, the longer it plays and the worse it sounds. Slow speeds are acceptable for spoken-word recordings (many early "talking books" were recorded at 16⅔ RPM), but not for music, where sound quality is critical.

Thomas Edison's first phonographs were hand cranked, which made a single standard speed virtually impossible. The listener cranked the machine at whatever speed "sounded right," which usually worked out to around 80 RPM. That was slow enough to get five minutes of material (then, as now, the average length of a popular song) onto one of Edison's five-inch cylinders, and fast enough to provide what passed in those days for decent fidelity.

When Emile Berliner invented the disc record in 1888, he designed it to meet the loose standards of the Edison cylinder— five minutes of playing time at 70 to 80 RPM. Formal standardization—at 78.26 RPM—didn't come until 1925, when the phonograph was married to the electric motor. 78.26 happened to be the speed a common, mass-produced 3600 RPM motor would yield if fitted with an equally common 46:1 gear.

Around this same time the original acoustic method of recording was made obsolete by a new, and far superior, electric system. The fidelity possible at 78 RPM could now be had at a much slower speed—33⅓. But the record manufacturers felt that the fickle public—then deserting the phonograph in favor of a newer novelty, the radio—would be put off by the cost of converting from 78 to 33⅓, and so, through the twenties and thirties, the process was used only in studios and radio stations. In 1931, RCA Victor badly bungled an attempt to put a cheap, imperfect 33⅓ system on the mass market, and no one tried it again until 1948, when Columbia Records introduced Dr. Peter Goldmark's new "microgroove" system. Columbia shrewdly pitched the new "LPs" to classical music collectors, pointing out that the longhair listener could now settle back and enjoy an entire movement of a symphony without the annoyance of changing the disc every five minutes.

Hoping to set 33⅓ as the new standard, Columbia offered the process free to any company that cared to use it. But RCA Victor, still licking its corporate wounds after the 1931 debacle, would have none of it, and promptly made what looked like another bonehead move; dumping an entirely new system—45 RPM— on the market. Just as Emile Berliner had adapted his disc to meet the standard of the Edison cylinder, RCA had designed the 45 to conform to the 78—it offered the same playing time, somewhat improved fidelity, and the dubious advantage of being more "convenient" because the discs were smaller. In presenting the 45, RCA unloaded some drivel about how 45 RPM was the optimum speed for sound reproduction, but it was revealed that in fact RCA had told its engineers to come up with any old speed so long as it wasn't compatible with Columbia's system. The big hole was apparently supposed to make the two types of records even more incompatible.

Thus began the so-called "war of the speeds." Since 45s offered few real advantages over the old 78s, most of the smaller manufacturers opted for the Columbia system. RCA, though, held out for 18 months, during which time industry sales volume dropped 25 percent as consumers waited for the giants to fight it out between themselves. Finally, in 1950, RCA capitulated—sort of. It began making 33⅓ records using the Columbia system, but it didn't discontinue the 45. Instead, it spent $5 million advertising 45 RPM as the preferred speed for popular music. In reality, of course, the speed didn't make any difference; a 7-inch record was simply more convenient for single tunes than a 12-inch one. Nonetheless, the public allowed itself to be duped, and in 1951 Columbia began making 45s too. Thus we ended with one speed and spindle size for popular songs, and another for symphonies. The 78, mercifully, was out of the picture by 1950.

Actually, the whole concept of constant turntable speed has been obsolete since the turn of the century. At a constant turntable speed, the velocity of the grooves moving past the stylus decreases as the record plays—the inner spirals of the track being, of course, much smaller than the outer ones, circumference-wise. If the groove speed were held constant instead of the turntable speed (in much the same way that a reel of film plays out at a steady 24 frames a second), it would be possible to record over 90 minutes of material on a single side, with greater fidelity and a lessened potential for damage to the record. A few phonographs designed on this principal were marketed in the early 1900s. But technology is one thing and show biz is another. For obvious commercial reasons—just imagine how much *more* crap Barry White would need to pad out an album—this line of development has never been pursued.

Please tell me about cabooses. Why are they called "cabooses"? Why are they always at the rear of the train? Wouldn't they be more accessible if they were directly behind the locomotive? Also, I've never seen anyone traveling from the locomotive to the caboose or vice versa while the train is in motion. Do they? How? Is there plumbing in a caboose? If so, where does it empty? Is there electricity? Could you watch Monday Night Football *in a caboose? Why don't passenger trains have a caboose?—Cliff N., Chicago*

In the old days, Cliff, you could have asked your father a

this stuff. Sometimes I long for the return of the nuclear family.

The caboose is in the back of the train mainly because the engine is in the front—that is, because you need somebody at both ends to throw switches and put out signal flares and do other railroad-type chores. In addition, the people in the back are supposed to keep an eye out for derailments, overheated wheel bearings, and other untoward incidents. On a typical cross-country freight you have a five-man crew, with the engineer, fireman (assistant engineer), and head-end brakeman in the engine cab and the conductor and the rear-end brakeman in the caboose. (Some railroads, I understand, have smaller crews.) They communicate by radio and under ordinary circumstances never travel from one end of the train to the other. If for some reason a trainman did feel the urge to visit his distant brethren, he would either have to get out and walk or, if he were in the engine, get out and wait until the caboose caught up with him. Certain uninformed Hollywood screenwriters have never grasped this signal fact, and one will thus occasionally see TV trainmen who run across the tops of the cars, or, even more implausibly, sling themselves from hand to hand along the sides. This invariably generates buckets of yucks among the nation's railroaders.

"Caboose" comes from the German *Kabuse*, meaning hut, and was first used in 1855 to describe the cabin cars of the Buffalo, Corning and New York Railroad. The caboose we know today, complete with cupola on top from which the crew watches the train, was invented in 1863 by one T.B. Watson, a conductor on the Chicago and North Western. Cabooses these days are admirably equipped, featuring (sometimes) refrigerators and air conditioning, with power suppled by a generator which may be run off the caboose's wheels, after the manner of a bicycle generator. There is a primitive john in the caboose, which empties onto the tracks. Passenger trains do not need cabooses because the crew can walk back and forth freely between cars and because passenger trains are much shorter to begin with. I suppose, by way of conclusion, that you could watch *Monday Night Football* in a caboose if you wanted to, presuming it was Monday night, but TV watching on the job is a practice upon which progressive railway management frowns.

I don't consider myself stupid (I read the Straight Dope), but I was curious why plastics can't be recycled. Or can they?—D.K., Urbana, Illinois

Sure they can. Problem is, there are dozens of kinds of plastic used in innumerable applications and they all have to be recycled separately. At present there's no practical way of sorting them. Some environmentalists have suggested that industries making extensive use of plastics for things like packaging—e.g., the food processing biz—settle on one or two basic varieties, to simplify sorting. Apart from that problem, plastics are excellent candidates for recycling, because most of the energy that goes into their manufacture is consumed during the initial formation of the polymers, the molecule chains from which plastics derive. As anyone who has ever owned one of those toy injection molders can tell you, many plastics are readily remelted and re-formed. It's estimated that recycling polyethylene, too cite one example, could save up to 90 percent of the energy involved in that commodity's original production. Sounds like Olivia Newton-John's got a great future ahead of her.

Is it possible to roll or loop a 747 or DC-10 loaded or empty? I have a bet with my roommate and he says the wings would shear off. I say it could because otherwise they would't allow it to fly people.—Todd J., Evanston.

I don't know that I quite follow you there, Toddles, but experience has shown it is never wise to inquire too deeply into the thought processes of the Teeming Millions. No one has ever tried to get fancy with one of the big birds, but there once was a Boeing test pilot who, in a moment of frivolity, took it into his head to execute a barrel roll in a 707. He made it, but he didn't exactly endear himself to his superiors. The consensus at Boeing seems to be that a 747 would probably survive a barrel roll, but to try it would be, and I quote, "an extremely foolish action." The problem is not so much with the strength of the wings, which are designed to stand much greater pressures, as with the skill of the pilot. Enough forward speed must be maintained during the roll to compensate for the loss of lift that occurs when, in effect, the wings cease to function. That happens when the wings are perfectly perpendicular to the ground—in the vertical position, they can no longer hold the plane up. In a small plane, the problem is minimal: the wings spin out of the vertical position in a split second. But in a larger plane that takes longer to roll, the margin for error is increased, and the fatal moment could be stretched out enough to pull the plane down.

Looping a 747 or a DC-10 would be trickier still. (Bear in mind that a "roll" means you flip to the right or left; a "loop" is roughly analogous to a backwards somersault.) You'd have the

262

problem of lift again, at the moment when the tail is down, but it would be harder to overcome, since the plane must be climbing, not merely maintaining its altitude, at the same time. One way to get a plane to climb is to make it go faster (increasing the speed increases the air pressure under the wings, which is what holds the plane up in the first place). But there's some doubt as to whether a 747 or a DC-10 could achieve enough forward speed to deliver the extra shot of lift that a loop would require. Boeing suspects its planes could make it, but since no one has ever been silly enough to try, there's no way of knowing for sure. So it looks like your bet is a draw.

Cecil, old buddy, even though I am receiving a doctorate this spring, the old adage that the more you learn the less you know still holds true. So tell me this: how does a gas station pump know when to turn off before spilling gallons of gas onto the pavement?—Ethel Pumper, Dallas

Pal, you're going to *need* a doctorate to understand the following, so cleanse your mind of distracting thoughts. In a gas pump handle you have two valves: the main valve, which is actuated by the oversize trigger you squeeze to make the gas flow, and the check valve, which lets gas flow out but won't let anything back in again, thus reducing fire hazard. In the seat of the check valve you have a little hole. To the backside of this hole is connected a Y-shaped tube. One branch of this tube runs down the nozzle and exits at the tip while the other runs back to a diaphragm connected to a release mechanism on the main valve. When you squeeze the gas pump trigger, gas running past the hole in the check valve sucks air out of the Y-shaped tube. (This is because of the Bernoulli principle: a moving stream of fluid tends to pull things in from the sides. Take my word for it.) As long as the end of the Y-shaped tube exiting at the spout is unobstructed, air is simply pulled into the tube and nothing much else happens. However, as soon as the gas in your car's fill-up pipe gets high enough to cover the end of the tube, a partial vacuum is created therein, which yanks on the diaphragm, releases the main valve, and shuts off the gas. If the gas happens to be especially foamy one day, it may actuate the release mechanism prematurely, with the result that you end up with less than a full tank of gas. Simple, huh? Sure, just like nuclear fission. Stick with English lit.

Chapter 14

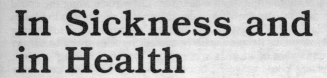

In Sickness and in Health

Due to our capitalist medical "system," there are a number of things that I can't get the answer to because I can't afford a doctor. First, I can wiggle my eyes. That is, I can make them shimmy rapidly a small distance back and forth. No one else I know can do that. Is it normal? Second, I can do something inside my body which results in a strange sensation. It feels like it is around my stomach or below. What is it?—W.C., Baltimore

First off, please don't mistake good old Uncle Cecil for a qualified diagnostician. If you think you have a problem, get it checked out. There are many ways of getting around the "capitalist medical system," one of which is called Not Paying Your Bills.

The eye condition you describe is normal, up to a point. It's called nystagmus, "the involuntary oscillation of the pupil," and we all do it when our eyes have to change focus rapidly. For example, when you're driving down the highway and turn to look at the telephone poles along the side of the road, your eyes jump from one pole to the next, keeping each in focus for a split second. However, when you can wiggle your eyes at will, it's a sign of something abnormal, although not necessarily dangerous. Medical science classifies at least nine different degrees of pathological nystagmus—it can be totally innocuous (a "parlor trick," as one medical dictionary describes it), or it can be a sign of brain damage, in which case you're dead by now. No doubt it's nothing to worry about, but I still wouldn't keep it up too long for the sake of amusing your friends. The muscles involved can be strained, and hurt your ability to keep your eyes in focus.

As for that strange sensation in your stomach . . . well, either you're belching, tightening the muscle that holds your guts in, or dying of any one of several hundred exotic diseases. There's no way to tell, sport—see a doctor if it bugs you.

Is there any way known to science that a male (age 24) could increase his height? I heard on a talk show recently that by way of a special operation, dwarfs and midgets were able to increase their height by as much as three inches! It had always been my understanding that once you passed the age of 21, you were about as tall as you were going to get. I realize that genes have quite a bit to do with growth patterns, but unfortunately, I come from a background of short-gened people. Can you fill me in so that maybe someday I could look the rest of the world square in the eye instead of square in the chest?—Jeff R., Chicago

I don't mean to be disrespectful, Jeff, but if you want to look people in the eye your best bet is to buy a periscope. There are a couple ways to increase height in people who have glandular or other health problems, but generally they are only effective

before age 21, and in any event they are not recommended for healthy persons who are simply short.

Perhaps the most drastic procedure is an operation used occasionally when one leg is significantly shorter than the other. Typically what happens is that the femur, or upper leg bone, is severed, and an intricate stretching apparatus is attached to both ends. Over a period of three weeks, during which time the patient is kept immobile, the implanted device is stretched out by means of an external crank, thus lengthening the limb by as much as two inches. The operation is quite risky; complications result about half the time. It is recommended only in extreme cases involving children or adolescents and in no event would it be used on both limbs simply to make you taller.

In cases where there is a gland defect—i.e., where the hormones secreted in your body are insufficient to induce normal growth—you can take snythetic hormones to make up for what your body forgets to supply. But this treatment is intended primarily for people who were "meant" to be taller, genetically speaking, not for people who are normal but short. In any case, I must emphasize, you can only do it while quite young. Allow me to elaborate.

Before the age of 21, your pituitary gland secretes large amounts of "growth hormone," or GH. There is an unpronounceable chemical name for this, but forget about that. Among other things, GH stimulates the growth of cartilage at the ends of your long bones (such as in your arms and legs), and this cartilage eventually hardens into bone. The areas where the cartilage forms are called "epiphyseal plates," and although they are quite spongy during youth, at age 21 or so they rigidify (or fuse, in medical jargon). Cartilage development ceases, and you don't get any taller. Once this occurs, no amount of GH will have any effect on your height. If you took synthetic GH as an adult, your hands and feet would become abnormally large, you'd develop an apelike jaw, and in general you'd look like a freak—but you'd be the same height.

True, ten years ago, while you were still in your teens, you could have dosed yourself with GH, and you might be taller today. But you'd have two potential problems. First, using synthetic hormones tends to suppress the production of natural hormones, meaning you're goofing up your body chemistry. Second, GH controls bone growth, so you could end up tall but spindly. You could administer muscle hormones, too, I suppose, but you must understand that you're horsing around with an extremely intricate system that is at best imperfectly understood today. You'd be taking an enormous risk of developing undesirable side effects just to gain a couple inches of height, and most doctors would say it wasn't worth the danger.

In short—I had not meant to stick a pun in there, but I see one has sprung up spontaneously—you are going to have to learn to like staring at chests. If you are choosy about your chests, I might say, this could work out quite advantageously. At any rate, you could have worse problems.

Recently, I discovered that I had hypoglycemia, or low blood sugar. On my doctor's advice, I've given up coffee, alcohol, and cigarettes because of their effect on my blood sugar. But I didn't feel comfortable asking my doctor how marijuana affects blood sugar levels. Could you tell me whether I need to give up the last of my simple pleasures?—Anonymous, Los Angeles

A good deal of research and federal money has been poured into the problem of how marijuana affects blood sugar levels. Some scientists thought, at first, that if marijuana significantly reduced blood sugar, that it might account for the furious attacks of hunger (known as "munchies," in vulgar street parlance) familiar to every marijuana user (known as "vipers," in vulgar street parlance). Millions of dollars and millions of "reefers" (vulgar street parlance for "marijuana cigarettes") later, the researchers concluded that dope smoking had no significant or consistent effect on blood sugar—and that, therefore, their hypothesis wasn't worth a hill of beans. Bad news for them, good news for you. Sounds like you could use some.

One of us is getting gray hair. He is only 22 and vain. Why is this happening? Does this mean he won't go bald? Do dark-haired people turn gray earlier or is it only more noticeable? There's some speculation that it means he's run out of pigment. Could this be true?—A friend, Tempe, Arizona

The phenomenon of graying is not very well understood. One of the few things that medical science knows for sure, though, is that there's no correlation between gray hair and balding—which gives your friend no guarantee one way or the other.

Hair color is determined by a pigment known as melanin that's distributed through the middle of the hair shaft. The range of color, from blond to brown to black, is determined by the number, size, and needless to say, color of the pigment granules. Darker hairs show higher trace amounts of copper, which indicates that the metal-based melanin molecules are more highly developed in dark-haired people That's about it for empirical observation; the rest is mainly speculation.

For some reason the cells that manufacture melanin, known not very imaginatively as "melanocytes," can slow down or stop completely. When this happens, the hair, naturally, begins to lose its color, turning yellow and then gray. Air bubbles, which may mysteriously work their way into the hair shaft, also contribute to graying by blocking the passage of the melanin. Graying seems to be genetically determined, but again, the connection is not all that clear. The process is the same for light- and dark-haired people, but the pigment loss, of course, is more obvious in darker hairs.

What can a hip, progressive, but (unfortunately) vain and balding disc jockey do to keep his hair from falling out? Please answer quickly, Cecil—my adoring public is counting on you.—J.P., Chicago

Got just the thing for you, J., straight out of an Egyptian papyrus dated about 1550 BC. Step 1: mix up a compound from equal parts of the fat of a lion, a hippopotamus, a crocodile, a goose, a snake, and an ibex. Step 2: apply liberally to your shiny spots. According to the modern medical science establishment, if you're suffering from "male pattern baldness" (which accounts for 95 percent of all cases), this preparation will work as well as any other remedy—that is, not at all. Male pattern baldness is thought to result from age, sex, heredity, and nothing else. At the moment, there's nothing you can do about it—although this may change in the not-too-distant future. (The remaining cases of baldness, or "alopecia," as scientists call it, result from diseases, scalp infections, drugs, radiation, and so forth. Many of these cases are temporary and can be reversed if diagnosis and treatment come early enough.)

Balding is caused by the shrinkage of the hair follicles, the tiny depressions in the skin that are responsible for nurturing hair. The follicles actually revert to their embryonic state, becoming smaller and less productive. The process is thought to be a perfectly natural one, triggered not by disease or infection but apparently by some action of the male hormone on the follicles in genetically-predisposed men. The follicles remain perfectly healthy, but somehow, they lose their motivation.

Admittedly, not everybody buys the idea that balding is normal. Some think it results from dietary deficiency. According to Adelle Davis (she died with hair) and her legion of vitamin-freak followers, inositol (a B-complex vitamin) and vitamin E may prevent baldness—it has been shown that animals deprived of these vitamins suffer from unusual balding, and Davis has reported instances of profuse hair growth after the administration of the B complex. The medical establishment pooh-poohs the vitamin business, though. Doctors admit that a dietary deficiency can *cause* baldness, but they protest that it's yet to be shown that an over-abundance of vitamins (which, if your diet is sound, is probably what you'd be getting if you took inositol or vitamin E straigh

268

from the bottle) will cure or prevent it. Of course, if the medical establishment is wrong, this won't be the first time—it certainly wouldn't hurt you to improve your diet or take a couple pills. There's currently on the market a vitamin formulation designed specifically to remedy baldness—and what the heck, you DJs have cash to burn, right?

Another promising line of therapy, just recently announced, involves a drug called Minoxidil, made by the Upjohn company. Originally used as a treatment for high blood pressure, Minoxidil was discovered to have an interesting side-effect: it promoted the growth of hair. In a year-long study by Dr. Richard de Villez at the University of Texas Health Science Center at San Antonio, half of the 56 participants reported partial or total recovery of their lost hair. Best results were achieved with those who had recently lost their hair, as opposed to guys who had been bald 10 years or more. There are a couple drawbacks. It takes about four months of twice-daily treatments before you begin to see much progress, and if you stop, within three months you're back where you started. In any case, before Minoxidil can be marketed, Upjohn has to get the approval of the Food and Drug Administration, which will probably take three or four years. In the meantime, all you can do is keep your hair reasonably clean, and avoid lots of friction and pulling.

There seem to be more balding women on the street these days. Are more women going bald or are more of them just going public?—P., Baltimore

The American Medical Association reports that hair-loss complaints among women have "increased markedly" over the last couple of decades. The reason is not well understood—sometimes I am hard put to think of anything the medical establishment *does* understand well—but a combination of factors is probably responsible, not the least of them being the increased attention we pay to hair and other cosmetic considerations these days. Women have always been susceptible to a hair-loss syndrome similar to the one that commonly afflicts men, though of course the female version occurs far less frequently and is usually less drastic, resulting in general thinning of the hair rather than vast, gleaming expanses of skin. There's also temporary hair loss, which can be caused by unusual stresses such as those that accompany high fever, childbirth, and surgery. To these age-old maladies, our modern lifestyle seems to have added a few more. Anti-cancer drugs are notorious for causing baldness, and the hormonal ups and downs produced by birth control pills are suspected of aggravating it, at least. Another known culprit is the mechanical abuse to hair and scalp inflicted by tight rolling, brushing with sharp bristles, and so on.

A new sense of social responsibility inspired by a new job has led me to make the crucial moral decision to cut my hair. This is no small matter, since I have been cultivating it for years now (ever since long hair was in style), and it has now grown to a truly astonishing length. But now, mindful of the O. Henry short story "Gift of the Magi," I'm wondering if I can't turn the situation to my advantage (and a substantial cash profit) by peddling my awe-inspiring locks to a wigmaker, as the young wife does in O. Henry's tale. Can you please tell me if there are any firms around that buy human hair? I'll be glad to give you 10 percent of the proceeds.—Alice M., Chicago

Ten percent of nothin', as Jean-Paul Sartre once observed, is still nothin'. Farrah Fawcett and the Clairol mafia have ruined the market for American hair by inspiring the huddled masses to keep their crops too clean—regular washing with most commercial shampoos strips the hair of its natural wax coating, which makes it too brittle to be sewn into wigs. Wigmakers are only interested in hair that originates in hygienically underdeveloped corners of the world—the dirtier, the better. So unless you've been particularly lax in your personal habits, your chances of making a profit on your next trip to the beauty parlor are virtually nil.

Is picking one's nose harmful? Sometimes when I pick mine, nasal hairs come out with the other stuff. In light of the filtering functions I have heard ascribed to these hairs, is there any damage to the olfactories?—Leo D., Dallas

The chief danger of picking your nose, Leo, is that you will gross your friends out of existence and wind up as a richly deserving social pariah. Your sense of smell is probably not in any great danger. The loss of some nose hair, whether by picking or otherwise, is normal; the missing hairs eventually grow back. On the other hand, nose hairs do indeed serve as filters, so if you are accustomed to picking with such vigor that your nostrils are entirely laid to waste, you may want to exercise some restraint. Fortunately, the nose is equipped with various other defenses besides nose hairs, notably the turbinate bones. These are essentially baffles

270

lined with mucous membranes in the nasal cavities that impart a swirling motion to inhaled air, causing any airborne dust to smack into the membranes and go no further.

There is one danger from nose-picking, however, and that is that you will break the skin somehow and give root to an infection, which could subsequently migrate inward—i.e., into the base of the brain. Blood from the nose (to be precise, from a triangular region of the face centered on the nose) drains to the rear of the head through the same vein used by the brain. If a nasal infection were to travel downstream and block this vein, an event rather ominously called a thrombosis, you'd have big problems. Not only would blood circulation be impaired, but any sort of surgical treatment might well result in disfigurement. Hence the high school injuction not to pick yer zits. Words to live by, Leo.

Having long ago abandoned the practice of wearing hard contact lenses in this fair but not terribly clean city I live in, and not being able to cope with the notion of plastic and glass sitting on the bridge of my nose, I tend to wear corrective lenses only when absolutely necessary. This means I'm walking around in a fog a fair amount of the time, which I'm not too wild about. What options apart from glasses and contacts do I have if I want to see all the time?—Clancy E., Los Angeles

If you're looking for ways to spend buckets of money *trying* to see better, Clancy, I've got good news for you. If you want something that actually works, it's another story. There are several methods of therapy that purport to improve vision without the use of glasses, but most of them are not highly thought of by ophthalmologists. One of the older ones is called the "Bates method," which was invented in the 20s by an English doctor named William H. Bates. Basically a system of eye exercises, the Bates method is said to strengthen the eye muscles and relax the eyeball, the theory being that tension distorts the eyes and causes improper focus. The British author Aldous Huxley praised the Bates method, but critics point out that Huxley died blind and claim there is no scientific evidence that the method is of any help whatever. An article in the *American Journal of Optometry* a while back flatly declared the method to be ineffective.

A somewhat more recently developed therapy is "orthokeratology," or ortho-k, as its fans refer to it. Ortho-k makes use of a series of special hard contact lenses, somewhat thicker and

flatter than ordinary lenses, supposedly to flatten the cornea and thus improve myopia, which is caused by an eyeball that is too elongated. A fairly expensive procedure ($1,100 as of a couple of years ago), ortho-k requires patients to come in and have their eyes examined every four to six weeks over a two-year period, during which time progressively flatter contact lenses are prescribed. After two weeks you graduate to wearing "retainer" lenses once or twice a week to maintain the improved eye shape.

There are about 300 doctors nationwide who practice orthokeratology, many of them in California. Proponents claim that some patients have shown dramatic improvement—from as poor as 20/1200 vision to 20/60 in five months. Many ophthalmologists say that ortho-k is worthless, though, and that any improvement from special lenses, which they consider to be simply ill-fitting, is only temporary. Little research on the topic seems to have found its way into the scientific journals. Cecil's mail on the subject has been mixed. Most of my correspondents say ortho-k has resulted in at least some improvement, but some say they still have to wear contacts, which they regard as disappointing in light of the high cost.

There *is* one medical procedure thought to be salubrious in extreme cases, an extraordinarily delicate operation called "keratomileusis," in which the lenses of the patient's eyes are surgically removed, frozen, and then actually reground and reimplanted. There are considerable risks involved, so this method (at which only a handful of doctors in the world are proficient) is rarely recommended, and then only in cases in which the alternative is virtual blindness or the use of prohibitively expensive lenses. Personally I think I'd rather squint.

I have a question about what seems to be a fundamental contradiction in all the hype about the advantages of aerobic exercise on one hand and the disadvantages of coffee and caffeine on the other. As I understand it, the idea in aerobic exercise is to get your heart pumping at an accelerated rate (say, 150 beats per minute) for a sustained period (say, half an hour). This supposedly strengthens your heart and enables it to beat at a slower rate the rest of the time. OK, but they also say coffee and caffeine are bad for you because (among other things) they make your heart pound too fast. Howcum it's good when aerobics makes your heart pound faster but bad when coffee does the same thing? Why can't you get a good workout by just trekking down to the local diner every morning and drinking a gallon of Maxwell House while doing the crossword puzzle in the New York Times? Or is this just another example of me-generation doublespeak?—Kathleen S., Washington, D.C.

Katie, my little catcus flower, I admire your moral tenacity on this issue, but I'm afraid you've fallen victim to the same pernicious reductivism (God, how I love this litcrit mumbo-jumbo) that afflicts the nation's weight lifters. That is, you focus myopically on the *parts* (for you, the heart; for weight lifters, the chest and limb muscles) rather than the whole. This is typical retrograde low-tech Chevy Impala-type thinking. We nonlinear postindustrial children of the Information Age, however, know that the important thing is the Big Picture, the *system*—the cardiovascular and pulmonary systems, to be precise. The important thing in aerobics is not to get the heart alone pumping faster, but to get the entire complex of heart, lungs, blood, and whatnot operating at max efficiency. Aerobics instructors sometimes focus on the pulse (heartbeat) because it's a quick-and-dirty way of finding out how hard your body is working during an exercise session. But the *true* measure of a good workout, as described in *Aerobics*, the 1968 bible on this topic, is *oxygen consumption*. In laboratory tests, they have you breathe into an air bag to compute how efficiently your lungs are working. Then they correlate that with electrocardiograms and numerous other technological miracles to determine what shape your bod is in. Needless to say, such fancy gadgetry isn't available at the average track or health club, hence the reliance on shorthand indicators like pulse rate. But merely getting your heart pounding from caffeine is like turning up the idle on your cough-and-wheeze Ford instead of getting an over-haul—that is, you may achieve some short-term gains, but you're still headed for long-term ruin. Plus caffeine may raise your blood pressure and do all sorts of other untoward things.

On a related note, one of Cecil's many admirers here at Straight Dope World HQ has inquired whether a fat person who loses a lot of weight isn't better off than a person who's been skinny all his or her life, since the fat person has been doing years of involuntary weight lifting—i.e., hefting his lardbucket self around every day. A beguiling thought if true, but Cecil is obliged to report that, unfortunately, it ain't. As a rule, as obesity increases, activity decreases—fat people frequently feel tired because their bodies are trying to ease the strain on the vital organs. So while they're carting around a lot more weight than average, they move a lot less than average. The net result is that the fat person probably performs less heart-strengthening physical work than an ordinary person, and as a result his heart is in worse shape. But suppose some ambitious fat person made a point of exercising energetically despite his condition. And suppose that person managed not to die of a heart attack in the process. And suppose finally that he managed to take off a lot of weight very suddenly. That person might well have an admirably muscular heart—*as long as he kept exercising*. If he stopped, though, the heart muscles would lose tone within a few weeks. Also, the blood vessels of our formerly fat person would probably be coated with atherosclerotic plaque, meaning we're potentially talking Infarct City. Wherefore abandon these puppylike excuses for not exercising—I swear, only the Teeming Millions could come up with the Drip-Grind Diet—and hump it on out to the gym today.

When a portion of the brain is removed, as in the case of Mr. Brady, Ron Reagan's press secretary, what do surgeons use to fill the space? Is it stuffed with cotton, gelatin, or left vacant?—Mr. P., Baltimore

In operating on a traumatized brain, one of the main objectives of the neurosurgeon is to relieve the pressure within the skull that may be caused by foreign objects, blood, or scar tissue. The *absence* of pressure is not considered a problem worth worrying about, especially in light of the fact that introducing foreign matter would greatly increase the chance of infection. When a portion of the brain is removed, the vacated space is occupied by the brain's natural juices. As for Mr. Brady, his physician refuses to discuss the particulars of his patient's skull, but he assures me

274

that he agrees with the foregoing in principle. It's a safe bet, in other words, that Brady does not have cotton in his head. If he did, he would certainly have been transferred to the budget office by now.

Is it true that by eating almost nothing but carrots and drinking carrot juice you can turn orangish in color? Is there a medical name for this?—Tom B., Chicago

Yup. "Carotene" is the red or yellow hydrocarbon pigment that gives carrots their characteristic cheery color, and also helps to brighten up egg yolks, sweet potatoes, and a variety of leafy vegetables. Intemperate carrot consumption will make the carotene build up in your bloodstream. Before you know it, your skin will take on a sickly yellow pallor, a grisly condition that superficially resembles jaundice. You've got carotenosis, you poor sap, and good luck to you. Fatal cases are rare, if that's any comfort: a London woman died from the disease in 1972, but she had to work at it.

Is there any way you've heard of of sleeping less? I'm envious of people who need only four hours a day.—D.E., Baltimore

There is this thing called an alarm clock that you may want to look into, D. I can personally testify that it does for oversleeping what the guillotine does for dandruff. If that's not good enough for you, you might want to pick up a copy of *Sleep Less, Live More* by Everett Mattlin. He basically suggests trying to sleep more efficiently. The deepest, most restful sleep occurs in the first four hours or so; during the last half of your sack time you're doing a lot of what is thought to be nonessential dreaming, and often you're half-awake anyway. So if you exercise regularly, avoid unnecessary stress, develop regular sleeping habits, and so on, eventually you may get to the point where you can drop off immediately, sleep like a rock for six hours, and awaken refreshed. It's worth a try.

I have this problem of being underweight. I'm a male, 22, 5'10", and weigh only 125 pounds. I don't know what the cause of it is, but whatever I eat and whatever I do I can't seem to gain any weight. I have taken some weight-gaining tablets and drinks, but they don't help. I have just started some body building, which might help, but I doubt it. People tell me my metabolism must be going too fast. So my questions are: (1) Is my metabolism going too fast? (2) If it is, when will it slow down? (3) Do you have any advice that will help me gain at least ten pounds?—R.E., Washington

I've heard this "fast metabolism" stuff for years, R., and as far as I've ever been able to discover it's bogus. Differences in basal metabolic rate (a measure of the rate at which the body burns energy while at rest) per unit of body weight among healthy individuals of the same sex are relatively minor. Major differences are usually accounted for by some disorder like hyperthyroidism. If you have any suspicions in this regard, convey yourself to a doctor. Illness aside, you may have poor eating habits or an excessively frantic lifestyle—stress tends to increase the metabolic rate. I have heard some other explanations for chronic thinness, too, but I'm not sure I buy any of them. For instance, one of my doctor buddies has advanced the novel proposition that body weight is related to the length of your small intestine—the longer it is, supposedly, the more food you absorb. Sure, doc. The most straightforward explanation is that people who have a hard time gaining weight (what we refer to as ectomorphs) simply have fewer muscle and fat cells to absorb the extra bulk than more athletic types. Fortunately, tests have shown that weight training can add new muscle cells, a process called hyperplasia. This is a lot more work than simply strengthening existing muscle cells, admittedly, but you can take some comfort in the fact that the new muscle cells stay with you all your life, even if you knock off weight training later on. What you need is a systematic weight gain program: eating (lots of carbohydrates, a fair amount of protein, no junk) plus weight lifting, with an emphasis on upper body exercises—six to eight repetitions per exercise with heavy weights. Increase the weight as soon as you can do more than eight reps. Patience is advised. The common wisdom among weight lifters is that you can gain about seven pounds of pure muscle a year. This may seem a little slow, but it can clearly be done, as long as you have the Proper Attitude. We'll have none of this wimpy "it might help but I doubt it" crapola, if you don't mind. Check out the next question.

I've been exercising regularly for the past few years—not for the alleged health benefits, but simply because I've learned people are attracted to muscles. I started with traditional weight lifting but gave it up because of the large amount of time required. Instead for the past two years I've been doing Nautilus. However, a couple heavy-duty, well-built jocks recently advised me to foresake Nautilus and return to weights for maximum bulk—which is what I really want. But my body is just beginning to take on the look I've wanted and worked for so long. What's a mother to do, Cecil? Should I continue with Nautilus or go back to classical weight lifting?—J.L., Chicago

P.S.: I'm 30 years old, 140 pounds, 5'6", in good health, with newly pronounced mesomorphic tendencies, although I used to be quite thin.

We enter here into a subject that is hotly disputed at the moment, J., and to tell you the truth, Cecil has a personal interest in it, although he has not been to the gym for a couple months on account of working on this damn book. First, for the benefit of the masses, a little background on what Nautilus is. The machines (there are more than 20 different devices for exercising various muscles, although it is the rare gym that has a full set) are advertised as the most intensive and therefore the most efficient method of weight training available. Nautilus offers a long list of supposed advantages over free weights, chief among which is variable resistance. Variable resistance means that during a given exercise you have to exert the greatest effort at the point where things would otherwise be easiest for you—say, past the midpoint of a bench-press-type exercise. Variable resistance is achieved by the use of cams, some of which are shaped like the cross section of the shell of the chambered nautilus, whence the name. Variable resistance means your muscles don't get to loaf at any point, and it reduces the incentive to cheat, e.g., by jerking the weight to overcome starting inertia. All this purportedly results in a more intense workout. Nautilus boosters claim you can get three times the results in one-tenth the time. This is undoubtedly hype, but it's true that a thorough Nautilus workout will take less time than a comparable free-weight workout.

The controversy comes in because body builders claim free weights are the only way to achieve championship form, whatever that means. There are lots of arguments in the muscle magazines on this score, most of them studded with pseudoscientific jargon backed up with very little reliable research. Fortunately, unless you have serious aspirations in the body building line, the arguments are irrelevant. Most body builders concede that in the early years of training you can achieve roughly the same bulk with either free weights or Nautilus—and since you seem to be doing OK with the latter, J., stick with it. Personally I prefer the Universal weight machines (similar to Nautilus but without the variable resistance feature), but I don't have any good reason for doing so. Whatever equipment you use, the important thing if you want to increase your physical bulk is to *regularly increase the weight you're lifting*. If you don't, you'll maintain muscle tone, but you won't put on extra muscle.

A final note: once you get to a certain point, what you want is not bulk so much as *definition*, i.e., well-shaped muscles with little subcutaneous fat. To achieve that, you've got to reduce the amount of fat in your diet. Striking results can be achieved this way. Take it from Cecil.

I haven't heard much about Linus Pauling's theories on vitamin C as a cure for the common cold lately, although I know several people who continue to down their C capsules religiously. Has any evidence been found to prove or disprove Pauling's claims? The whole business is beginning to look like a fad that has peaked. You have a fine skeptical mind, Cecil, so I know I can trust you to provide an unbiased opinion.—Kathy M., Los Angeles

Keep talking, sweetheart, you're worming your way into my heart. Although no hard data has yet been produced linking vitamin C to the prevention of colds, the fad, far from having peaked, has grown to epidemic proportions in recent years. Pauling, exercising some scientific discretion, claimed only mild preventive powers for C, but later vitamins A, B, D, and E were hauled into the fray, being touted as cures for everything from acne and impotence to cancer and heart disease. The theory behind megavitamin therapy, as it has been dubbed, seems to be that if a little is good for you, then a lot is *very* good for you, which is not only unscientific but downright dangerous. One of the oldest truisms of medicine is that any substance, innately beneficial or not, can be toxic when taken in large quantities. This isn't much of a problem with vitamin C, which dissolves in the body's water and passes out through the usual routes. But vitamins A and D, when taken in the massive doses prescribed by megavitamin therapy, are stored in the body's fat complexes and can easily build to poisonous levels. Vitamin A poses the most serious threat—an overdose can lead to a condition known as "hypervitaminosis A," with symptoms that strongly resemble a brain tumor.

The "recommended daily allowances" for vitamins set by the Food and Drug Administration are designed to keep intake well below the toxic level—if you follow the numbers, you've got nothing to worry about. But according to the megavitamin people, the RDA is the product of a conspiracy by the government, the American Medical Association, and the food industry to keep people sick and doctors rich. The Solgar Company, a vitamin manufacturer, won a ruling against the FDA a few years back, preventing the government from requiring prescriptions for large amounts of A, which was widely regarded as a triumph for the vitamin cultists. The controversy rages on, although the burden of proof, at this point, seems to lie with the pro-vitamin forces. The existing research is almost entirely on the FDA's side.

Still, vitamin C may have its uses as a cold cure. Much of the recent research on colds has centered on their psychosomatic side: emotional problems, such as nerves, stress, and depression, appear to play as large a part in bringing on colds as do the elusive germs. C might turn out to have no medical value, but it may well be effective as a placebo. If taking vitamin C makes you feel healthy, then—to some degree—you probably *are* healthy.

Tell me, Cecil—what are the hazards of disease which may be transmitted by towel litter against which we are warned by the labels on hot-air hand dryers?—Hypochondriac, Washington, D.C.

The chief maladies prevented by the use of hot-air dryers are poverty and unemployment among the owners and employees of the World Dryer Corporation, which, incidentally, no longer adorns its product with the famous piece of literature to which you refer. It seems that the references to disease and medical tests in that familiar ditty ("For your well being . . . we have installed electric hand dryers," etc.) were inspired by a Public Health Service study done in 1953 by one Paul E. Walker, MD, whose purpose was to determine whether hot-air drying could reduce bacterial contamination on the hands and forearms of surgeons and other operating room personnel after their usual antiseptic scrubbing procedure. Counting the number of bacterial colonies left by the hot-air drying method and the usual sterile-towel method, Dr. Walker concluded that hot-air dryers were indeed superior, as well as cheaper. Though he did not specify the types of bacteria he counted, and despite the obvious fact that the requirements of operating-room sterility and common bathroom sanitation are worlds apart, his report evidently fell into the hands of a creative copywriter who went on to warn millions of Americans about the "dangers of disease that may be transmitted by cloth towels or paper towel litter." This was a gargantuan leap of logic, in my humble opinion, but I suppose that's the sort of thing copywriters get paid for.

Your chances of catching something from a cloth towel— or from "paper towel litter," if you're in the habit of rooting around in it and wiping it all over yourself—are so remote as to be practically negligible. If you were to contract something, it would most likely be some sort of bacterial skin infection like impetigo (which isn't seen much anymore) or athlete's foot (the transmission of which is not very well understood). Of course, if a person with some monstrous infection just happened to precede you into the rest room, and just happened to dry his or her hands without bothering to wash them first, and thereby just happened to deposit a huge dollop of virulent pus on the very section of the towel that you just happened to use to dry the area around a gaping wound that you just happened to have, you would probably keel over and croak in about 12 seconds flat, so don't say I didn't warn you.

Some people at work have offered me $10 to drink a two-ounce bottle of Tabasco sauce. Now I am having second thoughts. Is it dangerous, other than a few minutes of discomfort? Should I drink a lot of water right afterward? Should I swallow the Tabasco all at once or maybe a spoonful at a time?—Anonymous, Los Angeles

I certainly hope you like Gatorade and cough syrup, A., because that's what you're going to be living on for a week after you try this stupid stunt. The vegetable oils in Tabasco are fairly potent skin irritants. In diluted form they produce the pleasantly fiery effect we associate with Mexican food, but straight down the hatch out of the bottle we're talking General Sherman meets Atlanta. At best your throat would hurt like hell for the rest of the evening; at worst you could end up with a mild chemical-type burn down the length of your esophagus. Admittedly the clinical literature on this topic is not as voluminous as one might like. One of Cecil's correspondents who tried it a while back says he promptly heaved his Cheerios, but he provides no further data. In an effort to expand the frontiers of knowledge, the Biomedical Research Team lately has been endeavoring to feed a quart of Tabasco to the associate editor here at Straight Dope HQ, but so far he has puppied out on me shamelessly, the worm, and scientific progress has been accordingly retarded. Should you try it—and I recommend lots of milk afterwards—make sure you have your estate send me a copy of the autopsy report. I like to keep my files up to date.

I read once, in some dusty and dimly remembered mystery, that subsonic sound (or sound that is much lower in pitch than can be heard) will cause acute anxiety to those within its range. It made an intriguing story. Is there any factual basis for this?—Barbara H., Evanston, Illinois

Infrasonic sound, to call it by its right name, has some effect on human "hearers," although it falls a little short of "acute anxiety." The frequency range of normal hearing is 10-24,000 hertz. Researchers have found that frequencies as low as one hertz (one cycle per second) have a definite effect on the inner ear, somehow short-circuiting its equilibrium and causing dizziness.

Infrasoncially-induced dizziness may not be the stuff of paranoid fantasies, but it may yet turn out to be a serious problem. In nature, infrasonic waves are produced only by earthquakes—in which event dizziness would probably be the least of your worries. But scientists have discovered that the waves can also be produced by forcing air into an enclosed space—an experiment you can duplicate with frightening accuracy by driving at high speeds with your car windows open. This should give you something to think about as you zip down the highway next summer.

Is it possible to contract herpes from a hot tub or spa? I heard that the high water temp supports the little devils and the water offers a medium for transmission. Say it ain't so.—J.M.S., Santa Monica, California

It ain't, strictly speaking. The herpes virus does not survive well in temperatures much above body heat. There's some indication that heat does encourage outbreaks in already-infected individuals, but that doesn't have anything to do with transmission. On the other hand, researchers at the National Institutes of Health found that the virus can survive for several hours on the plastic coated benches found *near* hot tubs at many clubs and spas. In fact, users of several spas in the Washington, D.C., area complained a while back that they contracted herpes without benefit of sexual activity, which to my mind has to be one of the all-time bummers. Fortunately, soap effectively annihilates the little suckers, so if you have any doubts, give your dub a rub, Bub.

My wife and I have been married for five years. She has a mild case of herpes, contracted years before we met and subject to intermittent outbreaks (usually related to stress). But although we take no precautions other than a little restraint occasionally, I have apparently never caught the virus, or at least I have never had an outbreak. Is it really possible that I'm clean? Or could I have herpes and not know it? Or could she not have herpes but something else causing similar manifestations even though it was diagnosed as herpes by two different doctors?—Name Withheld, Cave Creek, Arizona

Is it true that colds and flu and other germ-spread illnesses are most contagious before you get the symptoms rather than after? I have always written this off as a crackpot therapy, but now that I have a small child, I'd really like to know. If it's true, then I don't need to worry about him being around sick people, or infecting his little friends if he himself is sick. Can you find out for sure?—R.B., Monroe, Wisconsin

I realize that discussing kiddie sniffles and herpes simplex in the same breath is a bit—incongruous, shall we say, but we are dealing with the demon Virus here, which makes for strange bedfellows, to say nothing of making bedfellows strange. Starting with the simplest issues and working up: if you *look* contagious (sneezing, herpes blisters, or whatever), you almost certainly *are* contagious—that is, you are "shedding virus," as we clinicians say. On the other hand, it's quite possible to shed virus without exhibiting any obvious signs of disease. In the initial stage of a viral infection, in herpes called the "prodrome" and in other illnesses called "feeling like you're coming down with something,"

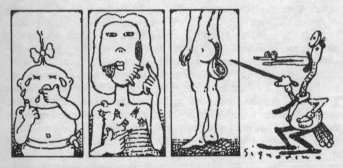

the only symptom you feel may be a tingling or aching sensation. Nonetheless, you can readily infect other people, and therefore it is best to lie low—in the case of a cold, staying home and scarfing OJ, and in the case of herpes, keeping yer paws to yourself.

It's also possible to have a "subclinical" infection, meaning one so mild that it goes from start to finish without the sufferer ever realizing he's sick. Unfortunately, you can still spread germs to others in this condition. With herpes, in fact, you can become what's known as an "asymptomatic carrier," which is roughly equivalent to being Typhoid Mary. Maybe that's the story with you, N.W. For obvious reasons, it's not known exactly how many asymptomatic carriers there are; I've seen estimates ranging from

1 percent to 50 percent of all herpes sufferers. On the other hand, maybe you just lucked out and never contracted herpes at all. The only way to tell for sure is to have tissue cultures taken every couple of months for, say, six months to a year. When herpes is in its inactive, or latent, stage, it's pretty much undetectable, but if you do have it, chances are it'll become active sooner or later and show up in the cultures. However, cultures aren't cheap, and presuming you're not planning any extramarital forays, it's not going to do you any good to know—herpes at present is incurable. It *is* possible that what your wife has isn't herpes but something with similar symptoms. Syphilis, for instance. If you have any doubts on this subject, by all means get another medical opinion.

If you've got further questions, you might want to call the Herpes Resource Center in Palo Alto, California, at 415-328-7710. If you don't feel like paying the toll you can call the VD National Hotline at 800-227-8922. Or you can write to the HRC at PO Box 100, Palo Alto, California 94302. They'll send you a booklet with Q&A about herpes, as well as a copy of their quarterly newsletter, called *The Helper*. At $20 a year it'll help keep you herpes sufferers abreast of new developments in treatment, among other things.

Everything I read on alcoholism, even from the AMA, focuses on social and familial trauma, with maybe a bit of liver damage thrown in. Could you approach alcoholism from a physical/vanity angle? To wit, the gum damage that tells a dentist you imbibe. The ever-drooping "alcoholic's ass" and other physical effects. The blotchy skin and red nose. I think such a rundown would be more effective than the usual warnings. Which of these conditions are reversible? Also, can you explain physiologically how "blackout" comes to happen more often and require less booze? Is this brain damage or lowered tolerance or what?—Anonymous, Chicago

If it's gory details you want, Cecil is always happy to oblige. Let's start with delirium tremens, which is marked by tremulousness, hallucinations, and localized or grand mal seizures, profuse sweating, rapid heartbeat, dilation of the pupils, and fever. Death rates among persons exhibiting these symptoms range as high as 15 percent. Next (and somewhat less commonly) we have Korsakoff's psychosis, a reduction of learning ability and memory span (particularly short-term memory), and Wernicke's disease, a reduction in mental acuity, characterized by disorientation, clouding of consciousness, poor comprehension, and weakness or paralysis of the eye muscles.

Moving right along, we have alcoholic amblyopia, partial loss of sight. The most dramatic instance of this is the sudden and permanent blindness that often accompanies the drinking of wood (methyl) alcohol. However, a slower-acting but equally serious form of amblyopia is often caused by nutritional deficiencies associated with ordinary grain alcohol. What happens is you substitute vitaminless booze for more wholesome foodstuffs, giving rise to numerous disorders. Another example of this is alcoholic polyneuropathy, a disease of the peripheral nervous system characterized by (among other things) numbness in the toes and fingers, a burning sensation on the soles of the feet, and tenderness of the calf muscles. In the severest cases you can lose the use of the hands and feet. Alcoholics can also get beriberi, a result of thiamine deficiency.

Then we have a number of generalized syndromes usually lumped under the catchall term alcoholic deterioration, including various combinations of the following: dilation of the facial capillaries, especially in the nose (the W.C. Fields effect), cirrhosis of the liver, alcoholic hepatitis, degeneration of the heart muscles resulting in eventual congestive heart failure, bloated appearance, flabby muscles (including alcoholic's ass), chronic stomach inflammation (in extreme cases, bleeding ulcers), pancreatitis, anemia and other bone marrow problems, low blood sugar (sometimes leading to sudden death), tremors (shaky hands), seizures, paranoia, emotional and behavioral problems, and so on. Some researchers believe that excessive alcohol produces premature aging, noting that many alcohol-related problems, such as gum disease, mental deterioration, etc., are similar to certain infirmities of the elderly.

How much of the above is reversible is open to question. With treatment most conditions can be improved, but some impairment usually remains. Interestingly, while we often think of alcoholics as people who've been hitting the bottle for years, there is evidence to suggest that very heavy drinking over a relatively short period—say, in college—can produce identical results, including permanent brain damage. Brain damage, incidentally, may well account for the increasing incidence of blackouts, but researchers aren't sure. Stick to tomato juice.

I can understand that drinking alcoholic beverages in the summer can make you feel hotter, but I also read that drinking in the winter also makes you colder. How can this be? And what is alcohol's effect on your body in temperate weather?—Anna M., Baltimore

Drinking makes you *feel* warmer no matter what the season, but its net effect is to cool off the body. Alcohol is what is known as a vasodilator—it causes the blood vessels to expand, particularly the capillaries located just under the surface of the skin. In doing so it overrides the body's normal heat regulating process, which also makes use of dilation. What happens when the blood vessels expand is that a greater volume of blood is brought to the skin surface, where the heat of the blood is dissipated to the surrounding air. That's why you take on a flushed appearance when you drink. Since most of your heat-sensing nerves are also located in the skin surface, drinking makes you feel superficially warmer in both summer and winter. In winter, however, heat is carried away so rapidly that the body's metabolic reserves are quickly exhausted, resulting in frostbite or hypothermia. Hence the danger of freezing to death after a midwinter binge.

Chapter 15

~~~~~~~~~~~~~~~~~~~~~~~~~~~~~~~~~~~

Language

In the course of an intellectual intercourse (no pun intended, as you shall comprehend shortly), an ardent friend of mine and I vainly attempted to derive the etymology of the loin-quivering word "horny." As you are the sultan of the urban smut scene, we have concluded that you are our last hope.—Ben Dover and C. Howett Fields, Los Angeles

If you were to apply your vestigial mental faculties to the problem, "Ben," it would probably occur to you that "horny" is vaguely related to "horn," the phallic possibilities of which are self-evident. The term dates from the 15th century. The horn/phallus link is also the reason some Eastern cultures prize the powdered horn of certain animals, notably the rhinoceros, as an aphrodisiac. Horns have also traditionally been associated with cuckoldry. One of the Teeming Millions informs me that in many European languages, being horny means you've been betrayed by your spouse. For instance, I'm told the Byzantine Greek word for cuckold, *kerasthoros*, means "horn bearer." My informant claims that this usage may derive from the practice of grafting the spurs of a capon (a castrated rooster) onto his comb, thereby creating horns. Sounds bizarre to me, but it makes a good yarn.

Can you tell me the derivation and meaning of the syllable wau, *as found in midwestern place names such as Milwaukee, Waukegan, Waupaca, etc.?—Mimi M., Chicago*

Not really. The Algonquin Indian languages that gave names to these and many other places in the midwest were oral, like all North American Indian languages. Place names like Milwaukee and Waukegan weren't written down by Indians but by white dudes who had no familiarity with the subtleties of the Indian tongue (some of them had a pretty shaky grip on their own languages, for that matter). The spellings have changed God knows how many times—Milwaukee, for example, first appears as "Melleoiki," which may or may not have meant "good land" in Chippewa.

Thus we have the *wau* syllable popping up in a slew of names that seem to have nothing in common: Waubonsee, from the name of a Potawatomi chief who attacked his enemies at dawn (*wapin*, "daybreak"); Waukegan, from *waukeegance*, a translation into Indian of the original name, "Little Fort" (the *-ce*, which meant "little" was dropped out of civic pride); Waupaca, where *wau* seems to come from the Potawatomi word for "white," *waub* (the same goes for Waupecan Creek, "white sand bottom"); Waukesha, "little fox"; Wausau, from *wassa*, "far away place"; and so on *ad infinitum* (Latin, "and so it goes").

There is a word used to describe the condition where you can't remember the word you want to use—I can't remember it. I think it starts with a. *Can you help me?—M.W., Phoenix*

I am surrounded by comedians. What you claim to be suffering from is *aphasia*. Strictly defined, aphasia is an impairment of the language function that is caused by brain damage. The word is used figuratively to describe that "I've got it on the tip of my tongue" condition. It's from a Greek root that means "to speak."

Whilst reading through a (fictional) account of King Arthur's childhood, we came upon the word fewmet. *The book explained that the droppings of the beast for which one might quest were fewmets, and that a knight on such a quest might carry some with him (one assumes for comparative purposes). The* Oxford English Dictionary *was consulted. It said that fewmets, with various spellings, refer specifically to deer droppings. The specificity of the reference moves me ask you, our illustrious illuminator, this question: does this imply that there are other, equally specific terms for the droppings of other beasts? That is, for every gaggle, pride, exaltation, flock, etc., there are left behind trails of things which have names? That there may have been a taxonomist hard at work naming all these creations and that his labors are forgotten should surely tug at the heartstrings of all sensitive* Straight Dope *readers.—Jim T., Chicago*

Ah, Jimbo, you are a man after my own heart. I wouldn't go so far as to say that every sort of animal caca has a name, but a surprising number do. We have *tath*, cattle dung; *spraints*, otter dung; *bodewash*, cow dung; the familiar *guano*, seafowl excrement used as fertilizer; *wormcast*, a cylindrical mass of earth voided by an earthworm; and *coprolite*, fossil excrement—e.g., dinosaur poop. For completeness's sake we ought to include *cowpies* and *buffalo chips*. A related word is *jumentous*, pertaining to the smell of horse urine. Nor must we forget *ichthyomancy*, fortune-telling with fish offal, or *spatilomancy*, fortune-telling by investigating animal droppings. Other milestones in the fecal vocabulary, as

long as we're on the subject, are *shardborn*, born in dung; *stercoricolous*, living in dung; and *sterquilinian*, pertaining to a dunghill. This last, I think, has many obvious applications in interoffice memo writing.

But let us not confine ourselves to excremental matters. There are an amazing number of obscure animal appurtenances that have names attached to them, a mere fraction of which we can relate here: *gleet*, hawk stomach phlegm (I am not making this up); *curpin*, a bird's behind; *numbles*, edible deer innards; *dowcet*, a deer testicle; *fenks*, leftover whale blubber used as manure; *axunge*, goose grease; *pulicous*, abounding with fleas; and *crapaudine*, a horse's ulcer. Useful verbs are *blissom*, to copulate with a ewe, and *caponize*, to castrate a chicken. For gourmets we have *ranivorous*, frog-eating, and *scolecophagous*, worm-eating. In the animal mania department there is *formication*, the feeling that bugs are crawling over you; *boanthropy*, the delusion that you are an ox; *cynanthropy*, the delusion that you are a dog; and *galeanthropy*, the delusion that you are a cat. Most of the preceding come from *Mrs. Byrne's Dictionary of Unusual, Obscure and Preposterous Words*, by Josefa Heifetz Byrne, a volume that no aspiring know-it-all dare be without.

A friend of mine said the other day he was going to "boogie on the slopes." I must have looked a little puzzled, because he amplified by saying, "You know, to make some moves in the snow."

288

*That set me to wondering about the origins of the word, "boogie,"
and to thinking that it might be connected with the French word*
bougir, *to move, or* bougie, *a movement. Am I right, and if not,
what is the origin of boogie?—Helen T., Los Angeles*

I think the French verb you mean is *bouger*, but in any case
there's no connection. Ultimately, "boogie" seems to come, via a
circuitous route, from the Latin *Bulgarus*, an inhabitant of Bul-
garia. The Old French term *boulgre* was used to refer to a member
of a sect of 11th-century Bulgarian heretics, and "bougre" first
appears in English writing in 1340 as a synonym for "heretic."
By the 16th century, "bougre" grew into "bugger," a practitioner
of vile and despicable acts including "buggery," or sodomy. "Bogy"
(or "bogie") first appears in the 19th century as an appellation for
the devil; later it came to be used for hobgoblins in general. Hence,
the bogeyman, which may be the source of the use of "bogey"
and "boogies" to mean "Negro." Shortly after these usages became
common (in the 1920s), there appeared boogie woogie music, and
I guess you can figure out the rest.

There's no need to be concerned about your friend, unless
he was using "boogie" in the old black slang sense to mean secondary syphilis. In that case, you might tell him that the snow of
Switzerland has no proven therapeutic effect, now matter how one
moves in it.

*My dictionary tells me that the obstetrical term "cesarean" is
derived from "the belief that Julius Caesar was born this way."
Who believes this, and why? Does anybody know how Caesar's
mother felt about it, given what must have been the rather primitive
state of anesthesiology at the time? Did the operation have more
than one survivor?—A Concerned Sister, Washington, D.C.*

Apparently the only people who believe in Caesar's untimely
arrival on this mortal coil are the people who write dictionaries.
This shocking error, which has even crept into that last bastion of
academic infallibility, the *Oxford English Dictionary*, seems to
have originated in the account Pliny gives of the Caesar family
name. The Caesars, a branch of the Roman Julii clan, supposedly
took their name from the verb *caedere*—"to cut"—in reference
to a forgotten ancestor who made his entrance through the side
door, so to speak. But like most noble Roman families, the Caesars
also traced their genealogy back to the gods, which doesn't say
much for their credibility. Julius's mother, Aurelia, actually out-
lived her husband by some years, and apparently became something of a Miss Lillian of her time.

The cesarean section, though, was well known in Caesar's day. The operation is alluded to in the Talmud and makes a brief appearance in the tenth-century Persian epic, the Shah-nameh; in 1608 the Venetian Senate passed a law requiring that it be performed on women dying in the last stages of pregnancy.

Not much hope was given to saving the mother. Even with the "anesthesia" of the time—in which the patient was either frozen, beaten senseless, asphyxiated, or pumped full of alcohol—the surgeons never really knew how to heal the gaping wounds they produced with their primitive instruments. On those few occasions when hemorrhage could be prevented, the patient inevitably died of infection.

The first successful cesarean—that is, in which the mother lived to tell the tale—is supposed to have been performed around 1500 by a Swiss pig gelder, clearly a man of experience and skill. His name has been forgotten, but the operation served to inspire several more centuries of butchery. Even by the middle of the nineteenth century, the mother was only given a 25 percent chance of survival. Today, of course, modern antiseptics and suturing techniques have made the operation routine.

Please tell me the etymologies of three words: joint, roach, and stoned. English is not my native language, and no one else will answer this question for me.—Marie-France M., Chicago

In the March 12, 1938 issue of the *New Yorker*, Meyer Berger begins a story about a dope-smoking party with the words, "It took weeks of dickering to get into a marijuana party, because I am not a viper, which is the Harlem word for a marijuana smoker." After thus assuring his genteel readers of his innocence, Berger goes on to provide them with many penetrating insights into the seamy, depraved underworld of the Harlem viper, and included among these insights are a few observations on marijuana jargon. "Viper vocabulary," Berger said, "changes fast—perhaps to confuse police." As examples of this fast-changing viper vocabulary, he cites, among others, the terms "joint," "roach," and "the Man" (a detective), all of which have changed so much that they're still being used today, more than 45 years later. Berger ends his story with some wonderfully hysterical comments on the psychotic horrors caused by dope smoking—murderous rages, schizophrenia, and the like.

The point of all this is that words like "joint" and "roach" were being used long before Meyer Berger ventured into Harlem with his bow tie, umbrella, and note pad—unfortunately, the people who were using them were not the sort who wrote regularly for the *New Yorker* or any other such publication. In the absence of literary citations, etymologies of slang words like this are nearly impossible to trace. Berger's written use of "roach" ("A pinched-off smoke, or a stub, is a roach") is the first I know of, and the only etymological explanation I can find for the usage (a rather tenuous one) is slang expert Eric Partridge's reminder that "roach" also refers to a stubby little freshwater fish of the carp family.

"Joint" seems to have come to its present meaning via a very circuitous route that started with the 19th-century American word "joinery," which referred to a specific part of a building. By the early 1800s "joint" had become a building; in 1870 it was used for betting parlors, in 1890 for opium dens, and by 1920 it was an addict's term for drug-related paraphernalia. "Stoned" appears to be as much of a mystery to etymologists as it is to me and you. If you're in the mood for some irresponsible conjecture, I'll pin the usage to the battered physical condition of one who has been physically stoned, as with real rocks. Alternatively, the derivation might have something to do with the 19th-century pub libation known as the "stone fence," a mixture of brandy and ale.

We all know that grown-up liberals are sometimes called "do-gooders," a rather self-explanatory term. However, that same do-gooder at a younger age might have been called a "goodie-two-shoes." Could you sort through the semantic thicket and tell us just where that term came from?—J.B., Dallas

"Little Goody Two-Shoes" was the heroine of a children's story of the same title, first published in 1765 and often attributed to that favorite of English graduate students everywhere, Oliver Goldsmith. The story, such as it is, concerns a poor waif who has somehow managed to make it through life with only one shoe. Finally rewarded with another, she scampers over hill and dale pointing at her feet and crying "Two shoes! Two shoes!" in so cloying a manner that her name has lived through the ages as a symbol of puerility. "Goody" is a contraction of "Goodwife," a form of address roughly equivalent to our "Mrs.," and now archaic.

A bunch of us were wondering where the term "86'd" comes from. We know about "can it" and "deep six" . . . but what about "86"?— Scott K., Los Angeles

Cecil presumes you are using the term "86" to mean "to put the kibosh on," generally said of some unusually retarded scheme or idea, such as anything thought up by the sales department, the

New York office, or that turkey who's angling for your job. The term derives via a roundabout route from a number code allegedly in wide use in 1920s diners and soda fountains. 86 supposedly

meant, "We're all out of the item ordered," said by the cook or some other honcho to a soda jerk or similar minion. By extension 86 came to mean, "Don't serve anything to the indicated party because he is either broke or a creep." (Presumably you see how a code would come in handy in such situations.) Bartenders later used the term in connection with any person deemed too hammered to serve additional drinks to, and eventually it came to have the all-purpose meaning we assign to it today.

Other lunch counter code numbers (I rely here on the *Morris Dictionary of Word and Phrase Origins*) include 82, I need a glass of water (80 and 81 at times meant the same thing); 99, the manager is on the prowl; 98, ditto for the assistant manager; 33, gimme a cherry-flavored Coke; 55, I crave a root beer; 19, I yearn for a banana split; and 87½, check out the babe over yonder. The expression for this last item in my youth, incidentally, was "sluts on the right," said by one adolescent stud to another while cruising in a Ford Mustang. Just goes to show you how our language is constantly evolving.

Of course he's jolly because he hasn't any lips, but who was that flayed "Roger" immortalized by the buccaneers on their skull and crossbones? What part of the skeleton are the crossbones taken from? Is he any relation to the "Roger" who is continually being evoked by fighter pilots and other military types?—Jeremy L., Baltimore

He's jolly because he hasn't got any lips? What kind of weird coastal humor is that supposed to be? I'll handle the witticisms around here, if you don't mind.

Jolly Roger, needless to say, bears no relation to Roger Wilco. The origins of the term are disputed. According to one theory, the buccaneers who operated around the West Indies in the 1600s used a red flag dipped in blood or paint, whichever could be gotten more conveniently. The French supposedly called this the *joli rouge*, which the English, with their traditional disregard for the niceties of pronunciation, corrupted in Jolly Roger. Later the term was applied to the familiar black-flag-cum-bones that began to appear in various forms around 1700. An alternative hypothesis involves certain Asian pirates whose chiefs held the title Ali Raja, "king of the sea." The English naturally thought that *they* were the kings of the sea, and appropriated the term, with suitable emendations, for their own use. Unfortunately, both these explanations, as one historian puts it, "are so plausible that neither can be accepted as correct," plausibility being an infallible indication of error in etymological matters. Some venture the opinion that Jolly Roger may simply derive from the English word "roger," meaning a wandering vagabond, noting that "Old Roger" was a popular canting term for the devil.

The bone of choice for the crossbones, I suppose, would be the femur, although what possible difference it makes is difficult to imagine. Once again, however, I think it would be wise not to inquire too closely into the matter.

I am curious about the origin of an English expression analogous to "turkey" in modern American usage, presumably referring to some obscure (to me) political personage, as in our "his name is mud (Mudd)." The word is "pratt" (from Pratt, I guess), as in "he must have felt right pratt," following some humiliating experience.—Sue H., Chicago

I hate to be a party pooper, but there's no great mystery to "pratt" (or, as it's more commonly spelled, "prat"), and what mystery there is is impenetrable. It's an old English slang expression that dates at least from the sixteenth century, translating roughly as "ass," as in buttocks, not donkeys. As with most scatological slang, no one is quite sure where it came from. The word survives in American English in "pratfall"—that is, to fall on your prat.

By the way, I should note that "his name is mud" was a

common expression well before Dr. Samuel Mudd took his famous, ill-fated pity on John Wilkes Booth (Mudd treated the broken ankle Booth suffered in his leap to the stage of Ford's Theater; for his trouble, he was sentenced to life in a federal prison). The phrase first appears in print in 1820, 45 years before Lincoln's assassination. It probably originates in another obscure bit of English slang—"mud" was an eighteenth century equivalent of our "dope" or "dolt" and was used through the nineteenth century by union workers as a rough equivalent of "scab."

A question that has been bothering me since the third grade: which is correct English—"He had got some" or "He had gotten some"?—Joseph M., Chicago

There's still some ambiguity on this point. Using "gotten" as the past participle of "to get" will get you laughed out of every University Club in England, but it is in common use in the U.S., if only in speech and informal writing. One could make the case, however—and believe me, I will—that the choice of two past participle forms allows for a wider range of meanings than is possible with comparatively impoverished British English.

But first a bit of history. "Gotten" is actually the older form of the word, dating back to at least the fifteenth century. The King James translation of the Bible, published in 1611, prefers "gotten" to "got," but it was written in a self-consciously grand, archaic style. Shakespeare, working at the same time, seems to prefer "got," which by then had become the colloquial style. The "got" vs. "gotten" battle raged throughout the 1600s, the colonists taking "gotten" with them to America, where it flourished, while the stay-at-homes eventually came down on the side of "got." When Noah Webster, a man much in favor of simplifying the language, published his first American dictionary in 1864, he firmly declared "gotten" to be "obsolescent," but few paid strict attention. In fact, I would venture to say that today *both* forms are proper, in both formal and informal usages, depending on the context. Permit me to quote A.H. Marckwardt, author of *American English* (1958): "... most Americans regularly make a very precise distinction between *got* and *gotten.* 'We've got ten thousand dollars for laboratory equipment,' means that the funds are in our possession—we have them. 'We have gotten ten thousand dollars for laboratory equipment,' means that we have obtained or acquired this particular sum of money. Few Americans would have the slightest question about the difference in the meaning of these two sentences. ..." In other words, *got* means you obtained something

294

in the indefinite past, and *gotten* means you *recently* acquired it. This seems like a useful distinction to be able to make, and therefore Cecil brazenly declares it *absolutely proper for all purposes, public and private.* If some fussbudget gives you a hard time about it, tell him (or her) he'll have to answer to me.

Where did the sentence, "Now is the time for all good men to come to the aid of the party" originate?—Lotte B., Phoenix

From the typewriter it came, and to the typewriter it shall return: the phrase was proposed as a typing drill by a teacher named Charles E. Weller. Incidentally, many modern typing books now use the variant "Now is the time for all good men to come to the aid of their country" instead, because it exactly fills out a 70-space line if you put a period at the end.

"Hoist by my own petard"—everybody says it, and so do I. But neither I, nor anyone else I've ever heard employ this particular cliche, has the slightest idea of what a "petard" is. The one plausible explanation I've come across holds that a petard was a sort of 19th-century animal trap, a rope and a bent branch arrangement that caught the desired beast by one leg and pulled it up into the air. Can you confirm or deny?—Robert B., Chicago

This choice cliche, like so many others, comes from Shakespeare—and as far as I know, he wasn't traipsing through the woods in the 1800s gathering metaphors. The particular line is *Hamlet*, act III, scene 4, lines 206 and 207: "For 'tis sport to have the engineer/Hoist with his own petar. . . . " The Melancholy Dane is chuckling over the fate he has in store for his childhood comrades, Rosencrantz and Guildenstern, who are plotting to have him killed. Deflecting his existential crisis for a moment, Hamlet turns the plot on the plotters, substituting their names for his in the death warrant they carry from King Claudius. He continues: "But I will delve one yard below their mines/And blow them at the moon." The key word is "mines," as in "land mines," for that is what a petard is (or "petar," as Shakespeare spells it—there was no orthodox orthography in his time). A small explosive device designed to blow open barricaded doors and gates, the petard was a favorite weapon in Elizabethan times. Hamlet was saying, figuratively of course, that he would bury his bomb beneath Rosencrantz and Guildenstern's and "hoist" them, i.e., "blow them at the moon." Dirty Harry couldn't have put it any better.

The word "petard," we note with a barely suppressed giggle, comes from the Middle French *peter*, which is derived in turn from the Latin *peditum*—the sense of which (heh, heh) is "to break wind." Which must mean either that the French had a serious gas problem in those days, or that the petard was of something less than nuclear impact.

My brand new Encyclopedia Britannica *says that William Faulkner's name was originally spelled "Falkner," without the "u." But it doesn't say why he changed it. How about some Straight Dope?—Karen T., Chicago*

He didn't change it—the printer who set up his first book did, by mistake, and Faulkner decided to live with the new spelling rather than hassle to correct the error. He drew the line, however, at *The Sound and the Furry*.

What does the G in G-string stand for? Is it related to the G in G-men (the FBI), or should that be gee!-string? The origin of this name isn't the local common knowledge I expected.—Suzanne S., Baltimore

Modern lexicography, believe it or not, is at a loss to account for the origin of the term G-string (which actually is often spelled geestring). One writer offers the dubious thesis that a G-string resembles a capital G in shape, comprehension of which requires a degree of mental origami exceeding my humble capabilities. The earliest known reference to G-string is in J.H. Beadle's *Western Wilds*, written circa 1878: "Around each boy's waist is the tight 'geestring,' from which a single strip of cloth runs between the limbs from front to back." From this we see that G-string originally referred only to the thong around the waist, which is precisely what a "girdle" was in its earliest form. Thus G-string may be an abbreviation of "girdlestring," the only difficulty being that no such word has ever come to light, that I am aware of, anyway. Alternatively, we may note that "string" was a common 19th-century synonym for "whip," which was of the same rawhide construction as the aforementioned prairie G-string, and that "gee" is an expletive frequently employed to accelerate one's horse. A "geestring" may thus have been a pioneer horsewhip later discovered to be useful in holding up one's pants, or the equivalent thereof. Finally, and rather unimaginatively, we can offer the pedestrian observation that a G-string (the string part, that is) bears a superficial likeness to the fiddle string of similar designation. However, this explanation does not appeal to me, and I trust the discriminating reader will not think it is so hot either.

Where did the phrase "side kick" originate?—M.L., Washington, D.C.

Around the turn of the century, "side kick" was pickpocket slang for the front pocket in a coat or a pair of pants. Some unknown poet of the underworld must have made the connection between the front pocket—the hardest to pick—and an inseparable companion. By 1920 "side kick" meant "friend," and around 1940 it took on its present meaning, "Gabby Hayes."

In view of the blizzards we frequently have here in the Great White Midwest, how about a vocabulary lesson? I've heard the Eskimos have nine words for snow. What are they?—Karen, Chicago

I have a lot more than nine words for snow, and I do not even need to resort to Eskimo. I have a powerful descriptive vocabulary.

However, if we must confine ourselves to Eskimo talk, I can still come up with quite a few terms, as long as you will let me throw in some words for ice too: *kaniktshaq*, snow; *qanik*, falling snow; *anijo*, snow on the ground; *hiko* (*tsiko* in some dialects), ice; *tsikut*, large broken up masses of ice; *hikuliaq*, thin ice; *quahak*, new ice without snow; *kanut*, new ice with snow; *pugtaq*, drift ice; *peqalujaq*, old ice; *manelaq*, pack ice; *ivuneq*, high pack ice; *maneraq*, smooth ice; *akuvijarjuak*, thin ice on the sea; *kuhugaq*, icicle; *nilak*, fresh water ice; *tugartaq*, firm winter ice; *nahauliq*, snow bunting.

If we wish to include peripheral items we may speak of *iglo*, snow house (igloo); *haviujaq*, snow knife; *puatlrit*, snow shovel; *uvkuag*, block of snow for closing the door of a snow hut. I imagine after-dinner chats in Eskimoland must get a bit monotonous after a while, considering the restricted range of subject matter. Fortunately, they have about 20 words for trout to liven things up with.

Most of the preceding words are from the dialect of the Umingmaktormiut, a tribe living in the eastern part of arctic America. Since the necessary diacritical marks are not available, the spellings are a little on the approximate side. However, Eskimos are not such hot spellers anyway.

The problem with trying to pin down exactly how many Eskimo words there are for snow and/or ice—or for anything, for that matter—is that Eskimo is what is called a "polysynthetic" language, which means you sort of make up words as you go along, by connecting various particles to your basic root word. For example, we may add the suffix *-tluk*, bad, to *kaniktshaq*, snow, and come up with *kaniktshartluk*, bad snow. By means of this system we may manufacture words that would fracture the jaw of an elk. To illustrate, I offer the word *takusariartorumagaluarnerpa*, a chewy mouthful signifying: "Do you think he really intends to go look after it?" It takes nerve to flog your way through a word of this magnitude. That is why Eskimos are so laconic— they're conserving their strength for their next foray into their godawful grammar.

In my spare time I have been attempting to construct an Eskimo sentence in my basement, such as will be suitable for the season. I have not got it perfected yet, but it is coming along pretty well, and with a coat of paint or two it might pass for the genuine article. So far I have: *kaniktshaq moritlkatsio atsuniartoq*. When completed, this sentence will proclaim: "Look at all this fucking snow." At present it means: "Observe the snow. It fornicates." This is not poetic, but it is serviceable, and I intend to employ it at the next opportunity. Anyone who feels it would alleviate his or her tension is invited to do likewise. Should it be felt that this is too burdensome a load of verbiage to be hauling around all the time, one may avail oneself of the timeless Eskimo interjection *anaq*, "shit." This is appropriate to a wide variety of situations.

Chapter 16

Fun and Games

During a slow moment in our Regulation of Gene Expression class at school the other day, the prof posed the following question: "What are the five ways of reaching first base without hitting the ball?" Most of us being graduate students, we had no problem coming up with four—a walk, hit by pitch, dropped third strike, and catcher's interference—but the fifth, if indeed it exists, remains an unknown. Can you enlighten us?—Geoffrey S., for Bio Science 447, Chicago

The Straight Dope, always willing to go that extra mile, not only gives you number five, but throws in number six, too, at absolutely no extra charge.

According to Official Rule 7.05 (h), the batter and base runners get one base "if a ball, pitched to the batter, or thrown by the pitcher from his position on the pitcher's plate to a base to catch a runner, goes into a stand or a bench, or over or through a field fence or backstop."

Alternatively, according to 7.05 (i), "on ball four or strike three, when the pitch passes the catcher and lodges in the umpire's mask or paraphernalia," the batter and runners are entitled to advance one base. That is, if they can stop laughing long enough.

I'm a rabid baseball fan, and often my friends depend upon me to provide the wisdom from on high when it comes to the grand old game. But the one thing people invariably ask is: "Why is the shortstop called the shortstop? I get all the other ones, but that's the weird one!" I've got enough problems with self-esteem as it is, and I don't need it undercut any further by not being able to answer that question. I look to you for the answer. I promise to credit you every time I repeat your reply.—Curt L., Los Angeles

That's the spirit. The origin of the word "shortstop" appears to have been lost in the mists of antiquity, but the absence of the facts has never prevented me from making something up, and the present case is no exception. I have here a Currier & Ives lithograph that purports to depict the first officially recorded baseball game, which occurred on or about June 19, 1846, in Hoboken, New Jersey, between the Knickerbockers and the New York Nine. Notwithstanding the fact that the Knickerbockers had made up the rules, they lost. This was not exactly what you would call a team of destiny.

Anyway, the print shows most of the infielders standing more or less on top of their bases, with the shortstop situated on the infield grass, perhaps 20 feet closer to home than his modern counterpart. Other sources confirm that this was the usual practice in the early days.

We may further note that the baseballs of yesteryear were fatter and, how shall we say, deader—that strikes me uneuphoniously, but you know what I mean—than they are today, and partook more of the bulbous quality that is commemorated nowadays in such phrases as "heave the old tomato, Jack." Moreover, this was the era before the introduction of the mechanical lawnmower, when infields were savage jungles that captured and ate innocent baseballs, or at least kept them from getting very far.

So it is not difficult to suppose that in the infancy of the game, there may have been a need for an infielder who could deal with short-range ground balls expeditiously, before they dribbled to a halt and got lost somewhere—who could "stop them short," you see. Sure you do. Later, of course, when the ball got livelier and the grass was more carefully attended to, the velocity of the average grounder would increase considerably, requiring the shortstop to retreat and join the other infielders in the wide arc that characterizes modern defensive alignment.

There are a couple holes in this theory, but I will leave it to the inevitable gang of malcontents to point them out.

While sitting in the ball park the other day watching the Orioles make mincemeat out of—oh, I think it was the Royals, my companions made fun of me because of my fear of the stray fly ball. I maintain that getting cracked in the head with one of those is no joke, and that it has laid a fan to rest more than a few times. My friends think I'm nuts, but I know you'll prove my fears have a foundation in truth. Can you help me show them I'm not par-

anoid, just cautious? Then maybe we can sit behind the home plate screen.—Susie O., Baltimore

Baseball may be the most statistics-crazed sport of them all, but the clubs seem strangely reluctant to keep records of fan fatalities, for some reason. You may have noticed the disclaimer printed on the back of your ticket, in which the management gracefully declines any responsibility for injuries you may suffer while in the park. There is some question as to whether that disclaimer would stand up in court, but so far it's worked pretty well: no lawsuits have been filed in anyone's memory, and so none of the clubs bother to keep tabs on the people who pass through their first-aid stations.

And so, faced with a shocking lack of documentation, I am forced to invent some of my own. It does happen: in an informal survey of major league clubs, I came up with a ballpark figure (grin) of three or four serious injuries to fans caused by batted balls per club, per year. Now, let us assume the absolute worst: that the fates decide to frown upon America's national sport, pushing the annual number of fan injuries up to a nice, round, easily managed figure of five. There are 12 teams in the National League, 14 in the American. With the help of some simple multiplication, we come up with a total, nationwide figure of 130 injuries each year. The combined attendance in 1977 (I know this is a long time ago, but that's the last time I figured it out, and I refuse to go through this twice) for all National and American League games was 38,703,975, which makes your odds for survival look fairly good: you'd have one chance in 297,723 of being beaned. If we break that down even further, we discover that—given a season consisting of 162 games—you could attend every Orioles game for 1,838 years (and wouldn't that be a thrill?) before the odds began to creep up on you. All of which sounds very comforting, even though it's completely meaningless.

All in all, looks like you'd be facing more of a threat by taking a shower, but getting hit by a ball is no picnic. A well-hit ball can easily achieve a speed of over 100 MPH, and that adds up to a lot of impact. By way of illustration, I am reminded of the sad story of Joe Sprinz. In 1939, the one-time Cleveland Indians catcher participated in a publicity stunt set up by the San Francisco Seals, a minor league team, in which he was supposed to catch a ball dropped from an airplane flying at an altitude of 1,000 feet. Joe did his damnedest, but the first four balls fell wide of the mark. Finally, on the fifth ball, Joe succeeded, but the impact knocked out four of his front teeth. Joe did, however, earn

himself immortality in the *Guinness Book of World Records*—
"World's Highest Catch"—so the sacrifice was no doubt worth it.

*What is the reason for the pitcher's mound in baseball? Also, are
there any regulations regarding the specifications of the dirt heap
in question?—R.H., Los Angeles*

The best way to understand the purpose of the mound is to
imagine the situation greatly exaggerated: picture yourself trying
to hit a fastball thrown at you from ten feet in the air. The angle
of the ball's path (and, I suppose, the force of gravity, to some
imperceptible extent) would make the task more difficult than it
would be if the pitcher were standing level with you. In short, the
height gives the pitcher an advantage. Over the years, baseball
men have tinkered with this and other variables in order to fine
tune the delicate balance between pitching and batting. Thus in
1879, it took nine balls (i.e., nonstrikes) to draw a walk; before
1887, the batter had the right to demand a high or low pitch; the
distance from pitcher's plate to home plate was increased from 45
to 50 feet in 1881, and again to 60 feet, 6 inches in 1893.

The mound first shows up in the rules of 1903. In 1963, to
adjust for a perceived pitcher's advantage, its height was changed
from 15 inches to 10. The rules also give specifications for such
things as the size of the pitcher's plate, or "rubber" (24 by 6
inches), the radius of the circle (nine feet), and the frontal slope
(one inch per foot over a specified range). Though these specs
appear in the official rules under the dubious heading "Suggested
Layout," they are considered law. Various other aspects of mound
construction are left up to the imagination, if any, of individual
team owners.

*My baseball cards from several seasons in the 50s refer to the
baseball team from Cincinnati as the "Redlegs." I seem to remember at one point this was because of the connotations of "Reds."
What exactly is the story?—Bruce M., Chicago*

When the team was first formed in 1890, it was known as
the Red Stockings—quite a mouthful for tight-lipped midwesterners, who soon shortened it to Redlegs, and then to Reds. The
official name of the company that owns the team now is "Cincinnati Reds, Inc."—although no one in the organization is exactly
sure when the change in names took place, thanks to the rather
casual record-keeping that prevailed in the early days of baseball.
But Reds they were through the 40s, until the sinister junior senator
from Wisconsin, Joseph McCarthy, started casting aspersions on

that end of the spectrum. Cincinnati being as all-American as any town you could name, and more so than most, the citizens quickly reverted to the older nickname. The situation was disturbingly similar to World War I, when sauerkraut became "victory cabbage" and frankfurters became "hot dogs" in order to avoid the taint of German militarism. After McCarthy fell from the scene, the team went quietly back to being the Reds (no outbreak of Bolshevik activity was immediately apparent), but among native Cincinnatians—and there are a few people who will admit to it—"Redlegs" remains the preferred appellation to this day.

Where does the baseball term "bullpen" come from?—Terry M., Los Angeles

All right, etymology fans. Here are three theories, arranged in order of preposterousness. You can stop when you've had enough:

1. The bullpen looks like a bull pen. That is to say, the area set aside for practicing pitchers bears an uncanny resemblance to the fenced-in spot where fighting bulls were kept before bullfights and rodeos. No doubt you've noticed the strange similarity between Fernando Valenzuela in the heat of warm-up and an enraged bovine preparing to dismember some hapless victim.

2. The bullpen looks like a bullpen. In the early days of this century, policemen were popularly called "bulls," out of respect for their towering strength and masculinity. Jail cells, particularly those crude arrangements of wire fence that were (and are) used to temporarily hold prisoners awaiting arraignment, were consequently dubbed "bullpens," i.e., pens maintained by the "bulls." After the Black Sox scandal of 1919, many of Chicago's beloved ballplayers, accused of throwing the World Series, had an opportunity to check out the similarity first hand.

3. It was all a cheap publicity stunt. One of the regulation features of early ballparks, supposedly, was a gigantic billboard advertising Bull Durham tobacco, inevitably located out in left field, near the pitchers' warm-up area. Hence the bullpen was the pen near the Bull. (Which, frankly, sounds like a lot of bull to me.)

My son plays on his college baseball team at the University of Wisconsin and has long had ambitions to break into the major leagues. The problem is that he is both left-handed and a catcher, for some reason a rare combination in the world of professional baseball. My sportswriter friends say that because of this the kid hasn't got a chance. Is this true? What accounts for this mystifying prejudice?—Don Y., Evanston, Illinois

As is my custom in matters of this nature, Don, I have consulted the Baseball Sachems, and the universal sentiment is that your son is doomed, baseball-wise, and had best prepare himself for a life of honest toil. As near as I can make out there have been but two left-handed catchers in the majors in the last 25 years, both of whom played, oddly enough, in Chicago, and both of whom caught just two games before moving on to more profitable employment: Mike Squires, Sox, 1980, and Dale Long, Cubs, 1958. The reason there are virtually no left-handed catchers apparently is that most batters are right-handed and thus stand to the left side of home plate (I don't mind admitting this caused me no end of confusion in the days of my youth), blocking the catcher's throw to second or third. Being a lefty myself, I have no doubt that any determined southpaw could overcome this minor handicap if given half a chance. However, unreasoning bigotry is rampant in the baseball biz.

I can't for the life of me figure out why tennis scoring is so screwed up. First you get fifteen, then thirty, and just when you think there's a pattern developing, the next point is called forty. I've been asking all the "experts," but they all just shrug and mumble. What do you say, Cecil?—Mary C., Phoenix

There's a reason for everything, my dear—in this case, the reason goes back to medieval numerology. The number 60 was considered to be a "good" or "complete" number back then, in about the same way you'd consider 100 to be a nice round figure today. The medieval version of tennis, therefore, was based on 60—the four points were 15, 30, 45 (which we abbreviate to 40) and 60, or game.

There's a common misconception that the equally puzzling "love," or zero, derives from the French *l'oeuf,* "egg," or, by extension, goose-egg or zero. Actually, it comes from the idea of playing for love, rather than money—the implication being that one who scores zero consistently can only be motivated by a true love of the game. Tennis originated in the 12th or 13th century in France, where it was called *jeu de paume* ("palm game"). It seems to have derived its present appellation from the French habit of calling *"tenez!"* before serving.

Has anyone of the Oriental persuasion ever played major league baseball in this country?—Judy H., Chicago

You betcha, gumdrop. Currently there's Lenn Sakata, infielder (mostly second base) for the Baltimore Orioles, who's an ethnic Japanese from Hawaii. There's also Mike K. (for Ken-Wai) Lum, who pinch-hit for the Chicago Cubs for a while after having played first base for the Atlanta Braves and I believe the Cincinnati Reds. Mike, who's also from Hawaii, is at least partly Chinese. Going back a few years we find Masanori Murakami, who pitched in 1964 and 1965 for the San Francisco Giants, where he compiled a 5-1 record. Previously a professional baseball player in Japan, Murakami as far as I know is the only native Japanese ever to have played major league ball in the U.S. Players with at least some Oriental ancestry include Mets pitcher Ron Darling (his mother was half Chinese, making him one-quarter Chinese), and Giants pitcher Atlee Hammaker (his mother was Japanese). There was also a player named Bobby Balcena who played seven games for Cincinnati in 1956, who I seem to remember was Filipino. However, unlikely as it may seem, I could be wrong. While we're on the subject of Orientals in macho American sports I should mention John Arnold, a return specialist and wide receiver for the Detroit Lions in 1979 and 1980. Born on an air base at Shizaka, Japan, Arnold had an American father and a Japanese mother and didn't get to the U.S. until he was in seventh grade. Play your cards right and you can parlay these amazing facts into big bux next time you visit the local tavern. Nothing like a little news you can use, I always say.

I knew a guy in college who could swallow lit cigarettes. Well, not really swallow them, but hold them in his mouth for what seemed like a pretty long length of time. He would then flip the cigarette back out and continue smoking. I have envied him all these years. It seems like a great way to pick up girls. How is it done? He used to say he had toughened up the inside of his mouth by chewing tobacco, but no one believed him.—Tom K., Chicago

Your friend was hip to an old magician's trick, sometimes used in sleight-of-hand routines. The performer would appear to take a lit cigarette from his mouth, hold it out in his fist, and make it vanish. What he'd really do is flip the cigarette back in his mouth, gripping it between his teeth and his lower lip, and hold it there, hopefully out of harm's way, until he was ready to reproduce it.

Unfortunately, that's all there is to the trick. The rest requires practice and three crucial props: a big mouth, a strong stomach, and a short cigarette. Not to mention a fairly wide masochistic streak. Inhaling the smoke can be a fatal mistake: not only will you choke, but the cigarette will heat up to an unbearable degree. Learn to breathe through your nose. Not only is it safer, but pretty soon you'll be able to talk like Rex Reed. Still, I feel duty bound to issue a Stern Warning to Youth. Don't try it unless you have an asbestos tongue. Believe me, there are better ways of picking up girls—have you tried wiggling your ears? It never fails.

However, you may (or may not) be interested to know that in some parts of the world, cigarettes are routinely smoked in reverse (hence the expression, "backward nations"). Among the lower classes in India, Korea, and some Caribbean islands, it's a common practice to put the burning tip of the cigarette in the mouth and draw air in through the unlit end. Again, the smoke is not inhaled, but blown back through the cigarette. In the Philippines, this peculiar custom is known as *bakwe*, and for some unknown reason it is practiced mainly by middle-aged married women. One earnest *bakwe* smoker told a correspondent for the *Journal of the American Dental Association* (apparently having no one better to unburden herself to at the time) that the main attraction of the habit is the delicious warming sensation it produces in the mouth, a tremendous boon during the rainy season.

I have long been mystified by ventriloquists. How do they do it? It seems impossible. Try to say "Sherry Lewis" with your mouth closed.—Joyce K., Seattle

It's "Shari," snookums, not "Sherry." We like to be punctilious about our spelling in this column. The trick in any case is not to say "Shari Lewis" with your mouth closed, but rather to say it without moving your lips, which are kept open about a quarter inch at all times. But there is more to voice-throwing than that. Ventriloquism relies on the fact that the ability of the human ear to locate the source of a sound without visual and other cues is very poor. What the ventriloquist does is supply misleading cues through the use of what we masters of deceit refer to as stagecraft and voice. Stagecraft consists of using gestures, eye movements, "patter," and so on to direct attention to wherever the voice is supposed to be coming from. Voice is the ability not only to talk without moving your lips but also to alter the pitch and cadence of your voice so as to create a second "personality," which you can then bestow on the object of your choice.

The talking-without-moving-your-lips part is easier than you might think. For starters, you learn to grin like an idiot at all times. This serves the dual purpose of baffling your audience and stretching your lower jaw muscles, making it easier to keep them motionless. There are only six tough sounds—the "labials," or lip sounds, *b*, *f*, *m*, *p*, *v*, and *w*. Essentially what you do is substitute some vaguely similar sound, talk fast, and let people hear what they want to hear. For *w*, for instance, we substitute *oo*. "Where" becomes "oo-air," "twenty" becomes "too-en-tee," and so on. Eventually you learn to run the sounds together to more or less eliminate the extra syllable. For *f* we substitute a *th* as in *think*, making the sound barely audible and putting most of the emphasis on the rest of the word. Thus the sentence "Why is Willie feeling funny?" becomes "Oo-eye is Oo-illie th*eeling* th*unny*?" You may think this sounds retarded, but we must have a positive attitude about this. There are other substitutions for other labials.

Having grasped the rudiments, we may then move on to the fine points, such as projecting your voice while drinking water. To do this you go out to some sleazy singles bar and get a beer stein that looks bulky but actually contains amazingly little liquid (no doubt you've come across these before). You raise the glass to your lips while concluding your spiel and pour the liquid into your mouth, making no effort to swallow. Since sound production takes place in the back and upper portions of the mouth, the liquid sloshing around your lower molars will not interfere. You time your rap in such a way that you finish at the same time you get done "drinking," whereupon you take your bow, swallow, and exit stage left. An infant could do it.

As a final touch, the ventriloquist must memorize a vast quantity of horrible jokes, which are to be sprinkled strategically throughout the act. For instance:

A: My great grandfather was killed 75 years ago in a parachute jump.

B: They didn't have parachutes 75 years ago.

A: I know. That's how he got killed.

The typical audience will be so appalled by this alleged witticism that any minor defects in your technique will pass unnoticed in the hail of tomatoes, beer bottles, and dead cats that will surely follow. Take it from an old trouper, kids.

On a recent pilgrimage to Troy Grove, Illinois to visit the home of Wild Bill Hickok, one of our company happened to mention that according to legend Wild Bill was shot while holding "black aces and eights." This hand has come to be known as the "dead man's hand." Is the story apocryphal, and if it is true, what was the fifth card in Wild Bill's hand?—Larry N., Chicago

You've settled on one of the few bits of Western lore that has some basis in fact. Wild Bill was indeed holding black aces and eights when he was plugged by Jack McCall on the fateful day of August 2, 1876, in the charming suburb of Deadwood, deep in the Dakota Territory. Bill's fifth card was the deuce of spades, which must have made for a pretty grim-looking hand. I'm surprised he didn't commit suicide.

John Ford got things a little confused when he tried to lay the curse of the Dead Man's Hand on one of the heavies in *Stagecoach*. Poor Luke Plummer found himself holding the appropriate black eights, but one of his aces was red—diamonds, to be specific. Luke's fifth card was the queen of hearts, all of which made for a much nicer composition than the real thing. John Wayne offed him anyway.

Hearts and diamonds I understand from Mike Jordan's song. Clubs look enough like clovers to satisfy me. But for understanding what spades are and why these four were chosen in the first place, I'm writing to you. I just bet you know.—Phoebe E., Montlake, Utah

Pretty safe bet, toots. The French invented the suit designations that are used today; each supposedly indicates one of the principal divisions of medieval society: the heart, *coeur*, the clergy; the club, *trefle*, the peasants; the diamond, *carreau*, merchants and tradesmen; and the sword, *pique*, the nobility. *Espada*, the Spanish equivalent of the French *pique*, has become our present day spade.

The symbolic significance of the nobleman's sword is obvious enough, but some of the other associations are a little obscure. Clubs can be interpreted in two ways: as walking-sticks or cudgels, the characteristic weapons of the lower class, who were frequently forbidden to own swords; or as cloverleaves, indicating agriculture. Hearts symbolize courage and virtue, which presumably would pertain to the clergy, the highest level of society. The diamond apparently was originally a paving tile, indicating the artisan-tradesman group, purveyors of material goods. Alternatively, there is the obvious connection between diamonds and money.

The early Italian designations, from which the French derive, are a little clearer: cups (the clergyman's chalice); swords; clubs or batons; and money. The Germans originally used hearts, acorns, bells, and leaves, which you occasionally still see in Eastern Europe. God knows what they stand for, but you didn't ask, so I won't have to make up an interpretation. The principal advantage of the

French symbols is that they were easy to draw and easy to recognize, which no doubt explains their subsequent popularity.

I've got a bet with my poker buddies. What hand did Steve McQueen lose to Edward G. Robinson's straight flush in the movie The Cincinnati Kid?*—John F., Washington, D.C.*

My usual cut on bets is 20 percent.

Robinson was showing the eight, nine, ten, and queen of diamonds; McQueen the ace of clubs, the ace of spades, the ten of clubs, and the ten of spades. On the call, Robinson shows the jack of diamonds for a straight flush, beating McQueen, who turns up the ace of diamonds for a full house. "You owe me five thousand dollars, kid," Robinson purrs, as McQueen breaks out in hives.

In the past few years I have heard different things about various games played in some colleges in the East. Dungeons & Dragons is one of them. What I would like to know is the different types and rules of these games, and where I can learn more about them.—R.C.M., Skokie, Illinois

The principal game played in colleges in the East—and everywhere else, for that matter—is called "Snoozing Your Way Through Four Years of Monotonous Drivel So You Can Collect a Piece of Paper That Entitles You to Make Twice as Much Money as the General Run of Mankind While Doing Half the Work." I played it, and see where I am today—a famous author and certified Beautiful Person. Most profitable damn nap I ever took.

I suppose, however, that you are referring to what are loosely called "fantasy games," a relatively recent offshoot of the military games that have been around for eons. Dungeons & Dragons (or D&D, as it is more familiarly called), is far and away the best-selling of all such games, presently claiming some 400,000 devotees—I use the word advisedly—worldwide. Quite frankly I have some reservations about bestowing further publicity on this demented pastime, but a devotion to the noble principles of journalism demands that the facts be exposed, come what may.

D&D was invented in 1974 by one Gary Gygax, whose father was a violinist for the Chicago Symphony Orchestra. (This strikes me as significant, somehow.) Gary moved at an early age to Lake Geneva, Wisconsin, where his minions today are cranking out D&D rule books, D&D miniature playing pieces, and all sorts of other dubious D&D paraphernalia to palm off on a gullible public. By means of guile and threats of violence it happens I have managed to get my hands on a couple of those sacred rule books, and let me tell you, R. buddy, this game is weird.

The basic idea in your run-of-the-mill Go Fish-type game is to get all your opponent's cards or all his checkers or some other readily graspable commodity, but this is not the case with D&D. Here is a quote from Mr. Gygax on the subject: "The ultimate aim of the game is to gain sufficient esteem as a good player to retire your character—he becomes a kind of mythical, historical figure, someone for others to look up to and admire." A lifetime of Parcheesi does not adequately prepare you for this.

To play D&D you need at least two acolytes, who play under the guidance of a vaguely Mansonesque personage called the Dungeon Master (DM). By means of various murky protocols involving the use of charts and dice, each player establishes the persona

of the "character" he or she will manipulate in the game, who typically ends up (if male) being an antisocial cutthroat of some sort, or (if female) possessed of large, grapefruit-like breasts. I deduce the latter from studying the illustrations in the book. Apart from predictable characteristics like strength and intelligence, players also have to determine such baffling minutiae as their likelihood of contracting communicable diseases or becoming infested by parasites. I am at a loss to comprehend the significance of such things, but that is what the rule book says.

The preliminaries having been dealt with, the players are led through an imaginary dungeon devised by the DM, in search of treasure or something similar. On the way, they will encounter various obstacles and evil creatures, which they will have to defeat or evade.

The concept seems simple enough: it is the application that

throws me. There are two main problems: (1) there are one billion rules, and (2) the game requires nonstop mathematical finagling that would constipate Einstein. The rule book is laden with such mystifying pronouncements as the following: "An ancient spell-using red dragon of huge size with 88 hits points has a BXPV of 1300, XP/HP total of 1408, SAXPB of 2800 (armor class plus special defense plus high intelligence plus saving throw bonus due to h.p./die), and an EAXPA of 2550 (major breath weapon plus spell use plus attack damage of 3-30/bite)—totalling 7758 h.p." Here we have a game that combines the charm of a Pentagon briefing with the excitement of double-entry bookkeeping. The lure of this sort of thing is beyond my comprehension.

If you wish to know more about Dungeons & Dragons, for some reason, you can find D&D paraphernalia at many hobby and game stores, or you may write to Mr. Gygax's company, TSR Hobbies, Inc., at Box 756, Lake Geneva, Wisconsin 53147. Among numerous other things, they offer a monthly magazine called *The Dragon*, which I understand is principally useful in obfuscating such portions of the game as you think you already understand. Lotsa luck, buddy.

According to my father, who misspent his youth as thoroughly as I am trying to misspend mine, pinball machines didn't always have flippers. When he was a boy, he says, the machines allowed you only the use of the plunger—you shot the ball up to the top, and then watched helplessly as it rolled down the board. Is this true? (Not that I doubt my father, but he is given to strange flights of fancy.) If so, was this supposed to be fun, or what?—B.F., Morton Grove, Illinois

Show some respect, my son. We children of the 1980s, constantly on the prowl for "kicks" and "action," require nonstop razzle-dazzle if we are not to become bored. But our ancestors were more easily amused. They were still able to take pleasure in the majestic forces of nature, such as gravity. This explains the appeal of flipperless pinball, which is actually a modern variation on the age-old game of bagatelle. It was said to have been invented by the ancient Greeks, who used to amuse themselves between Socratic dialogs by rolling balls down the side of a hill, aiming for holes dug along the route. By the time the Renaissance bloomed, the game had been adapted to tabletop play: the object was still to drop balls in holes, but the balls were propelled from the bottom of an inclined playing board by means of a cue stick. The holes were protected by an arrangement of pins, which sealed off the easy shots. The game remained popular through the end of the nineteenth century, when interest began to flag.

Pinball as we know it began in 1930, when David Gottlieb— a name that should be revered by every pinball aficionado— designed a small (16x24 inches) coin-operated bagatelle board he named "Baffle Ball." Instead of a cue stick, the game used a built-in plunger, the same simple but elegant device that survives today. For a penny, the player enjoyed the spectacle of shooting seven balls to the top of the machine and watching fatalistically as they rolled down and fell (or didn't fall) into the scoring holes. Soon, the players developed a technique politely known as "nudging," which consisted of slamming the board from side to side in an effort to influence the ball's progress. Nudging did not become the fine art it is today until 1933, when the British Hardinges Company introduced an alarm bell that went off with a deafening roar whenever the machine was "tilted."

Pinball increased in popularity through the 30s and the manufacturers vied with each other to give the game more action and greater ball control. In 1933, the Rock-Ola Company (now remembered as a manufacturer of prophetically-named jukeboxes) introduced a game called "Juggle Ball," which featured an early prototype of the flipper in the form of a metal rod that ran the length of the board and could be used to point the ball from hole to hole. The Bally Manufacturing Company countered with "Fleet" in 1934, the first board to use the electric kickers called "solenoids" responsible for the frenetic action of today's games. But Bally's greatest triumph came in 1936, when the scoring holes were first replaced by bumpers on a board titled, with great originality, "Bumpers."

Unfortunately, all was not well in the world of pinball. Just as the game was riding the first crest of its popularity, authorities began a nationwide crackdown on slot machines. The greedy manufacturers of the one-armed bandits promptly invaded the previously unsullied pinball industry, and began marketing a bastard version of the pinball machine known as the "bingo." These machines were nothing more than thinly-disguised slot machines that took advantage of a loophole in the law defining gambling devices. To qualify as a gambling device, a machine had to offer a "thing of value"—money, merchandise, or tokens—as a reward. What bingos offered instead was the chance at free games. You could play a game for one coin (nowadays it's a quarter or more but for a long time you could find dime machines), or you could put in two coins and increase your free-game payoff if you won

312

(odds were printed on the backboard). I'm told that ten coins yielded the optimum payoff, but there were also many other tantalizing payoff gimmicks, called features, which you could activate by feeding in still more coins. Twenty coins gave you an odds-on chance to win something.

The game itself was a 20 or 25 hole playing field with posts. The numbered holes corresponded to lights on the backboard which in turn comprised a bingo game. Three, four, or five in a row on the backboard won a specified number of free games. If you put in the maximum number of coins and won 300 games you'd have to stick around all day to work them off, but in many of the sleazy venues in which bingos were found the proprietor was always glad to "take the free games off" and convert them to cold cash. Three hundred freebies at two bits per (it was less in the early days, of course) would thus net you $75.

Needless to say, this emphasis on money was a gross perversion of the original spirit of pinball, which celebrated athletic grace and determination. The authorities were quick to recognize the change. By 1935, bingos had been banned in New York, but not before they had driven legitimate pinball purveyors to the brink of bankruptcy. The death blow came on January 21, 1942, when—after the New York cops decided it was too much trouble to make the distinction between bingos and pinballs—Bronx magistrate Ambrose J. Haddock ruled that "all pinball machines are illegal even if they reward the player with nothing more substantial than amusement." In subsequent raids, 3,252 machines were confiscated and destroyed and their metal parts (including 3,000 pounds of balls) given to the war effort. Other cities followed New York's example.

But the manufacturers of true pinball machines did not give up. In 1945 after the war ended Bally went back into production with a game designed to add a new element of ball control. Called "Nudgy," the board featured a button on the side, which, when pressed, would jerk the entire playfield backwards, sending the ball back to the top of the machine. It was a dismal failure, apparently because the players resented this electronic intrusion on their carefully honed nudging skills. It took the far-reaching mind of one Harry Mabs, a designer for the Gottlieb company, to come up with the ultimate ball control device—one that added a new element of skill to the game without impinging upon the player's pride. The "flipper," as Mabs christened his movable bumper, first appeared in October 1947 on the Gottlieb game "Humpty Dumpty." This historic machine featured six flippers, which were gradually reduced to two in subsequent models as the players developed greater facility. The flipper proved to be the salvation of the industry. Although pinball continued to be illegal in many jurisdictions for decades afterward, the flipper made it clearly a game of skill and not of chance, and it attracted many dedicated sportsmen, such as myself, whose interest in the game was purely aesthetic. Of course, if you won 300 free games, that was OK too.

Pinball has been eclipsed by the video game in recent years, and some have rashly predicted its demise. True fans know, however, that no wimpy microchip can match the pulse-pounding pleasures of pinball: the lights, the action, the scantily-clad maidens on the backboard. Video games may come and go; pinball alone endures.

Spring is in the air, and it's time to start making those vacation plans. We really want to get away from it all this year, head some place where the Big Mac fears to tread, where there aren't any motels, or roadside reptile zoos, or souvenir stands. But every

state park we've been to seems to be filled with Country Squires, camper trailers, and folks lusting to "get back to the earth." Where's the real wilderness, Cecil? The unspoiled virgin territory? Where can a person go for a little peace and quiet?—Nature Lovers, Santa Monica, California

I'd recommend rowing out to a little fun spot in the South Pacific, 48 degrees, 30 minutes south, 120 degrees, 30 minutes west. You won't find any Big Macs there. In fact, you won't find anything at all. You'll be 1,660 miles from the nearest land, half-way between Pitcairn Island (of *Mutiny on the Bounty* fame) and Cape Dart, Antarctica—smack in the middle of the emptiest area on the face of the earth, with 8,657,000 square miles of pure, unadulterated water to enjoy. You might want to bring some cards, in case watching the waves gets a little dull. You wanted peace? You wanted quiet? Shut up and deal.

Your discussion of pinball has brought to mind dim memories of an unusual game in which two players faced each other over a single board. The idea was to keep the ball on your half of the machine to rack up points. A bad shot would send it to the other player's side. This was an unusually compelling game, but I haven't seen it in many years. What happened to it?—Roger S., Chicago

You're probably thinking of *Challenger*, a game that D. Gottlieb and Company brought out in May 1971. The radically redesigned playfield apparently went against the grain of the company that traditionally has been the most conservative of pinball manufacturers, and after a brief run it was dropped from their line.

In the mid-70s an Indianapolis company called Komputer Dynamics (sic) announced a modified version of *Challenger* titled *Invasion Strategy*. A solid state, printed circuit game, it featured eight flippers (four for each player), two balls, and electronic sound effects. Unfortunately, Komputer Dynamic's business sense proved to be on a par with its spelling, and after scoring a success at the 1975 Chicago trade show, the company went under, taking the game with it. *Challenger* and *Invasion Strategy* are virtually impossible to find today, although a couple may yet be lurking in some dusty arcade.

Cecil, how about something for us Scrabble freaks? A list of all the usable two-letter words would be fantastic!—Mel R., Phoenix

Oh, me no do it. If so, it do me in.

315

Chapter 17

≈≈≈≈≈≈≈≈≈≈≈

Rock 'n' Roll, Etc.

My friend attended your typical inner-city sleaze high school in the late 60s. I attended your average insulated isolated sterile high school in the suburbs. Despite these similarities we learned two different versions of the lyrics to "Louie Louie" by the Kingsmen, inasmuch as the words are unintelligible. Can you, dear Cecil, separate our virginal teenage sexual fantasies from the "real" and "official" lyrics?—Barbara K., Robin D., Chicago

Funny you should bring this up, girls. It just so happens that I attended a seance last Sunday and had the opportunity to discuss this very topic with some of my friends from the afterlife. Bob Denver, AKA Maynard G. Krebs of TV's *Dobie Gillis*—who, as I'm sure you'll recall, died tragically when a radio fell into his bathtub—said that one of the lines of the song is, "I fuck a girl endlessly." Jerry Mathers of *Leave it to Beaver*, who was blown apart in Vietnam (some people think he grew up to be Alice Cooper, but that's just one of those silly myths), opined that another line is, "I shoot a wad into her hair." Paul McCartney recalled that he always used to sing, "Tell her I'll never lay her again." It pained me to shatter their illusions—as it pains me, believe me, to shatter yours—but the "real" lyrics to "Louie Louie" are about as racy as a Neil Simon script, and almost as dumb. What's more, we have the assurance of the man who wrote the song, one Richard Berry, that the Kingsmen did not spice it up in the studio. The song was about seven years old when the Kingsmen recorded their version in 1963, and the fantastic legend that grew up in its wake—a legend that even an FCC investigation couldn't kill—seems to have sprung solely from their extraordinary lack of elocution.

Berry, who spoke on the subject a while back to a Los Angeles interviewer named Bill Reed, explains the song as the lament of a seafaring man, spoken to a sympathetic bartender named Louie. Here, without further ado, are the "official" published lyrics: "Louie Louie, me gotta go. Louie Louie, me gotta go. A fine little girl, she wait for me. Me catch the ship across the sea. I sailed the ship all alone. I never think I'll make it home. Louie Louie, me gotta go. Three nights and days we sailed the sea. Me think of girl constantly. On the ship, I dream she there. I smell the rose in her hair. Louie Louie, me gotta go. Me see Jamaican moon above. It won't be long me see me love. Me take her in my arms and then I tell her I never leave again. Louie Louie, me gotta go." (By Richard Berry. Copyright ©1957-1963 by Limax Music Inc.)

Note the subtle shifts of temporal perspective, and the refreshingly arbitrary substitution of the objective case for the nominative and possessive in pronominal situations. As a rock lyricist, Mr. Berry was clearly far ahead of his time.

I would like to get a little info about what's involved in making the "music" that's sold by Muzak, which is impossible to avoid if you go into any McDonald's, elevator, etc. It's all around us, but so mysterious. I'm told that it's made in Japan, by heavily sedated Oriental musicians.—Bob F., Los Angeles

Muzak is recorded by studio musicians, so we may safely deduce that a good deal of it is produced under the influence of drugs. The corporation claims to use recording facilities "all over the world," so we might also wish to conjecture that some of it is made in Japan. Basically, though, the people who make Muzak

are the same musical free-lancers who do commercial and pop-record sessions. They crank it out at a clip of roughly 200 new tunes per year, and the company maintains a library of some 10,000.

Founded in the 1920s and now part of the Westinghouse group, the Muzak Corporation offers two basic programming services—one for office environments and one for industrial. The music (I use the term loosely) is arranged, produced, and on rare occasions even written to company specifications—measures deemed necessary to ensure the proper "stimulus progression"—and is programmed, with the aid of a computer, to counteract the vicissitudes of the typical worker's daily routine. According to Muzak theory, the average Joe's spirits slacken around 10:30 AM, pick up in midday, and decline again around 3:00. Accordingly, Muzak gets pretty bouncy in mid-morning and mid-afternoon, and downright perky around midnight for the bleary-eyed boys on the graveyard shift. It is programmed in blocks of 15 minutes, with the peak excitement (another loosely applied term) coming at the end of each segment. In most places—have you ever noticed?—it's on for 15 minutes and off for 15. I know of no scientific study proving that people can be driven stark raving mad by, say, 17 continuous minutes of Muzak, but for some reason the company thinks it's better this way.

Ever since I heard the Willie Dixon tune Hootchie Cootchie Man *with the lyrics:*

> *I've got a black cat's bone*
> *I've got a mojo tooth*
> *I've got a John the Conqueroo*
> *I'm gonna mess with you,*

I've been obsessed with a craving for a John the Conqueroo. Where can I get one?—Wesley R., Chicago

A "John the Conqueroo," also known as a "High John de Conquer," is the root of the St. John's-wort plant. In southern American black folklore, this root is used to cast or break evil spells—thus all the references to "root rubbing" in blues songs.

Where do you get one? Look around—the St. John's-wort (*Hypericum majus*, *Hypericum kalimanum*, or any of the 23 other *Hypericum* species) is common to the Northern Hemisphere. Look for an herb with yellow, flesh-colored, or purplish flowers; there are usually five petals on each flower. *Hypericum* shrubs generally have cylindrical seeds and clustered stamens.

By the way, if someone casts an evil spell on you with a John the Conqueroo, you might be able to counteract the spell with a Jack, a red cloth shaped in a cylinder and filled with dirt, coal dust, and a silver dime.

Did Glen Campbell really play lead guitar on "Eight Miles High" by the Byrds?—Phil D., Los Angeles

Not likely. When Glen Campbell first arrived in Los Angeles, a fresh-faced country boy from (where else?) Delight, Arkansas, he worked as a studio musician for a number of high-powered acts, including Johnny Cash, Dean Martin, and the Mamas and the Papas. For a few months in 1965, Campbell was a genuine Beach Boy, filling in for Brian Wilson (who had suffered a nervous breakdown) when the group went on tour. Campbell was soon replaced by Bruce Johnston—a lucky break for Glen but a serious blow to music lovers, since Campbell then signed with Capitol and began churning out the ersatz country hits that infected America's airwaves for many years thereafter. So Campbell's studio career was, presumably, finito by the time the Byrds released "Eight Miles High" on *Fifth Dimension* (1966). Roger McGuinn, in any case, ain't talking.

Why are some musical instruments made in different keys? If the tenor saxophone, a B-flat instrument, and the piano, a C instrument, both play the note C, they would in fact be producing different tones. The tenor saxophonist would have to transpose to D for the instruments to be sounding the same tone. Why don't they just build instruments so that a C (or any other note) is the same tone for all instruments?—Robert B., Glen Burnie, Maryland

Before we get into this, Bob, let me explain to the befuddled masses what we're talking about here. First of all, the true C is the same tone on whatever instrument it is played, namely 263 cycles per second. However, a true C is not necessarily *called* C on all instruments. On a tenor saxophone, which is known as a "transposing" instrument, everything is shifted down a tone (well, actually a tone plus an octave, but let's not quibble). That is, if you play a "C," you actually get a B-flat; if you play a "G," you get an F, and so on.

The reasons for this have to do with the difficult nature of the sax. On instruments with a linear arrangement of notes, such as a piano, transposing keys is easy—you just shift your fingers up or down the keyboard. On instruments like the sax and the cornet, however, the notes are obtained by various combinations of valves scattered all over the instrument. Changing keys would mean having to completely rethink your fingering. To avoid this difficulty, saxophones are made in a number of different ranges, soprano, alto, tenor, and baritone being the most common. Essentially, instead of your doing the transposing, the instrument does it for you. Thus if you think a tenor (B-flat) sax is too low for a given tune, you can get an alto (E-flat) sax instead. Using the identical fingering, you'll find the melody comes out about a half-octave higher. For ease of nomenclature, when sax players talk about playing a "C," they are talking about a particular valve combination (which is the same for all saxes), *not* the actual tone that is produced.

Most saxes today are either E-flat or B-flat, but years ago there were also C and F instruments, the former being called a "melody saxophone." Although it enjoyed some popularity in the 20s and 30s, it is rarely seen today. When C saxophones were still used, it made sense to write all sax music as though C were the home key—after all, C is the easiest key to sight-read, due to the absence of sharps and flats in the signature. Also, when they first invented this system, it seemed pretty obvious that on a C sax a "C" came out C, on a B-flat sax "C" came out B-flat, and so on. Admittedly, now that C saxes are uncommon, it seems a little perverse to have to choose between a B-flat and an E-flat as the result of playing a "C," but having known a few sax players in my day, I must say it seems only appropriate.

From time to time the question of the relative popularity of Elvis vs. the Beatles comes up. What makes it more difficult is the fact that the Beatles had the most number one records but Presley had the most top ten records. Since Presley cheated by being around longer, it is impossible to resolve just who was really more popular. So the problem is, who was on top the longest with the most consecutive hits?—Nancy W., Chicago

Elvis Presley first broke *Billboard's* top ten on February 22, 1956, with "Heartbreak Hotel," and stayed there through "Return to Sender" in the fall of 1962. Elvis had 29 consecutive releases in the top ten before he broke his streak with "One Broken Heart For Sale," which peaked at a miserable number eleven in the winter of 1963. Elvis regained the hearts and souls of his followers with his next release, "Devil in Disguise," but from there on it was all downhill for ol' swivelhips, who spent the next six years polluting the screens of drive-ins across the country in what is widely regarded as the most boring series of movies ever made. Elvis, his mind apparently irreparably damaged by his Hollywood experience, returned to the top ten with the loathsome "In the Ghetto" in 1969.

The Beatles had eight consecutive top ten songs (from "I Want to Hold Your Hand" to "P.S. I Love You") when some shady operator at MGM records dug up the old Tony Sheridan tapes ("My Bonnie" and "Why") and tried to inflict them on the record-buying public. Knowing a ringer when it saw one, the aforementioned public held "My Bonnie" down to a deserved number 26. The lovable moptops recovered their equilibrium with "I Feel Fine" (December 1964) and hit 1.000 for the next six years, until "Let It Be" simultaneously spelled splitsville and the end of an era in 1970, leaving the score at 22 consecutive hits.

Since the Beatles' last single reached number one, it seems reasonable to assume that their string would have continued had they not broken up, whereas Presley clearly suffered a severe falling off in popularity after his six years in the limelight. But rationalize as we might, the final results remain Memphis 29, Liverpool 22.

We have a Beatle trivia question on which a dinner-for-four wager rides. The question is this: on the Sgt. Pepper song "A Day in the Life," what instruments are used for the crescendo after the singer says, "I'd love to turn you on"?—David W., Chicago

The crescendo is the product of a full-scale 41-piece orchestra, conducted by one P. McCartney, with Mal Evans soloing on alarm clock.

*What were the circumstances surrounding the death of Sam Cooke?
I only know he was shot in a hotel room.—Steve D., Evanston,
Illinois*

Sam Cooke, one of the biggest r&b stars of the late 50s and early 60s, met his sad end in the lobby of the Hacienda Motel in Los Angeles on December 11, 1964. Clad only in a top coat, he was shot and then beaten by Mrs. Bertha Lee Franklin, the motel manager.

The chain of events leading up to this bizarre incident apparently began in a quiet Hollywood bar, where Cooke met Linda Boyer, a 22-year-old Eurasian, and took her on a tour of Tinseltown night spots. The former gospel singer from Chicago was beginning to crack under the pressures of his career; with the death of one of his three children the year before, drowned in his swimming pool, Cooke had reportedly become a heavy drinker. When Boyer accepted Cooke's offer of a ride home, he took her instead to the Hacienda, where the couple registered as "Mr. and Mrs. Sam Cooke."

Once in the room, Cooke undressed and forced Boyer to do the same. When he stepped into the bathroom, she panicked, grabbed her clothes and his, and fled. Cooke, in a rage, ran to the reception desk where he accused Mrs. Franklin of hiding the girl, and began to slap her when she couldn't answer. Franklin snatched a gun from her desk and fired three shots, striking Cooke once in the chest. She then picked up a piece of wood and beat him to the floor. Boyer was later found in hysterics, crouched in a phone booth half a block away from the motel.

In accordance with the James Dean principle, Cooke's first posthumous single, "Shake," became a hit, reaching the number seven spot on *Billboard*'s chart where his last release, "Cousin of Mine," had only managed a 31. There's nothing like sudden death to give your career a good shot in the arm—ask Jim Croce—but of the other six Cooke singles RCA released in 1965, none made the top ten. Cooke's last side was "Let's Go Steady Again"—a rather poignant appeal from a dead man, but evidently not poignant enough. It was number 97 for one week.

*When I was growing up in the glorious 50s and early 60s, we
could go to our local record store and listen to anything we wanted
before we bought it. Now, even with the expanded music scene,
no store will let you listen and you can get burned buying shit.
Who's responsible for these changing policies—record compa-*

nies, the stores? What can we do to get the moneygrubbers to change back?—Steve W., Los Angeles

Back in the glorious 50s and early 60s, most records were three minutes long and most record players were worth about 25 bucks. Listening booths didn't represent much of an investment then—you didn't spend much time in there, the inventory of records was small, and if you damaged a record accidentally, your friendly dealer would just put it back on his rack, secure in the knowledge that the eventual purchaser's victrola would plow through the scratch like a switchblade through a leather jacket.

Times have changed. It would take you 30 to 40 minutes to listen to the typical pop album today. If you're like most, you'd want to hear it on the finest sound equipment, and you'd probably want to listen to a fresh copy of the record. (Even if you didn't, the "expanded music scene" makes it virtually impossible for dealers to keep sample copies of each release on hand for listening.) Of course, you wouldn't *think* of purchasing a record that had already been played. So, either you get burned buying shit or the dealer gets burned with a lot of abused stereo equipment, hacked up records, and frazzled nerves.

At the end of the movie Citizens Band, *there is a copyright notice for the song "Happy Birthday." This is appalling. How could somebody copyright a song that's been part of the common culture for centuries? Is this some smart lawyer's idea of a quick buck, or what?—Barbara T., Chicago*

They could copyright it because they wrote it: two sisters, Mildred J. and Patty S. Hill, published the song in 1893 under the title, "Good Morning to You." It was no chartbuster, but reissued in 1936 with a new set of slightly ill-fitting lyrics— "Happy Birthday to You"—it became, shall we say, rather popular. Under the present laws, the song will be protected by copyright until 1996, at which time anyone can sing it who damn well feels like it. "Happy Birthday," lest we forget, was the first song to be performed in outer space, having been given a stirring rendition by the Apollo IX astronauts on March 8, 1969.

I am wondering why record companies used to, on a double album, sandwich sides one and four on one disc, and put sides two and three on the other. This really has me confused.—Andrew W., Rockville, Maryland

Andrew, I am going to try to remain calm, but . . . I mean . . . even a brain-damaged freaking ORANGUTAN COULD

323

FIGURE OUT . . . sorry. Ahem. Look. Get a copy of the groovy rock opera *Tommy*, which has sides one and four on one disc and sides two and three on the other. Notice how E-Z it is to stack it on your automatic record changer so that sides one and two play all the way through. Then all you have to do is flip the whole thing over to get sides three and four. Keen, huh? Cripes, they're gonna have to start putting instructions on the toilet paper if this keeps up.

Who composed the musical score to the old-time Flash Gordon *television serial?—Glenn Y., Los Angeles*

The *Flash Gordon* theme is taken from *Les Preludes* by the well-known Hollywood composer Franz Liszt. American movie makers have always held a deep reverence for composers whose works lie in the public domain.

I remember reading once that the group the Diodes recorded "Red Rubber Ball" to get back at its composer, Paul Simon, for saying that he hated punk rock. This brings to mind a question: must a group or singer get any sort of permission before recording somebody else's song? Or do you just have to pay royalties after the fact? Is asking permission beforehand just a professional courtesy?—Curly L., Fair Lawn, New Jersey

Surprisingly enough, if somebody is determined to do a cover version of your song, it is well-nigh impossible for you, Joe Composer, to stop them. In general, the right to record somebody else's song is called a "mechanical license," and usually it's negotiated in a routine manner between representatives of the copyright holder and the would-be cover artiste. (Outfits like The Harry Fox Agency in New York generally handle the publisher's side.) However, in the rare event that negotiations fail, the copyright laws contain provisions for a type of mechanical license called a "compulsory license," which, in effect, gives anyone the right to record any song he or she wants to, as long as notice is given to the song's copyright owners within 30 days after the recording is made and before it is distributed. Compulsory licenses were written into the copyright laws in 1909 in an attempt to break up a monopoly in the piano-roll industry—an industry which has since been pretty well broken up, period. So why negotiate at all? Mainly because the law dictates higher royalty rates and stricter payment schedules for compulsory licenses than you can obtain with the negotiated kind.

But hey, you say, I've just written a couple of can't-miss

tunes that I'm sure will rocket to the top of the charts as soon as I can get them recorded. Do I now have to worry that music industry vultures will steal them before I can make my pile? Don't fret, bucky. The composer's one inalienable right is to decide who will record his song first. Bob Dylan pulled this one in the notorious case of "Mr. Tambourine Man": the song was originally set to be issued in a version that Dylan had recorded live at a folk festival, but Dylan wasn't happy with the results. Unfortunately, his contract with Columbia didn't give him the right to decide on what material the company released, so Bob didn't seem to have much of a choice. But then, the Poet of Our Generation remembered his first issue rights and denied a mechanical license to his own record company. The album was killed.

Meanwhile, the Brothers Four, a once beloved folk group that had fallen on hard times, had recorded a highly commercial cover version of the song—a guaranteed comeback. But when Dylan's anticipated first version failed to appear, the group was caught between the proverbial rock and a hard place, unable to release their dynamite single. It sat in the vaults until Dylan issued his approved version some months later—but in the meantime, the Byrds had recorded *their* cover version, and that was the one that went to the Top of the Pops. Such are the vagaries of fortune.

For a more detailed discussion of licensing (and lots of other stuff besides), see *This Business of Music*, by Sidney Shemel and M. William Krasilovsky. Of this extraordinary volume even Cecil is in awe.

I once saw the Alvin Ailey dance group perform a piece entitled "The Ballad of Phoebe Snow." As I recall, the handbill listed this piece as having been created sometime in the 60s. Is this the same Phoebe Snow who had the hit song "Poetry Man"? What's the connection, if any?—Kent R., Chicago

You bet, Kent—Phoebe Snow is a pop singer, "a rolling stone gathers no moss" is a Mick Jagger-Keith Richards lyric, and Western Civilization dawned circa 1963. People nowadays have the historical awareness of tree squirrels.

Phoebe Snow was the invention of the advertising department of the Delaware, Lackawanna, and Western Railroad, which has long since been merged into Conrail. She was created in 1900 by artist Penrhyn Stanlaus, and her name and garb—always white from head to foot—were chosen to symbolize the cleanliness of DL&W trains, which burned "smokeless" anthracite coal instead of the soft bituminous coal used by most other roads at the time.

325

The ad campaign—a very famous one—also employed actresses who appeared as Phoebe at special events and civic celebrations (a la Ronald McDonald), as well as jingles that eventually became so popular they were sung from the Broadway stage:

> Says Phoebe Snow about to go
>   Upon a trip to Buffalo
>   My gown stays white from morn 'til night
> Upon the road of anthracite.

When the government prohibited the use of anthracite coal in steam locomotives during World War I, Phoebe was retired, but she reappeared in white military garb during World War II to dramatize the Lackawanna's contributions to the effort. In 1949 the DL&W inaugurated its first streamliner passenger run—Hoboken, N.J. to Buffalo, N.Y.—and the train was named the Phoebe Snow. After merger with the Erie railroad in 1960, Phoebe's run was extended to Chicago; she died of the disappearing railroad blues in 1966.

Cecil, what was the Big Bopper's real name?—S.H., Baltimore
The Big Bopper, who made a hit of "Chantilly Lace" and died in a plane crash along with Richie Valens and Buddy Holly, was in real life a disc jockey and program director at KTRM in Beaumont, Texas. His real name was J.P. Richardson.

I'm a Jimi Hendrix freak. To this day I think his genius has seldom if ever been equalled. What I'd like to know is, what did Alan Douglas have to do in order to be able to strip down and remix the tapes for the posthumous Hendrix album Crash Landing? *What kind of legal proceedings took place? Could Douglas have been stopped from doctoring up the tapes? Maybe I'm just being overly touchy, but I think the tapes should have been issued as they were found, or not at all.—H.D., Los Angeles*

The tapes from which *Crash Landing* was culled were owned by Hendrix's family (hereinafter referred to as "the estate"), which had been supplying Warner Brothers with the material used for the first posthumous albums, which are generally regarded as having been of pretty poor quality. When Warner rejected the final offering, it suggested the estate hire Alan Douglas, who had produced sessions for the live Jimi Hendrix, to review a collection of tapes warehoused in New Jersey to see what he could make of them. Douglas and his compatriots listened to the unmixed multitrack recordings with everything but Hendrix's voice and guitar tracks "potted down." After some four months of reviewing the sessions, which totalled about 500 hours, they selected the numbers that "stood up off the tapes" as superior Hendrix performances, edited them down to eliminate miscues, meanderings, and musical tangents, and then hired a crew of session musicians (only one of whom had ever met Hendrix) to record new rhythm tracks for them.

The problem, as I understand it, was that Hendrix was given to recording with almost anyone. The rhythm tracks on some of those tapes were abysmal, and—while admitting to being somewhat spooked by the prospect—the producers have pointed out that their decision to re-record them does not stray very far from the recording practices used and accepted by live musicians.

In any case, the effort was pretty successful commercially, which, in the music business, is pretty close to successful, period. The critics—although they, too, were spooked a little—agreed that *Crash Landing* was far superior to the earlier posthumous Hendrix releases, which Warner subsequently withdrew from the market. Several other remixed albums were released later. Listen, after that Jim Morrison business a few years ago, nothing in the pop music racket surprises me.

Steely Dan's "Do It Again," Lynyrd Skynyrd's "Sweet Home Alabama," Journey's "Wheel in the Sky," Dire Straits' "Tunnel of Love," and several other songs that I know of all have one thing in common: the Big Wheel, or a variant of the Big Wheel, in the lyrics. One can either watch the Wheels, or just accept the fact that they "go round" or "keep turnin'." We would like to know just what the Big Wheel is, where it can be seen in its natural habitat (is it native to North America?), and whether you have to be a musician in order to see it.—Chas A., Chuck L., Chicago

You might also have mentioned Creedence Clearwater Revival's "Proud Mary," and Peter, Paul, and Mary's "The Great Mandella" (sic), subtitled "The Wheel of Life." The Big Wheel, AKA the great circle, the mandala, etc., is one of those classic symbols so vague as to be susceptible to almost any interpretation, having been used at one time or another to signify cosmic unity, the Godhead, society, fate and/or fortune, the universe, space, time, space *and* time, the seasons, the sun, and the Zodiac, to say nothing of a certain brand of piston rings. The Swiss psychologist Carl Jung regarded mandalas (intricate drawings generally involving circles, used in various Hindu, Buddhist, and northern Californian rituals) as the symbol of the Self, the totality of the psyche, or, as he put it, "Formation, Transformation, Eternal Mind's eternal re-creation." No doubt this clarifies matters for you. According to my trusty Micropaedia, Jung thought the spontaneous production of mandalas "is a step in the individuation process . . . and represents an attempt to integrate hitherto unconscious material by the conscious self." The astute reader will at once recognize that this precisely describes the act of writing rock and roll songs. In view of the fact, however, that the Big Wheel metaphor has been in more or less continuous use for some 20,000 years now, one must frankly inquire whether the novelty of the thing might be starting to wear off. Perhaps it is time to transfer the focus of creative effort to some less cliched geometric figure—say, the icosahedron. Just a thought.

Chapter 18

Money

What's the most expensive thing in the world?—H.B., Baltimore

Some years ago what was then the Atomic Energy Commission held a special clearance sale on an element called californium-252, which they were letting go for a mere $1,000 per microgram, or about $350 billion per pound—just slightly higher than the price of sirloin.

In looking over the instructions that were so thoughtfully included along with Form 1040, I see that "embezzled or other illegal income" is specifically mentioned as a type of income one must report. How long has this been in there? If someone were to report illegal income, would the IRS notify other authorities, or would they be happy just to get their cut?—Loren B., Dallas

The IRS has been listing "embezzled or other illegal income" for years, but they don't really expect the nation's criminals to comply. It's just that income tax evasion is often the only thing prosecutors can pin on big-time crooks. The notice prevents the bad guys from arguing that nobody told them they were required to report their ill-gotten gains. If anybody was actually dumb enough to send in a list of his swag for the year, the folks at the IRS say they'd promptly alert the appropriate authorities.

Why do grocery store coupons always say "cash value one twentieth of a cent"? Why should anybody care?—Tony W., Phoenix

Coupons are given a cash value in order to comply with laws in a few states that classify them with trading stamps. As I assume you know, the cost of trading stamps to the merchant is always incorporated into the price of his merchandise. Since you're paying for them whether you want them or not, some jurisdictions require that the stamps be redeemed in cold cash if the customer so demands. Coupons are a little different than trading stamps, of course, but the law is the law. The cash value is set high enough to be legal, but low enough so that nobody will actually bother to collect the things.

My question concerns the term "legal tender." I remember reading years ago that certain huge amounts of loose change can be rejected by a cashier as payment. But what are these amounts? I ring on a register all day long and have frequently encountered people who make purchases of $5 or more with nothing but dimes, nickels, and pennies. To suggest an extreme example: could you force a car dealer to take $10,000 worth of nickels? Or pay your ex-wife's alimony with an enormous sack of pennies? Another thought: can you buy a newspaper with a 25-cent postage stamp?—Mike J., Chicago

You can buy a newspaper with a Tootsie Roll, Mike, should that medium of exchange be acceptable to all parties to the transaction. In fact, during the Civil War, when coins were scarce, people used postage stamps enclosed in brass frames instead. But neither Tootsie Rolls nor stamps are "legal tender"—that is, officially recognized as legal payment for debts. Unfortunately, that's about as far as we can go in the way of definitive statements on this subject. Legal tender happens to be one of the curious anomalies of U.S. law. At one time there were definite limits to how much small change you could legally unload on the people you owed money to—25 cents in the case of "minor coins" (the penny and the nickel) and $10 for "silver coins" (the dime, quarter, and half-dollar). In 1933, however, in the course of getting the U.S. off the gold standard, Congress offhandedly declared that all U.S. coins and currency were legal tender for *all* debts, which would appear to repeal the earlier limits. There is evidence to suggest that this was accidental, though, and the contradictory statutes have been permitted to remain on the books, perhaps in the hope that someone would bring them to a court test. No one, as far as I can tell, ever has.

Matters were further complicated when the U.S. ceased to make silver coins, having chosen to use cupronickel-clad copper instead. The $10 limit, on the face of it, applies (or applied, anyway) only to silver coins. It is at least arguable, then, that while you might not be able to force your ex-wife to accept more than $10 in pre-1965 (i.e., silver) quarters, you *could* pay her off with unlimited amounts of post-1965 coins. This is not a hypothesis I would be prepared to defend tooth and nail, frankly, but such of the Teeming Millions as are of a sporting nature are free to make use of it if they wish.

How are coins taken out of circulation when they get worn? I know there's an elaborate procedure for culling out worn paper money, but I've never seen anything about coins.—Dave K., Baltimore

Coins are usually pulled from circulation nowadays only when they are so worn, bent, or mutilated that they will no longer run through the automatic sorting machines at local banks. Such coins are sent to a branch of the Federal Reserve, the Denver Mint, or the U.S. Assay Office in New York for credit. Coins that don't jam the machines can circulate indefinitely.

What is a "Swiss bank account"? In what ways and under what circumstances would it behoove me to have one? Who would I contact to arrange the deal?—Ann H., Washington

A Swiss bank account, dollface, is an account in a bank in Switzerland. It seems to me you could probably have noodled this out for yourself. Most likely what you are really interested in is the legendary *numbered* Swiss bank account, made famous in innumerable trashy novels. Such accounts are misleadingly named,

since all Swiss bank accounts (and, for that matter, all American bank accounts) are numbered; the difference with the ones in question is that they are referred to solely by number, rather than by name and number, in the course of the bank's internal bookkeeping operations. The bank does keep a list of depositors' names, of course, but access to it is restricted. The supposed advantage of this is that no one will be able to bribe some clerk to reveal the size of your balance, which may be useful if you happen to be, say, the deposed ruler of a large Middle Eastern country.

The usefulness of numbered accounts is greatly exaggerated, particularly in light of the trouble you have to go through to get one. The secrecy for which Swiss bankers are renowned extends to *all* their accounts, not just numbered ones; under Swiss law, the disclosure of any information about an account, including such elementary facts as whether it even exists, is a crime, except as ordered by the Swiss courts. Numbered accounts have been so closely associated with the stashing of ill-gotten gains that Swiss bankers are extremely reluctant to open them anymore, especially if you insist on having statements sent to a post office box or some similarly fishy destination. You must open such accounts personally in Switzerland, you must have references, and you must convince the bank that you have a legitimate reason for wanting one (originally they were intended to prevent the Gestapo from learning about illegal German foreign deposits during the 1930s). Finally, the minimum balance for such accounts is usually in excess of $25,000.

This is not to say that Swiss bank accounts in general do not have their uses. Swiss bankers will perform many highly specialized financial services not widely available elsewhere, such as the purchase and storage of precious metals. With some types of accounts, it's possible to note on your checks which foreign currency you want them to be paid in, which greatly facilitates international commerce. And finally—let's face it—the secrecy laws do make Swiss banks a favored haven for boodle, although various international agreements in recent years have made them less attractive to criminals than they used to be.

As a devoted reader of Sherlock Holmes I've noticed that there must be some difference between "guineas" and "pounds," but I've never really been able to figure out what it is. How about a little elementary deduction, my dear Cecil?—Audrey V., Chicago

When in doubt, Audrey, try the dictionary. Mine says a pound is equal to 20 shillings, a guinea is equal to 21—or at least they used to be, since guineas and shillings, strictly speaking, aren't around anymore.

The guinea hasn't existed as an actual unit of currency since 1813, when the last guinea coin rolled off the production line at the English mint. The coin was first issued in 1663, when the crown authorized the Royal Mint to manufacture 20-shilling gold pieces "in the name and for the use of the Company of Royal Adventurers trading with Africa." Forty-four of the coins—which bore an image of a small, white elephant, the Royal Adventurer's trademark—were the equivalent of one pound of gold. The coins came to be known as guineas thanks to the British mind's great gift for association: they were minted of gold imported from the Guinea Coast of West Africa. The name stuck to later coins of the same gold value, minted from different stock.

By 1695, the price of gold had climbed enough to make the guinea worth 30 shillings. William III answered this inflationary trend by fixing the value of the guinea at 21 shillings, 6 pence in 1698. The extra 6 pence were finally lopped off in December 1717, fixing the coin at its traditional value of 21 shillings. The British never tired of reforming their monetary system though, and in 1817 they introduced a new, improved coin, fixed at the easy-to-use value of 20 shillings—the pound. The guinea survived only in the popular imagination, a shorthand way of saying, "one pound and one shilling." Nowadays, if the term is used at all, it's used in come-on advertising, "only one guinea" being the British equivalent of our "only $9.98." If you look fast, it looks cheap.

The humble shilling went the way of all metal on February 15, 1971, when yet another monetary reform act went into effect. The system went to a decimal basis—a pound became one hundred pence, and shillings, thruppence, tuppence, and ha'pennies went out the proverbial window.

Coming home from a restaurant dinner tonight, the subject of tipping came up and with it many unanswered questions. Naturally, our thoughts turned to you, Cecil. (1) What is the origin of tipping? (2) Who determined the 15 percent figure? (3) Why do cabdrivers expect a tip when their job is to provide door-to-door service? I can understand giving a tip if the cabbie has to handle luggage, but they expect one regardless.—Karen G., Chicago

The origin of tipping is lost, like so many things, in the Mists of Antiquity. There's evidence that tipping goes back at least to the age of the Romans, but human nature being what it is, it could just as easily date from the invention of money.

Luckily for us, etymologists have managed to come up with a selection of deeply fascinating etymologies for the phrase "to tip." The dullest and most likely has it coming from the Latin *stips*, meaning "gift." In the days of Geoffrey Chaucer and Middle English, "to tip" meant simply "to give"— as in "tip me that cheate" ("give me that thing"), immortal words penned by one Samuel Rowlands in his 1610 *Beadle of Bridewell*.

The most charming explanation refers us back to the days of Dr. Johnson and his eighteenth century circle of wits. Upon entering his local coffeeshop for a session of epigram-flinging, Dr. Johnson (or rather, one might presume, his flunky, Mr. Boswell) would drop a few pence in a box labeled "To Insure Promptness" ("T.I.P."—get it?) in order to encourage a greater display of vigor on the part of the generally listless attendants.

Tipping spread from England to colonial America, but after the revolution it was frowned upon (temporarily) as a hangover from the British class system. One only tipped one's social inferiors, which, lest we forget, did not exist in the brave new world. Unfortunately, the working class eventually got around to swallowing its pride, and tipping returned with all the fervor it possesses today. Even the Communist countries have not entirely succeeded in eliminating the practice. These days, of course, taxi drivers and waitpersons depend on tips for a substantial part of their income. If you didn't tip, presumably they'd expect to be paid more, and your restaurant bills and taxi fares would consequently be higher. The fifteen percent standard is mostly a question of what the market will bear. In New York, the figure these days is twenty percent; European restaurants generally add a ten percent gratuity to the bill.

On the way home this morning I stopped to pick up two one-dollar bills which I assume someone lost in an alley. Reflecting on the decreasing value of the dollar led me to consider this question: is it worth it to pick up a penny? That is, considering the amount of energy expended and the cost of food required to provide said energy, can the penny be considered a profit?—Nick L., Chicago

Let's not make this any more complicated than we have to. The Scientific Research Team here at Straight Dope HQ has proven that a proficient penny-picker upper can probably pick up a particular penny in five seconds. On an hourly basis this works out to $7.20 per hour. Minimum wage, by comparison, is $3.35 an hour. Wherefore, if perchance a penny appears, pounce upon that puppy promptly, Poopsie. And pass that spittoon on your way out. Please.

I've heard that if you don't mind being put on the subversives list, you're free not to pay the federal tax on the phone bill on the grounds that you're opposed to military spending, etc.—and that the phone company won't cut off your service. Is that true?—Matt B., Baltimore

I hesitate to predict what giant bureaucracies will do in every instance, but in general the answer is yes, the phone company won't cut off your service if you don't pay your federal tax. On the other hand, it *will* tell Uncle Sam all about you and your lonely struggle against the war machine. What happens next varies. Some folks claim they've never heard a word from the government. Others have had the unpaid taxes deducted from their income tax refunds. Why don't you try it and let me know?

I believe that Babe Ruth's salary level in the late 1920s (around $100,000 annually) stood for some time as the highest in the history of sport when one took inflation and the tax rates into account. Judging by the astronomical wages being paid these days in baseball, it would seem that someone must have passed the Sultan of Swat by now. What was Ruth's highest salary and what would its current equivalent be?—Gary B., Chicago

In his top year salarywise (actually it was two years, 1930 and 1931), Ruth pulled down $80,000 per. However, salary accounted for only a fraction of his earnings. In 1927, for instance, the year he hit 60 homers, he took in $70,000 in salary and at least $110,500 in other income, including his World Series share, cash from a movie and a barnstorming tour, and so on. Add in payments for personal appearances, endorsements, investments, and other lucrative sidelines, and some estimate that Ruth cleared nigh unto $300,000. During the 15 years he spent with the Yankees, Ruth earned approximately $850,000 in salary, with maybe another $5–600,000 for exhibition and barnstorming fees, World Series shares, and other baseball income. Nonbaseball earnings are estimated at between one and two million bucks, giving us, conservatively speaking, a total of $3 million for Ruth's prime earning years. To figure out what this would be worth today, we note that $1 in 1930 would buy $5.91 worth of stuff at today's prices (as of April 1983, actually), and that the top federal income tax rate in the late 20s and early 30s was 5 percent, whereas today it is 50 percent. This means that Ruth's $80,000 salary would be the current equivalent of $898,400—which happens to be almost exactly what Reggie Jackson gets today from the California Angels, excluding bonuses (Jackson's got a four-year, $3.6 million contract). As for career earnings, Ruth's chief rival nowadays would have to be Muhammed Ali, who earned $69 million between 1960 and 1981. Figuring an average top income tax rate of 70 percent during the Ali years, and using the 1972 Consumer Price Index as our benchmark, Ruth's salary works out to the equivalent of $23.8 million. Clearly, when it comes to Ali, Ruth is pale by comparison.

Dimes, nickels, and pennies I've seen—but how about a mill? They get plugged on Green Stamps and box tops a lot. Are they extinct?—Martin F., Los Angeles

No mills have ever been minted. Defined by the 1786 law that established U.S. coinage as "the lowest money of accompt, of which 1,000 shall be equal to the federal dollar, or money unit," the mill has been the bastard child of the system since its beginning. Even in those pre-inflation days, the smallest coin ever issued was the half-cent. At one time, some states issued "mill tokens" that were used in collecting sales taxes, which, in 1935, prompted Secretary of the Treasury Henry Morgenthau to ask Congress for a license to make a coin to replace the states' homemade substitutes. Unfortunately, they thought he was kidding.

I once read that as head of the Soviet Union Leonid Brezhnev took home as his monthly salary the U.S. equivalent of $700. I was astonished for two reasons: first, something like the president's salary in the Soviet Union seems like it ought to be a state secret, and second, Brezhnev was a sports car aficionado, so how did he support his habit on $700 a month? They couldn't all have been gifts from Nixon and other heads of state. It occurred to me that his salary was merely pro forma. I know, for example, that members of the Central Committee and Supreme Soviet have access to a floor of the GUM department store in Moscow which is closed to the general public and stocked with quality items from the West, which rather dents the whole "we're all comrades over here" *notion. Cecil, what's the lowdown on Soviet big-shot salaries and perks?—Jonathan L., Los Angeles*

When it comes to compensating the elect, Jon, the Soviet Union is run pretty much along the same lines as the city of Chicago—i.e., what you don't get in salary you make up for in freebies, graft, and under-the-table boodle. Brezhnev's official salary was said to be 900 rubles (the equivalent of $1,200 in the early 70s, about $720 now). This was not particularly high by the standards of Soviet officialdom; top scientists and military men were hauling down around 2,000 rubles per month. But such comparisons are meaningless. What's important in the Soviet Union is not cash per se but *blat*—Russian for "clout." Top Russky leaders and their families have access to a wide range of goodies for which they pay little or nothing, whereas for your ordinary Joe Doakski, the same items are either outrageously expensive or simply

unavailable. (The Russians, by the way, do not exactly go around broadcasting this stuff. What follows was gleaned from the writings of various nosy journalists, notably the *New York Times*'s Hedrick Smith.) A whole bureaucracy has been built up to administer the system of privilege. For instance, there's a department of the Communist Party Central Committee known as the *Upravleniye Delami*, the "Administration of Affairs," which maintains a vast system of apartments, dachas (country houses), guest houses, car pools, and servants for the exclusive use of top Soviet honchos. Special clinics and hospitals for the elite are run by the "Fourth Administration" of the Ministry of Health. There are something like 100 special shops and stores in the Moscow area alone, ranging from tailors to high-class groceries, reserved for big shots. Probably the best known of these is "Section 100," a special elite-only clothing store on the third floor of Moscow's GUM department store. All these shops and services are organized into a strict hierarchy—the higher you are in rank, the wider selection of goods you get and the less they cost you. For example, a Soviet-made Fiat will cost the average schmo in the Soviet Union about 7,500 rubles and requires a two- to three-year wait; ranking Soviet bureaucrats can get the same car for 1,370 rubles in a couple days (not that they necessarily need one; the top 20 Russian leaders get chauffeur-driven Zil limousines).

Brezhnev himself had a swank Moscow apartment as well as a mansion near the village of Usovo about 20 miles from Moscow that had formerly been used by Khrushchev and Stalin. He also had a hunting lodge at Zavidovo, which I believe is in central Russia, and had access to government guest houses and other facilities throughout the Soviet Union. (Incidentally, Brezhnev was known for his collection of expensive luxury cars, not sports cars. Most of them in fact were gifts from foreign leaders.)

Still, while Soviet leaders are clearly not hurting, it should be noted that the difference between the top and bottom rungs of society is less extreme in the U.S.S.R. than it is in much of the West. Furthermore, the Russian leadership frowns on conspicuous consumption, lest the masses get restless. Brezhnev did, after all, live in a Moscow apartment, not a Russian version of the White House. So let's not get too smug, kids.

Publishers Clearing House, Reader's Digest and the like are constantly giving away millions for free. Why? What do they get out of it? This question is really burning a hole in my brain.—Doug W., Irvine, California

I don't want to tax your brain unnecessarily, Doug, especially in view of the fact that holes are being burned into it, but surely you must remember that the Reader's Digest Association, Inc., publishes a magazine entitled *Reader's Digest*, to which it is anxious to have people subscribe. Similarly, Publishers Clearing House is in the business of drumming up subscriptions for its many publisher clients. Million-dollar sweepstakes giveaways have been shown to be a pretty good way of doing this, and it is not hard to see why. I have here a very impressive letter from Reader's Digest that is chock-full of fascinating gimcrackery, including two "computerized sweepstakes cards," a personalized computer-printed cover letter, and a "Super-Bonus" card with a gold "bonus box." I am supposed to scratch the box with a coin to reveal the Super-Bonus prize (a Cadillac Seville, as it turns out) that I could win in addition to the $250,000 Grand Prize. For those too poor to supply their own coin, a shiny new nickel is helpfully provided. We note that the letter skillfully obeys the Five Golden Laws of Direct-Mail Marketing: (1) *Grab the recipient's attention with official-looking verbiage*. The Reader's Digest letter is covered with things like "Urgent you reply by Jan. 30" and "Attention Postmaster. Requested delivery date is on or about..." It looks like a subpoena or a tax refund. (2) *Cram the letter full of eye-catching gimmicks*. The more items a letter contains (up to a point), the higher the response rate. If I remember correctly, the optimum number of items is five to eight. The Reader's Digest letter contains seven items. (3) *Get the recipient involved by giving him/her something easy 'n' fun to do*, in this case using a coin to uncover a secret prize. An alternative tactic is having the recipient paste a sticker on an entry card. (4) *Give the recipient something of value so he/she feels obligated to participate*. You don't think Reader's Digest *really* figured nobody could come up with his own nickel, do you? Significantly, the nickel was plainly visible to the recipient through a window in the envelope. (4) *Force the recipient to make a clear choice between subscribing and not subscribing in order to enter the sweepstakes*. The Reader's Digest letter contains two envelopes to return your sweepstakes entry in. One says YES—enter my subscription, and the other says NO— I do not wish to subscribe. Reader's Digest is legally obligated to treat entries equally whether you subscribe or not, but most people— and let's face it, the average sweepstakes participant is a TV-addled bozo who barely has brains enough to spit—do not realize this. "There does seem to be a lurking feeling that if I do order the product I will win," a Reader's Digest spokesman was recently quoted as saying. Ergo, lots and lots of subscriptions.

Devious? You bet. If it's any comfort to you, though, the publishers often think they're getting screwed too. A magazine executive who has had dealings with Publishers Clearing House recently told Cecil, "They make themselves a bloody fortune. Literally for every name they supply you, a magazine publisher loses between $1 and $1.50. If we were to go through Publishers Clearing House and offer a six month subscription for $10, we would get $2.50 out of that $10—they get the other $7.50. As you can imagine it costs us more than $2.50 to send out six issues." So why do it? For starters, you hope your loss-leader subscribers renew at the regular price—although the renewal rate for such readers is notoriously poor. More important, says my informant, "you can hype your circulation," in hopes that you can increase your ad rates based on higher readership. "Ad agencies [from whom publishers try to extract ad orders] don't care where you get your circulation numbers from," he says. In the long run, however, "it just doesn't pay," he concludes. Words of wisdom for all you budding magazine entrepreneurs.

We were sitting around the kitchen table the other night discussing Big Oil and its impact on the Republic, and we got into the matter of Standard Oil in its various corporate incarnations. I thought Teddy Roosevelt and the Trust-Busters broke up the Standard monopoly at the turn of the century, and that all the various Standards (Indiana, California, Ohio, etc.) were all separate companies now. However, you go all over the country and you see the same Standard Oil logo everywhere. Also, when Johnny Cash used to do those dumb commercials, he said "you expect more from Standard," not "you expect more from Standard of Indiana." So presumably all the different Standards benefit from the same commercial. Is there some kind of conspiracy here? Are all the Standards separate or not? Or are they all owned by the Great Combine that (some of us think) owns everything in the country?—Fred Z, Chicago

A complicated question here, Frederick, so we'd best start with a little history. Prior to 1911, Standard Oil of New Jersey was an enormous holding company that owned, directly or indirectly, about 100 subsidiary corporations involved in the production, refining, transportation, and marketing of oil around the world. In 1906, Standard controlled 86 percent of total U.S. refining. However, in that year the government started an antitrust suit that eventually resulted in the Supreme Court's order that the company divest itself of 33 of its affiliates, representing 57 percent of its net value at the time. This still left Jersey Standard the nation's second largest industrial corporation, and today, as Exxon, it ranks number one. The orphaned companies didn't exactly die on the vine; after a period of consolidation, they emerged as huge companies in their own right: Mobil (formerly Standard of New York) is the 2nd largest industrial organization in the country; Standard of Indiana is the 8th, Standard of California the 9th, and Standard of Ohio the 25th.

One of the early conflicts among the Standard progeny was who would get to use the widely recognized Standard brand name for advertising purposes, since everybody had a roughly equal claim to it. A series of court battles had the practical effect of dividing the country up into several carefully defined regions, in each of which the local oil company got exclusive use of the

Standard name. Outside their home regions, though, the companies were required to use some other name. Thus at a Standard of Indiana gas station outside the company's 15-state home region in the Midwest, you'll find the familiar torch-in-an-oval sign, but it'll say "American" or "Amoco" instead of "Standard," American Oil Company being Indiana Standard's foreign alias. (When Johnny Cash did those commercials for Indiana Standard in the 70s, he had to make different versions for use in different parts of the country.) Similarly, Standard of California markets under the name Chevron, and Standard of Ohio under the name Sohio. For many years, Standard Oil of New Jersey used the name Esso (S-O, Standard Oil, get it?) in the East and South, and Enco and Humble elsewhere. The firm fought in the courts for years for the right to use the Esso name throughout the country, but after its last appeal failed in 1969 it gave up, and in 1972 changed both its brand name and its official corporate name to Exxon. Several of the other Standard descendants have also abandoned the Standard name. Standard Oil of New York, long known as Socony, changed its corporate name to Mobil in 1966; Standard Oil of California officially became Chevron in 1984. Even Standard of Indiana, long the holdout, has begun to downplay the Standard name; most of its stations in the Midwest now say Amoco.

So much for advertising. The question of who *owns* Standard Oil goes a little deeper. It's important to understand that the intent of the antitrust action in 1911 was to break up the concentration of *management*, not the concentration of ownership. At the time of the break-up, it's true, there was some controversy over whether the courts had accomplished even that. Many critics charged that old Standard bosses simply appointed junior executives as "officers" of the newly emancipated subsidiaries while they ran things from behind the scenes. Whatever the case may have been then though, there can be little doubt today that the various companies generally conduct their affairs independently of one another.

But ownership is another matter. If you owned 1 percent of Standard stock before the break-up, you ended up with 1 percent of the trimmed-down Jersey Standard Company plus 1 percent of each of the 33 affiliates. So if you were a Rockefeller, you still controlled enormous amounts of capital—it was just spread around more. Before 1911, John D. Rockefeller and associates not only managed Standard Oil, they pretty much owned it as well, through a complicated system of trusts and holding companies. They didn't necessarily own the stock personally, but they controlled the people and institutions that did. After the Supreme Court ruling, this situation remained essentially unchanged. It was only through the passage of time, as additional issues of stock were sold to outsiders and the companies drifted apart, that Rockefeller influence diminished. As late as 1929, though, the Rockefeller family was able to quash a rebellious Standard of Indiana board chairman in a proxy fight by marshaling shares owned by the several Rockefeller foundations and the heirs of old Rockefeller associates.

It's unclear today how much stock in Standard Oil's descendant companies is owned by the Rockefellers or their foundations, banks, and subsidiaries. Standard of Indiana, for example, professes to be unable to identify *any* large blocks of Rockefeller stock, but admits that a great many shares are held by nominees or trusts that conceal the identity of the true owner. A Congressional report a while back said that as of 1960, 1.2 million of Indiana Standard's then 36 million shares were owned by Rockefeller-controlled foundations. Large holdings in other oil companies were reported as well.

In fairness, it must be said that owning a lot of stock does not necessarily mean you get to run the company—that is, unless you own at least 51 percent, which is not the case here. Shareholders, even major ones, have little say in the day-to-day operations of their companies unless they can contrive to get themselves elected to the board of directors, which by and large the Rockefellers have not done (in the case of ex-Standard affiliates, anyway). Moreover, in Indiana Standard's case at least, 1960's 36 million shares had grown to 150 million in 1979. Unless Rockefeller minions have been extraordinarily busy, the family's relative share of the action has diminished considerably. In short, the rich are still pretty rich, but their influence in the nation's oil industry has been substantially diluted.

Chapter 19

════════════════════════

Food and Drink

Can you find out what "Reg. Penna. Dept. Agr." means and why it's all over our food? Who cares what Pennsylvania's department of agriculture thinks? They can't keep anybody's food out of Pennsylvania, anyhow—it's a burden on interstate commerce. And why does this mysterious mark appear on food sold in Canada?—Kelly K., Chicago

The people of Pennsylvania, apparently, are incurable do-gooders. In 1933, they became concerned about the quality of the new, mass-produced baked goods that were infiltrating their state and passed the Pennsylvania Bakery Law to ensure that all products met their exacting standards for cleanliness and honest weight. The law requires every baker—that is, virtually anyone who applies heat to his product, including makers of spaghetti, macaroni, pretzels, breakfast foods, potato chips, or what have you—to pass an inspection and obtain a license from the Pennsylvania Department of Agriculture in order to do business in Pennsylvania. State agents make periodic inspections of registered plants to make sure that the employees are still washing their hands. Because of a similar law in Connecticut, many packages also bear a license number from that state.

Pennsylvania, no matter what its burden on interstate commerce, has every right to decide what baked goods can and cannot be sold within the state. Rather than make up a separate package for Pennsylvanians, most manufacturers incorporate "Reg. Penn. Dept. Agr." into their standard design—and that includes Canadian as well as overseas operations ("Reg.," by the way, stands for "registered with," not "regulated by," in case you were wondering). Naturally, Pennsylvanians find it impossible to dispatch agents to every bakery in the world, so they have developed a network of contacts with other state (and foreign) agriculture boards, all of which are happy to keep tabs on domestic production for the sake of clean-living Keystoners.

Was the orange named orange because of orange, or was orange named orange because of oranges? You want me to repeat the question?—Pete B., Washington, D.C.

Spare me. The noun preceded the adjective, deriving ultimately from the Sanskrit *naranga*, "orange tree." It is thought that the initial *n* may have been dropped in French or Italian as it was assimilated into the definite article—i.e., *une narange* became *une arange*, and *una narancia* became *una arancia*. The first English use of the word "orange" as a color adjective appears to have been in 1620.

Here is a question that has plagued me ever since I was breaking up with my last girlfriend and wandered around my empty apartment in a daze staring fixedly at random objects. Once I stared fixedly at the back of a box of Jell-O. I saw something that made me stare at another box, and another (my old girlfriend liked Jell-O). Anyway, here's the question: why is it that every Jell-O package says not to add fresh or frozen pineapples? And why is there no pineapple-flavored Jell-O, only orange-pineapple? Occasionally I still sink into morbid brooding about this, particularly when having trouble with my new girl friend. Only you can help.—Bill R., Dallas

Man, does Ann Landers get letters like this? If you put fresh pineapple in your Jell-O, you'll end up with pineapple floating in Kool-Aid. Pineapples naturally contain a chemical substance that

inhibits jelling. Cooking the fruit drives the substance out, and that's why only fresh and fresh-frozen varieties are prohibited.

None of this has anything to do with the question of why there is no pineapple-flavored Jell-O. General Foods generally decides such things on the basis of consumer preference surveys. To date no great yearning for pineapple Jell-O has been detected, so they don't make it.

While I was munching on a slab of Juicy Fruit today, two questions filtered from mouth to mind: who invented the stuff, anyway? And what's it made of?—G.A., Baltimore

The chewing gum habit goes back to the Indians, actually. Such a deal: they give us gum, tobacco, and Manhattan island; we give them firewater, syphilis, and Frank Sinatra. Oh, well. New England tribesmen chewed on a gum-like substance taken from the pulp of the spruce tree to keep their whistles wet on long hikes through the woods. The practice was quickly adopted by the first white settlers, but strangely enough it was a hundred years or so before a wily capitalist came along to size up the commercial possibilities. In 1848, John Curtis set up shop in Bangor, Maine, manufacturing "State of Maine Pure Spruce Gum" from a stove-top plant. Curtis's success was not overwhelming. There was one serious problem with "Pure Spruce Gum"—namely, that it tasted entirely too much like pure spruce. Curtis experimented with adding other flavors to the mixture, but nothing seemed capable of disguising the essential sprucidity of his product. By 1850 Curtis had thrown over spruce gum in favor of paraffin, a petroleum by-product that had the advantage of being tasteless, but wasn't up to the spruce stuff texture-wise. (Spruce gum didn't entirely disappear, though; I'm told you can still get it in New Hampshire today, tasting as rank as ever.)

The next breakthrough came on December 28, 1869, when Patent No. 98,304 was issued to William Finley Semple of Mount Vernon, Ohio. The visionary Semple laid claim to the idea that a functional chewing gum could be made from rubber, combined with unnamed "other articles." Semple apparently never discovered what the other articles were, because there is no record of his product ever entering the marketplace. He was, as we shall see, a man ahead of his time.

The scene now shifts to Staten Island, New York, 1870. Thomas Adams, a commercial photographer (no relation to the present writer), has spent the last two years of his life experimenting with a strange substance he has imported from Mexico, the sap of the Chiclezapote tree. Adams hopes to develop the goo into a substitute for rubber. But he has failed again and again. He sits at his workbench a broken man, staring blankly at the wad of chicle. Suddenly, on a blind impulse, no longer caring for the consequences, the despondent Adams reaches out, tears off a slimy corner of the mocking mound, and pops it into his mouth. Eureka! The Chiclet is born!

Little did Adams realize that the Mexican Indians had been chewing chicle for centuries, having no use for it in the form of automobile tires. No matter. Adams scooped up his chicle and went out to look for backers. Many scoffed, but the undaunted Adams opened his plant anyway. Success was instantaneous. By 1890, Adams' six-story factory employed 250 workers.

Unwittingly, Adams had spawned a national craze. Gum chewing, like hula hoops and the Beatles, swept the country, and was soon being condemned as evil by politicians, clergymen, and women's groups. The *New York Sun* editorialized in 1890: "The habit has reached such a stage now that makes it impossible for a New Yorker to go to the theater or the church, or enter the street cars or the railway train, or walk on a fashionable promenade without meeting men and women whose jaws are working with the activity of the gum chewing victim. And the spectacle is maintained in the face of frequent reminders that gum-chewing, especially in public, is an essentially vulgar indulgence that not only shows bad breeding, but spoils a pretty countenance and detracts from the dignity of those who practice the habit." However, when it became clear that no definite link between gum chewing and white slavery could be established, the furor died down.

Today, William Finley Semple has been vindicated. Most gum is now made from latex rubber, taken from the sapodilla tree of Central and South America. The dried latex is kneaded into a hot mix of sugar and corn syrup, delicately flavored, and then pressed and cut into neat little strips, ready to rot the teeth of the nation.

Why doesn't water work to soothe your mouth after eating spicy hot Chinese, Indian, Mexican, etc., foods? Is it true that water actually makes the burning sensation worse? What, if anything, does work?—Robert R., Chicago

If you had been paying attention in sixth-grade science class like you should've, Bobo, you would already know the answer to this question, which can be summed up thusly: oil and water don't

mix. The fiery spices in the foods you mention are oil-based, and thus mix readily with the cooking oil and/or natural juices the food simmers in. When you eat the stuff, the oil coats your tongue and throat, and for complicated molecular reasons that we need not discuss right here, repels all efforts to wash it down with water. Water doesn't actually make the burning sensation worse, but by eliminating all other distracting tastes I suppose we might say it purifies the agony. There are many ways of eliminating the problem. A quart of Drano, for instance, will do wonders. If this seems a bit drastic, you have two basic choices: dilutants (more oil) and solvents (such as alcohol). Best dilutant I know of is milk, which generally works like a charm. If this is not sufficiently macho for you, you can try some alcoholic beverage appropriate to the occasion. A good jolt of tequila, for instance, in a Mexican restaurant. Then again, you may feel that the cure is worse than the disease.

Please answer a question that came up over a (three-fourths empty) bourbon bottle the other night. What's the difference between "age" and "maturity" in hard liquor?—Ed D., Chicago

Freshly distilled whiskey is unfit for drinking—about as palatable as crude oil. Once it comes out of the still it goes into storage, and only properly becomes whiskey with the passing of time and completion of a series of chemical changes. Bourbon and rye, for instance, are stored in white oak containers that have been carefully charred on the inside in order to let chemicals contained in the wood mix with the brew, and to permit oxygen to enter through the pores of the staves. The barrels are systematically heated and cooled—this is called the "breathing process"—first forcing the liquid, under pressure, to expand into the pores of the wood, and then to draw oxygen back as the liquor is allowed to cool and condense. The faster the "breathing," the faster the chemical changes take place. The liquor is said to be "fully matured" when the process has run its course. "Maturity," then, is a relative measure, the degree to which the chemical changes have been completed, while "age" is a simple linear measure of the time the liquor has been in storage.

What is the origin of the custom of drinking tequila after licking salt off your hand and afterwards biting into a slice of fresh lime? What does the salt do, anyway? Is it true that tequila is made from the same plant as mescaline?—Linda T., Los Angeles

Get ready for this. Mescaline is made from what the plant botanists call *Lophophora williamsii*. Tequila is made from several species of the genus *Agave*. The term "mescal" is used as an informal name for both types of plant, even though they are of different genera. So, while you could say that both tequila and mescaline are manufactured from the mescal plant, you couldn't say they are manufactured from the *same* plant. To add to the confusion, tequila is classified as a Mexican brandy, and the generic name for Mexican brandies is . . . *mescal*! Aren't you glad you asked?

Mexicans have long known that a little sodium chloride on the tongue can help to mollify the fiery flavor that characterizes much of their food. They use salt when downing chile peppers, for example. By the same token, citrus juices of various kinds have long been used to kill the aftertaste of the more potent forms of alcohol. American blacks, for instance, at one time cut their port wine with lemon juice. The Gallo wine company noticed this and began marketing Thunderbird, a white port-citric acid mixture. Anyway, when tequila came to the U.S., the salt and lime (or lemon) bit came with it.

Apart from the fact that all the light beers say "less calories" rather than "fewer calories," I am irritated that they never tell us whether the alcohol content is also reduced. What is the alcohol content of, say, Pabst Extra Light (50 percent fewer calories) and how does it compare with regular beer?—Roland E., Chicago

Believe it or not, you are dealing in classified information.

If you asked the friendly folks at the Pabst Brewing Company about this, they'd cordially invite you to sue them before they'd tell you anything. Fortunately, you didn't ask Pabst, you asked me. Alcohol is the prime factor in determining the calorie content of beer—the carbohydrate and protein percentages hardly matter at all. This, perhaps, is the source of Pabst's guilty secret: the advantages of drinking a light beer seem to pale somewhat when you realize that you'll have to drink twice as much in order to get a buzz on.

The alcohol content of "regular" American-made beer varies between 3.6 and 3.8 percent by weight, depending on the brand (European beers are significantly heavier, containing about 5 percent alcohol). For each 12-ounce can of Pabst Blue Ribbon you guzzle, you'll be absorbing between 100 and 150 calories, depending on which tests you prefer to believe. The average light beer, by contrast, contains between 3 and 3.4 percent alcohol by weight and boasts an average of 96 calories. But like the name says, Pabst Extra Light is *extra light*, and if we take the ad's claim of "half the calories" at face value, it would have to check in at 50 to 75 calories per can. Given that range, an educated guess puts Extra Light's alcohol content in the area of 2 percent by weight, give or take a few tenths in either direction. Might as well switch to Kool-Aid.

One morning, not having anything better to do, I tried to calculate the Recommended Daily Allowance for protein using the nutritional info they put on the labels of breakfast foods. The milk had 9 grams of protein per serving, which supposedly was 20 percent of the RDA for protein, making the total RDA 45 grams. The cereal, however, read 3 grams for 4 percent of the RDA, making the total RDA 75 grams. Then I remembered that all proteins are not alike in amino acid content, and figured maybe the RDA was scaled to reflect the amino acid makeup in a particular food item. This hypothesis went down the drain when I examined the protein content for fruited and plain yogurt. Clearly the proteins in these two products ought to be identical, yet by my calculations the protein RDA in the one is 50 grams and in the other it's 40 grams. What gives?—Chuck A., Loyola University, Chicago

The problem with you college kids is that you lack the discipline necessary for sustained mental effort. We have here a case in point. As you correctly surmised, there isn't any RDA for protein as such, because how much protein you need depends on the so-called *quality* of the protein you propose to eat—i.e., the extent to which it contains the proper proportions of the eight amino acids adults need to maintain health. Now, if you had given a little additional thought to the problem, you would have realized that the reason the two varieties of yogurt have different percent-of-RDA figures is that in the fruited kind, the high-quality protein of the yogurt is diluted with frivolous strawberries, or whatever. Plant products tend to be shy of one or more critical amino acids (vegetarians have to be a bit careful about what they eat for this reason). It's as simple as that.

What do the letters K, R, and U mean on various food and other packages? For example, Chun King Rice has a small letter K, Clorox Scrub Cleaner a U, Dow's Ziploc storage bags a U, and so on.—Frank N., Baltimore

The circled R, as I think most of the civilized world knows by now, stands for registered trademark. The K, circled K, and the circled U are all meant to indicate the product is kosher. Therefore, Frank, what you have in your closet there is a box of kosher storage bags. This may strike you as taking this kosher business a bit far, but allow me to explain. A product is "kosher" if a rabbi determines and certifies that it meets the requirements of Jewish dietary law, which is no mean feat in these days of additive-laden, prepackaged foods. In addition to the familiar prohibitions against pork and mixing meat and dairy substances, the law contains strict provisions for the slaughter and preparation of virtually all animal products. The most innocent-looking ingredient—an emulsifier, an oil, a dab of gelatin—can mean the difference between kosher and nonkosher, even if it merely comes in contact with something that will eventually be eaten (which is where things like oven cleaners and plastic bags come into play). Because some rabbis are more finicky (or more thorough, depending on how you look at it) about enforcing these strictures than others, the matter of who is doing the certifying is a matter of some moment. Thus we have a plethora of codes signifying kosherness. The unadorned K, being a simple letter of the alphabet, can be used by anyone who wants to claim his product is kosher. The circled K, on the other hand, is a registered mark and can only be used with the permission of its owner, the Organized Kashruth Laboratories of New York, a private certifying concern. The circled U is similarly controlled by the Union of Orthodox Jewish Congregations of America, the undisputed heavyweight of kosher-certifying organizations. Some smaller organizations have marks that you may find on locally-distributed products. It's not a matter of one product being more or less kosher than another, but who says so and whom you want to believe.

What does it mean to say that a pickle is "kosher?" Is it just the way they taste, or are kosher pickles really kosher?—Andy P., Chicago

They'd better be, kiddo, or they'll incur the wrath not only of the above-mentioned religious organizations but also of various state and federal agencies. "Kosher" has a very specific meaning, and to put it on a product that doesn't conform to the Jewish dietary laws constitutes a serious violation of food labeling regulations. So don't try it.

Some of the confusion about pickles, I suppose, arises from the assumption that the Torah doesn't have much to say about them—pickles are, after all basically vegetables, which the dietary laws don't cover. But modern science has stepped in to cloud the issue. Polysorbates, derived from animal fat, are sometimes added to the pickle brine as an emulsifier. Anything derived from animals, no matter how remotely, is covered by the laws.

The procedures for having a product certified as kosher are fairly standardized. The manufacturer writes a letter describing the product to whatever Jewish organization in his area has the appropriate authority. Specific potential problems with the product are identified, an inspection of the plant is conducted, and an agreement is reached as to how the quality of the ingredients is to be controlled and how often the plant is to be reinspected. Once all that has been worked out, the authority issues a letter of permission, whereupon, I need hardly add, everything's kosher.

My hard-drinking friend from Purdue and I are in a state of disagreement. She insists the original (and hence "true") boilermaker drink consists of a shot of whiskey dropped, glass and all, into a mug of beer. Being from a more modest drinking background, I have only experienced these concoctions under the name "depth charges," and am familiar with the shot of whiskey with a beer chaser as a boilermaker. What's the straight dope on this, and should I stay away from women who can consume quantities of liquor in excess of their body weight?—C.M., Oak Park, Illinois.

To tell you the truth, C., I'd never heard of dropping a shot glass of whiskey into your beer before now, and at first I assumed it was just some moronic custom confined to no-mind Purdulians. However, an ex-bartender buddy of mine informs me that the practice is actually widespread, God help us. He (the ex-bartender) also backs up your friend's contention that this is the original boilermaker. On the other hand, a veteran liquor salesman of my acquaintance says that your friend is full of crap—the true boilermaker is and always has been the good old shot-and-a-beer. To further confuse matters, most bar guides list a "depth charge" as a weird confabulation of brandy, applejack, and grenadine, or alternatively, gin, Pernod, and something called Kina Lillet. In short, who knows?

The term "unsweetened" on an orange juice can, I have been told, means that the OJ within is no sweeter than an industry-set standard. Supposedly it's permissible to add sugar to substandard orange juice to bring it up to that level and still call it "unsweetened." On the other hand, I've heard, truly superior OJ says "no sugar added." This means that "unsweetened" is virtually a sure sign that sugar has been added. Is this true? Also, what's the story on "100 percent concentrate"? And is the fetuslike tumor on the bottom of a navel orange in any way different from the rest of the orange?—Will W., Colgate, Maryland

According to our federal protectors, any product attempting to pass as "concentrated orange juice" or "orange juice concentrate" must contain, by weight, 11.8 percent orange juice solids after being diluted for consumption. Ready-to-drink "canned orange juice" must contain 10 percent solids. These solids are essentially fruit sugars and associated citric acids—the stuff that's left over after you squeeze the juice out of the fruit and remove the water. Substandard juices are generally adjusted for taste, color, and sweetness by blending with other juices; if any foreign sweetener is added, the label is supposed to say so clearly. In other words, the theory you outline above is jive—if the label doesn't say "sugar added," the presumption is that no sugar has been added. Terms like "unsweetened," "no sugar added," and "100 percent" have no special, technical meanings in this regard. They are merely hype used by various packers to emphasize the wholesomeness of their products and make the other packers look like poison-peddling scumbags.

Of course, some packers and repackers of orange juice—most often the distributors of regional and private-label brands—have been known to bend the rules, but unfortunately these bad apples (I know, poor choice of words) can't be detected by close label reading. In any case, they're not much of a problem. Something like 95 percent of the orange juice concentrate sold at retail in the U.S. is packed in Florida, where state standards actually exceed federal standards and are strictly enforced. They take their orange juice seriously in Florida.

The common navel orange appears to have arisen naturally as a mutation of the Brazilian orange variety known as the Selecta; its existence is recorded at least as far back as the 17th century, and it was brought to the U.S. in 1870. The "fetuslike tumor" you mention might more accurately be described as a tumorlike fetus, though it is properly called the navel. It is a secondary, rudimentary orange that will never get to grow up, poor little fella. Proportionally, it contains less pulp than the mature fruit, but the pulp is quite similar in composition to the mama fruit and is eminently edible, if you're into that kind of thing.

What is carob? Where does it come from? Is carob healthier than chocolate? Why is it more expensive? How many calories in an ounce of carob? How much sugar, and what type?—Eddie E., Los Angeles

I can see you have a fiery curiosity, my son, although carob seems like a strange thing to get passionate about. It is basically a chocolate substitute made from the roasted and ground pods of the carob tree, a Mediterranean evergreen that goes by the name *Ceratonia siliqua*. It is not healthier than chocolate in itself; both carob and chocolate are basically nonnutritive flavorings. Carob has 51 calories per ounce to cocoa powder's 98; it has a somewhat larger proportion of carbohydrates, but less protein and fat. You don't use enough of it to make the sugar content worthy worrying about. What's significant is that carob is naturally sweeter than (or, perhaps more accurately, not as bitter as) chocolate, so you don't have to use as much sugar with it in recipes. Refined sugar, which does little for you besides rot your teeth, is the major ingredient in many chocolate recipes. Supposedly you can use half as much sugar when you substitute carob. Carob is still a specialty item, which accounts for its cost.

Having ventured one or two carob delicacies in my day, I must say that carob makes for a pretty vague approximation of chocolate, and American tastebuds do not take to it with unanimous delight. However, it is worth experimenting with, as long as you are not determined to eat it.

On our vacation to the wilds of Wisconsin, we noticed some of the locals picking cattails from the swamps. My husband asked them why, and the terse midwestern reply was, "eat 'em." Is this on the level? If so, how do you cook them—roast the tips like hot dogs?—R.B., Chicago

Cattails are one of the enduring favorites of the Euell Gibbons crowd, and can be enjoyed in at least three different ways. The favored cut of the cattail is the inner portion of the stem, called, for unknown reasons, "Cossack asparagus." The outer covering of the stalk is removed by pulling down on the leaves that cover it, breaking off the shell near the roots and exposing anywhere from one to twelve inches of the succulent white pseudo-asparagus. It can be washed and eaten raw, chopped up for salads, or cooked in a stew. The best plants for harvesting are the younger sprouts, two feet tall or so, in the early spring, but the stems are edible all summer long.

Some woodland epicures also collect the pollen of the cattail, which starts to flow in the middle of the summer. The powder is used as a seasoning, or mixed with flour for pancakes, cookies, and so on. Finally, the roots can be dried, ground up, and used as flour. In the spring, the roots are covered with small, potato-like bulbs, which can be boiled, dipped in butter, and served up to the delight and amazement of your city slicker friends.

Ever since I was a kid, I have seen references to sarsaparilla. All the kids in western and nineteenth-century stories were always drinking it. It seemed to be very popular, and I've always wondered: how come you can't get it today?—Garth G., Phoenix

Sarsaparilla is still around, but it takes a little poking to turn it up. The drink, which tastes a great deal like root beer, is still popular in some parts of the U.S.—the folks in Pittsburgh, I understand, are crazy about the stuff. Although none of the major soft-drink manufacturers markets a national brand, all continue to make the flavor base available to any local bottler who cares to market sarsaparilla on his own. Many cities have a specialty store or two that carries these brands; ask around.

You might think that sarsaparilla would be made from extract of the sarsaparilla plant, a tropical vine distantly related to the lily, but you'd be wrong. It was originally made (artificial flavors have taken over now, of course) from a blend of birch oil and sassafras, the dried root bark of the sassafras tree. Sassafras was widely used as a home remedy in the nineteenth century—taken in sufficient doses, it induces sweating, which some people thought was a good thing. Sarsaparilla apparently made its debut as a patent medicine, an easy-to-take form of sassafras, much as Cocoa-

Cola was first marketed in 1885 as a remedy for hangovers and headaches.

Why isn't sarsaparilla popular anymore? Basically, it just lost out to cola, like almost every other flavor you could name. Root beer, sarsaparilla's closest cousin and once America's most popular soft drink, now accounts for less than 4 percent of the national market. Sarsaparilla's share is too small to be measured.

Why, in a bag of M&Ms, are there always lots of "dark browns" and "yellows," but only a few "light browns" and "greens"? And what does "M&M" stand for, anyway?—Rob G., Evanston, Illinois

M&M stands for the two confectionery geniuses, Mars and Murrie, who founded the firm back in 1928 in Minneapolis, Minnesota, which also happens to be the home of the 3M company (why does this seem significant?). M&M is now a wholly owned subsidiary of Mars (hmm . . .) Candy Corporation, manufacturers of such venerable teeth rotters as Milky Ways, Three Musketeers, and . . . Snickers. Shoot. For a second there I thought I had evidence of another Illuminati plot.

M&Ms are colored strictly for eye appeal. Contrary to popular mythology—generations of pre-schoolers have lusted after the elusive "greens"—there's no difference whatever in flavor between the colors. M&M's market research has revealed that one particular blend—roughly 60 percent dark brown, 30 percent yellow, and 10 percent "other"—is irresistible to the candy consuming public.

The last time I ate a popsicle I noticed that the wrapper said ". . . Twin Pop, a quiescently frozen confection . . ." Can you find out what this vaguely alarming phrase means? Please respond quickly! My freezer is filled with QFCs, and I'm afraid to eat another one until I find out.—S.M.F., Mesa, Arizona

The phrase "quiescently frozen confection" is simply the legal definition of a Popsicle, used in the various state and legal codes that regulate the production and distribution of food. Legislators, it seems, are too embarrassed to drop words like "Popsicle" into the middle of their carefully honed legalese, so a little linguistic obfuscation is necessary. Besides, "Popsicle" is the registered trademark of Popsicle Industries of Englewood, New Jersey—which is to say that there are many popsicles, but only one Popsicle, as licensed for manufacture by the parent company.

"Quiescent" means "at rest," and that's pretty much how

Popsicles are frozen—a blend of colored water and flavor is poured into a mold and run through a refrigerator. That's as opposed to the "overrun" method of freezing, which is used in making ice cream and similar products. Ice cream is constantly stirred and agitated as it is frozen, incorporating a fair amount of air into the end product, which increases its volume but not its weight. Fudgesicles fall into still another category. Since they contain a small amount of milk (as well as water), they become "quiescently frozen *dairy* confections," and are subjected to yet another set of rules and regulations.

OK, Popsicles and Fudgesicles I understand. So what's the difference between a Creamsicle and a Dreamsicle?—C.S., Chicago

The sherbet-like shell of the Creamsicle is identical to that of the Dreamsicle, but the payoff inside is ice cream in the former, ice milk in the latter. The difference in price, last time I checked, was about a nickel.

A friend of mine who brews beer told me something quite startling recently. He said he read in a brewer's magazine that Budweiser uses chicken hearts *in their beer. Is this true? Why do they use them? Does anybody else? I assure you this is not a case of professional jealousy—we can't stand Bud anyway—Sparky H., Chicago*

Why are alcoholic beverages exempt from having to list their ingredients? How can the consumer tell if a beer has preservatives, chemical additives, or artificial flavors and colors? Mass consumption of alcohol is unhealthy enough without also having to ingest assorted chemical horrors.—Steve N., Phoenix

There is no question that a disquieting amount of chemical smegma goes into the nation's beer (not to mention its wine and liquor), but Uncle Cecil must humbly confess that he does not know exactly what goes into which. That's because the booze industry has successfully resisted all attempts to force it to list ingredients, on the ridiculous grounds that doing so would be too expensive. The real reason, needless to say, if that if you, Joe Consumer, knew what kind of sludge went into your favorite brand, you would probably drink a lot less of it. I don't know about chicken hearts, but some brewers use seaweed extract as a foam stabilizer, and some wine makers use fish glue to prevent cloudiness. Queasy as these things sound, they're probably harmless, which is more than you can say for some additives. In the mid 60s, for instance, about 50 people died when brewers began putting cobalt sulfate into their products as a foaming agent. Beverage manufacturers don't intentionally murder their customers, of course. But the fact is that a fair number of people are allergic or otherwise sensitive to booze additives, and in the absence of labeling the only way to find out if there's anything bad in a given brew is to take a hefty swig of it and see if you keel over.

Anheuser-Busch claims that Budweiser contains only natural

ingredients: water, barley malt, rice, hops, yeast, and tannin, an anticloudiness agent that is mostly removed from the final product. They say there's no chicken hearts or anything else. On the other hand, Miller, Anheuser's chief competitor, uses quite a bit of chemical goo. We can prove this by performing the following easy 'n' fun test for the presence of foam stabilizers. Get two clean beer glasses, and into each put one drop of milk diluted 70-to-1 with water. Then pour Bud into one glass and Miller into the other. Unless the manufacturers have changed their formulas in the last couple weeks, the head on the Bud will die like a dog within two minutes (which it should—even a tiny trace of milk is deadly to beer foam), whereas the one on the Miller won't, indicating the presence of false drugs.

The preceding exercise in handy home chemistry is supplied by the Center for Science in the Public Interest, a consumer group based in Washington, D.C., that recently made a not-very-successful effort to get manufacturers to voluntarily reveal their ingredients. I don't mean to single out the Miller company, but you may be interested to know that Miller Lite contains propylene glycol alginate, water, barley malt, corn syrup, chemically modified hop extracts, yeast, amyloglucosidase, carbon dixoide, papain enzyme, liquid sugar, potassium metabisulfite, and Emka-malt, whatever that is. I would venture to say that light beers as a class tend to have more additives than others, simply because they'd be totally flat and tasteless otherwise. For more info on this subject, see *Chemical Additives in Booze*, available for $4.95 from the Center for Science in the Public Interest, 1775 S Street NW, Washington, D.C. 20009.

I would appreciate a scientific answer to this question if there is one. In making chocolate chip cookies, why is it important to add one-half teaspoon of water? Any real reason? For years the recipe on packages of Nestle's semi-sweet chocolate chip packages told you to do this, and the recipes on other brands still do.—Linn V., Santa Monica, California

There is only one way to obtain a "scientific answer," Linn, and that is to conduct a scientific experiment. Which I did, under the controlled sterile conditions of my own humble kitchen. Following the Scientific Method, as laid out by countless generations of high-school chemistry teachers, I prepared two batches of the peerless cookie, one with the mysterious half teaspoon of water, and one without. End difference: zip. But the batch with the water seemed to make a less glutinous batter—it mixed better, came off the spoon with less resistance, and was, in general, noticeably more docile.

Chapter 20

TV and Movies

One evening during an orgy of hard-core trivia, we were suddenly and frustratingly stumped by a truly baffling item. Even the most devoted trivia freaks among our friends drew blanks when we presented them with this one. If you can answer it for us, Cecil, we'll finally be able to sleep nights. What the hell was the name of Dudley Do-Right's horse?—The Smithies, Chicago

Dudley's horse was named Horse. That's it—Horse. Bet you could kick yourself, huh? Now you can go back to worrying about the important things in life, like the Middle East crisis, nuclear war, the situation in El Salvador, and where Bullwinkle went to college. Answer on request.

A bunch of us former Mouseketeers were sitting around reminiscing about the good old days with Annette, Roy, Cubbie, Lonnie, and the whole gang. Many golden memories came flooding back, but none of us could recall with certainty the different themes the show had every day. There was "Circus Day," of course, and who could forget "Fun With Music Day"? But what were the others, and when did they fall chronologically? As a former Mouseketeer yourself, no doubt, you should have no trouble with this one.— Evelyn W., Los Angeles

There are certain episodes in our past that we try desperately to forget, Evelyn. If you must know, "Fun With Music Day" fell on Monday, Tuesday brought "Guest Star Day" (usually some washed-up vaudevillian on the order of Morey Amsterdam), Wednesday was "Anything Can Happen Day" (i.e., the Mouseketeers cheap it out), Thursday was "Circus Day," and the week reached a grand climax on Friday with "Talent Round-Up Day," which generally meant Cubby and another of his crummy drum solos.

Please help my friends and me solve a point of great confusion and save us from having to sit through five years of "Fugitive" reruns. We would like to know if there were several different endings to the "Fugitive" series shown in different regions of the U.S. In the Midwest, we seem to recall, the last episode revealed that Kimble's best friend had murdered his wife after a lovers' quarrel, while on the East Coast a friend saw a version in which the crime was pinned on the infamous "one-armed man." Are we crazy, or were there really different endings? And what was the West Coast ending?—Susan N. and Jim M., Chicago

You are crazy. Only one ending was filmed for the ABC series, and it went, ahem, something like this:

After four seasons of searching, Inspector Gerard (played by the incomparable Barry Morse) finally manages to catch Johnson, the mysterious "one-armed man" (played by the sublime Bill Raisch). But Gerard, an incurably suspicious sort, still has doubts about Dr. Kimble's innocence, and he leaks the news of Johnson's capture to the press, hoping to lure Kimble into his clutches. Kimble (played by the unspeakable David Janssen) falls for it like a ton of bricks and turns himself in. But meanwhile, Johnson has escaped, leaving Kimble, nearly annihilated by the irony of it all, to plead with Gerard for one last chance to clear himself. A fine fellow after all, Gerard relents and allows Kimble to search for the one-armed man, while he follows at a discreet remove. Kimble tracks Johnson to an amusement park, where, during a terrific fight atop a water tower, the one-armed man confesses to having killed Kimble's wife, Helen (played by the inconspicuous Diane Brewster). As the fight rages, Gerard looks on from below. Finally, Johnson is about to kill Kimble, and it falls to Gerard, who has not heard the confession, to make the final judgment. After a heart-stopping pause, the crack of a rifle shatters the night sky: Johnson is dead, and Kimble, relatively vindicated, is free to leave the series and become a contract player at Universal.

For some reason the other day I happened to think about the chimp who used to appear on the old Today *show with Dave Garroway. His name, etched in my memory forever, was J. Fred Muggs. However, I also have a dim recollection of J. Fred having a girl friend, but I can't remember her name for the life of me. My friends insist I'm making the whole thing up, so I can only*

360

throw myself on your tender mercies. Did J. Fred Muggs have a lady companion, and if so, what was her name?—Mandy R., Washington, D.C.

Heartfelt pleas like yours never fail to move me, and so it gives me great pleasure to report that J. Fred did indeed come equipped with a female consort. Her name—mellifluous and beguiling, as befits a creature of her tremendous delicacy and charm—was Phoebe B. Beebee.

I just realized the other day that I have never understood how they walked upside down in the spaceship in the movie 2001: A Space Odyssey. *It looked like they walked around the inside of a cylinder. How'd they do it, Cecil?—Paul S., Skokie, Illinois*

This may disappoint you fans of high-tech special effects, but several sequences in *2001* made use of a technique that had once been used in a Fred Astaire movie, of all things. One number in Stanley Donen's 1951 musical *Royal Wedding* required Astaire to dance over the walls and ceiling of his London apartment, an effect accomplished by mounting the entire apartment set inside cylinder. The set was turned on rollers as Astaire danced, hopping from floor to ceiling as the apartment revolved underfoot. The camera, bolted to the "floor" of the apartment, turned with the set—and so, on the screen, the set appeared to be perfectly sta-

tionary: Astaire was dancing on the ceiling when the ceiling was actually the floor, if you follow me.

Stanley Kubrick used the same gimmick several times in *2001*. There's an early scene in which a stewardess carrying a food tray steps into a sort of cylindrical vestibule and proceeds to walk up the wall, with the result that she pivots through 180 degrees and ends up completely upside-down. Later, aboard the Jupiter mission, we see one of the astronauts jogging a couple times around the cylindrical interior of the spaceship. In both cases the set rotated while the actor remained more or less stationary. The Jupiter mission set was 38 feet in diameter and was mounted on a steel framework much like a ferris wheel. "The camera was on a gimbaled mount [attached to the moving set], and the [camera] operator was in a gimbaled seat," Kubrick has been quoted as saying. "As the [set] rotated at three miles per hour, the camera was constantly adjusted by the operator to keep the actor in the picture. The effect on the screen is that the camera is standing still and the actor is walking up and around the top and down the other side." Combined with the already shifted perspective of the dope-crazed members of the audience, the effect is irresistible. For pictures of the sets, see Jerome Agel's *The Making of Kubrick's 2001* (1970).

What is a gaffer? According to my dictionary, a gaffer is an old man, but I've yet to see a movie whose credits didn't mention such a creature. What do old men have to do with the making of movies?—George C., Phoenix

You Arizonans are so literal-minded. The gaffer is the head electrician in a film production unit, and is charged principally with taking care of the lighting. He is aided in this effort by his number-one assistant, the "best boy," who also gets to be in the credits a lot of the time, right next to the "key grip" and the "second grip," the head handyman and his chief helper, respectively. None of these is a title I would be eager to insert in my resume. However, the electricians at least get to yell such satisfying cinematic admonitions as "slap a jelly on the baby" ("please be so kind as to affix a gelatin filter to one of the 500-watt lamps"), which more than makes up for minor embarrassments of nomenclature, to my way of thinking.

I don't understand TV scheduling. I would assume that since a greater number of the Teeming Millions is awake from 9 to 10 PM than from 10 to 11 PM, more of them are ogling the idiot box during the earlier hour. This means that during the last hour of prime time (10–11 PM in New York, 9–10 PM in Chicago), many more people are watching in the Central zone than in the Eastern zone, allowing a far greater number of Buttoneers, Popeil Pocket Fishermen, and tubes of Tickle Deodorant to be sold in the Midwest than on the East Coast. Accepting this, which any sensitive and thoughtful individual would, why on earth does West Coast TV operate under the East Coast schedule?

As an addendum, Cecil, if you are called upon to destroy my assumptions, please be merciful and don't employ your laserlike wit to grind me into pulp.—Allan S., Evanston, Illinois

Don't snivel, Allan, we just had the floors waxed. The present system of network scheduling is the result of the four timeless factors that govern all human endeavors: geography, technology, inertia, and greed. It's true, as you say, that TV viewership nationwide starts to fall off pretty rapidly after 10 PM; indeed, peak viewing occurs between 8 and 10. However, since the prime time schedule lasts three hours (8–11 PM in the Eastern and Pacific zones, 7–10 in Central and Mountain), the networks have the whole country pretty well covered. More people tend to watch the first two hours of prime time on the coasts, and the last two in the heartland, but in the end it all averages out. By concentrating on the peak periods, however, we lose sight of the real genius of TV scheduling—namely, dragging out the evening as long as possible, so there'll be more hours to cram commercials into. No matter where he lives, the average schmo would probably go to bed around 11 if left to his own devices. Many people like to cap off their day with the news, though, so it doesn't take much to convince them to stay up an extra half-hour to catch up on the latest jive from Five, or whatever. At the same time, the networks historically have tried to begin entertainment programming as early in the evening as possible. When nightly 15-minute newscasts first started in the late 40s, CBS's show appeared at 7:30 Eastern time, and NBC's at 7:45. In 1954, though, ABC began rolling its entertainment programming at 7:30. The ratings for the CBS and NBC news shows promptly dropped like a rock, and soon they were rescheduled for 7:15. (Network news expanded to a half-hour in the 60s, at which point 7 became the starting time.)

Given their demonstrated love of the buck, if there were no other problems to worry about, the networks might well end up running prime time programming from 7 until 11 all across the country, with news at 6 and 11. But there is one big problem: the time zone differential. Broadcasters first had to deal with this in the early days of network radio. Recording devices were quite primitive then, and there was also some philosophical opposition to recording, which many felt deceived listeners somehow. As a result, all network shows, including the news, were broadcast live. An 8 PM broadcast in New York was thus heard in Chicago at 7. 5 PM was too early for California, though, so the folks in New York did every show all over again three hours later specifically for the West Coast, updating news programs where appropriate. This enabled the West Coast to operate on the "normal" (i.e., New York) schedule. When regular TV news broadcasting began in the 40s, voice recording was no longer a problem, but videotaping hadn't been perfected yet, so the idea of simultaneous broadcasting to the Eastern and Central zones, with a rebroadcast for the Pacific zone, was retained, with some modifications. Today the early feeds for the evening network newscast are transmitted at 6:30 PM and 7 PM Eastern time. (The two feeds are for the convenience of the local stations, which can pick the one they want to use.) A later feed is sent to the West Coast, where it's kept in the can until broadcast time, which is either 6:30 or 7 PM Pacific time. Network correspondents are kept on hand in case there're any late-breaking stories.

In our advanced age, of course, it would be possible for Chicago to record the New York transmissions and delay them for an hour, as Mountain zone stations do now (they generally broadcast the network news at 5:30 or 6 local time). By the same token, New York could start broadcasting the network news at 6 local time, making possible a four-hour prime time schedule. But the feeling is that people are used to the current schedule, and trying to re-educate them would be more trouble than it was worth. Also, the more recording and rebroadcasting you do, the greater the chances that some fumblethumbs is going to erase the tape or something. Besides, those guys in New York probably figure that people in the Central and Mountain zones are simple folk who like to rack out early after a hard day of mowing the alfalfa. In any case, we're probably going to be stuck with the present system for the forseeable future.

Did John Wayne ever serve in the military?—Bert D., Dallas

The closest Wayne ever came to military action was a three-month entertainment tour of Pacific bases that he went on in 1944. His childhood dream—to become a naval officer—was never realized, although he did come close to receiving an appointment to Annapolis. Later, during World War II, he was rejected for military service. He was never a cowboy, either.

Whatever happened to Dooley Wilson, who played Sam in Casablanca?—*R.S., Phoenix*

Dooley scored his last film credit in 1951 with the release of *Passage West*. What with the revival of interest in *Casablanca* in recent years, he could probably have made a fortune playing it again on the talk-show/nightclub circuit, but he blew his chance by dying in 1953.

The finale of The Pirate (1947), *with a score by Cole Porter, is a number performed by Gene Kelly and Judy Garland called "Be a Clown." In* Singin' in the Rain (1952) *Donald O'Connor does a famous routine to a song called "Make 'Em Laugh," whose music is identical to that of the earlier song and its lyric nearly so. Its authors, however, are listed as Nacio Herb Brown and Arthur Freed, who wrote the rest of the movie's score. How come? Were there any lawsuits? Both movies were produced by Arthur Freed, which may mean something.—Elizabeth B., Chicago*

Arthur Freed, the producer responsible for most of the MGM musicals of the 40s and 50s, began his career as a songwriter. "Singin' in the Rain" was part of Brown and Freed's score for MGM's first "all talking, all singing, all dancing" musical, *The Hollywood Revue of 1929* (the song has since been used in five other films, counting *A Clockwork Orange*).

In 1952, Freed decided to use his songbook as the basis for an original musical, as he had done with Jerome Kern's songs in 1946 (*Till the Clouds Roll By*) and George Gershwin's in 1951 (*An American in Paris*). Freed assigned Betty Comden and Adolph Green to build a screenplay around the available material, with Stanley Donen and Gene Kelly to direct. When the time came to shoot, Donen decided that Donald O'Connor needed a solo number, and couldn't find anything that worked in the Freed catalog. Donen suggested that Brown and Freed write a new song, pointing to Porter's "Be a Clown" as the sort of thing he thought would fit in at that point in the script. Brown and Freed obliged—maybe too well—with "Make 'Em Laugh." Donen called it "100 percent plagiarism," but Freed was the boss and the song went into the film. Cole Porter never sued, although he obviously had grounds enough. Apparently he was still grateful to Freed for giving him the assignment for *The Pirate* at a time when Porter's career was suffering from two consecutive Broadway flops (*Mexican Hayride* and *Around the World in Eighty Days*).

Who wrote the now-famous theme for the Laurel and Hardy series? Was the theme already a part of the public domain as a symbol of "somebody who has a screw loose" before the series started, or is its source solely from the Laurel and Hardy comedies?—Marty M., Washington, D.C.

The theme, called "The Cuckoo Song," was written by Marvin Hatley for a morning radio program broadcast from a small studio on the Hal Roach lot, where the Laurel and Hardy comedies were made. Stan Laurel thought the melody sounded appropriately ridiculous and used it in one of the team's early sound shorts. A preview audience responded enthusiastically (today, if we were writing for *Creem*, we would call it a "hook"), and the song became their permanent theme. At the height of their popularity, Laurel and Hardy would be met on their public appearance tours by huge crowds whistling the song in perfect unison, which must have been a sight to stir the blood.

How much was Humphrey Bogart paid for making The Maltese Falcon *and* Casablanca? *I hope it was a lot.—Leslie B., Chicago*

Bogart was under contract to Warner Brothers at the time he made his two most famous films—he was paid by the year, not by the picture. In 1941, the year of *Maltese Falcon*, Bogart received $96,525, which also covered his appearances in *High Sierra* and *The Wagons Roll at Night*. In 1942, he was paid $114,125 for his performances in *All Through the Night*, *The Big Shot*, *Across the Pacific*, and *Casablanca*. Even by the pre-inflationary standards of the time, it wasn't exactly what you'd call "a lot." Bogart had only established himself as a box-office draw (and a moderate one at that) with *High Sierra*; the biggest stars of the 40s—Gable, Cagney, and Cooper—were making three or four times as much. For those two years, Bogie actually checked in at somewhat below Mickey Rooney ($158,083 in 1941; $156,166 in 1942).

Here is a matter that has not been on my mind for quite a while now, that isn't a matter of life or death, and that doesn't have 50 bucks riding on it: tell me, what are the differences between Cinerama, Panavision, and Super Panavision? Are any of these simply trade names for ordinary 70mm film?—Bruce L., Western Springs, Illinois

366

You might have mentioned CinemaScope, Metroscope, Ultra Panavision, or any of about a dozen other cinematic breakthroughs while you were at it, Bruce; the movie industry has never been at a loss for grandiose titles for its dubious products. All of the above refer to various widescreen techniques intended to help Hollywood meet the TV challenge of the 50s. The earliest, Cinerama (1952), required three projectors flashing onto a huge curved screen to give the illusion of depth. 1953 saw the debut of CinemaScope, which was the first of several processes to use an anamorphic lens. Such lenses squeezed the unusually wide screen image like an accordion so that it would fit onto an ordinary 35mm negative—i.e., everything got skinnier. When projected, a reverse anamorphic lens stretched the compacted image back out to its original width. In some instances, the stretching was done in the lab, meaning you used a 35mm negative to make a 70mm print, which was then projected with an ordinary 70mm lens. Panavision appeared on the scene a year or two after CinemaScope, and eventually offered three techniques: ordinary Panavision, which uses a 2.35:1 anamorphic lens to squeeze a wide image onto a 35mm negative; Ultra Panavision, with a 1.25:1 lens and a 65mm negative; and Super Panavision, with an ordinary 1:1 lens and a 65mm negative. 65mm, incidentally, is the size of the film used in the camera. When the film is processed, a 5mm sound stripe is added and what the movie houses get is 70mm wide.

In the early days of wide-screen projection, 70mm prints were often preferred because they produced a screen image with less grain. As film stocks improved over the years, though, this advantage began to disappear, and today most movies, wide screen or otherwise, are both shot and printed on 35mm stock. The wider film is still used on occasion for movies involving a lot of special effects, since the bigger negative is easier to work with in the lab and the image holds up better during the numerous duplications that are generally required.

None of the aforementioned 'Scopes and 'Visions is exactly what you would call a trade name for 70mm film. A process called Todd-AO (1:1 lens on 65mm stock, 70mm print) was widely identified in the public mind with 70mm, but the trade name, such as it is, would probably have to be the stock number assigned by Eastman Kodak, which makes the stuff. Mercifully, I forget what it is, and if you know what's good for you, you will too.

What is the name and purpose of the scissors-top contraption which is clicked shut just before a movie scene is filmed?—Marcia W., Chicago

It's called a clapboard, and it enables the filmed action to be synchronized at some later date with the recorded sound—i.e., you jiggle the tape around until the sound of the clapboard clapping lines up with the picture thereof.

Is there some kind of rational, intelligible pecking order to Hollywood and TV screen credits? Specifically, are there quantitative measurements that apply to the term "star," "costar," "also starring," "guest star," and others? Why, in some TV series, are some actors credited "as" their characters (e.g., Charles Haid "as" Renko in Hill Street Blues), *even though others in the same series are not? And are there industry guidelines on type size with respect to job performed?—Bruce R., Riverside, California*

Apart from indicating in a vague way the relative clout of the players in a given production, the terms "star," "costar," and the like have no intrinsic significance. For instance, while it is usually true that "starring" in a movie means that you play a leading role, one will occasionally see something like "Cecil Adams in *The World's Most Fascinating Newspaper Column* starring Slug Signorino," in which case the latter personage clearly has a subsidiary, and we might even say a hopelessly insignificant, part. What's important in the movie biz is not the terminology but the *order*, and in the case of the advertisements the relative *size* and *position*, of the actors' names. These things are generally worked out in extraordinary detail well before filming starts in negotiations between the production company and the individual actors' agents.

The type size to be used for each name in a movie ad is usually expressed in percentage terms, with 100 percent being the size of the movie title itself. Big stars often insist on having their names appear at 100 percent (or bigger, if they can swing it, which usually they can't), and it works down from there. If you ever happen to be negotiating some macromazuma deal with Fox you might want to bear in mind the crucial distinction between the "art" title and the "billing box" title. The art title is the name of the movie as it appears in fancy (and often humongous) lettering in the middle of the ad, whereas the billing box, where the title sometimes appears again, is that indecipherable smudge of print at the bottom of the ad. If possible, you want to get the size of your moniker pegged to the size of the art title.

Once you get past the top stars, any number of terms, such as "also starring" and/or "costarring," may be used to designate the supporting or "featured" players. Agents for supporting actors use considerable ingenuity to try to make their clients stand out, and thus one often sees "introducing" or "featuring" or "as." "Guest star" is mostly used (along with the even more awesome "*special guest star*") to indicate a one-shot appearance in a TV series.

Actually, one of the trickier jobs in putting together the credits is giving people *equal* billing. Simply putting the names side by side won't do; since people read from left to right, the guy on the left will appear to have top billing. One famous solution to the dilemma was used in *Towering Inferno*. Paul Newman's name appeared above Steve McQueen's, but McQueen's was farther to the left—both in the same size type, of course.

There are a few industry guidelines that the unions insist on: in most cases, every actor with a speaking part in a movie has to be listed in the screen credits. The name of the screenwriter must be the same size as that of the director and producer, and all three must be no less than 15 percent of the average size of the art title in advertisements. In the screen credits (I omit certain subtleties here), the writer appears first, the producer second, and the director third. Since many writers often come and go in the course of a production, there's an arbitration process to decide who gets what billing. "Story by" generally indicates the first person to have gotten his mitts on the script, and "screenplay by" means the guy who administered the final indignities. All in all, it's probably easier to decide who gets to stand where on the reviewing stand at the Kremlin.

I'm sitting here placing cold compresses on my eyes after being suckered into another 3-D movie. After being tortured as a child with those ridiculous candy-wrapper glasses, you'd think I'd learn, but nooooo. Though this latest entry, Space Hunter, *is the most natural, i.e., it isn't hitting you in the face at every turn with special effects, it still falls victim to current technology. Is there a reason, save Foster Grant's special interest, that we must suffer through the present form of projection? Why can't a coherent 3-D image just appear on the screen?—John F., Evanston, Illinois*

I note from your stationery, John, that you are a college student, and thus a man of towering intellect, so I assume you already understand why it is necessary to have two separate film images, one for each eyeball, in order to create the 3-D effect. At the moment this means you need glasses, but I have heard tell of an experimental 3-D screen that makes glasses unnecessary. (Supposedly it works along the lines of those novelty photos where the image changes as you look at the thing from different angles.) However, this process is not yet commercially practical. The main problem with *Space Hunter*, in any event, was not the glasses but the print. Years ago 3-D required two separate projectors, which were hard to keep properly aligned and in sync. To eliminate such problems, *Space Hunter* used a new process in which both images were printed on the same piece of film. Unfortunately, since you were still using the same old 35mm stock, each image got to be only half as big as before, and consequently was a lot fuzzier when it got enlarged to big-screen size. In addition, since you only had one light source (as opposed to two with the old 3-D system), the screen image was a lot dimmer. The result was eyestrain and migraine headaches for viewing audiences around the country.

Here's a killer for you: on the late, fondly remembered TV show Kung Fu, *what were the names of those aphorism-crazed monks who instructed David Carradine in the mysteries of the Oriental martial arts? This question is much harder than the names of the Seven Dwarfs, although superficially similar.—Esther F., Towson, Maryland*

That may be a stumper in the suburbs, Esther, but this is the big time. The head of the Shaolin monastery where Kwai Chang Caine (Carradine) studied was Chen Ming Kan. The subsidiary monks were the Masters Shun, Teh, Yuen, Wong, Sun, and Po. It was Master Po, you'll recall, who was Caine's best friend (Caine affectionately called him "Old Man"; his nickname for Caine was, touchingly, "Grasshopper"). When Po was murdered by the Emperor's nephew, Caine saw no choice but to give said nephew a solid thunder kick to the groin, thus necessitating Grasshopper's sudden emigration to the U.S.A.

This may seem like a silly question but it's important to me. I have always wondered if the animals used in movies and television are really killed in "death scenes," or whether they are trained. Also, when two animals are fighting on a television program, such as you used to see on Walt Disney, are they really fighting or is that also the result of training? How do you train a dog and a snake to fight but not kill each other—that is, to pretend viciousness? It's hard to believe it's all faked.—Peggy M., Chicago

P.S.: How would you like to get together some time and talk about animal instincts?

Your library or mine?

Practically all American film and television producers cooperate with the American Humane Association's program to curb deliberate violence against animals. When any potentially dangerous scene is being filmed, a representative of the AHA is on the set to make sure nothing untoward happens.

Most animal fight scenes are the products of camera trickery. One of the most frequently used devices is what's known as a "matte shot," or split screen. If a dog is supposed to attack a snake, for example, the director will first make a shot of the dog "fighting" with its trainer. Then, without moving the camera, the scene will be shot again, this time with the snake and its handler occupying the opposite sides of the frame. The two shots are finally printed together—in a "matte"—with the appropriate areas blocked out. When the film is projected, the snake and the dog appear to be facing each other in a single image.

If a fight scene has to involve actual contact between the two animals, a different technique is used. For a fight between two dogs, let's say, the trainer will use two animals that know each other and allow them to fight for a few seconds while five or six cameras record the scene from different angles. When all of the footage is edited together, the fight seems to last much longer than it really did. Other shots of one dog wrestling a dummy—or his trainer dressed in a dog suit (no kidding)—may also be cut in. When a dead animal is needed, like the cat in *The Sailor Who Fell from Grace With the Sea*, filmmakers generally use these selfsame dummies.

Naturally, all these dog suits, dummies, and trick shots are expensive, and there are always producers willing to cut costs by going for the real thing. Thanks to the AHA, this seldom happens in the U.S. (one notable exception was a film called *Born to Kill*, which used genuine footage of cockfighting), but foreign productions are impossible to monitor. Producers, of course, are under no legal obligation to have an AHA representative on the set, and sometimes a film will get away from the watchdogs, as happened some years ago with Arthur Penn's *The Missouri Breaks*. For some reason, the producer refused to allow an AHA rep on the film's location in Billings, Montana—and the shooting left one horse dead from drowning, another crippled after being purposely tripped by wires (a practice specifically prohibited by an agreement between the AHA and the major studios), and several others injured in a stampede sequence. Consequently, *The Missouri Breaks* made it onto the AHA's "unacceptable" list, a continually updated index of offending films. For more information, write the AHA's California office, 14144 Ventura Boulevard, Suite 260, Sherman Oaks, California 91423.

This has been bugging me for years and now I've finally run out of patience. If you don't tell me the answer I'll go nuts and start voting for Republicans. Can you tell this ignorant slut who still calls films "movies" just what in the world is a "mise-en-scene"? This will make film criticism a trifle less impenetrable and make me more confident at parties that feature white wine.—C.L.A., Chicago

Don't fret about it, honey. The only guy I ever knew who understood what mise-en-scene meant also used to use the word "albeit" in casual conversation. Talk about your alien beings. Originally a theatrical term meaning a stage setting (literally, "putting-in-scene"), mise-en-scene is often loosely translated as "direction," which unfortunately tends to convey the purely mechanical notion of blocking out the actors' movements so they don't get in each other's way. In its most significant sense, mise-en-scene means the aggregate effect created by art direction, placement and movement of camera and actors, lighting, and other visual elements in a given scene. By extension, but somewhat more vaguely, mise-en-scene can refer to the dominant visual features of a film or film genre, e.g., the typically cramped, somber mise-en-scene of the *film noir*. Mise-en-scene, according to some theorists, is the principle vehicle by which a film's "meaning," such as it is, is conveyed, and as such is supposedly imposed on the film by its director, who may also call him/herself a *metteur-en-scene*, "putter-in-scene." One may refer to a director's mise-en-scene in the sense of his/her characteristic visual style, such as Fritz Lang's use of harsh lighting and sharp angles. Or Walt Disney's use of primary colors and four-fingered rodents. Such are the trademarks of genius.

This question has puzzled me for a long time. Why isn't there a Channel One on television?—Sandy C., Mesa, Arizona

I'm glad to see we're finally getting around to the Fundamental Mysteries, Sandy, instead of wasting time on the irrelevant drivel that usually preoccupies this department's readers. It turns out there *was* a Channel One once upon a time—in 1945, to be precise, when the Federal Communications Commission first allocated broadcast television frequencies. Later, however, the FCC repented its generosity and decided that TV was hogging too much of the broadcast spectrum (each TV channel requires a bandwidth 600 times as wide as an individual radio station does). So the Channel One band (44 to 50 MHz) was reassigned for use by people with mobile radios. Considering how things have turned

out, they would have done well to reassign Channels 2 through
13 while they were at it, thus sparing the nation such horrors as
Green Acres, arguably the worst blow to civilization since the
sack of Rome by the Huns. But there is no point in dwelling on
these things.

Chapter 21

≈≈≈≈≈≈≈≈≈≈≈≈≈≈≈≈≈

The Phone Company

Why do all phone numbers in TV shows, movies, etc., have the prefix 555? Is it an FCC regulation?—Mary Jane, formerly of Lawrence, Kansas

Believe it or not, there are a few pinheads out there with nothing better to do than sit down and call every number they see on television or in a movie. "Hello, is Kojak there?" they say, chuckling at the sublimity of their wit. Generally, Kojak is not there, which causes a great deal of inconvenience for the poor sap who is. In one case several years ago, a *Peanuts* strip carried a number that turned out to belong to a family in Moline, Illinois. Over 50 calls, ranging from plaintive requests to speak to Snoopy to less plaintive requests of a considerably darker nature, were logged in one evening.

Up until a few years ago, the phone company maintained a service that provided fictional (i.e., unused) numbers to producers and writers. But it soon developed, in this wide, wonderful country of ours, that there wasn't a single number that wasn't in use somewhere. The "555" gambit was created in 1973—no matter where you are, dialing the 555 number plugs you into directory assistance, where a legion of professionally trained operators awaits to answer the particular crankiness of your call. 555 isn't an FCC regulation, but simply a convenient creation of Ma Bell.

Television and radio ads soliciting subscriptions to the Wall Street Journal *and several other publications give a free "800" number subscribers may call, "except in Nebraska." I have personal knowledge that Nebraska does have some commercial activity which might be well served by the* Journal. *Why won't the* Journal *pick up the tab for inquiring Cornhuskers?—Steve L., Chicago*

The *Journal* doesn't care about Nebraska because the Strategic Air Command is headquartered there. But here, let me elaborate a bit:

If you pay close attention to the sort of ad under consideration here, you'll notice that two 800 numbers are often given, one for the residents of a particular state—the state where the answering facilities are located—and one for everybody else. This is because the recipient of the calls pays for them according to two different rate schedules: one for intrastate calls, which are regulated by the state commerce commission or its equivalent, and one for interstate calls, which are the domain of the Federal Communications Commission. For a long time using two numbers was the only way to keep the two types of call separate. But sometimes—particularly on radio, where speed and comprehensibility are of the essence and there is no visual means of offering a second number—using two numbers just isn't possible. The response of some advertisers was simply to write off the population of the bothersome state.

Today, I should point out, there is an alternative. AT&T recently began offering so-called "single number service," which eliminates the need for two numbers through the magic of high technology (the *Wall Street Journal* uses such numbers in some of its ads). But single number service is pretty expensive and not many companies have signed up for it. So the "except in..." business continues.

Nebraska is the state most often selected for this singular humiliation because Omaha, its most populous city, is the world capital of the WATS marketing business. It seems that in the early 70s, Northwestern Bell, the local phone company, began an aggressive campaign to lure WATS customers into the area. One of the company's selling points was—and remains—the presence of the Strategic Air Command in nearby Bellevue; because of SAC's communication needs, they say, the Omaha area is blessed with extraordinary trunk-line capacity and switching facilities, which make it virtually impossible that incoming calls will be "busied out" before reaching their destination. The practical value of this "advantage" is somewhat dubious, but in any case there are others, including Omaha's central location, which means a convenient time zone and low rates for calls from the coasts; its labor pool, a sizable body of potential operators who work cheap and speak in a "neutral" midwestern accent (i.e., they're not blacks or hillbillies); and, of course, Nebraska's relatively sparse population—if you're going to write off a whole stateful of potential customers better Nebraska than, say, Ohio.

Omaha is now home to at least three of the country's biggest WATS answering services, which take orders for such clients as the *Journal* on a contract basis, and to various in-house facilities operated by hotel, car-rental, and credit-card companies. In the rich-get-richer way of capitalistic enterprise, the volume of business being done there allows Northwestern Bell to offer what is

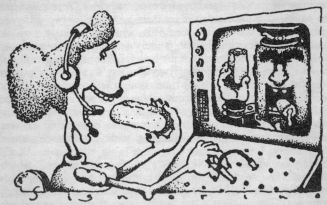

now undoubtedly the greatest advantage of them all, a range of special facilities and services that other phone companies cannot provide. For example, while it can take weeks to get a new 800 line installed in many places, Northwestern boasts that at its "Direct Response/Reservation Center"—a specially-equipped area of northwestern Omaha where the proprietors of WATS answering operations can look out their windows at each other—lines can be opened and closed within hours, sometimes minutes. They don't say what happens if the Russkies try to immobilize our air defenses by offering free Twinkies on national TV, but I suppose they have provided for that eventuality one way or another.

Everybody knows that (1) telephone service is usually not interrupted when electric power goes out and that (2) you can talk on the phone while soaking in the bathtub without electrocuting yourself. Why? What's so special about the way telephones are powered?—Vicki T., Los Angeles

Instead of being wired to your house electrical line, most telephones are powered by storage batteries located at the telephone company's central headquarters. The storage batteries, of course, are themselves charged by the local electric company line.

but when possible, the phone company, in its infinite wisdom, tries to connect to two different power sources—in case the generator supplying one line goes out, they can fall back on the other. If everything fails, the batteries can usually supply enough current to cover short breaks in service. Should there be a longer interruption, many of the central stations are equipped with diesel generators that can be pressed into action with a flick of the switch.

All of this complicated re-routing of electricity is made necessary by the happy fact that the telephone runs on a much smaller current than that supplied to homes by the power company—a happy fact because that's what keeps you from roasting your eyebrows when you're phoning from the tub. It takes a mere 100 milliamps of current flowing through your bod to bring on a killer dose of "ventricular fibrillation," as they call it in the trade. Your heart stops beating and starts to quiver like an emotionally distressed bowl of Jell-O, cutting off the flow of blood to the brain and other vital organs. The electrical outlets in your home pack a whopping 15 amps; your humble telephone carries less than a tenth of a milliamp. That isn't much, but under some circumstances it might be enough to do a little damage, so underwater telephony should still be approached with caution. No deaths have ever been reported from this sort of thing, but there's a first for everything.

How is it that some companies and businesses have telephone numbers that spell out their names and/or services, such as T-I-C-K-E-T-S for ticket services? Is this for businesses only? Is it expensive like custom license plates?—Sue Ryan, Chicago

Phonetic telephone numbers became feasible in some cities a few years ago when local phone companies began replacing their old electromechanical switching equipment with computer-controlled electronic toys, which simultaneously made possible such modern conveniences as call forwarding and three-way calling. "Feasible," though, is not the same thing as "easy." There are two conditions here, plus a catch. The conditions are, first of all, that the first three letters of the desired number must designate an existing exchange within your area code, and second, that the number cannot already have been assigned to another subscriber. If you, Sue Ryan, resident of area 312, wanted S-U-E-R-Y-A-N (783-7926), for instance, you'd find that there is a 783 exchange on the south side of Chicago, but that 7926 is already assigned. You can try to work out a trade with the present assignee if you want, but the phone company will take no part in such negotiations.

If the desired number is available, it's yours at no charge, whether you're a business or not (in Illinois, anyway). The catch is that you have to pay "trunk mileage" charges to have incoming calls transferred from the remote exchange (i.e., 783) to the exchange that serves your telephone (that's where the electronic switchgear comes in). The charges, as one might suppose, vary with distance.

If the preceding doesn't suit you, you can apply for an 800 (incoming toll-free) number. The exchange restrictions don't apply, and since only businesses use 800 numbers, there are many more number combinations available. Unfortunately, it'll also cost you a buncha bux.

Is there a special technique needed to win on any of those "call-to-win" contests offered by various radio stations? If so, what is it?—Jeanne, Los Angeles

Thousands have already amassed wealth beyond their wildest imaginings by simply following the Cecil Adams foolproof phone-blitz method (patent pending). Three easy steps lead to success: (1) Call your friendly local telephone company service representative. Tell her that you want 25 new telephone lines installed in your apartment. Enjoy her expressions of shocked disbelief. Assure her of your sincerity. Send her money. (2) Arrange your 25 brand new telephones around the kitchen table. Invite 25 friends over and arrange them around the 25 brand new telephones. Place your radio in the center of the table, tuned to your favorite schlock-rock station. Now sit back and wait, tapping your toes to the Clearasil commercials as the excitement and suspense mount to a fever pitch. (3) The moment the jock gives the vaguest intimation that a "call-in" is imminent (listen for key phrases like "Wow! Looks like Michael Jackson is gonna have another *hit album*!"), you and your friends pounce on the telephones, dialing madly—and instantly jam the switchboard! You can't miss. Within weeks you'll have the world's largest collection of promotional T-shirts and Michael Jackson albums—the envy of teeny boppers everywhere!

Why is there no Q on the phone dial? Z is also missing, but it's the last letter and there's no room for it anyway.—Emi D., Baltimore

The exclusion of *Q* and *Z* dates back to when the phone company began replacing human operators with mechanical switching equipment, which necessitated the use of dials. Bell wished to retain its folksy exchange names (since discontinued), but for reasons we'll get to in a moment elected to assign letters to only eight of the ten available digits. At three letters per number, that meant two were destined not to make the cut. Since Z was the last letter anyway, it was an easy one to eliminate. The selection of the other came down to deciding which of the remaining 25 was the most useless, the principal candidates being Q and X. The records of the debate within the phone company on this weighty topic are lost to history. But it seems clear that since *Q* must always be followed by *U*, except in the case of un-American aberrations like QAtar, it lends itself to fewer letter combinations than *X* (although the possibility of ending up with brain-damaged appellations like XAnadu, XErxes and XRay strikes me as a pretty strong counterargument). In any case, *X* was chosen for telephonic immortality while *Q* was consigned to the obscurity in which it presently resides.

The obvious question in all this is why the phone company didn't assign letters to the number 1, which would have permitted the entire alphabet to make the trip. It turns out that Bell wanted to reserve 0 and 1 for special "flag" functions when used in the first couple of positions in the dialing sequence. 0, of course, is used to signal the operator, while 1 is used in such shorthand numbers as 411 (directory assistance), 611 (phone repair), 911 (emergency dispatch), and 011 (international long-distance access). In many parts of the country it's necessary to dial 1 before dialing a long-distance number. Also, if you'll notice, the second digit of every area code is either a 0 or a 1. Assigning letters to the number 1 would have meant that it occasionally would be used as one of the first two digits of an ordinary local call, which would have fouled up the routing system. So that's why schoolchildren today can leave each other urgent messages to call Walter Cronkite at QUincy 5-2000.

We're having a debate where I work concerning how those excru-ciatingly dull phone recordings for the correct time of day are made. A secretary friend of mine contends that a monotonic woman was forced to sit in front of a microphone for 12 hours straight reading off the time at ten-second intervals. This tape, once made, could be distributed nationally to any city which adheres to a 24-hour-a-day framework, and the monotonic woman would quickly achieve national fame. The woman certainly deserves recognition for her ability to suppress bodily functions (in even the mildest forms) for 12 hours straight. Anyway, could you clear this up?—Rhonda L., Ridgewood, New Jersey

What do you mean, "any city which adheres to a 24-hour-a-day framework"? What do they have in Ridgewood, New Jersey—a 23-hour day? At any rate, the origin of the time-of-day recording wasn't quite so heroic as you make it out to be. (I base the following remarks on the set-up in Chicago, but the folks at New York Bell say things worked similarly there, and I presume the same is true of other major cities.) In the early days of the century, time was a free service, with operators individually answering each call. That got to be too much of a burden, though, and the service was discontinued in 1918. It was resumed in 1928, when a group of unfortunate wage slaves was put to work reading the correct time at 15-second intervals into a mike. Half an hour

was all they could take before their minds cracked. Some years later Bell switched to a recording featuring the voice of one Mary Moore, an employee of the Audichron Company from Atlanta, Georgia, who had graduated from Vassar as a drama major in 1939. Ms. Moore achieved immortality by reading each segment of the time-of-day message—i.e., the hours, minutes, and seconds—separately, just once. The pieces were subsequently assembled into a coherent, if boring, whole by an ingenious playback device, a modern version of which is still in use today. In the offices of the typical recorded-message company (the government made Bell turn time, weather, and other such services over to independent outfits in 1983), you'll find a machine (sometimes two machines—one is used for back-up) with two spinning magnetic drums. One has the hours and minutes recorded on it, the other has the seconds. These generate the message you hear. The machine is periodically synchronized with the radio time signal issued by the National Bureau of Standards in Boulder, Colorado. That's all there is to it.

I always thought Touch-Tone telephone exchanges worked by detecting the unique combination of notes produced by the Touch-Tone buttons, while standard-dial exchanges counted the slow, even sequence of "clicks" made by the dial rotating back to rest after dialing. Now there are a number of push-button phones on the market that are claimed to work on rotary-dial lines. Owning one would thus not only save you the expense of renting your phone from the phone company, but also save the additional charge levied for a Touch-Tone line. My question is, how does a push-button telephone work on a rotary-dial line?—P.D., Chicago

Easy. First you have to remember that "push-button" does not necessarily mean the same thing as "Touch-Tone." True Touch-Tone push-button phones, supplied by Ma Bell and various other manufacturers, work pretty much as you describe—they send a series of high-frequency beeps down the line that are detected by special switching equipment at the phone company's central office. The push-button phones made by some other manufacturers, however, are merely faking it. The miracle of the electronic micro-processor permits them to convert push-button impulses into the "clicks" that a standard-dial phone would make. So you can get away with using a cheaper line.

There are a few drawbacks, though. For one thing, a fake Touch-Tone phone is not going to save you any dialing time. After you get done punching buttons, you have to wait several seconds until the phone gets done sending the click sequence down the chute. In addition, you don't get the asterisk (*) or pound-sign (#) keys, which only work on legit Touch-Tone lines. So you couldn't bank by phone, should you have some primal urge to do so. On the other hand, something like 75 percent of the telephone exchanges in the U.S. are rotary-dial only, so if you ever move out to the boonies and miss the convenience of your Touch-Tone phone, you can take comfort in knowing that you do have an alternative.

Chapter 22

~~~~~~

Leftovers

Whilst cruising through the countryside the other day, I noticed that most of the barns were painted red. Why is this? Also, what is the origin of the New York City nickname, the Big Apple?—Marsha N., Baltimore

Barns were originally painted red because back in pioneer days there wasn't much choice. Farmers mixed their own paint, preferring a nauseating blend of skim milk, lime, linseed oil, and iron oxide—a mixture that hardened quickly and wore well. The red color was a side product of the iron oxide. After the advent of Sears Roebuck and modern factory-mixed paint, barns stayed red in order not to disappoint the tourists.

The etymology of "Big Apple," sad to say, lacks the classic clarity of the answer to the first part of your question. Of the many theories advanced, the most reasonable seems to be that the phrase originated in show-biz circles. "There are many apples on the tree," an old saying supposedly runs, "but only one Big Apple." Recognizing the inescapable wisdom of this sentiment, vaudevillians, jazzmen, and other wormy entertainment types dubbed New York, the most important performing venue of them all, the Big Apple.

How was gas rationing handled during World War II?—Bob M., Phoenix

Poorly. Actually, gas wasn't what they were rationing at all. The main purpose of the restrictions on gas purchasing was to conserve tires. (And you thought those bureaucrats were stupid.) Japanese armies in the Far East, you see, had cut the U.S. off from its chief supply of rubber.

There were four rationing classifications. An "A" classification, which could be had by almost anyone, entitled the holder to four gallons a week. A "B" classification was worth about eight gallons a week. "C" was reserved for important folk, like doctors, and the magic "X" went to people whose very survival required that they be able to purchase gasoline in unlimited quantities—rich people and politicians, for example.

Rationing was handled through the federal Office of Price Administration. To get a classification and rationing stamps, citizens appeared at the OPA office in person and swore to the high heavens that they (1) needed gas desperately and (2) owned no more than five automobile tires (any in excess of five were confiscated by the government). Each driver was given a windshield sticker that proclaimed his classification for all the world to see. Theoretically, each gallon of gasoline sold was accounted for. The buyer surrendered his stamp at the point of purchase, and the vendor forwarded the records to the OPA.

Gas rationing began on a nationwide basis on December 1, 1942. It ended on August 15, 1945. Speed limits were 35 MPH for the duration. For a short time in 1943, rations were reduced further and all pleasure driving was outlawed.

Recently I adopted the arguably worthwhile habit of reading the New York Times. *But, speaking purely as a bumpkin, mind you, I am puzzled by the small print which follows 95 percent of the by-lines in the paper: "Special to The New York Times." How special can these be, since many of the writers appear almost daily in the paper? And most of the stories, while informative, strike me as rather run-of-the-mill. What is so "special" about them? Or is this just another case of hype stripping a word of all meaning?—Mike K., Chicago*

Clearly, Mike, you have not had much experience with the *New York Times*, in which *every* story is special, simply by virtue of having appeared in that newspaper's distinguished pages. This is what is known as the New York Times Mystique. I am mindful of the experience of a journalist acquaintance of mine, who applied for a job as a *Times* sub-editor of some sort, only to learn that the pay was $12,000 per year, or something equally dismal. Upon complaining that sewer scrubbers in Borneo make more money, he was told, in rather wounded tones, "But you'd be working for the *New York Times*!" I mean, like, whoopee.

When accompanied by a by-line, "Special to The New York Times" means, as one might suppose, that the story was written exclusively for the paper by one of its own correspondents, rather

than by one of the wire services, say. The precise origin of this practice is lost in the Mists of Antiquity, but apparently the paper at one time wanted to demonstrate what an amazingly large staff of ace reporters it had. Nowadays they do it mainly because that's the way they've *always* done it, inertia being one of the principal determinants of *Times* editorial policy. One *Times* copy editor I happened to chat with about this one time was still miffed by the fact that the paper had stopped using the line "By Wireless."

When "Special to The New York Times" appears *without* a by-line, it usually means that the story was contributed by a "stringer," one of the paper's overworked, underpaid part-time correspondents. Occasionally, though, it means that what you're reading is basically a rewritten press release. (Many of those little squibs you see in the *Wall Street Journal* that say "By a Wall Street Journal Staff Reporter" are also rewritten press releases.) An unusual twist was given to the "Special to..." tag by the Chicago *Sun-Times*. The old *Chicago Journalism Review* once reported that "Special to the Sun-Times" over a story on an out-of-town sports event sometimes meant (and maybe still means, for all I know) that the reporter had *watched the game on television,* thus giving new meaning to the term "electronic journalism." Le this be an inspiration to all you hustling journalism students.

I fly in and out of O'Hare Airport in Chicago frequently and have always wondered why the O'Hare baggage code is ORD Can you tell me?—Carl A., Minneapolis

During World War II the Army and the Douglas Aircraft company built and operated a military airport at "Orchard Place," an unincorporated area in the northwest suburbs of Chicago. Known as Douglas Field, the airport was deeded to the City of Chicago for commercial use after the war, when it was officially designated Chicago Orchard Airport. Hence ORD. Later the name was changed to Chicago-O'Hare International Airport, after "Butch" O'Hare, a war hero and son of a Chicagoan who had apparently been murdered by the mob. That's the Toddlin' Town for you.

Whenever life gets too tough on my ego, I comfort myself by thinking back on my glory days—i.e., 1965—when I got two 800s on my SATS. Yeah, I know: pathetic. But it's been a slow 20 years. Now this friend of mine has made things worse by insisting that he knows someone who scored 810 on one of his SATs. They must have changed the scale, I said. No, countered my friend (hah!), we all know that you don't need to get all the answers right to score 800. OK, I conceded. Well, this guy, my friend continued, got everything right, so they had to give him more than 800, and besides, I saw his score report and a letter from the College Entrance Examination Board confirming that there had been no mistake, so there! Gee, I don't want to call my friend a liar, but I maintain that it is impossible to score 810 on a scale of 800. Was the scale changed, is this whole report bogus, or would the CEEB actually do such a thing?—A.K., Santa Monica, California

This seems like a pretty trivial thing to get worked up about, A., but I suppose after two decades of non-achievement your sense of proportion starts to get a bit frayed. Be that as it may, you'll be happy to know that there is no such thing as an 810 score on an individual SAT test, 800 being the scholastic equivalent of the speed of light. I am assured on this point by an official of the admissions testing program of the Educational Testing Service of Princeton, New Jersey, which administers the Scholastic Aptitude Test. He concedes that a typographical error might possibly have resulted in someone getting an 810, but says that under no circumstances would a letter have gone out "confirming" the error. You might want to invite your friend, therefore, to cough up his alleged evidence.

All this is not to say that somebody might not have *earned* a score above 800—quite the contrary. Unadjusted scaled scores in some years ranged as high as 840, due to a process ETS calls "equating," which we'll discuss anon. The 800 maximum is an arbitrary limit that ETS imposes mainly to keep neurotic geniuses like yourself from complaining that they got ripped off. The idea behind the present SAT scoring system is that scaled scores should be equivalent from one year to the next—in other words, so that getting a 650 in the verbal section requires the same amount of brainpower in 1983 as it took in 1965. The problem, obviously, is that the difficulty of the tests fluctuates from year to year, as does the caliber of the test-taking population (until recently, as I'm sure you're aware, America's college-bound seniors were getting progressively dumber each year). So every year ETS has some students take a special SAT section consisting of questions from tests given in previous years. The results don't affect the students' scores, but they do give ETS a statistical basis for establishing the relative difficulty of a given test, which is then used to "equate" this year's scoring scale with those of earlier years.

The one drawback to this otherwise admirable system is that a perfect score on an "easy" test might earn you only 801, whereas a perfect score on a more difficult test might be worth 840. If such scores were reported without adjustment, the people who got only 801 might complain that they got lower scores through no fault of their own. Now, a rational person might object that it doesn't make any conceivable difference, since *either* score is enough to guarantee you admission to virtually any college in the country. Unfortunately, as you can surely attest, A., high school prodigies are not rational. Hence the 800 maximum.

Finally, I should point out that even if somebody did get a score ten points higher than yours, the difference is statistically meaningless. ETS states that only scoring differences in excess of 65 points indicate a genuine difference in ability.

Why is Death Valley denominated a national monument, rather than a national park? With over 500 square miles of its area below sea level, it hardly comports with the popular idea of a "monument." Are large numbers of trees strictly necessary for the "park" designation?—Steven L., Chicago

You may not realize this, Stevo, but you are expressing a notion that is considered highly retrograde in progressive park management circles, whose adherents have spent decades trying to extinguish the misguided "popular idea" of what ought to constitute a national monument (or, for that matter, a national park)—that is, a collection of curiosities that tourists are supposed to come and gawk at for a couple hours before heading off to the KOA campground. National monuments were originally intended to preserve sites of historical or scientific interest, without regard to their value as tourist attractions. Death Valley, which among other things holds the record for hottest temperature ever recorded in the Western Hemisphere (134 degrees Fahrenheit), certainly qualifies in this respect, although it is not without its scenic aspects besides. Unfortunately, the use of the term "monument" has tended to obscure the original purpose of the designation in the public mind.

The distinction between parks and monuments is a bit arbitrary and mostly reflects the different ways in which the two are chosen. National parks and most other national reserves are created by act of Congress. National monuments, on the other hand, are selected at the sole discretion of the president from among available federal lands, under the authority of the Antiquities Act of 1906. As its title suggests, the act was intended mainly to protect areas of historical and anthropological value, such as Indian ruins—that is to say, places associated with activities of man. As something of an afterthought, a line had been included in the act permitting the designation of sites containing "other objects of historical or scientific interest," meaning fossils and whatnot. Prior to 1906, many such sites had been badly damaged by souvenir hunters.

However, Teddy Roosevelt, who was president at the time of the act's passage, promptly construed "objects of scientific interest" to mean things like mountains, and designated as the first national monument Devils Tower in Wyoming, a striking volcanic formation that you may recall from the movie *Close Encounters of the Third Kind*. This choice, although not unreasonable, tended to perpetuate the idea that the government was mainly in the business of preserving scenic wonders. Thus no one paid much attention to areas that were scientifically interesting but not particularly scenic, such as the prairies of Iowa and Illinois, virtually none of which now remain in their native state. Proponents of Everglades National Park in Florida in the early 1930s had a similar problem; the big swamp was mainly saved because it, unlike the prairies, was unusable for any other purpose. Equally unusable Death Valley was designated around the same time.

National monuments are generally smaller than national parks and less diverse in terms of the number of "attractions" they contain. Death Valley National Monument, though, is huge, and some have suggested that Congress upgrade its status to national park, the absence of trees notwithstanding. National park and national monument are just 2 of roughly 15 terms applied to various sites administered by the National Park Service, which include national lakes and seashores, recreation areas, battlefields, memorials, and so on. All of these are to be distinguished from the national forests, which are overseen by the U.S. Forest Service, a division of the Department of Agriculture. They chop down trees—lots of trees—in national forests. But that's a subject for another day.

Someone told me Ireland allows artists to live tax-free. Now suppose my dream comes true and I'm the next DeNiro, Winkler, Redford, or whoever and I make a zillion dollarrs and buy a little mansion in Ireland (southern Ireland, of course) and even go so far as to give up U.S citizenship. Can I escape taxation, or is it all just a dream (the Ireland tax part, I mean)?—Zachary S., Los Angeles

The provision of the Irish income tax laws you refer to is intended for the relief of *artists*, you cretin, not no-talent freeloaders from Los Angeles. By artists we mean writers, sculptors, painters, musicians, and other persons of delicate creative sensibilities, such as myself. By musicians, I should further clarify, we mean—how shall I put this—makers of *music*, as opposed to worthless trash. The post-1976 work of Steve Miller, for instance, is specifically exempted. Furthermore, the Irish authorities have wisely adjudged that the movies are, ipso facto, not art. Nor, for that matter, is most of what we might laughingly refer to as "popular culture." Indeed, there is some sentiment in Ireland that so-called entertainers deemed to have significantly retarded the advance of civilization, such as Donny and Marie, be taxed at confiscatory rates, and in extreme cases, shot down like dogs. In many respects Ireland is a remarkably progressive country.

I should point out that even if you *are* a bona fide artist living in Ireland—the Arts Council of Ireland makes the decisions on these things—you still have to pay taxes (usually) on income earned in the United States. The friendly folks from the Internal Revenue Service and I have been poring over these statutes for the last hour or so, and near as we can make out—I emphasize the tentativeness of the following judgment—you have to pay a flat 30 percent tax on royalties on books and whatnot sold in the U.S. That's if you're an Irish citizen residing in Ireland, you understand. American writers living in Ireland pay ordinary U.S. income taxes, as a rule, although they needn't pay any Irish income taxes. I omit certain complications here, but you get the idea. For more info on the preceding, call the nearest Irish consulate and ask for the handout entitled "Tax Relief for Writers and Artists."

As a casual dance-goer, I've often wondered: how are dances written down and passed along? Is there some sort of choreographic notation, the way there is for music? Or do dances just disappear when no one can remember them anymore? That hardly seems fair.—Karen B., Wilmette, Illinois

Every choreographer, it seems, has his own eccentric system of dance notation, generally imponderable to anyone but its author. The one system that has received anything like wide acceptance is known as Labanotation, after Rudolph Laban, who developed his unavoidably complicated method for recording and preserving dances in the 1920s. Labanotation is tied to a musical score: off to one side, graphic symbols of the various body parts (head, torso, right arm, left arm, etc.) appear, describing the position and direction of each member at that particular point in the piece. The symbols are accompanied by various code words describing the particular "quality" of the movement at that moment ("fluid," "swept," etc.). Since very few dancers can read Labanotation scores, a company that wants to reconstruct a piece will often call on the Dance Notation Bureau of New York—an organization that acts as a clearinghouse for scores and provides a "certified dance reconstructor" who will fly out to your provincial theater, appropriate Labanotations in hand, and instruct the backwoods chorines in the subtleties of their interpretation. All for a nominal fee.

There seems to be a convention in Spanish-speaking countries that most newspapers in the United States follow but never explain. This is the use of a man's second-to-last name as the name he is usually referred to by: for example, the president of Mexico, Miguel de la Madrid Hurtado, is called President de la Madrid; the late premier of Chile, Salvador Allende Gossens, is referred to as Premier Allende. Is this last name his wife's name perhaps? If not, what is it? If it is, why isn't it hyphenated? This may very well be something they teach you in Spanish 101, but there didn't seem to be any place I could easily look it up.—Randy G., Dallas

Obviously, Randy, you're unfamiliar with *The Chicago Manual of Style*, which is chock-full of meaningless trivia like this. From the manual we learn that the second-to-last name in most Spanish personal names is the father's name (*apellido paterno*), and the last name is the mother's maiden name (*apellido materno*). Thus José and Maria, whose father is Pedro Santiago Lopez and whose mother before she was married was Luisa Rodriguez Castillo, would be José Santiago Rodriguez and Maria Santiago Rodriguez. Male chauvinism being a long-standing tradition in

Spanish-speaking countries as elsewhere, the two would be Senor Santiago and Senorita Santiago on second reference. Furthermore, according to the manual, "a woman keeps her maiden name after marriage but drops her mother's family name and replaces it with *de* plus her husband's family name" (you're writing this down, right?). Thus José and Maria's mom is known as Luisa Rodriguez de Santiago.

The Spanish equivalent of the hyphen you occasionally see in English last names (e.g., Olivia Newton-John) is the Spanish *y* ("and"), as in José Ortega y Gasset. This system results in occasional oddities. One of my distinguished journalist colleagues, for instance, has a friend with the enchanting name Evangelina Rocha y Wodehouse, said friend having had a Mexican father and an English mother. Persons who think this practice demonstrates an uncharacteristically liberated point of view (you know, wife's name getting equal billing and all) should keep in mind that a woman's maiden name is really her *father's* last name. In one sense, then, the use of dual last names simply signifies the union of two male lineages.

While we're on the subject of naming peculiarities, we might also make mention of our friends the Vietnamese. As you may know, the usual practice with Oriental names is to put the family name first, followed by the given name. The Vietnamese do it that way, too; trouble is, Vietnam, in addition to its other privations, suffers from an acute lack of variety in family names, with half the people in the country having "Nguyen" stuck somewhere in their monikers. (I exaggerate, but not much.) Thus it has become common and correct to refer to a Vietnamese by his or her given name: Nguyen Van Thieu, President Thieu. A little tardy to find this out, I suppose, but better late than never.

Here is a question that will satisfy the curiosity of anyone who has ever read an Agatha Christie novel or seen one of her books as a movie or play. What is known about her mysterious "disappearance"? (1) When did she disappear? (2) Where was she (at home, on a trip, etc.)? (3) Was foul play suspected? (4) How old was she? Could she have been senile? (5) Could she have engineered her own disappearance? (6) Is she now presumed dead?—Linda D., Baltimore

Inasmuch as Agatha Christie was buried in an English churchyard in 1976, I think it's pretty safe to assume she's dead. However, you never know with these mystery writers. In any event, the famous "disappearance" you refer to occurred some 50 years earlier, and if she was senile at the time it is surely the most protracted case of that disorder in the history of medicine. Mrs. Christie disappeared on the evening of Friday, December 3, 1926, from her home near a small town in Berkshire, England. She was an established mystery writer even then; her seventh effort, *The Murder of Roger Ackroyd*, was on the best-seller lists. Nonetheless, she was known to have been nervous and depressed. Her mother, to whom she had been quite close, had died some months earlier, and perhaps more important, her husband Archie, a handsome war hero, was having an affair with a woman named Nancy Neele, which he made little effort to disguise. On the day Agatha disappeared, in fact, Archie had gone to the home of some friends to spend the weekend with his inamorata. Around 9:45 PM Agatha announced she was going out for a drive. The next morning her car was found abandoned several miles away, with some of her clothes and identification scattered around inside. There was an immediate uproar in the press, with speculation that Mrs. Christie had committed suicide, been murdered, lost her memory, or simply constructed an elaborate publicity stunt. Agatha had written several confusing letters to her husband and others before vanishing. One, to her brother-in-law, said she was simply going for a vacation in Yorkshire; another, to the local chief constable, said she feared for her life. A quarter mile from where her car was found there was a lake called Silent Pool that Agatha had used in one of her

books; one of her characters had drowned there. The police promptly had the lake dredged, without result. Hearing of the husband's infidelities, the police tapped his phones and followed him wherever he went. They also organized 15,000 volunteers to search the surrounding countryside.

As it rather anticlimactically turned out, Agatha had gone to Yorkshire after all, specifically to a health spa in the town of Harrogate, where she signed in on the morning of Saturday, December 4, under the name, significantly, of Teresa Neele. As the days passed and her picture continued to appear in the newspapers, several of the guests recognized her, but she laughed off suggestions that she was the missing author. Finally someone notified the police, who grabbed her husband and rushed up to have him identify her, which, on Tuesday, December 14, he did. Mrs. Christie's comment was, "Fancy, my brother has just arrived."

The Christies immediately went into seclusion, and several doctors were called in; they put out the story that Agatha was suffering from amnesia brought on by grief over her mother's death. Virtually no one believed this, though, and Agatha's subsequent refusal ever to discuss the matter—she made no mention of it in her autobiography—has fueled speculation among mystery buffs that continues to this day. The most plausible explanation is that she simply wanted to get away from a bad situation and embarrass her husband at the same time. At any rate, the two were divorced in 1928 and she later married archaeologist Max Mallowan.

ABC recently aired the movie classic, The Wizard of Oz, *which brings to mind something I first heard in high school. A friend of mine had collected several of the Oz books by L. Frank Baum, and he said the one entitled* The Wizard of Oz *was in fact a satire of the French Revolution. the Tin Man, the Scarecrow, and the Lion represented different members of the royalty, and the various witches were somehow opposing factions—or maybe it was the other way around. I know* Animal Farm *satirized the Russian Revolution; did* The Wizard of Oz *do the same for the French Revolution? If so, what characters represent which actual people?—Cameron G., Phoenix*

This is the first I've heard about a connection between *The Wizard of Oz* and the French Revolution, Cam, and frankly it sounds to me like typical lettuce-brained adolescent raving. The story *I* got was that the book was an allegorical treatise on the Populist movement in the U.S. in the 1890s. This interpretation strikes me as being about as wacko as your friend's, but since it was published in an allegedly scholarly journal (Littlefield, *American Quarterly*, 1964), I will present it without comment (more or less) in all its ridiculous majesty.

The Wizard of Oz, published in Chicago in 1900, was written by L. Frank Baum, an endearing dreamer and general nutcake. Baum had been a reporter and editor at newspapers in Chicago and South Dakota, where he had been in a position to observe the Populist agitation for agrarian reform. The Populists felt they were getting screwed by eastern capitalists who controlled the gold supply, among other things, and one of their principal demands was for the free coinage of silver, which would make for "easy money." Supposedly this was represented in *The Wizard of Oz* by Dorothy's silver shoes (they only became ruby slippers in the movie version), which gave her a "wonderful power," could she but recognize it. You'll recall that Dorothy treks all over Oz via the Yellow Brick Road, which represents the gold standard, the ultimately illusory route to salvation.

The Tin Woodsman represents the ordinary workingman, reduced to a dehumanized, heartless machine by eastern capitalists. The Scarecrow is the midwestern farmer, whose bumpkinesque facade conceals his native shrewdness. The Cowardly Lion represents politicians in general and specifically William Jennings Bryan, who was endorsed by the Populists for president in 1896. Bryan was a pacifist given to windy oratory, but deep down he was a brave man. Dorothy herself represents the Little Guy, naive but feisty.

The Emerald City represents Washington, D.C., and the Wiz is El Presidente, who appears awesome but is really an ordinary guy. He sends Dorothy out to do battle with the Wicked Witch of the West, namely the malign forces of nature in the American West. On the way Dorothy and her buddies are attacked by the winged monkeys, who represent (very subtle metaphor here) the plains Indians. Dorothy finally conquers the Wicked Witch with water, representing the power of irrigation, believe it or not. Finally, Glinda, the Good Witch of the North (representing Cecil Adams, symbol of universal righteousness), tells Dorothy she has had the power to return home ever since Page 16, thereby implying that she has frivoled away an entire book's worth of adventures for nothing. Our heroes learn they should look within themselves rather than to the government for the solution to their problems. The End.

The main problem with the preceding interpretation is that taken in aggregate it does not make a damned bit of sense. I mean, why should the forces of nature (the W.W. of the W.) be so hot for the free coinage of silver (i.e., Dorothy's footwear)? Baum was given to occasional satirical touches in his work, I admit, but he was primarily a storyteller rather than a political commentator, and the bits of symbolism stuck into his books for the most part don't add up to anything. However, far be it from me to discourage the English majors of the world.

From time to time I have heard about a legendary performer on the French vaudeville stage at the turn of the century named Le Petomane. It seems, incredibly enough, that this man actually made a living out of trained flatulence. Unfortunately, try as I might, I can find no more than a fleeting reference to this maestro of sulphur dioxide. Could you tell me more about him, and how he did it?—Curious in Baltimore

I think it is poetically appropriate that Joseph Pujol, better known as Le Petomane (which we may loosely translate as "the fartiste") should emanate from France, without doubt the most pretentious nation on the face of the earth. Le Petomane performed his unique act from 1887 to 1914, and became one of his country's best-known vaudevillians. At one point he was earning 20,000 francs a week, compared to 8,000 for his contemporary Sarah Bernhardt. It is pleasant to contemplate these things while suffering through the latest Jean-Luc Godard movie.

Joseph Pujol, born in Marseilles in 1857, owed his remarkable career to an extraordinary ability to control the muscles of his abdomen and anus. As a youth he discovered he could take in via the rectum as much as two liters of water, which he could then expel at will. Later he found he could do the same thing with air. At first he employed this talent solely for the entertainment of his friends, obviously a very refined and intelligent bunch, but after working quietly for some years as a baker, he was encouraged to give public performances. The first of these, in Marseilles in 1887, met with some initial skepticism, *petomanie* ("fartistry") being something of a novelty even for the French, but within a few days Le Petomane's winning manner and solidly professional performance had won audiences over. From then on it was one triumph after another.

Le Petomane arrived in Paris in 1892, and was promptly hired by the Moulin Rouge, the famous music hall. He became an immediate sensation. In a typical performance, he appeared on stage in red cape, black trousers, and white cravat, with a pair of white gloves held in the hands for a touch of elegance. Having explained that his emissions were odorless—Le Petomane took care to irrigate his colon daily—he would proceed with a program of fart impressions, as it were: the timid fart of the young girl, the hearty fart of the miller, the fart of the bride on her wedding night (almost inaudible), the fart of the bride a week later (a lusty raspberry), and a majestic 10-second fart which he likened to a couturier cutting six feet of calico cloth. Later, having inserted a tube into his nether orifice (offstage, of course—Le Petomane had a high regard for the delicacies of his audience), he would smoke a cigarette right down to the b—well, pretty damn far. He could also blow out candles and stage footlights. By way of grand finale, he would attach an ocarina to the tube and play popular tunes such as *O sole mio*, with which he would invite the audience to sing along.

An immensely popular figure in his day (even the king of Belgium snuck into Paris incognito one night to see him), Le Petomane was the subject of numerous articles, poems, and caricatures in popular magazines. One cartoon depicted little cherubs holding his coattails aloft while elaborate melodies issued from his hindquarters. (Actually, Le Petomane could produce only four notes without the aid of an instrument—do, mi, sol, and the octave do.) He bought a house filled with servants for his family, and in 1895 opened his own theatre. He went on foreign tours, sued a false female imitator (she had a bellows concealed in her skirt), and in general enjoyed a profitable career until 1914. Two of his sons (he had ten children) were disabled in World War I, however, and afterward he did not have the heart to return to the stage. He resumed his former career as a baker, and died surrounded by friends and family in 1945 at the age of 88. Mel Brooks would be lucky to do as well.

Lefties, southpaws, sinistrals, and other right-brained folk have to put up with right-handed design in everything from school desks to revolving doors to bound books. Given our minority status (though exactly how minor, no one seems to know ... do you?), I can almost understand the dearth of left-handed fielder's gloves and scissors. But one major omission in the anti-lefty campaign puzzles me. I stuff my billfold into my pocket every day with amazing ease; if there is only one back pocket, it's on the left, and that's also where you'll find the button or flap to slow down the pickpockets. How in the world did Fashion, the Right-Handed Establishment, and Levi-Strauss manage to do such an obviously levophilic thing?—Andy W., Washington, D.C.

Pockets have always tended to be placed on the left side, for reasons that have little to do with the free expression of minority rights. The Roman toga is said to have had just one pocket, which was invariably on the left, and in fact the Latin word and latter-

day heraldic term *sinister*, "on the left side," is supposed to have derived from *siniis*, "pocket side." No one knows who exactly decided to put the wallet pocket on the left (wallet pockets and hip pockets in general came into fashion in the 1890s), but the reason for doing so is obvious; you may extract your wallet from your pocket with your left hand, but you fish the money out and tender it to your creditors with your right. By such means as these are left-handed people coopted into cooperating with a right-handed world.

Wallet pockets are not the only example of deceptively even-handed gestures to lefties. The design of most telephones (as exhibited in such features as the placement of the cord) is intended to encourage the user to pick up the receiver with the left hand—at first glance, another apparent sop to the bruised sensibilities of that underused member. However, if a left-handed person attempts to jot down a note while on the telephone, he quickly discovers that he has been made the victim of an outrageous fraud, since it is necessary to shift hands clumsily. The only mechanical device of any consequence that I am aware of that consistently favors the left-handed person is the manual typewriter. Anyone who has ever pondered the daft arrangement of keys on that invention, though, is invited to form his own opinion of the mental stability of the designer.

Estimates of the number of lefties in the world vary widely; 8–10 percent is the most commonly accepted figure. At least one researcher has claimed that the number would be as high as 34 percent were it not for the program of oppression inflicted on incipient lefties by parents, primary school teachers, and other instruments of juvenile terror. There is a revolutionary movement waiting to be born here, I think.

MORE UNSOLICITED COMMENTARY
FROM THE USUAL COLLECTION OF BUTTINSKYS

Your discussion of left-handed fashions contains an error. The hip pocket on men's trousers appears to have originated during the latter part of the Civil War as officers switched from the long, formal frock coat, which contained pockets in the coat's tails, to the shorter sack coat, which was similar in cut and length to the modern sports coats. Pockets were added to the trousers to make up for the scarcity of pockets on the sack coat. In the numerous documented specimens I have examined, the pockets on the hip of Civil War officers' trousers were invariably on the right side. In addition, trousers issued by the U.S. Army during the 1870– 1880 period had hip pockets on both sides. My guess is that the left-only hip pocket was just a bit of fashion variation that happened to catch on.

On the topic of the frequency of left-handedness, it might be observed that many lefties, particularly those not genetically related to another left-handed person, show evidence of ambidexterity, or skill in using both hands. Some psychologists believe that the ambidextrous left-hander might actually have been a right-hander but for minor biochemical "accidents" during development. Such people may prefer one hand for writing and another for throwing, making it hard to establish the "true" frequency of left-handedness.—Michael C., Elmhurst, Illinois

The hip pocket may well have been invented by U.S. Army tailors, but according to most fashion historians it did not become generally fashionable until the 1890s, as I wrote. The custom of putting your wallet in your left hip pocket obviously depends on your having a wallet, as opposed to the somewhat larger billfold, which 19th-century men kept in one of their inside coat pockets. In prewallet days it wasn't particularly critical where you put the hip pockets, but today it is clearly more sensible to place the main one on the left. These things are not entirely capricious.

You're right about the difficulty of establishing true left-handedness; for that matter, it's difficult to establish true right-handedness. One researcher estimates that if you considered a wide range of motor skills—writing, throwing, batting, eating, and so on—only about 7.5 percent of the population would turn out to be "pure" right-handers. Moreover, there is some dispute about what true left-handedness means. A few years ago a couple researchers at the University of Pennsylvania claimed to be able to detect two distinct kinds of left-handed writers—those who mirror the way right-handers hold their pencils, and those who "hook" when they write, i.e., curl their hands around so the pencil points toward the bottom of the page. The latter group, which is thought to comprise about 60 percent of all left-handed writers, is considered the hard-core element, in the sense that their neurological organization (according to the theory, at least) is substantially different from that of the general run of mankind. You undoubtedly recall that in humans you have what we call "contralateral neural control"—this scientific jive just slays me—in which the left side of the brain controls the right side of the body, and vice versa. In addition, in most people—righties and nonhooking lefties, anyway—the writing hand is located on the opposite side of the body from the brain's language center. In hooking left-handers, though, the writing hand and the language center supposedly are *both* located on the left side. This means that one side of the brain is taking care of business on both sides of the body (writing on the left, everything else on the right), which means it has to work harder than usual, which means it ends up either (a) extremely adept, or (b) extremely beat. This may explain the statistically documented fact that lefties tend to be either geniuses or idiots. Being a hooking left-hander myself, I think this also explains some of the more striking features of my own career over the last 10 years. You can draw your own conclusions.

Index

A

ABC (network), 363

Adam and Eve: belly buttons in, 1; and myth of ribs, 1; 95–96

Adams, John Quincy, 135

Adams, Thomas (chewing gum inventor), 345–346

additives: in beer, 356–358; in kosher products, 350–351; in toothpaste, 174–175. *See also* propylene glycol alginate

adhesive tape: how it works, 117

advertising of autos, 189–90; of cigarettes, as grounds for suit, 224–225; claims for toilet paper, 176–177; of diet beverages, 193–195; of H.J. Heinz Co., 195–196; and Phoebe Snow, 325–326; of Post cereals, 147–149; of razor blades, 183–184; of Standard Oil, 340–341; subliminal, 187–189; and sugarless gum, 174; in tobacco industry, 191–192; and WATS telephone service, 375–376

aerobic exercise: and heart muscle, 273–274

Africans: variation in characteristics of, 100–101

afterimage, 235; causes of, 85–86

age: of whiskey, 347–348

Agel, Jerome, 362

air curtains, 178

air fresheners: nasal anesthetics in, 182–183

airplanes: circular patches visible from, 245–246; rolling and looping stunts in, 262–263

airport security systems, 245

air travel: and radiation, 236–238

Airwick (air freshener): and nasal anesthetic, 182–183

Alamo: Mexican perspective on, 104–105

alcohol, 222; as antidote for spicy food, 347; and citrus juice, 348; and drowning, 211–212; effect of, on body heat regulation, 284–285; percentage of, in light beer, 348–349; and spontaneous human combustion, 206–207. *See also* whiskey

alcoholism: physiological effects of, 283–285

Algonquin Indian languages: and U.S. place names, 286–287

Ali, Muhammad: lifetime earnings of, 336

Alice in Wonderland: and Cheshire cat, 7–8

almonds: cyanide in seeds of, 213

alopecia (baldness): causes of, 268–270

alpha particles: from smoke detectors, 234

alternating current: and electric chair, 220

aluminum: reaction with ketchup, 121; reaction with silver, 121; and senility, 216; in space, 128

Alzheimer's disease: and aluminum, 216

amblyopia, alcoholic, 284

American Express cards: significance of name C.F. Frost on, 180–181

American Health, 216

American Humane Association, 370–371

American Journal of Optometry, 271

American Medical Association, 269

American Museum of Natural History, 9–10

Amoco (American Oil Co.), 341

American Tobacco Co., 191
americium-241: use in smoke detectors, 233
amino acids: and protein quality, 349–350
amnesia, retrograde: and decapitation, 221
amphetamines, 115
AM-PM: designation of, 130–31
amygdalin: and cyanide poisoning, 213
anal sacs: infections of, in cats, 12
anesthesia: early methods of, 290; and suicide, 204
anesthetic, nasal: in air freshener, 182–183
Anheuser-Busch: and beer additives, 357
animals: domestic, 250–252; hypnosis of, 13; terms relating to, 287–288; treatment in movies, 370–371
animal droppings. See excrement
animal products: kosher rules concerning, 350–351
Anne, Princess, 138
Antarctica (South Pole), 10, 165, 315
antiperspirants: and senility, 216
antitrust actions: and Standard Oil, 340–342; in taxi industry, 193; and tobacco industry, 191. See also piano-roll industry
anus: of Le Petomane, 394–395; and sex, 66–68
aphasia: defined, 287
Appel, Kenneth, 126
Apple, Big (NYC nickname): origin of, 382
Aramaic: and Jesus's name, 35
Aristophanes, 75
Arizona, 186, 202; divination of water in, 168–169
Armada, Spanish: and Ireland, 111–113
Arm & Hammer baking soda: and Armand Hammer, 198–199
Army, U.S., 77; and pants pockets, 397
Arnold, John, 305
Arnold, Larry, 206
arrest, power of jurisdictional questions, 146–147; by concert security guards, 151–152
artists: Irish tax policy regarding, 388
ascorbic acid. See vitamins
Asia, 251–252; as continent, 166
asphyxiation: and drowning, 212; from painting of skin, 221–222
Astaire, Fred: in Royal Wedding, 361
astrology: and Jesus, 34–35
AT&T: and WATS service, 375
Atchison, David Rice, 134–135
atheists: swearing of oaths in court by, 145–146
Atomic Energy Commission: sale of californium-252, 329
Audichron company (time recordings),

380
aurora borealis, 163
autos: cost of, in Soviet Union, 336–338; Leonid Brezhnev's interest in, 336, 338; marketing of, 189–190; as taxicabs, 192–193. See also traffic

B

Babylonians: and timekeeping, 125
bacteria: and corpses, 93; and foot odor, 244–245; and flatulence, 80; and hand drying, 279–280
bagatelle, 312
Balcena, Bobby, 305
baldness: causes of, 268–269; and graying, 267; in women, 269–70
Bally Manufacturing Co., 312
barns: origin of red color of, 382
Barruel, Augustin de, 45
Baryshnikov, Mikhail, 96–97
basal metabolism. See metabolism
baseball: earnings of Babe Ruth, 335–336; injuries from fly balls in, 300–302; left-handed catchers, 303–304; Oriental players, 304–305; origin of shortstop, 299–300; and pitcher's mound, 302; ways to reach first base in, 299
Bates method (of vision improvement), 271
bathtubs: electrocution in, from telephone, 376–377; Millard Fillmore hoax, 108
bats: and rabies, 31–32
Baum, L. Frank, 392–393
Beach Boys, 319
"Be a Clown": similarity of, to "Make 'Em Laugh," 365
Beadle, J.H., 296
Beatles, The: and "A Day in the Life," 321; Top Ten hits of, vs. Elvis, 321
Beebee, Phoebe B., 362
beef: quantity per cow, 186
beer: additives in, 356–358; in boilermaker, 351–352; effect on bubbles in mug of, if dropped from Empire State Building, 131–132; explosion of cans of, 245; fastest method of cooling, 119–120; light, calorie content of, 348–349
belly buttons: in cats and dogs, 1; defects of, 89–90; innies vs. outies, 89; lint in, 80–81
Bentley, Dr. J. Irving, 206
Berger, Meyer, 290–291
Berliner, Emile (inventor of disc record), 259
Bernard of Gordon, 68
Bernhardt, Sarah, 394
Bernoulli principle, 263
Berry, Richard ("Louie Louie" author),

Clement VII (Pope), 75
clitoris: cancer of, 68–69; and tickling, 208
Close Encounters of the Third Kind, 387
cloud seeding, 158
coal: as fuel in locomotives, 325–326
Coca-Cola, 354–355; company policy on bottles, 197–198; and diet beverages, 194–195; pH of, 121; and subliminal advertising, 187
cockroaches: history and habits, 18–19; extermination, 19–21; and microwave ovens, 25; post-mortem, positioning of, 24–25
coffee. See caffeine
Coke, Edward, 139
coins: and mills (monetary unit), 336; in Britain, 332–333; removal from circulation, 331; as legal tender, 330
cold: adaptation to, by Eskimos, 91–92; sensation of, in wood vs. metal, 118; in space, 127–128. See also freezers
College Entrance Examination Board, 385
Columbia Records: and "Mr. Tambourine Man," 325; and introduction of 33⅓ RPM records, 259–260
Columbus, Christopher: and maize, 102–103
combustion, spontaneous human. See spontaneous human combustion
commercials. See advertising
Communist Party: perks for members of, in Soviet Union, 336–338
compulsory license (in recording), 324
conception: by two women, 59–60
concerts: legal rights of attendees, 151–152
Concorde: radiation detection equipment on, 236
condensed milk cans, 190
Congress, U.S., 154, 231, 330, 336, 387; and draft, 140–141; mourning observances of, 151; and presidential succession, 134–135
Connecticut: and registration of baked goods, 343
Constitution, U.S., 147; and draft, 140–141; 2nd amendment, 141; 13th amendment, 140; 17th amendment, 106; 20th amendment, 134
Consumer Reports: report on smoke detectors, 234
Consumer's Research: report on razor blades, 183–184
contests: sweepstakes, 338–340; winning 'call-to-win' type, 378
continents: why Europe and Asia count as two, 166
Cooke, Sam: circumstances of death, 322
cookies, chocolate chip: use of water in, 358

Coolidge, Calvin, 135, 126
cooling: of beer, 119–120
Coon, Carleton, 101
copyright: of "Happy Birthday," 323; of personal names, 144–145; and piano roll industry, 324; and private correspondence, 153; and recording licenses, 324; of titles, 144. See also Franz Liszt
Coriolis effect: and bathtub drains, 161–162
corn: meaning of term, in various countries, 102–103
corpse: of cockroaches, 24–25; exhibition of, 203; John Wilkes Booth's body, 114; preparation for burial of, 92–93; in sideshows, 114; Elvis Presley's body, 143–144; vampires: signs of, 39
correspondence: publishing of, 153
cosmic rays: hazards of, 236
coughing: and "sparks," 95
coupons: cash value of, 329–330
covert entry. See burglary, court-authorized
cows, 287; McDonald's consumption of, 186–187; peristalsis in, 81
"Crash landing" (posthumous Hendrix album), 327
Creamsicle: vs. Dreamsicle, 356
credits, screen, 368
cremasteric muscle, 84
Crockett, Davy, 105
crocodiles: and tears, 4–5
cuckoldry: and "horniness," 286
"The Cuckoo Song" (Laurel and Hardy theme), 366
Curtis, John: and spruce gum, 345
cyanide: in fruit seeds, 212–213
cylinder records, 256–258

D

dance notation for, 389
dancers, male: jumping by, 96–97; toe-dancing by, 97
Darling, Ron, 305
Darwin, Charles, 98, 208
Davis, Adelle, 268
Davis, Jacob (of Levi Strauss), 175
"Day in the Life": orchestration of, 321
"dead man's hand," 307–308
death: from alcholism, 283–284; from bread-only diet, 209–210; from bullets and knives, 203–204; from carotenosis, 275; from cosmic rays during air travel, 238; from cyanide in fruit seeds, 212–213; from drowning, 211–212; by electric chair, 220; from falling in elevator, 205; from fire, 233;

405

Frederick the Great, 108–109
Freed, Arthur, 365
freezers: in grocery stores, 178
French Revolution: and Illuminati, 43–46; *Wizard of Oz* as satire of, 392
French's (mustard), 182
Freud, Sigmund: and orgasm, 70
Frost, C.F.: and American Express, 180
Fudgesicles: freezing methods for, 356
Fugitive, The: plot of final episode, 360

G

Gaels: origin of, 112–113
"gaffer": defined, 362
Gallego culture: and Ireland, 113
Gallo company: and Thunderbird wine, 348
Gary, Indiana: effect on weather of, 158
gasoline: operation of gas station pumps, 263; rationing during World War II, 382; relation of mileage and tire inflation, 254–255
gas, waste: and plumbing: 253. *See also* flatulence
General Foods: and Jell-O, 344–345
General Motors, 189, 190, 193
genetic defects: anticipated, from cosmic rays during air travel, 238
genetic residue: of male, in female following pregnancy, 62
genetics: chemical basis of traits, 122. *See also* chromosomes
Gestapo: and Swiss bank accounts, 332
Gillette (razor blades), 183–184
glass: as solar filter, 163–164; why it's transparent, 120
"glow-in-the-dark" effect. *See* luminescence
gold: in British coins, 333
Goldfinger: and lethality of skin painting, 221–222
goldfish hermaphroditism, 71
Goldsmith, Oliver: and goodie-two-shoes, 291
Goldwater, Barry: tattoo of, 84–85
goodie-two-shoes: origin of term, 291
Goodyear tires, 254
Gottlieb, David: and pinball, 312
Gottlieb, D. & Co., 313, 315
"got" vs. "gotten," 294–295
Grand Rapids Press, 215
Grant, Ulysses, 135
Grape-Nuts cereal, and truth in packaging, 147–149
gravity, 253; and black hole, 200; at center of earth, 165; effect of, on bubbles in mug of beer dropped from Empire State Building, 131; and falling elevator, 205
Greeks: and bagatelle (pinball

predecessor), 311–312; and designation of continents, 166; and halo, 41; and philtrum (space between ridges under nose), 78
Greeley, Horace: and electoral college, 134
J.R. Gribbon: and "Jupiter Effect," 160
grills, barbecue: hazards of burning newsprint in, 223–224
Grosvenor family: and Cheshire cats, 8
growth hormone. *See* hormones
G-spot, 69–71
G-string: origin of term, 296
GTO: significance of letters, 189
guano (seafowl excrement), 108, 287
guillotine: consciousness of victims following use of, 221
guineas vs. pounds (in England), 332–333
gum, 174; sugarless, advertising claims for, 174; history of, 345–346
GUM department store (Moscow): Soviet perks and, 337–338
Gygax, Gary: and Dungeons & Dragons (game), 309, 310, 311

H

H: significance of, in Jesus H. Christ, 33
Haddock, Ambrose J.: and pinball, 313
Haken, Wolfgang, 126
hair, 210; cat, shedding of, 9; nasal, function of, 270; genetic basis for color of, 122; graying of, 267; growth patterns of, 97–98; human, use in wigs of, 270; loss of, 267–269; pubic, function of, 64; and shampoo, 178–179. *See also* razor blades; wool
hairballs: in cats, 9
halo: depiction of, 40–41
Halley's comet: and Nostradamus, 51, 53
Hammaker, Atlee, 305
Hammer, Armand: and Arm & Hammer baking soda, 198
hamburger: McDonald's consumption of, 186–187
Hamlet: and "petard," 295
handgun: lethality of, vs. rifle, 203–204
"Happy Birthday": copyright status of, 323
Harding, Warren, 136
Harrison, George, 140
Harrison, William Henry, 136
Harry Fox Agency, The, 324
Harvard Medical School Health Letter, 79
Hatley, Marvin, 366
Haymarket Riot (Chicago): and May Day, 43–44
Health Research Group: and hazard of smoke detectors, 233
heart: deterioration of, in alcoholics,

284; effect of caffeine vs. exercise on, 273–274; and ventricular fibrillation, 377

heartbeat, 8, 65; during aerobic exercise, 273–274; number of, in lifetime, 88

heat transfer: and fastest method of cooling beer, 119–120; in wood vs. metal, 118

height: average, during time of Christ, 34; effect of, on temperature, 165; of Eskimos, 91; methods of increasing, 265–266; variation of, in Africans, 100

Heinz Co., H.J.: and 57 varieties, 195–196; and ketchup, 182; and Illuminati, 196–197

hen. See chickens

Hendrix, Jimi: posthumous recordings of, 327

Henry II: Nostradamus's prediction of death of, 52

heredity, 267, 268; and Alzheimer's disease, 216

hermaphroditism: in goldfish, 71

Herod's Evil, 216–217

herpes transmission, 281–283; in spas and hot tubs, 281

Herpes Resource Center, 283

Hertz, John (taxi entrepreneur), 192–193

"He's So Fine": litigation involving, 140

Hickok, Wild Bill: and "dead man's hand," 307–308

highway traffic, 28–29

Hill, Mildred and Patty (authors of "Happy Birthday" melody), 323

hippoptamus: and "spray," 12

Hiram Walker: and promotion of Canadian Club, 185

Hitler, Adolph: Nostradamus's predictions regarding, 52

Holly, Buddy, 326

"Hootchie Cootchie Man": and John the Conqueroo, 318

Hoover Institute, 226

horizon, distance to: on earth and moon, 157–158; variation in, 167–168

hormones: growth, as way to increase height, 266; and hair loss, 270; sex, and male nipples, 93–94

"horny": etymology of, 286

horses, 39, 288; and Catherine the Great, 109–110; Dudley Do-Right's, name of, 359; hypnosis of, 13; injury of, on movie sets, 371

hot tubs: and herpes transmission, 281

Houdini, Harry: secrets of, 41–42

houseflies: extermination of, saving of cosmos resulting from, 22–23

Houta, Marshall, 222

Humble (Standard Oil alias), 341

Huxley, Aldous: and Bates vision improvement method, 271

hydrostatic shock: from bullets, 204

hyoid apparatus: and cat purring, 7

hypnagogic myoclonus (twitching while falling asleep), 90

hypnosis: of animals, 12–13

hypoglycemia: effect of marijuana on, 267

hypoxia (tissue oxygen starvation): and drowning, 212

I

ice: and dinosaurs, 10–11; Eskimo words for, 297–298; in space, 127–128

ice cream: freezing of, 356

ideomotor action: and dowsing, 169

Igorot (tribe), 77

Illinois: boundary idiosyncrasies of, 167; and Lincoln-Douglas debates, 105–107; and nuclear waste, 230–232

Illuminati (world's oldest conspiracy), 43–46; and H.J. Heinz, 197

implants, penile, 56–57

Incas: and invention of the wheel, 251

income: illegal, and IRS, 329; illegal, and Swiss bank accounts, 332; of Soviet officials, 336–337; of Babe Ruth, vs. other sports figures, 335–336

incubi: and nocturnal orgasm, 62

Index of Prohibited Books, 75

India, 100; timekeeping in, 124

Indians, American, language of: and "wau-," 286–287

infection: and brain surgery, 274; of nose, dangers of, 271; viral, 281–283

infibulation: of females, 72; of males, 73–74

infrasonic sound: effects of, 281

inositol (baldness preventive), 268

intelligence: of cats vs. dogs, 5–6

Internal Revenue Service, 154, 388; and illegal income, 329

intestine, 204; effect of length of, on weight, 276; generation of flatulence in, 80; and peristalsis, 81; problems of, in cats, 9; and yoga purificatory practices, 50–51

Invasion Strategy (pinball game), 315

iodine: human need for, 217–218. See also potassium iodide

Ireland: artist tax policy of, 388; seasons in, 170–172; and Spanish Armada survivors, 111–113; timekeeping in, 124

irrigation devices (self-propelled boom), 245–246

Italy, 52; and terrorism, vs. U.S., 226, 227; use of chastity belts in, 72; use of long *s* in, 111

itching, spot: causes of, 90–91

407

J

Jackson, Reggie: earnings of, 336
Janssen, David, 360
Japan: subways in, 27
Japanese: in American baseball, 305
jeans, blue. *See* Levis
Jell-O: and pineapple, 344–345
Jesus Christ: birthdate of, 34–35; and halo, 41; height of, 34; origin of name, 35; significance of *H* in "Jesus H. Christ," 33–34
Jewish dietary laws, 350–351
Jews: and Exodus, 35–37; in Ireland, 113
John XXIII (pope): and Fatima, 38
Johns Hopkins Hospital, 56, 59
Johnson, Lyndon, 135
Johnson, Samuel: and tipping, 334
John the Baptist: birthdate of, 35
John the Conqueroo: origin of term, 318–319
"joint": etymology of, 290–291
Jolly Roger: origin of, 292–293
Joshua bar-Joseph: as name for Jesus, 35
Journal of the American Dental Association, 306
jumping: in male dancers, 96–97; as means of saving self in falling elevator, 205
Jung, Carl: and mandala, 328
"Jupiter Effect," 159–160

K

K, circled (kosher symbol), 350–351
Kaskaskia (Illinois township), 167
Kelly, Gene, 365
Kemmler, William, 220
keratomileusis (operation on eye lens), 272–273
ketchup: bottles for, vs. mustard, 181–182; and H.J. Heinz, 195–196; reaction of, with aluminum, 121
"key grip": defined, 362
Khrushchev, Nikita, 228, 338
kidneys (animal): contaminants in, 218
Kimble, Dr. Richard (*Fugitive* hero), 360
Kingsmen: and "Louie Louie," 316–317
Kinsey Institute: and Vatican pornography collection, 74–75
knife: as cause of death, 203–204
koan (Zen Buddhist riddle), 49–50
Komputer Dynamics (game company), 315
Korsakoff's psychosis: and alcoholism, 283
Kosher: certification process, 350–351; pickles, 351
Krantz, Kermit, 70–71
Krasilovsky, M. William, 325

Kubrick, Stanley: and special effects in *2001,* 362
Kung-Fu (TV show): names of monks in, 370
Ku Klux Klan, 226

L

Labanotation (for dance), 389
Ladas, Alice Kahn (G-spot author), 70
landslides, electoral, 135–136
La Porte, Indiana: weather anomaly in, 158
Laurel and Hardy: musical theme of, 366
lawn: danger of chemicals used on, 26–27
lead, danger of: in food, 219; in tuna cans, 222; in condensed milk cans, 190
lease, 99-year: origin of, 138–139
left-handedness: and baseball catchers, 303–304; and brain organization, 397–398; and wallet pocket, 396
legal tender: law regarding, 330–331
Legman, Gershon, 75
L'Enfer (pornography collection in French National Library), 76
Lenin: and Illuminati, 226
lens: contact, in orthokeratology, 271–272; surgery of, 272–273
Les Ballets Trockadero de Monte Carlo (drag ballet), 97
Les Preludes (Flash Gordon theme), 324
Levis: origin of pocket stitching in, 175
licensing: of song recording rights, 324–325
life, meaning of, 27
Life Savers: "sparking" of, 129–130
light: passage of, through glass, 120; and phosphors, 242–243; scattering of, in atmosphere, 170
lights, electric: and energy conservation, 249–250
lightning: effect on television, 166–167; heat vs. sheet, 170
lime: tequila and, 348
Lincoln, Abraham, 113, 135, 294; purpose of debates with Douglas, 105–107
liquid: cooling of, 119–120; glass as, 120; and peristalsis, 81; in space, 127–129
listening booths, record store: demise of, 322–323
Liszt, Franz, 324
liver: contaminants in, 218–219
llama: as beast of burden, 252
London, 6, 76; Nostradamus's prediction of Great Fire of, 52
Long, Dale, 304
Long Beach mummy, 203

effects in, 361–362; and subliminal advertising, 187–189; and 3-D, 369–370; use of animals in, 370–371; use of phone numbers in, 374; widescreen techniques for, 366–367

MPLSM marks on mail, 256

"Mr. Tambourine Man": recording of, 325

Mrs. Byrne's Dictionary of Unusual, Obscure, and Preposterous Words, 288

Mudd, Samuel, 294

"mud, his name is": origin of, 293–294

Muggs, J. Fred, 360–361

mummy, 34; found in Long Beach, 203

Murakami, Masanori, 305

muscles: deterioration of, in alcoholics, 284; development of, and weight training, 276–278

mustard: bottles for, vs. ketchup, 181–182

Muzak theory, 317–318

"My Sweet Lord": litigation regarding, 140

N

Nader, Ralph, 233–234

Nakache, Patricia, 130

names, personal: legal right to, 144–145. *See also* surnames; titles

Napoleon: and Nostradamus, 52

National Academy of Sciences, 217

National Aeronautics and Space Administration (NASA), 128, 236

National Association of Broadcasters, 188

National Bureau of Standards, 381

National Institutes of Health, 281

national monuments: vs. national parks, 386–387

National Museum, U.S., 77

National Park Service, 387

Nautilus. *See* weight lifting

navels. *See* belly buttons

Navy, U.S.: disposal plans for nuclear submarines, 229

NBC (network), 363

Nebraska: and 800 telephone numbers, 374–376

nerves, 91; and cremasteric muscle, 84; and itching, 91; optic, role of, in afterimage, 85; pinched, 86; in vagina, 70–71

nests: of chickens, 3; of pigeons, 15–16

neurapraxia, 86

Newman, Paul, 369

Newfoundland: timekeeping in, 124

news broadcasts: scheduling of, 362–364

newsprint: in barbecue grills, hazards of, 223–224

New York (city and state), 9–10, 113,

193, 195, 196, 222, 334, 345, 350, 380, 389; and Canadian Club promotion, 185; flea circuses in, 7; nuclear waste generated in, 231; origin of "Big Apple" nickname, 382; and pinball, 313; and TV scheduling, 363–364. *See also* Empire State Building

New Yorker, 290

New York Times: and Illuminati, 46; "Special to the New York Times," significance of, 383–384

Nicholas and Alexandra: exhibition of corpses of, 114

nipples: why men have them, 93–95

Nixon, Richard, 135, 241; mourning plans for, 150–151

nocturnal orgasm, 61–62

No Deposit, No Return, 214–215

None Dare Call It Conspiracy, 46

noon, reckoning and significance of, 124, 130–131

Northwestern Bell, 375–376

nose: picking, dangers of, 270–271; ridges beneath, 78; and yoga purificatory practices, 51. *See also* anesthetic, nasal; smell

Nostradamus: accuracy of prophecies of, 51–53

"Now is the time for all good men...": origin of, 295

nuclear bomb: effects of, on Chicago, 228

nuclear power plants: disposal of spent fuel from, 230, 231

nuclear reactor: breaching of, in ocean, 228–229

Nuclear Regulatory Commission, 230, 233–234, 243

nuclear war: locale least affected by, 232; predicted by Nostradamus, 51–53

nuclear waste: disposal of, 229–232; in ocean, 228–229

nuclear weapons: and plutonium, 231; procedures for launching of, 239–241

numbered accounts: at Swiss banks, 331–332

number codes: in soda fountains, 291–292

numbers, significance of: to ancients, 125–126; in Middle Ages, 304

numbness in limbs, 86

nystagmus (oscillation of eye pupils), 264

O

obesity: and heart, 274

Occidental Petroleum Corp. 198

ocean, 160–161; nuclear pollution of, 229

O'Connor, Donald, 365
Odorama, 246
Office of Price Administration, 383
O'Hare airport: significance of ORD baggage code, 384–385
oil companies, U.S.: advertising, ownership, and control of, 340–342
oligopoly: in tobacco industry, 191
Omaha, Nebraska, 239; and WATS telephone-answering industry, 375–376
O'Malley, Joseph P., 222–223
Omnibus Crime Control and Safe Streets Act, 150
omphalocele (defect of navel), 90
O'Neill, Tip, 134
"opponent process" nerve cells, 86
orange: etymology of word, 344; navel, 353; juice, regulations concerning, 352–353
ORD (O'Hare airport baggage symbol): significance of, 384–385
Organized Kashruth Laboratories, 350
orgasm: in female animals, 64–65; and Grafenberg spot, 69–71; nocturnal, 61–62; and tickling, 208
Oriental surnames. See surnames
Orientals: in American baseball and football, 305
orthokeratology (vision improvement therapy): efficacy of, 271–272
ovens: injuries from, 213–215
Ovid, 75
Owen, Richard, 140
oxygen: consumption, and health, 273; lack of, and drowning, 212
oysters: cadmium concentration in, 219

P

Pabst beer: calories in, 348–349
Pacific Ocean: most remote spot in, 315
pain, sense of: and itching, 91
Panavision: mechanics of, 366–367
parallax: in pigeons, 17–18
Passover: and Easter, 126
Pauling, Linus: and vitamin C, 278
penis: surgical creation of, 58; cancer of, 68–69; of corpse, 92; enlargement of, 56–58; and Herod's Evil, 216–217; and "horniness," 286; implants for, 56–57; infibulation of, 73–74; of pigs, 60–61
Penn, Arthur, 371
penny: effect of, if dropped from Empire State Building, 225–226; as legal tender, 330–331; rewards of picking up lost, 334–335
Pennsylvania Department of Agriculture: inspection and registration program of, 343–344

pentachlorophenol: hazards of, 219
Pepsi Cola: marketing efforts for, 194
peristalsis (swallowing mechanism), 50–51, 81
permissive action link (nuclear weapon safety catch), 240
Perry, John, 70, 71
perspiration: and belly button lint, 80–81; effect of painting of skin on, 221–222
pesticides: and cockroaches, 18–22; effects of, on pets, 26–27; in foods, 218
"petard, hoist by one's own": origin of phrase, 295–296
Le Petomane (flatulence virtuoso), 394–395
Pett, Grace, 206
Pettingill (ornithologist), 17
phalloplasty (surgical creation of penis), 58
Philip, Prince, 138
Philip Morris (cigarettes), 192
Philippines: cigarette smoking customs in, 306; tailed tribes of, 77–78
Phillips, Mark, 138
philtrum (space between ridges beneath nose), 78
phonograph records. See records and recording
phosphors: and luminescence, 242–243
phosphorus: and matches, 117; and spontaneous human combustion, 207
photocopiers: radiation hazards of, 235
photography: in public, law regarding, 152–153
piano-roll industry: and copyright laws, 324–325
Pican Corporation, 189
pickles, kosher: regulation of, 351
pigeons: and head-bobbing, 16–18; hypnosis of, 13; milk of, 16; raising of babies, 16; and urban environment, 15
pigs: orgasm in, 64; sex organs of, 60–61
pinball: history and development of, 311–314; two-man version of, 315
Pindar, Peter, 8
pineapple: effect of, on Jell-O, 344–345
pipes: ability of rats to climb, 29–31. See also plumbing
Pirandello, Luigi, 27
Pirate, The, 365–366
pitcher's mound: purpose of, 302
Pittsburgh, 193, 196; and sarsaparilla, 354
Pius XII: and message of Fatima, 38
Plagemann, S.H., 160
plague(s): bubonic, 31; of Egypt, 36–37
plastics, recycling of, 261–262
Playtex, 87

411

Vietnamese surnames. *See* surnames
Vikings: in Ireland, 113
Virgin, Blessed: and Fatima, 37
virus transmission, 281–283
vision: and afterimage, 85–86; methods of improving, 271–272; loss of, from alcohol consumption, 284; of pigeons, 17–18
vitamins: as baldness preventive, 268; and common cold, 278–279; deficiency in bread-only diet, 210; effect of deficiency in alcoholics, 284; megavitamin therapy, 278; overdose danger, 278
vocal cords: and cat purring, 7; ability to carry two notes simultaneously of, in certain individuals, 79
vote: in presidential elections, 135–136

W

Wales, Prince of: how to become, 137–138
Walker, Paul E., 279
wallet: and pocket location, 395, 396
Wall Street Journal, 374, 375, 384
Warner Bros. records, 327
Warner-Lambert company (makers of Trident gum), 174
Washington, D.C., 1, 281, 358
Washington, George: vote for vs. other presidents, 136
water: and bread-only diet, 209–210; in chocolate chip cookie recipe, 358; Coriolis effect on, in drains, 161–162; divination of, 168–170; and drowning, 211–212; and plumbing, 253; and spicy foods, 346–347; and spontaneous human combustion, 207; and wool, 118; and wrist-slashing, 204
Waters, John, 246
WATS (wide answering telephone service) lines, 375–376
Watson, T.B., 261
"wau-," significance of, in place names: Milwaukee, Waubonsee, Waukegan, Waukesha, Waupaca, Wausau, 286–287
Wayne, John, 308; military service of, 364–365
weather: effect of cities on, 158; in Ireland, 171–172; and seasons, 171–172
Weather Service, U.S.: measurement of snow by, 162–163
Webster, Nesta: and Illuminati, 45
weight: at center of earth, 165; effect of obesity on heart, 274; methods for gaining, 275–276
weight lifting: by chimpanzees, 2–3; free weights vs. Nautilus, 276–278;

and weight gain, 276
Weinhold, Karl August, 74
Weishaupt, Adam (Illuminati founder), 44
Weller, Charles E., 295
Weller, Newton, 167
Wernicke's disease, 283
Westinghouse, George: and first electric chair, 220
Westinghouse group, 318
wet dreams: in women, 61–62
whales, 288; depth of excrement of, 3–4
wheel: failure of New World to invent, 250–252; as metaphor, 327–328
Whipple, Beverly (G-spot author), 70
whiskey, 351; age vs. maturity in, 347–348. *See also* Canadian Club
wigs: use of human hair in, 270
wilderness: most remote spot on earth, 315
Wilkinson (razor blades), 183
Wilson, Brian, 319
Wilson, Dooley: post-*Casablanca* career of, 365
Wilson, Robert Anton, 46
Wilson, Woodrow, 135
wintergreen. *See* Life Savers
wiretapping: and covert entry; law regarding, 150
"wishing": for water, efficacy of, 169
Wizard of Oz, The: as satire of Populist movement, 392–393
wool: ability to cope with moisture of, 118
World Dryer Corporation: and diseases from paper towel litter, 279
World Health Organization, 219
World War II, 75, 188, 385; and John Wayne, 364–365; and Levis, 175; and rationing, 382–383
wormhole: and black hole, 201

X

Xerox machine: danger of radiation from, 235

Y

yellow: as color for taxicabs, 192
Yellow Cab company, 192–193
Yellowlees, D., 74
yoga: and cremasteric muscle, 84; purificatory practices of, 50

Z

Zen Buddhism. *See* Buddhism
Zionism: and Illuminati, 45
Zulus: and barbecue grill design, 224

About the Author

One of the world's legendary recluses, Cecil Adams, author of THE STRAIGHT DOPE and reputedly the world's smartest human being, has never been photographed or interviewed. In fact, only a handful of people have ever met him, giving rise to his reputation as the Howard Hughes of American journalism.

All Cecil's dealings with the public are handled by his editor and confidant, Ed Zotti, who has been sworn to secrecy. Consequently, little is known about Cecil's private life. Even Zotti says he doesn't know where Cecil managed to learn so much stuff.

On the Lighter Side...

30   TA-49